FILM AND THE LAW

Described by Richard Sherwin of New York Law School as the law and film movement's 'founding text', this text is a second, heavily revised and improved edition of the original *Film and the Law* (Cavendish Publishing, 2001). The book is distinctive in a number of ways: it is unique as a sustained book-length exposition on law and film by law scholars; it is distinctive within law and film scholarship in its attempt to plot the parameters of a distinctive genre of law films; its examination of law in film as place and space offers a new way out of the law film genre problem, and also offers an examination of representations of an aspect of legal practice, and legal institutions, that have not been addressed by other scholars. It is original in its contribution to work within the wider parameters of law and popular culture and offers a sustained challenge to traditional legal scholarship, amply demonstrating the practical and the pedagogic, as well as the moral and political significance of popular cultural representations of law.

The book is a valuable teaching and learning resource, and is the first in the field to serve as a guidebook for students of law and film.

Film and the Law

The Cinema of Justice

Steve Greenfield
Guy Osborn
and
Peter Robson

·HART·
PUBLISHING

OXFORD AND PORTLAND, OREGON

2010

Published in the United Kingdom by Hart Publishing Ltd
16C Worcester Place, Oxford, OX1 2JW
Telephone: +44 (0)1865 517530
Fax: +44 (0)1865 510710
E-mail: mail@hartpub.co.uk
Website: http://www.hartpub.co.uk

Published in North America (US and Canada) by
Hart Publishing
c/o International Specialized Book Services
920 NE 58th Avenue, Suite 300
Portland, OR 97213-3786
USA
Tel: +1 503 287 3093 or toll-free: (1) 800 944 6190
Fax: +1 503 280 8832
E-mail: orders@isbs.com
Website: http://www.isbs.com

British Library Cataloguing in Publication Data
Data Available

ISBN: 978-1-84113-725-4

Typeset by Compuscript Ltd, Shannon
Printed and bound in Great Britain by
TJ International Ltd, Padstow, Cornwall

PREFACE

Film and the Law: The Cinema of Justice is a product of many ideas, thoughts, conversations, conference papers and articles that have taken place over the past two decades. It is the product of not just an academic collaboration, but of a friendship that has been developed and nurtured over this period. All three of the authors came to the area with a background not only in the law, but also of seeing law in a broader social context. Perhaps more importantly, the book is underpinned by our love of film, and our understanding of the possibilities, potential and problems of film. The book charts a journey, a journey from the early interventions in the area, via our first book together and to this current text. It is certainly the case that the area we mapped out initially has changed and developed in many ways. At the same time, we as scholars have also changed and developed, and this text reflects these changes.

Richard Sherwin described *Film and the Law* as the 'law and film movement's founding text'. Whilst flattered with the description, we have had to ask ourselves whether there is a 'movement' and also, if there is, how we answer the 'so what?' question. We firmly believe that recent work by ourselves, and others, has further answered this question. Whilst it seems a grand term, there is a film and law movement in so far as we have begun to see a number of threads and ideas emerge outside of our original template, and this is to be celebrated and further encouraged. One thing that we can say with some certainty is that the sheer volume of published work has continued to grow at a significant rate. Since 1996, there have been some 13 books written in the field of law and film. In addition, nine edited collections of essays in the area have been published, and, on at least seven occasions, learned journals have had special law and film focussed issues. To this substantial thematic film and law focus can be added a whole raft of individual essays, and it is clear that a major body of scholarship is now available for analysis. Whilst much of the work has been in English, scholarship has also been encountered in French, German, Italian and Spanish. All of this work is noted in the Bibliography, and we very much hope that this will act as a useful resource for those working in the field. Areas, movements and ideas do not stand still, and we as scholars have had to move on, reformulate and re-think and also to move our research in ways we had not originally anticipated. Two good examples of this are the explorations in British law films, as part of a broader movement with European colleagues to highlight national significance, and the development of work considering the influence of law films.

Whilst the authors have many synergies in approach, our routes into the area are slightly different, although complementary. Robson's interest arose from very practical political concerns in the early 1990s around the funding of legal services for the poor. Popular culture seemed to have an apparent ability to demonise lawyers in such a way as to help deny legal assistance to the oppressed in our society. Legal funding for poor and vulnerable people was threatened, and the villains of the piece appeared to be lawyers. The problem was that some 'fat cats' were making a good living out of the poor. Whilst this was a theme that had been noted some 20 years earlier, the solution being proposed was not some kind of properly funded national legal system to assist the poor and modestly off, but rather a curtailing of the already inadequate provision for legal aid. Where did the perception that lawyers were self-serving hypocrites rather than servants of justice and the greater public good derive from? Popular culture and the media seemed to play a part.

One of Robson's initial examinations of popular fiction was prompted by the observation, by one of Grisham's minor characters in *The Client* (1993), to the effect that litigation had replaced health care as the focus of those concerned with victims of accidents. This was followed with the aside that it is easier to get a lawyer than a doctor. That observation did not seem to ring true with the lives and experiences of those lawyers with whom Robson, in particular, had worked and taught. A more systematic examination was begun of other images of lawyers in film and television and a simplification of lawyering to crude stereotypes was noted—although not as dangerous as the kinds of lawyers Grisham portrayed. The first fruit of the examination of Grisham, by Robson, suggested that Grisham was in fact rather more critical of the system of law provision under capitalism than had at first been imagined. Although Grisham's analysis was found to be somewhat unspecific, by this time the whole area of the different ways in which law was represented in modern life had emerged as a more viable canvas.

Working independently at the outset, Greenfield and Osborn began from the proposition that law meant little without a sense of context. Inspired by Osborn's experience at Bar School, and Greenfield's love of *The Trial of the Incredible Hulk* (1989), they enrolled on a short course as part of the University of London's extra-mural programme, taught by Vincent McGrath. Here was a lawyer who clearly loved film. Attendance at this short course coincided with a move towards modularisation of the law degree at the University of Westminster, and a desire, strongly supported by the then Head of School, Professor Michael Gunn, now Pro-Vice Chancellor at the University of Derby, to teach law 'in the round'. After some debate as to desirable level, approach and position within the degree pro-gramme, the module that was developed was aimed squarely at first-year students at the very beginning of their studies. Its aim was to take a critical view of law and lawyers and to challenge preconceptions, using the module's position at the beginning of the law course to avoid the tyranny of 'finishing school syndrome', and, as an antidote to the tagged-on luxury of other potential critical responses to law curricula hegemony, such as philosophy or jurisprudence.

The module aimed to be accessible, empowering, and fun, whilst at the same time introducing students to critical approaches to the law. It was an example of the symbiotic link between research and teaching and allowed Greenfield and Osborn to test out their ideas. The approach was to take film as a text with which to carry out innovative and radical teaching within the LLB syllabus, and the films used were an amalgam of what was available and accessible and did not pretend to be a comprehensive overview of all law films, but was necessarily selective.

When we joined forces and examined, in greater depth, the range of films that had been produced utilising lawyers and the justice system we discovered they were both more extensive and varied than had originally been thought. They were, though, principally about American murder trials with recognisable plots and common characteristics for the participants. Some of these ideas were explored in conference papers at various locations. In due course we were contacted by Michael Asimow, who made us aware of his recently published work with Paul Bergman, *Reel Justice*. This and the other 1996 collections, edited by John Denvir and Richard Sherwin, provided the stimulus for us to develop our examination of films rather further. This collaboration bore fruit in a number of papers culminating in *Film and the Law* in 2001. As we indicated in the Introduction to that work, the analysis was part of our joint and individual desires to map out an area, but also to provide possible food for thought and act as a catalyst for future research and teaching initiatives.

Since that publication we have continued working on film and other aspects of popular culture and, although this is technically a second edition of our original book rather than a wholly new work, our perspective and approach has altered through the individual and collaborative work we have undertaken in the intervening years. There are significant changes, alterations and additions as can be seen by a cursory comparison of the two texts. We noted in 2001 that whilst we had started to provide a route map, there was much more work to be done, and the intervening years, and this text, lie testament to an attempt to address that.

The essence of there being a range of scholars from distinct disciplines with different goals for their commentaries has meant that we are confronted by many approaches in the scholarship. It ranges from the most limited remarks and use of film in a professional training environment to highly dense theoretical engagement within literary or film theory. The material may be common, but the goals and conclusions are not. It is little wonder that those engaged in some areas within this very broad field have expressed frustration and occasionally concern that their particular interests are ignored by others working on law and film. Such has been the extent of these types of debates that they figure in our examination of the themes that can be discerned within law and film studies from whatever quarter. There seems likely to continue to be a continued debate about the most appropriate focus for scholarship. Whilst none of us is so arrogant as to think that our way is the only true path, there is nonetheless an understandable resentment at others 'passing off' as law and film scholarship something we deem to be trivial, opaque or irrelevant. As we have indicated previously, we have not sought to hide our perspective on the purpose of law and film for us. We continue to hold the view that for us the principal interest lies in uncovering the ideology of film. We do recognise that for others, other goals inform their practice. For us, though, law and film is part of the ongoing struggle against oppression rather than some exercise in aesthetic scholasticism.

The scholarship now extends to a vast number of books, journals and articles. The approaches differ. The styles differ. There is a palpable recognition in some quarters that there are only partial descriptions of the many varieties of films involving law and justice. There remains still a need for many areas to be described and mapped out. Whilst a number of conflicts have been aired as to what kind of issues should be prioritised there are no clear signs that any consensus exists or is likely to be achieved as to what the best way forward is. We will in the ensuing chapters be indicating the focus we have been working on and where our work will be focused in the future. At least one of our goals in providing this brief overview of scholarship has been our genuine wish for there to be as much inter-connection as possible between those working in this novel field. We hope the area will not be fragmented with different scholars failing to benefit from the insights of others, or finding developments impenetrable or trite. From our experience it should be possible for anyone coming to this field afresh to be able to grasp what law and film has to offer without having to undergo retraining in several different disciplines. That said, a richer perspective is likely to be gained by those with the time, and inclination, to read and view as widely as they can.

Finally, we are often asked, to paraphrase David Byrne of Talking Heads: 'How did we get here?' More specifically, we are often asked the question, perhaps for want of anything else more incisive to ask: 'What is your favourite (law) film?' Similar variations of this include 'Which film got you into this?', or, 'If I had to watch one law film, which would it be?' Self-evidently, there is no easy answer to this, and the book shows how many films have touched all the authors in one way or another. However, for all of us there are key films that mean something very specific to us. Whilst *Brothers in Law* (1957) was the first film that introduced him to the arcane world of the Bar on a Saturday afternoon in the late 1970s or early 1980s, the first time Osborn saw *Young Mr Lincoln* (1939) this crystallised many ideas for him. When it was shown as part of Vincent McGrath's course, as part of the Birkbeck extra-mural programme, on 35mm film to a group of seven or eight interested film buffs, not only did it show a whole host of interesting ideas for future development and analysis, it also made clear why film is so important and how passionate film buffs and scholars are about their subject. In fact, he recalled seeing the film years before, but had not picked up on the legal resonance or the wider cinematic pedigree of the film. At the time, to paraphrase Lincoln, he may not have known what a law film was, but he knew what a good film was, and this was all that was great about the cinema.

Robson also has fond memories of Ian Carmichael's portrayal of Roger Thursby as being instrumental in him thinking of law as a world of light-hearted amateur-ish incompetence—which is an image which has been constantly reinforced subsequently. For sheer all-round excellence, however, he selects *The Accused* (1988). It has everything from the opening shots, through the plea-bargain and resulting alternative court action, to the stark post-finale statistics on the incidence of rape and levels of conviction. In its crisp 90-minute structure it combines so many elements which could provide a full course without using another film. It is a reality-based film, with all the conventions we associate with the cinema of justice along with portrayals of women in a changing macho culture. Add to this the rare, but omnipresent issue of class being raised and its sheer watchability, and we have a film with which all law and film courses should start.

Greenfield notes that the sheer volume of law films that have been discovered and watched since we started in this area of work makes selection of one or two key, or influential, or indeed favourite, films hard—harder even than the construction of this edition! Of course much depends on time, place and the emotional feeling of the viewer and some films such as *In the Name of the Father* (1993) are, whilst worthy, very much a product of their time. Others, such as *The Verdict* (1982) offer us a picture of a complicated character, Frank Galvin, who combines professional and personal failings yet remains committed to the idea of justice within a framework of dirty realism. To this author, this film stands the test of time because of the immense performance of Paul Newman and a plot focusing on civil law that marks it out from the usual criminal law fare. He gives two more interesting examples. First, the Swedish offering *Solstorm* (2007) providing us with a beautifully crafted film linking together ideas of law, justice and religion, without the usual gamut of Hollywood stars. It also reminds us of the importance of national cinema beyond America, a growing area of interest for law and film scholars. The second film is *The Rising: the Ballad of Mangal Pandey* (2005), a Bollywood film that covers the Indian Mutiny of 1857. There are interesting legal points concerning the rule of the East India Company but it fits squarely into the sub-genre of courts martial films that have not been subject to the same detailed analysis as courtroom drama. Importantly it is also based upon a most significant incident in Indian political history and reminds us of these events. This group also raise questions about the production of films based on 'true' events and how these contribute to our knowledge of history.

What we are all agreed upon is that film is a vital and important resource, and an area that is increasingly important. This book carries on the journey and we hope that others will use it as a point of departure to develop further research, teaching and study.

Finally, thanks are due to Jurga Gradauskaite who helped with the checking of sources and materials. All errors, unfortunately, are ours.

Steve Greenfield
Guy Osborn
Peter Robson

CONTENTS

Contents

1

Film and the Law: an Orientation

Film and the law appears to be thriving. As the text illustrates, significant developments have occurred in many aspects within the field. Significantly we have had a shift further towards both the theoretical and the empirical. At the same time the numbers of scholars teaching and researching in the area has increased. This chapter seeks to provide an initial orientation of these developments, many of which will be interrogated in greater depth in later chapters. As part of this we seek to set down some markers as to the *purpose* and *prospects* for work in this area, and to chart how work in the area has been impacted upon by both the theoretical, and the empirical.

Law and Film Scholarship

The scholarship on law and film is both extensive and diverse. Since many of the films examined recur in different books and essays, and in differing contexts, we must be careful not to assume that the specificities of their discussion do not vary accordingly. Given especially that much of the initial work in the field emanated from the United States, it is important to note that much of the individual work that has been undertaken reflects the distinct legal framework in which it takes place, as well as local educational structures. This might seem an obvious point, but very few writers presage their remarks by emphasising the particularity of their situation. Almost no writers indicate the nature of their approach or the limited applicability of their remarks. Writers it seems to us imply by their silence that their comments are capable of being universally applied. They may, perhaps, hope that this is the case. It may be that since film is a global phenomenon, any comments are assumed to have the same properties. This we consider limits the effectiveness of scholarship. Failing to acknowledge the specific cultural situation means the context is not revealed. What may pertain in one jurisdiction in terms of the politics of the judiciary, or the reputation of practising lawyers, may be entirely different in another jurisdiction. Just because we tend to watch the same cultural products does not mean they have the same resonance to every audience.

Thus when we come across work on some feature of law, such as the jury, any remarks need to be limited to those systems where there are very similar institutions. Failure to limit the scope of comments has not in the past been helpful.

Recognising the specifics of different legal cultures and popular cultures was not a feature of the early work on law and film, largely because of the hegemony of Hollywood and the Anglo-American adversarial jury-centred system. Given that a significant proportion of the scholarship on law and film takes place outwith the United States the distinct nature of other legal cultures needs to be noted. Otherwise any scholarship speaks only to the American and ignores all the other states with legal systems.

There are very basic differences in focus between those working in American law schools and their colleagues in other jurisdictions, especially as far as becoming lawyers is concerned. The role of education in this process, and where law and film sits as a discipline, needs to be explained. In the United States most of the students are studying law as a graduate course with a view to practice rather than, say, the British model where law is taken as a *possible* route into practice. After graduation in this model, law students are required to undertake a postgraduate year of professionally orientated study. In Europe there is a very different set of arrangements, with students opting between private practice, the prosecution service and the judicial profession. There has also been considerable interest from those with no direct contact with law teaching or the legal profession, and their interests are rather different from those engaged in teaching and research within legal academia.

Scholarship has flowed from various different questions addressed in relation to film. The interests of scholars have been quite distinct and it is crucial to understand the parameters of these rather different goals. This should address the problem that has emerged in various critical commentaries on earlier works. Whilst our work has sometimes been highly praised, it has also been subject to critique—this has largely focused upon an alleged failure to fully address the concerns of film theory, or for not including television in a study of law and film.[1] It is unhelpful, we submit, for critics to lament the fact that the book or article in question is not the one the critic personally would have written had he or she been writing on, for instance the films of Alfred Hitchcock or Sidney Lumet, the film theory of Jacques Deleuze or the history of the much underrated *Carry On* ... canon.

By seeking to organise the broad literature on the relationship between law and film in the chosen method, we hope that the distinctive contributions of scholars will be recognised, and that participation be encouraged, even where it fails to contribute to, for instance, the development of legal doctrine or film theory. The work, for instance, of Mike Nevins, in drawing attention to the possibilities of B Movie Westerns to provide an alternative location for discussing the nature of justice, should not be dismissed because he does not contribute in this work to debate on whether these films were influential in changing the public mood on the death penalty, or policies in relation to judicial appointments.[2] By the same token, Nevins' description of the films, made between 1928 and 1934, will provide a valuable resource for anyone taking on the task of a comprehensive history of

---

[1] Moran, L (2004).
[2] Nevins, F (1996a).

lawyer films from the birth of cinema, without adding to debates on how music and lighting contributed to the aesthetic pleasures to be derived from law films of this era.[3] In this way work can be considered on its own merits, outside of any particular critic's own agenda or hobby-horse, although obviously, where relevant, work may be subject to critique.

At this juncture we also believe that law and film studies will benefit from a critical appraisal of what has been achieved, what gaps there are in coverage, and how the area might develop in the future. By its very nature, there is no guiding body in a position to prescribe what might be done, in the way that the Critical Legal Studies Movement, for example, may have proposed a reading of the law of tort or contract.[4] We offer this assessment in the spirit of academic commentators who have worked extensively in the area and who are keen to encourage both a greater volume of work as well as a more engaged kind of scholarship. We are attracted by the idea that the political aspects of this part of practice need to be expressed less obliquely. Long-time radical singer Pete Seeger, in the context of another part of culture, outlined his musician father's view that 'The necessary question to ask is not "Is it good music?" but "What is the music good for?"'.[5] We have been concerned for a number of years at the way in which the diversity of approaches in law and film studies threatens to overwhelm its founding principle of engaging students in a liberating intellectual and socially significant process. There is a danger that, in the climate in which scholarship operates in the major areas of activity, it will become impenetrable in its language and arcane in what it seeks to illuminate, and therefore its ideology is rendered opaque.

Law and film is now a relatively mature discipline and has changed markedly since we first produced teaching materials, articles and conference papers. There is a fabulous wealth of material, demonstrating a broad range of aims and methods. Some of these show the way in which the use of film can supplement legal study and involve truly imaginative approaches to areas of scholarship. Others show a use of language that may prove baffling to the beginner and involve an opaque methodology. These comments on the current state of law and film studies outline reasons why some of these developments have taken place, and the problems and differences that have emerged. The relevant areas can be divided into questions of methodology, issues of theoretical engagement and the use of language.

Methodology

Decisions about what the subject matter is, and how enquiry should be carried out, were largely overlooked in the early scholarship. Here was a new (to lawyers) resource—film—highlighting a range of questions in relation to the practice of law.

---

[3] Nevins, F (2004).
[4] Kairys, D (1990).
[5] Wilkinson, A (2006).

Exactly what one did with this new resource was determined by one's traditional method of analysing texts for their meaning. Film was no different. It was simply another text that had both clear meaning on its surface as well as other rather more oblique significance and potential meanings. Thus we had *The Man Who Shot Liberty Valance* (1962) seen as a metaphor for two different concepts of the nature of law.[6] A more modern and innovative example is to use *Judge Dredd* (1993) to demonstrate how law is divested in figures of authority. We can use films as examples of the source and authority of law; in one version law is shown as emerging organically through the will of the people whilst in the other law is vested in and dispensed from some authoritative source. A slightly different approach is identified by Spelman and Minow through *Thelma and Louise* (1991).[7] The discussion here is a central theme which crops up in both legal discourse as well as, more broadly, the role of confidence and specifically the ordeal posed by a rape trial.

Much of the early work was relatively modest in its goals; exposing problems with evidence, looking at the accuracy of the legal rules and the realism of portrayal of the personnel presented on screen, for example. A key point in this swathe of work was accuracy and realism, contrasting screen law with 'real' law. However, there was little attempt to explore the *consequences* of any identified gap between film and practice. This is understandable given the enormous and complicated nature of the task involving psychological enquiry and empirical survey. The causal relationship between media portrayals and subsequent beliefs or actions is controversial and highly problematic. Perhaps the location of law as a postgraduate vocational discipline explains the concern of US academics with realism in practice. Undergraduate legal education is less concerned with legal practice so ideas and theories of law may come more to the fore. However, there are UK examples of the realist school. Greenfield and Osborn (1996) adopted a critical approach to two films based on real life events, *In the Name of the Father* (1993) and *Let Him Have It* (1991), and their framework was not just to identify flaws and inaccuracies, but to offer some tentative thoughts about the significance of the portrayals. The methodology was to analyse a wide range of non-legal materials that outlined the events. This extended to interviewing the late Iris Bentley (sister to Derek, the central figure in *Let Him Have It* (1991)) to determine how those close to the 'story' felt about the cinematic version of their lives. Iris had mixed views on the film, unhappy with some of the inaccuracies but pleased to keep the case in the public eye. She had nothing but praise for Christopher Ecclestone, who played Derek.[8]

There has, however, been work that has sought to draw rather more elaborate conclusions from the material. A couple of examples illustrate such perspectives. For example, in his examination of the making and re-making of the film

---

[6] Denvir, J (1996a).
[7] Spelman, E and Minow, M (1996).
[8] Greenfield, S and Osborn, G (1996).

Cape Fear (1993), Richard Sherwin draws conclusions about the nature of shifts in American society and the role of lawyers between the late 1950s and the 1990s.[9] His comments appear perceptive and well grounded at the general level, although not necessarily supported by data on levels of respect for lawyers and their changing societal role. The problem, though, is the way in which the cinematic evidence is used as a key to the *zeitgeist*. How does a trend become significant? How many films should we be looking at? What period of time might we observe? What about the issue of changes in different generations' perceptions of earlier films?

There are other concerns where we move beyond the imprecise boundaries of *zeitgeist*. Mark Tushnet examines the film *Class Action* (1990), not in terms of its significance as an illustration of class politics or professional ethics, but as a site for psychoanalytic discussion.[10] He reads the film as a struggle between father and daughter. Indeed, this motif of the relationship between parent and child, and in particular father and son, runs through many of the films that deal with law and film. Austin Sarat, for his part, looks at a range of issues in *The Sweet Hereafter* (1997). He analyses the film for its potential to illustrate psychoanalytic perspectives drawn from Lacan.[11] What is interesting in both these examples is that they use the specific perspective of Lacan in relation to the law of the father, notwithstanding its contentious nature.

When law and film started, the role of the first scholars was to provide a supplement to legal education. As we outline in Chapter 2, legal education has traditionally been dominated by professional concerns. Films were used to highlight and emphasise, thus an early complaint was of the absence of any kind of clear theoretical perspective informing the analysis. The work looking at different kinds of films had a tendency to be highly descriptive, a problem which stemmed from the nature of the task which scholars were addressing. As has been explained in greater detail elsewhere, this was a subsidiary role.[12] The film texts were examples of these ideas in action though more recently the films themselves seem to have become the focus of critical attention. This shift into a cultural or film studies framework alters the nature of the scholarly enterprise. It may produce more rigorous 'film' scholarship but does it advance our understanding of such issues as gender, ethnic or class oppression? This is an area we return to in later stages of the book in specific chapters.

Jessica Silbey has pointed out that this splitting of emphasis between 'law' and 'film' is somewhat akin to the 'law in literature/law as literature' bifurcation. She suggests that work like that of Chase, and the essays in the *Legal Reelism* collection, are effectively 'law-in-film' akin to the 'law-in-literature' approach. The central effort here is to see how debates within law are conducted within film.

---

[9] Sherwin, R (1996b).
[10] Tushnet, M (1996).
[11] Sarat, A (2000).
[12] Osborn, G (2001).

5

How does law order our world in film? Within this broad field of 'law-in-film', Silbey notes scholarship that looks at how film shapes our expectations of law and justice in the world at large. Her characterisation of the other mode of scholars in the field is to suggest that 'film-as-law' is a study of filmic practices that are as 'pervasive and effective as legal ones in the ways in which they influence and inspire social order'.[13] Although relegated to a footnote, this does seem a bold and tantalising proposal. It resonates with some of the work that Meyer, Sherwin and Silbey herself have conducted.[14] The suggestion that film can have an impact upon our perceptions of reality is crucial for an understanding of law and popular culture, and is a point made by many commentators such as Macaulay, Sherwin and Denvir.[15] It remains a bold and controversial claim though it was not really borne out by the empirical research on perceptions of law.[16] Interestingly, a related debate could ensue about the very title of this book—is it *Film and the Law*, or *The Law in Film*?

It goes without saying that we make a distinction between what we take to be the main thrust of a text rather than its title. Hence there are two works focusing on women's portrayal in film. One is entitled *Framing Female Lawyers: Women on Trial in Film*, the other *Framed: Women in Law and Film*.[17] It is clear from the content that the authors have rather different interests. Lucia provides an overview of how women were represented in mainstream Hollywood cinema as lawyers on screen during the 1980s when there was a spate of films starring women lawyers. Kamir, on the other hand, looks at the representation of women as a whole from the silent film through to modern times. She selects principally art house films and gives only limited coverage to popular cinema. Thus, though the book titles are, as noted, strikingly similar, the 'framing' concept was used some years ago by Helena Kennedy in her influential overview of how women were treated under the legal system in Britain, the nature and style of the analysis are remarkably different.[18]

It is also worth noting that the tendency of writing to come from a single discipline, principally from lawyers, is not universal. A trend of scholarship has emerged in Spain where the interests and concerns of legal and film studies scholars are effectively split. This bifurcated approach is encountered in its most thoroughgoing form in *Images and Justice: Law through Film* (Imágenes y Justicia: el derecho a través del cine).[19] Here the authors selected 21 individual films, with two separate commentaries for each film. There is a legal commentary from the magistrate author, and a cinematic one from the journalist author. In the other works in the *Derecho y Cine* series there are examinations of individual films with

---

[13] Silbey, J (2007a).
[14] Silbey, J (2001); Sherwin, R (2000); Meyer, P (2001a).
[15] Macaulay, S (1987); Denvir, J (2004); Sherwin, R (2000).
[16] Asimow, M *et al* (2005); Salzmann, V and Dunwoody, P (2005).
[17] Lucia, C (2005); Kamir, O (2006).
[18] Kennedy, H (1992).
[19] Nieto, FS and Fernández, F (2004).

a mix of legal, social and cinematic analysis.[20] English language scholarship, as we have noted, tends to be somewhat more oblique in acknowledging its perspectives. This introduction seeks to clarify the contexts in which the work appears and the paradigms within which the essays and books operate. The recognition of the divergent methodologies of the authors writing on law and film should, we feel, lead away from sterile counter-posing of works with possibly similar titles but different goals.

Silbey also points to another stream of activity in law and film, centred on the storytelling features of law and film. There is, admittedly, a parallel between the way in which trial lawyers seek to construct a narrative and the way in which some cinema is narrative in its form. We have previously interrogated this link between storytelling and the role of stories in 'the law' and film. This common feature of storytelling, though, neither exhausts what is involved in the operation of the justice system, nor what occurs in film. Much day-to-day legal practice is involved in negotiating between parties as to how future relations will be conducted. There will be discussions about how past conduct has not met stipulated criteria. When allied to the complex enterprise of drafting documents to encompass these scenarios and prevent against undesired outcomes it is hard to see why this set of practices should be portrayed as storytelling. The narrative convention in film may be dominant but much 'art house' and even mainstream cinema takes a very different approach.

The question, however, for us, is not so much whether or not the characterisation of law as storytelling is inadequate, but rather whether the range of studies Silbey identifies as 'law-in-film' can be usefully contained within a single framework. We suggest that different methodologies are at work. Different interests and foci exist. Just as legal scholarship ranges from the doctrinal black letter, through socio-legal, to philosophical analysis, so too law and film has its distinct constituents. The problem lies in failing to recognise that the distinct approaches come with different sets of criteria of relevance. When scholars shift between different approaches without acknowledging this change, they run the risk of their work being misinterpreted or critiqued for failing to do something that it was not trying to do. Descriptive work or taxonomic surveys often cover extensive amounts of material without appearing to engage explicitly with theory. Theoretical insights are sometimes premised, as we have noted, on very limited evidence. These limitations need to be addressed in the pursuit of richer scholarship. Whether that is turned, as we would wish to see it, towards demystification of the politics of law in film, is a separate issue.

Having highlighted the heterogeneity of the scholarly approaches in the field, it is worth looking at the scholarship in a slightly different way. At the risk of seeming to construct ever more taxonomies, it seems worth stepping back and looking at the themes that recur in these writings. Law and film scholarship can

---

[20] Robson, P (2007b).

also be looked at in terms of the specific topics that have attracted the attention of scholars. The issues here have emerged within writing that it geared very clearly towards the practical as well as much more theoretical approaches. Probably as a result of the status of legal education as the standard prestigious route into the potentially lucrative field of legal practice, in the United States there has been relatively little soul searching as to the value or function of this kind of scholarship. Its value has been assumed to be worthwhile through its ability to provide more rounded lawyer citizens much as literary lawyers were lauded a century ago.[21] At worst it is going to produce lawyers who can engage effectively with the new multi-media age in which litigation is conducted.[22]

One can divide the published material in terms of the major recurring themes. Most of the work centres on the way law and lawyers appear in fictional work. From the earliest days when lawyers appeared in films, concern has been expressed by the legal profession (and censors) as to the kinds of images being portrayed. How the images have altered and how different groups have been featured forms a major part of the scholarship to date. Rather less attention has, hitherto, been paid to analysing how these images are constructed. Finally, the question of reflection on where the scholarship is taking us has been of ongoing concern to some. This theme is so crucial that we feel it merits a separate discussion that we undertake in the next chapter. Our own assessment of what we feel to be the most important areas we discuss at greater length later in the book. For the moment we describe what the thrust of the scholarship has been hitherto. We leave our assessment of the value of the work for the moment as well as where we hope to move in future research to achieve our aims in relation to our reading of the political nature of law.

Language

Although this might be seen as the least significant complaint, the question does need to be addressed. Due in part to the nature of academic specialisation, and perhaps for the less worthy goal of academic *kudos*, there is a tendency towards written obfuscation. Journals expand in both size and numbers and the contents are aimed at specialist audiences. Those lacking the background in a discipline need not start to read. People who may have thought they were interested in law and literature or critical studies have only to open the journals catering to these areas to find a bewildering array of language and style unfamiliar to the standard educated reader. The solution, as always, is to purchase a dictionary. Academics cannot be expected to dumb down. Whilst the foregoing is no more than an argument for a more explicit recognition of the need for clearer signposting of

---

[21] Gest, J (1913).
[22] Sherwin, R (2000); Sherwin, R, Feigenson, N and Spiesel, C (2006).

methodological questions in scholarship, there is always the danger that it might be seen as seeking to be prescriptive. This is not the intention, nor the expectation. Our own work has focused previously on both classification and the question of impact of popular culture.[23] This has been conceived of within a broadly material- ist framework. These are the areas that seem to us to be worthwhile exploring in seeking to uncover the way in which law exercises power and who benefits from such an exercise.

There is no reason to suppose that scholars will want to abandon their very different approaches to the field of law and film studies. Although we have noted that there has been pressure to achieve academic 'respectability', there are also countervailing forces at work. Academics value the freedom that they have to follow their own instincts and react to any purported orthodoxy.[24] In addi- tion, many of those who have written on law and film are involved principally in other areas. The suggestion that there be an agreed orthodoxy is unlikely to appeal to many of those already working in this area. For those coming into the area, however, a clearer guide as to what is being examined and to what purpose would surely assist in the development of law and film studies as a serious area of scholarship.

There is no professional external pressure on the area, other than that exer- cised indirectly. That is to say, it does not seem likely that professional bodies will start to require their members to attend courses on law and film. That said, courses orientated to law and film run in the United States have attracted continuing professional development recognition by dint of being offered by approved providers. They are also offered in Britain for the Scottish legal pro- fession. There is also the experience from France and Portugal. In the former, a week-long law and film studies course has been provided as part of French judi- cial training by the *Institut des Hautes Études sur la Justice* (Institute of Advanced Studies on Justice) in partnership with the *École Nationale de la Magistrature* (National School of Judicature). It is entitled *L'Image de la Justice dans le Cinéma Européen* (The Image of Justice in European Cinema). This looks at how lawyers and law systems have been presented in the cinema of France, Germany, Italy and the United Kingdom. In Portugal, lawyers have arranged to undertake pro- fessional development work on law and film under the auspices of the Catholic University of Portugal.

Thus, despite the threats and dangers that attend this new area, there are rea- sons to be cheerful about the future. There is also the question of the role and significance of television. Some of the early work on images of lawyers in popular culture in the 1980s was carried out in relation to television and this continues to be the focus of some work. Material on television provides a dual problem of accessibility and extent. The nature of weekly appearances and the possibil- ity of extensive character and issue development during the runs of these shows

---

[23] Greenfield, S, Osborn, G, and Robson, P (2001); Asimow, M *et al* (2005).
[24] Bradney, A (2006).

requires a rather different kind of reading from 90–120 minute one-off films which have dominated law and film studies hitherto. If the opportunity to debate the issues of methodology and theoretical approach is seized, and vigorous debate ensues, then law and film studies may escape marginalisation.

Empirical Work and Causation

At an International Institute of Sociology of Law Workshop held in Oñati, Spain, in 2002, a number of us working in the field observed that what actually underpinned much of our work was the assumption that popular culture was significant. In particular, it helped to determine how legal culture operated or was understood. This was an attempt to answer the 'so what?' or 'why does it matter?' questions that can be posed to those engaged in the analysis of film and the law. Both Stewart Macaulay and Lawrence Friedman, amongst others, have sought to explain the significance of popular culture.[25] A key question is the extent to which contemporary knowledge and understanding of the institutions of law and the personnel of the justice system is drawn from the media. This includes not just the reporting through television, the internet and the print media, but more specifically popular representations of law, legal personnel and justice that can be found throughout literature, television and film. Here we are drawn into the area of cultural studies which, like film studies, is fraught with theoretical pitfalls for the non-specialist and we make no claims here to distinguish between variants of high and low culture. There is, though, some sense that previously clear lines are becoming more blurred as new means of creation and distribution permit greater flexibility and interpretation of works. At the Oñati workshop we discussed the way forward and there was consensus in a number of areas. We determined that further work was required. One area of debate concerned the image of lawyers. Was the reputation of lawyers in films in decline? Did the various depictions accurately reflect this? Were the images unrealistic?

Whilst there might be conflict between scholars about the significance and meaning of legal films, the input of the viewing public seemed to be absent. What appeared to be lacking were any concrete studies of what the viewing public were actually gleaning from law films. Bearing in mind that establishing the influence of popular culture on how law is perceived is notoriously difficult, we determined to undertake a modest piece of empirical research into this area. In addition to highlighting film and news, we also included television in our survey of first-year law students across the globe. It is important to note that what we understand as a first-year law student has different resonances in the various jurisdictions. The results of this were published in 2005 and confirmed the suggestions of the

---

[25] Macaulay, S (1987); Friedman, L (1989).

earlier writers as to the significant role of the media and popular culture in shaping people's perceptions of law, justice and lawyers.[26] This is work we have continued to undertake in a small-scale way, and are in process of developing further empirical studies. We are, as previously, seeking to do this work across borders. The 2005 study looked at law students' perceptions in six different jurisdictions: Argentina, Australia, England, Germany, Scotland and the United States. We hope that we will be able to maintain a similar kind of breadth to avoid the assumptions and claims of any studies being too narrowly focused on the common law adversarial version of law practice. More broadly this reflects our attempts to move away from the American hegemonic position, something that we have already attempted to address.

The Heterogeneous Goals of Law and Popular Culture

One of the current concerns is the direction in which law and film seems to be moving. For example, some colleagues are more committed to the film studies part of the enterprise than with the insights for law students. David Black, back in 1999, bemoaned the lack of rigour of lawyers engaging with film. We have written about this on a number of occasions and sought to clarify our doubts about the direction away from a concern with the impact of film to their cinematic qualities.[27] James Elkins provides a robust rejoinder[28] to the kind of complaint raised initially by Black, and more recently Moran and his colleagues.[29]

There have been calls for a much greater engagement with film studies and a critique of both the nature of law and film scholarship, and the prevailing 'orthodoxy'. Seymour, for instance, bemoaned the fact that in the burgeoning literature of film and law there was a tendency to reduce films to a resource for specific legal issues, points or questions in which the specificities of film disappeared.[30] This can best be understood by looking at the different streams from which law and film studies emerged.

David Black has expressed what he perceives to be a difference in the focus between film studies and legal scholarship.[31] Black has suggested that we have, in fact, two realms of scholarship: one tied in to professional concerns, the other free floating. On one hand we have legal scholarship which, Black argues, 'has the very constant and identifiable goal of education toward, or commentary upon, an existing professional regime ... Legal studies ... has a constant and identifiable

[26] Asimow, M *et al* (2005).
[27] Greenfield, S, Osborn, G, and Robson, P (2007).
[28] Elkins, J (2004).
[29] Moran, L *et al* (2004).
[30] Seymour, D (2004).
[31] Black, D (1999).

telos', and where film is used to gain 'access to important legal issues'.[32] On the other side of an apparently unbridgeable divide, he posits, there is film studies: 'Unlike legal education, film studies has no clear-cut relation with an overriding and constant goal. The study of film is, or hopes it is, a valuable academic discipline in its own right.'[33]

Black's approach echoes the debates about the nature and purpose of the study of law since it emerged in the 19th century as a subject for degrees in universities.[34] This debate re-emerged, with some vigour, when law schools in Britain commenced full-time education in the post-Second World War era,[35] and the vocational/academic issue continues to exercise law teachers and lawyers to this day in a variety of forms. Black's approach is, nonetheless, based on a misperception of the nature of legal education. In simple terms much of what is covered in law schools has little to do with inculcating legal doctrine and much to do with intellectual skills, and little that is learned in the law school makes real sense without an understanding of context.

---

[32] *Ibid*, 133.
[33] *Ibid*, 133.
[34] Robson, P (1979).
[35] Osborn, G (2001).

2

The Penetration of Law and Film

This chapter has as its principal focus the development and use of film within the law school, although references are made to the application of film in other disciplines. As we have noted, the vast majority of the scholarship on law and film has its source in those teaching in law schools. Like many other professionally orientated areas of teaching, the syllabus is somewhat constrained as to what is deemed significant, and appropriate, by the relevant external body, in this case the legal profession, which has its own interests and goals. However, there is a greater degree of freedom today than was previously the case when subject areas and assessment were far more prescriptive. It is this close relationship with the professions and the consequent link between the theory and practice of law that has often provided the impetus for using film in a variety of ways. Black argues that the use of film in law and film studies is 'to elucidate and enrich areas of legal practice and interpretation'.[1]

Whilst it is clear that many have sought to break away from these professional and ethnocentric confines, we do not concur with Black's general view of law and film scholarship. These notions of commentary and critique provide the context within which our own, and others' work has generally operated. This can be seen both in the developments we describe in this Chapter, as well as more recent expansion of law and film studies in other European countries, which are a most welcome addition to the field. This Chapter first considers some of the issues that the traditional framework for English legal education throws up before considering the development of popular culture and the emergence of law and popular culture. This is then married to the use of film generally within higher education before exploring the ways in which it has been used within law teaching. Finally we review the film and law courses that we are aware of through contacts and academic writing.

The Framework of Legal Education

Law has always rather uneasily straddled the divide between the intellectual and the professional. That the legal profession exists provides law with a vocational

---

[1] Black, D (1999: 129).

edge, despite the fact that further practice-oriented study and professional training are required before qualification. Originally the governing bodies ran the professional training courses themselves, though these are now operated independently, but subject to a regime of inspection and approval. The Law Society Finals course, taught by the College of Law, became the Legal Practice course, which is now run by both universities and private providers in addition to the College of Law. The Bar Finals course became the Bar Vocational course and is also run externally by approved bodies as well as the Inns of Court School of Law. The 'conflict' between the university law schools and the professional bodies lies in the content of the law degree, and how far the syllabi, and assessment of it, can be independently determined. The legal profession is largely concerned with the knowledge and competencies with which law graduates approach the next stage of training. The professions have insisted that certain subjects must be studied and passed for the award of a qualifying law degree (QLD). These are the traditional areas of law—administrative law, contract law, tort law, equity and trusts, land law and criminal law—with the more recent addition of European law. The legal profession is not the only influence on the curricula, as heed must be paid to the Benchmark Statement in Law produced by the Quality Assurance Agency.[2] There may of course in addition be university-specific local requirements that must be met. This might include, for example, a requirement that a free elective must be offered in each year of study, with the rationale being that a student has the opportunity to study a different subject to their main area of study to enrich their educative palette. The professional requirement of core subjects at the expense of other law subjects or indeed other areas from different disciplines was subject to a withering critique by Peter Birks, Basil Markesinis and others in *What are Law Schools For?*[3].

In the same text, Goodrich further argued that while law schools trained the soul, this took the form of '[instituting] a culture of law through a hierarchical conception of knowledge and through a variety of techniques of separation, isolation and fear'.[4] Some 10 years later Watt, who had contributed to Birks' original collection, argued that the soul of legal education was still in need of redemption in a piece that attempted to search out this very soul and to identify areas that illustrate this. His survey explores a variety of areas and approaches, and centres upon a belief that a law and humanities perspective to legal education should be incorporated or adopted. In particular it should show context, be aware of broader meaning and, crucially, 'engage imagination':

> My hope is that a decade from now, when we look back on the tenth anniversary of this special issue on the subject of legal education, we might sum up the focus of modern law school education in a different word (to pedagogy): 'imagination'.[5]

---

[2] See www.qaa.ac.uk/academicInfrastructure/benchmark/honours/law.asp, last accessed 18 February 2010.
[3] Birks, P (1996).
[4] Goodrich, P (1996: 68).
[5] Watt, G (2006).

Others have taken up this clarion call. Notably, Tony Bradney has argued for a broader and more contextual curriculum, both for the good of the law school as an entity but also for the health of the legal academics that inhabit it.[6] The inter-disciplinary field of law and film is itself a part of the broader law and popular culture movement which can be viewed as part of the socio-legal studies tradition.

Law and Context—the Role of the Socio-legal Imagination

The meta-rules which determine what counts as compelling in such a system, of arguing by analogy from previous examples, has been the source of much of the controversy within socio-legal studies from the 1930s in the United States and from the 1960s in Britain. Class, race and gender emerged as major factors in attempts to trace how the process of decision making within common law jurisdictions is affected. These aspects of the broader socio-legal movement are dealt with within the context of law and film below. Such critiques do not, how-ever, seek to deny the reality that the framework within which this class, racial or gendered justice is meted out has the flavour of law and legality. It has been one of the underlying themes within critical legal work that the process of creating law from raw social and economic power is one which goes on scarcely noticed in many Western parliamentary democracies. Class, gender and racial interests almost disappear in the construct of law. Since the seductive notion of human rights is presented as a function of the concept of the rule of law, this examination of the sources of the power of law has been even more muted at the end of the 20th century. The progressive focus within the academy has shifted significantly from the structural to cultural. The relationship between the political economy and the law has been displaced by a concentration on the workings of cultural artefacts. The expansion of law teaching into areas such as law and literature and law and culture has, of course, other adherents. These areas are not by any means the preserve of the radicals. There is, nonetheless, a strong stream of work from writers previously associated with radical critiques of law and its relationship to the political economy. This expansion of work in the area of law and culture is to be welcomed and it is hoped that it will develop more broadly into all areas of popular culture.

For example, Goodrich and Murphy have provided their readings of develop-ments leading away from materialist critiques of the legal process into the work of critical legal studies. These are valuable records, albeit dense and highly personal. The starting point which the movement assumed was the political and intellec-tual bankruptcy of positivist accounts of law. As accounts of the developments

---

[6] Bradney, A (2003).

in theoretical writing on law Goodrich and Murphy offer, not surprisingly, somewhat different emphases. The conclusions, or at least tone, seem rather different. Goodrich suggests that critical approaches within legal scholarship have not really passed beyond a passive reproduction of the core legal curriculum. Goodrich suggests that critical legal scholarship 'has had only indirect and hesitant effects upon law because it has not studied or engaged with law...'[7]

There is then the paradox of a highly prestigious body of work and group of scholars whose engagement is with each other rather than the object of critique, law and its institutionalisation of class, gender and ethnic hegemonies. This successful professional trajectory, which Goodrich describes with justified pride, does not disguise the fact that re-engagement with fellow radicals is, as Goodrich hints, surely crucial. Merely establishing a congruence of agendas is, of itself, however, not enough according to Murphy.[8] There is a need to be clear what critique is actually *for*. The post-modern commitment within much of CLS is an obstacle to engaging effectively with those strands of analysis which are universalistic in thrust. It is in this context of critical self-examination that the work which has developed within CLS on law and literature seems in danger of failing to heed the warnings of Goodrich and Murphy by providing a distinctive and impenetrable world, forbidding to those outwith its language and unable to grasp its political potential. The area of law and popular culture is one where the potential to galvanise, and also be meaningful, relevant, and most crucially understandable, for both academic teachers and students, is overt. These are its great strengths.

Popular Culture and Law and Popular Culture

There are three distinct issues that we need to explore here. First, the emergence of popular culture as a subject of study within cultural studies. Second, the argument that it is useful, desirable, or even vital that law students should have some understanding of cultural values and events which includes those located within popular culture. Finally we need to examine the developing area of law and popular culture as arguably this is a place that law and film could successfully be located. Much, however, depends on the type and extent of the law and film work and indeed the nature of the law and popular culture framework in which we want to place it. As we will see at one point, engaging aspects of popular culture can be examined (legally) from a doctrinal black letter perspective.

Cultural studies is widely believed to have been instigated via the work of Hoggart and Williams, and cultural studies as an area of study can be said to have

---

[7] Goodrich, P (1999: 360).
[8] Murphy, T (1999: 266).

arisen through the British cultural studies movement.[9] In terms of its coverage, Turner notes that:

> It would be a mistake to see cultural studies as a new discipline, or even a discrete constellation of disciplines. Cultural studies is an interdisciplinary field where certain concerns and methods have converged; the usefulness of this convergence is that it has enabled us to understand phenomena and relationships that were not accessible through the existing disciplines.[10]

It is sometimes difficult to see where cultural studies ends and popular culture begins or, indeed, if there is any real distinction at all. Storey argues that popular culture is part of cultural studies, but that it could also be seen as part of areas such as history and literary studies. When we think of popular culture as lawyers, a further problem can be identified. Not only is there a hurdle of establishing a 'law and ...' element within the context of a predominantly black-letter tradition within the law school, but also the difficulty of confronting debates in some quarters (both inside and outside the legal academy) as to the relevance of popular culture itself. This rejection, or marginalisation, of popular culture is charted by Turner in his exemplary history of British cultural studies. As Newman notes, echoing Redhead's point about 1980s dominant traditions:

> [p]opular culture theorists have claimed that their field has been ignored by elitist scholars, who view popular culture as not worthy of serious study, *because it is popular* ... This attitude toward popular culture has prevailed since Matthew Arnold's *Culture and Anarchy* (1869). Popular culture began to receive scholarly attention in the 1960s and 1970s, but the 1980s saw a resurgence of the 'back to basics' movement in education exemplified by the Harvard Core Curriculum.[11]

The role of the arts and culture as part of the education of lawyers has long been recognised as important by some commentators.[12] The early rationale for inclusion of subjects beyond the day-to-day courtroom forensic and document drafting skills of the practitioner was to ensure that lawyers were fully rounded individuals capable of empathising with their clients. Ray Browne suggested rather more strategic thinking at a conference of scholars on popular culture in 1993 when, noting that law is the matrix in which the forces of development and restraint collide and play out, he argued that 'lawyers are the machine operators who keep the conflicting forces from overheating and destroying the central core. Thus, lawyers can and should be very much interested in the culture in which these forces operate.'[13]

Popular culture has become established as an area of academic analysis for a number of different disciplines, yet study of the relationship between law and popular culture has been rather slow to develop. There are a number of reasons for this. First, the law school curriculum is to a large extent still based around the

---

[9] Hoggart, R (1958); Williams, R (1958).
[10] Turner, G (1996: 11).
[11] Newman G (1990: 270).
[12] Robson, P (1979); Chase, A (1986b); Friedman, L (1989).
[13] Browne, R (1993: 7).

doctrinal or 'black-letter' tradition and its hegemony can be seen in the many textbooks and casebooks that are produced:

> The black letter tradition assumes, of course, that the law is predicated upon a rational and coherent body of rules that, once identified and applied, will provide the answer to the problem. However, whilst such an assumption might underpin much teaching, even a cursory incursion into legal study reveals a labyrinth of confusion and non-conformity.[14]

This is partly because the legal academy is resistant to change, often isolated from the wider scholastic community, and perhaps possesses an innate conservatism that militates against progression. That said, there have been some significant shifts within the law curriculum, although many of these have been influenced by professional demands. As noted above, the requirement to study a swathe of subjects is determined by the professions so that the law degree retains its status as a qualifying degree. This element has increased with the introduction of skills as well as new substantive subjects such as European law. However, it is illuminating at this juncture to consider the recommendations of the Ormrod Report almost 40 years ago, which argued that:

> In the scheme of training for the practice of the law, the objectives of the academic stage should be to provide the student with:
>
> (i) a basic knowledge of the law, which involves covering certain 'core' subjects;
> (ii) an understanding of the relationship of law to the social and economic environment in which it operates; and
> (iii) the intellectual training necessary to enable him to handle facts and apply abstract concepts.[15]

Ormrod hints at a wider appreciation of law, and that law should be viewed within its broader socio-economic context. There have been a number of developments that have attempted to satisfy this aim. However, even these have at times been treated with suspicion and academics have had to battle for acceptance, notwithstanding the fact that these subjects may actually be very traditional in their teaching and learning methodology:

> Both Family Law and Labour Law are, for example, good examples of this phenomenon; both are responsive to societal and legislative changes. However, a key aspect of such 'new' subjects is not so much the subject matter itself but the approach adopted. For example, Labour Law could be seen on one level as a particular sub-strata of contract, tort and EU Law, although on another it might be seen as a heavily politicised course and the approach and coverage would reflect this accordingly. Similarly, as recounted below, any new subject can be reactionary and mundane and not necessarily as vibrant and dynamic as the area might suggest; 'new' does not necessarily equate with 'critical' or 'contextual'.[16]

---

[14] Osborn, G (2001: 165–66). See also Sugarman, D (1991).
[15] Ormrod (1971: 94).
[16] Osborn, G (2001: 168).

The area of 'law and popular culture', whilst of comparatively recent origin, is a further example of a shift toward a more contextual approach. Within the broad field of law and popular culture there is a conundrum: there is no obvious body of law and to a large degree the delineation of subject matter is highly subjective. This is further compounded by the fact that popular culture is itself a loaded term, and this perhaps accounts for the lack of academic treatment it has received. This is notwithstanding the fact that, as Lawrence Friedman suggested:

> Popular legal culture and popular culture are related to one another in two important respects. First, popular culture gets its ideas of law, or at least some of them, from popular legal culture. In other words, popular culture *reflects* popular legal culture.[17]

Friedman's point neatly illustrates one of the crucial aspects of law and popular culture, and one that is exemplified in law and film particularly, that much understanding of law is gleaned from cultural *representations* of the law. Recent years have seen the emergence of a number of courses and modules that attempt to draw upon this relationship, as detailed in part below. Of course these do not necessarily share any particular characteristics, and use differing approaches and coverage.

The status of popular culture, and cultural studies, exacerbates this situation as cultural studies have embraced popular culture.[18] The question for lawyers is whether it has yet become academically respectable to study law and popular culture? Perhaps even more problematic is defining exactly what law and popular culture may mean. Defining the terms is perhaps a logical point to start, and we need to organise the terms of popular culture and legal culture and what we may expect from interaction between law and popular culture. Friedman defines legal culture as 'ideas, attitudes, values and opinions about law held by people in a society'.[19] A narrower view of legal culture could, however, be constructed. This could refer to the working culture of the profession itself, that is to say the norms and values that underpin the working of the law. As a means of clarification we term the broader notion as external legal culture, and the narrower profession-based perspective as the internal legal culture. One of the most interesting theoretical perspectives in this area is determining the relationship between the ideologies of the cinema and the law, or, more bluntly, exploring why and whether the cinema provides any messages about law and lawyers. In many ways, though, this is rather pre-emptive, as we first need to determine what films, and more broadly popular culture, are saying, if anything, about law and lawyers. We would firmly argue that this is indeed the first task, to determine the nature of the portrayal before this can be linked into wider theoretical debates. Tied in to this is the idea of genre, and how genre theory can be applied to legal films, and this is explored later in the book.

[17] Friedman, L (1989: 1592).
[18] See generally Storey, J (1994).
[19] Friedman, L (1989: 1579) citing his previous work, Friedman, L (1985).

In a sense much of the intricate theoretical debate concerning the ideologies of culture, and in particular that related to the cinema and high/low culture debates, has bypassed many of those working on the relationship between law and popular culture, often for purely practical reasons. As Redhead points out, 'it is patently difficult to maintain expertise in both legal theory and cultural studies'.[20] There have, however, been a number of strands of work produced—some more firmly rooted in social theory than others. Thus, in areas concerning gender, race and ethnicity and sexuality the role of film in challenging stereotypes has been considered in a range of literature. The theoretical framework of such studies has included equal rights liberalism as well as various strands of feminism. One area of the law and popular culture relationship concerns the legal regulation of issues within contemporary cultural life and is often more akin to traditional black-letter legal analysis. As Redhead observes:

> Case law history across a whole series of 'traditional' and 'emerging' pedagogic areas of legal study including sports law, licensing law, intellectual property law, heritage law, privacy law, obscenity law, entertainments law, media law and computer law, testifies to the increasing importance in the law school curriculum of law and popular culture.[21]

Lawyers familiar with traditional subjects such as tort, contract and criminal law have been able to apply these concepts to the cultural industries themselves, and the products of such industries. This has led to claims for the autonomy of subjects such as sports law as opposed to the concept of sport and the law. Entertainment law has also begun to emerge as an academic subject at both undergraduate and postgraduate level as well as within legal practice courses, though it has a far longer history within law schools in the United States. On one level these are subjects that are often inherently interesting exactly because they are concerned with popular culture. If we accept, for these purposes, the definition of popular culture as the culture of everyday life, then cases and statutes in these areas are enticing precisely because they are part of our cultural life. Cases involving Napster and other file-sharing sites, the George Michael dispute, the OJ Simpson trial and others attracted massive media attention that highlighted legal disputes that would not have been present if the cultural status of the participants had been different. This stresses the importance of popular culture to our daily life and widespread interest in the regulation of this culture. Law that governs popular culture becomes tagged with the populist cloak.

A further approach analyses how popular culture portrays the internal legal culture, and how this then affects the external legal culture. Simply, what does film and/or television show us about the law and how does this alter public perceptions of law and lawyers? This view of one narrow subject matter of popular culture is encompassed in wider debates about what popular culture is and how it

---

[20] Redhead, S (1995: 30).
[21] *Ibid*, 30.

works. Berger draws a convenient distinction between two camps within cultural studies:

> The difference between popular culture critics (many of whom are critical theorists) and scholars who study and analyze the mass media per se is that popular culture critics tend to focus much of their attention on texts—specific works and specific genres—in contrast to mass communication scholars, who are more interested, generally speaking, in the way mass-mediated works affect attitudes, values, beliefs and related concerns in audiences. Mass communication scholars tend to see themselves as social scientists, and their approach is (or at least was) essentially social psychological, measuring effects, using participant observation and other such techniques. Popular culture critics draw much of their theory from literary theory, philosophy, rhetorical theory, and related areas.[22]

Much of the work by lawyers, particularly in the area of film and law, straddles this divide. For example, there are numerous examples of work concerned with the *effect* of popular culture. In the legal sphere this is often concerned with legal liability for entertainment products that cause 'harm' and in the past this has revolved around the legitimacy of the censorship of material. This idea of harm, whether to individual or society morals, has been the basis for the regulation of entertainment products including books, films or music. More recently this has moved forward to consider whether such products can lead to injuries to third parties caused by those consuming the cultural products, both the copycat scenario and through the influence of behaviour. There have been allegations against different media including books, films, videos and music, most significantly the litigation surrounding the film *Natural Born Killers* (1994).[23] However there are major legal difficulties to surmount for claims to succeed, particularly with respect to causation. The other area that has interested film and the law scholars has been to identify the meaning of the film. This approach is more akin to cultural criticism, but has as its aim to chart these messages upon the public perception of law and lawyers. This subject is explored in more detail below, but it is important to recognise that this work does have links with both cultural and mass communication studies and other work in the area of law and popular culture; although on a purely one-dimensional level cinematic portrayals of law can be used as a teaching aid to replace or add to traditional teaching materials.

The Use(s) of Film

Law is obviously not the only subject area where films may be used in a variety of ways as part of a teaching and learning strategy. Comer discusses the use of *The Lion King* (1994) to 'help undergraduate management and organizational behaviour

---

[22] Berger, A (1995: 162).
[23] *Byers v Edmondson* 712 So.2d 681 (1999).

students learn and apply such fundamental leadership concepts as bases of power and leadership skills, traits and behaviours'.[24] She indicates that the student feedback appreciated the use of the film. Hudock and Gallagher Warden note the use of films to teach family systems theory and explore the contribution that fiction film may make to the development of perceptual, conceptual and executive-level skills.[25] Interestingly, they also raise the point that students may become subjectively involved with the plot or characters that can be positive in that it indicates that the student has personal issues that need to be addressed. Thus what might be seen as a negative point of using film can be turned into a positive outcome provided it is recognised and supported in an appropriate environment.

Berger and Pratt promote the use of two David Mamet films, *Glengarry Glen Ross* (1992) and *House of Games* (1987), to enhance the teaching of business-communication ethics.[26] There is also widespread evidence of the use of films on psychology courses, group counselling and English as a foreign language for example.[27] Perhaps most surprising is the use of silent film to teach French. Bloom argues that the absence of speech 'can lead students to compensate for it with prolific discourse',[28] furthermore the films can contribute to the student appreciation and knowledge of the cultural history in which the film is set. Champoux raises some interesting points around the construction of film and the characteristics a film may contain which offer a different experience for students:

> The unique characteristics of film making add to its communication power. Focusing techniques, editing, framing of shots, camera angles, sound, and the like, help a director make a powerful statement of a subject. These techniques also let a director create an experience that often goes beyond what we can experience in reality. Viewers are not passive observers. Their responses add to the power of film. Cinema's ability to create a unique experience gives it unbeatable power as a teaching tool.[29]

This raises the interesting point that we do not just enhance the experience of students through the use of film, but expand their knowledge and understanding. This is not just information gathered in a different and arguably more accessible format, but both a deeper and broader awareness, albeit from a different jurisdiction. To illustrate one example of how the use of close-up shots may increase our understanding, Champoux uses *Twelve Angry Men* (1957). He argues that the close-up shots 'show the emotions each juror felt during their decision-making process in a murder trial. Ordinary vision would have difficulty seeing the emotions of each person's face as he spoke'.[30] Drama is emphasised by this technique, and whilst Champoux uses this as an example in terms of decision making in the context of organisational behaviour and management, it clearly allows us to

---

[24] Comer, DR (2001: 430).
[25] Hudock, A and Gallagher Warden, S (2001).
[26] Berger, J and Pratt, C (1998).
[27] King, J (2002).
[28] Bloom, M (1995: 31).
[29] Champoux, J (1999: 207).
[30] *Ibid.*

penetrate the jury room. This is important, as little is written in the UK on the jury experience which leaves such films as an important source of information. But the close-ups will also demonstrate an indication of the difficulty that some jurors have, and the weight of the burden such a public function may carry. Tyler and Reynolds also draw upon *12 Angry Men* (1957) to consider group theory. As they note, the example of the father and son relationship could be examined 'from varying perspectives including a psychodynamic perspective, a social learning perspective, or a behavioural perspective'.[31] The use of films can of course apply to the teaching of many disciplines besides law as many of the same benefits will apply. Furthermore law films that handle important moral or ethical problems can contribute to education generally. For instance, the problems of backstreet abortions, especially in a narrow intolerant moral climate, can be effectively highlighted through such films and *The Cider House Rules* (1999) and *Vera Drake* (2004).

Film and Law Teaching

As teaching has become subject to greater analysis from both theoretical and bureaucratic perspectives, those in the classroom have been expected to spend greater time reflecting not just about course content but also the modes and methods of delivery. Universities are expending greater efforts and funds into both staff development and electronic resources for students; e-learning environments and programmes abound. Law teachers are more likely now to be faced with an interactive white board than the traditional blackboard, whilst overhead projectors sit quietly gathering dust in the corner, superseded by a range of electronic alternatives. Contemporaneously, the shift from analogue to digital and the development of the World Wide Web has enabled access to a much wider range of materials. However, it would be a mistake to assume that it required the invention of the VHS video recorder for films to be used within law teaching. Millard Ruud, a law professor at the University of Texas, wrote in 1958 of the existence (and in its fifth year) of 'The Townes Hall Film Forum', a vehicle to show films to both law and non-law university students. These films were selected for both professional and cultural interest. This latter category illustrates a point we consider further later, namely the importance of understanding the context to law. As Ruud observes: '[i]t is self evident that a student's understanding of the workings and policy of a rule of law bears a direct relationship to his understanding of the fact situation with which the rule deals'.[32] Whilst there are undoubtedly many of us who would argue that students need to understand the context in which the fact

---

[31] Tyler, J and Reynolds, T (1998).
[32] Ruud, M (1958: 552–3).

situation arises to fully understand the rule and application of law, this is a radical approach in terms of the use of film.

Perhaps the most obvious use of film in the study of law is as a simple audio-visual teaching aid to illustrate particular points. These could even be fairly 'black letter' areas of law such as using *A Civil Action* (1998) to discuss environmental law and causation in tort. Clips can also be used to illustrate legal skills such as advocacy, and there are a number of fine oratorical performances that could be utilised for critical analysis, comparison and learning. The final courageous closing speech, or the rigorous cross-examination, are often the hallmarks of the great courtroom drama especially in capital cases such as *A Time to Kill* (1996). Students can be asked to view the positive and negative aspects of such advocacy and measure it against the theoretical perspectives. Whilst these scenes may be overly melodramatic and contrary to elements of court protocol or procedure, they often possess great examples of timing and eloquence, Anthony Hopkins' closing argument in *Amistad* (1997) being a case in point. Certainly Anthony Hopkins' (Adams) appeal is a stirring and emotional one and could be utilised in terms of illustrating delivery of text and message.

Beyond the more simplistic clips, whole films can be used to draw attention to broader ethical and moral issues and the consequent interaction with law. Examples of how film could be used at this level include using *Philadelphia* (1993) to illustrate discrimination in employment, *The Verdict* (1982) for medical negligence or *A Civil Action* (1998) and *Erin Brockovich* (2000) for environmental disasters and corporate responsibility. In addition, ethical topics abound in law films, from narrow legal ethics such as codes of conduct, *Cape Fear* (1991), through to issues such as the legitimacy of capital punishment in *Let Him Have It* (1991), *The Green Mile* (1999) and *Dead Man Walking* (1995). Similarly great moral dilemmas are often a mainstay of law films, with examples such as racism, *To Kill a Mockingbird* (1962), *A Time to Kill* (1996), *Mississippi Burning* (1988); police corruption, *Serpico* (1973); vigilantism, *Deathwish* (1974); sexual harassment, *North Country* (2005); abortion, *Vera Drake* (2004); and homophobia, *Philadelphia* (1993).

The principal (methodological) approach in relation to doctrinal law issues involves discerning the legal issue embedded in the film's narrative. Reading films which have a courtroom drama at their centre is generally straightforward enough. The writing, which has addressed the issue of how film has represented a particular area of law, has been extensive and is currently thriving. It can be expected to flourish in the future because of its ability to connect with the core attribute of accessibility. As various writers in the 1990s pointed out, film provides an entry point into a discussion of the nature and development of doctrine that is most attractive for those involved in teaching.[33]

---

[33] Denvir, J (1996a).

Writers have also sought to show how misleading film versions of law have been and we see this most clearly in *Reel Justice*.[34] In the first major text to examine legal films systematically the question of accuracy was a clear and acknowledged function of the work. Thus Bergman and Asimow structured their book to cover the narrative of films, the legal issue raised and what the law actually said. They suggest, for instance, that 'it's important to know how Hollywood bends the rules to inject drama or humor into trial movies'.[35] How much, they wonder, of what you see in trial movies is 'real'?

Nevins has questioned the usefulness of this approach. What time frame does one adopt, he wondered—the law then or the law now? Whilst he does highlight the limitations of this method, it is, nonetheless, not difficult to see why the image/reality issue strikes a chord for law teachers. In courses where one is seeking to indicate fundamental principles, the demonstration of the absence of such principles may be seen as helpful. For instance, Paul Bergman's discussion of memorable courtroom 'sleights of hand' such as the throwing by Atticus Finch of a water glass to Tom Robinson provides a similar kind of perspective on the way in which film and actual courtroom practice diverge.[36] This tactic was repeated in *Suspect* (1987), which demonstrates common themes and ideas that contribute to the idea of genre.

Whatever the merits of the criticism, the range of areas where writers have sought to highlight the nature and, often, shortcomings of film coverage, has included divorce law,[37] criminal law,[38] rape,[39] Admiralty law,[40] corporate misconduct,[41] and public interest lawyering.[42] This ongoing interest in using film within doctrinal courses will continue to attract scholarship, whose principal concern is the meaning and accuracy of the representation of the specific legal issues covered in the films. The value of this form of scholastic aid is not, however, likely to be pervasive across the curriculum since filmmakers have their topics dictated largely by expectations of marketability. Crime dominates. Within crime, murder dominates.[43] The extent and nature of civil or minor criminal issues are few and far between, although there have been a significant number of films with a civil law theme.[44]

For anyone, however, teaching a course on landlord and tenant law, if there is to be use of cinematic material it is limited to one broad farce from the 1990s about a slum landlord, *The Landlord* (1991).[45] The potential for critical engagement in

---

[34] Bergman, P and Asimow, M (1996).
[35] *Ibid*, xviii.
[36] Bergman, P (1996a).
[37] Asimow, M (2002).
[38] Meyer, P (2004).
[39] Projansky, S (2001b).
[40] Bolla, A (2000); Corcos, C (2000).
[41] Robertson, M (2005).
[42] McCann, M and Haltom, W (2008).
[43] Robson, P (1996b).
[44] Chase, A (1999).
[45] See also Robson, P (2005).

doctrinal issues has not been seized, particularly by commentators, although the possibility was noted from the beginning.[46] Johnson and Buchanan suggest that beneath the comfortable bland surface of legal doctrine as it is taught, a whole range of conflicts operate.[47] They argue that one of the functions and possibilities for looking at popular culture is to strip away this mask of neutrality. Furthermore, films can be used to promote critical discussion around controversial issues with students enjoying a greater freedom to engage by utilising the inevitably controversial characters. Kamir argues that:

> Films have a unique way of touching people's hearts and allowing them to employ their emotions in the process of seeing, listening, and understanding, discussing and analysing. Analysis of film from a new perspective is an exciting, intriguing and challenging experience for students, who take it home with them and share it with families and friends, thereby continuing its work. The intersection of law and film adds a personal aspect to professional legal training, making it more human, specific and meaningful. Further, the study of jurisprudential issues through film makes them less abstract and intimidating and more concrete and intuitive. Teaching law-and-film, therefore, becomes an important avenue for bringing the humanities into legal studies.[48]

Kamir indicates the opportunities to use film. Specifically, she notes a human, contextual approach. The point of extending the method of study is to encompass other non-lawyers who may have different perspectives and thoughts which will provide the opportunity for a broader reflection. Ashford noted the promotion of a deeper learning during his first-year human rights law module by utilising films. The area was sexuality and rights, and the issue was the practice of 'cottaging'. The excerpts, and Ashford quotes from the script in his piece, beautifully illustrate some difficult notions of sexuality and identity. Here, the use of excerpts from a Home Box Office (HBO) mini series made concrete and understandable something that his students had struggled to articulate:

> The short excerpt allowed students to finally understand the issues with students commenting at the end of the lecture that they wished I had shown it earlier as it made a difficult concept straightforward in a way that previous academic explanations had failed to.[49]

In addition a further highly desirable outcome was that the students' imaginations had been fired. Whilst not as yet taught as an explicit module, the Law on Film Group at Sunderland is a bold attempt to encourage contextual awareness, of staff and students, via an extra-curricular activity. Importantly, much of the impetus came from the students themselves after being invigorated by the use of film in a more limited sense on modules such as the one noted above.

---

[46] Chase, A (1986b).
[47] Johnson, R and Buchanan, R (2001).
[48] Kamir, O (2005b: 275).
[49] Ashford, C (2005).

These same kind of tensions between inculcating practical lawyering skills and the academic aspects of legal education encountered in Britain have also featured in the United States. The focus on skills, in confrontation with intellectual development, is eloquently described by Elkins as the 'practicalist virus'.[50] Elkins has a much greater focus on teaching students who are planning to become lawyers.[51] He explains that the concerns of film theory are not what his course is focused on. He approaches the films as texts in the lives of those whose central study is the law and the role of lawyers. Denvir talks of the advantage of the level playing field which discussing film seems to provide as opposed to the exalted position of the law teacher as repository of wisdom which is the standard academic–student relationship.[52] He also argues that film can teach students much of value, and that often areas and issues that are not concentrated upon in the curriculum can be covered. Key 'lessons' that film teaches us include that justice counts, that the status quo needs to be questioned and, on a very practical level, that we ought to choose our employers carefully. The first two are particularly important:

> I think there is another message that study of movies provides for law students: the practice of law is fraught with ethical consequence. Every day movie lawyers are confronted with the choice of fighting for justice or permitting the unjust system to prevail. To me this 'popular' image of the practice of law is especially valuable because it subverts the 'professional' image of the lawyer as a technically proficient craftsman that students imbibe in other courses.... My point is not to defend the accuracy of the hyper-moralistic popular image of the lawyer, but to insist on its importance as an antidote to the amoral image so dominant in the rest of the law school curriculum.[53]

Stone indicates that his approach is to work with films 'which present complex ideas, interesting moral questions, ambiguous and subtle and psychological themes, challenges to settled beliefs, and creative ambition—films that explore the nexus between psychology and morality, character and context'.[54] Like Denvir, he discovered that students who are alienated from the law school classroom are confident in working with film and engaged by this a process which allows them to conceptualise and debate their own ideas around justice.

Law and Film Courses

In the early, pioneering, American courses looking at law in film, the emphasis was on how film might be used to enhance the process of teaching law. Bergman and Asimow, for example, have a clearly articulated 'legal education' goal. They

---

[50] Elkins, J (2004: 824).
[51] *Ibid.*
[52] Denvir, J (1996a).
[53] Denvir, J (2004: 183).
[54] Stone, A (2000: 588).

seek to provide a guide as to how Hollywood bends the rules to inject drama or humour into trial movies.[55] The aims expressed by Nevins share this concern; to draw attention to features of good practice through the medium of film.[56] Film is the vehicle for this enlightenment as a result of its availability and apparent accessibility to student lawyers. While the concern of law educators to engage their students' attention, and hence the use of law films, is presented with pride in some quarters, the imputation that film is simply understood and decoded because a film only takes 100–120 minutes to view is treated with some concern by others.[57] There is, however a significant difference in undertaking what Bergman and Asimow, Laurence and Denvir talk of by way of 'livening up' their courses with film and claims to develop theory:

> Educators generally choose films and plays emphasizing professional ethics and client counselling. Such dramas focus on either the legal system or on the attorney and his or her role in the drama. Therefore they lend themselves to use in both professional responsibility courses and in studies of the justice system or alternative resolution.[58]

In this more limited area the use of film to draw attention to moral dilemmas and ethical issues for prospective law practitioners does not purport to add to theory. It does, however, serve the purpose of embedding and signposting points and also acts as a natural break within a class to ensure that material is absorbed. Even on a more mundane level, film clips can contribute to a positive teaching strategy. Certainly the experience of Hauserman, in her Introduction to Law module, bears this out with increased student attendance and a greater degree of useful participation.[59]

Teachers using film clips, for whatever reason, as part of their law teaching on traditional courses, can afford to ignore a detailed analysis of films. It is the development of law and film courses that has provided the impetus for a more elaborate critical comment on films and the struggle to deal with issues related to film theory. Although 'law and film studies' have sprung principally from the interests of law teachers, the true picture of what has developed and what has been done is, however, rather more complex. There is also work which makes links between 'legal films' and areas of legal and social theory, with the aim of illustrating concepts and perspectives mediated through film. The discrete law and film courses have a radically different approach: they seek to use legal films as the source of critical analysis of the law. Both the substantive content of the films and how the various issues are dealt with cinematically may be important.

For example, Greenfield and Osborn's original law and film module was devised as a first year undergraduate elective. It originally aimed to develop general

[55] Bergman, P and Asimow, M (1996).
[56] Nevins, F (1996a).
[57] Black, D (1999).
[58] Corcos, C (1993: 502).
[59] Hauserman, N (1995).

transferable skills and to provide a medium to introduce a limited form of critical jurisprudence at an early stage in the law programme.[60] Films were used to replace texts that are often inaccessible to students at that point in their academic life. In terms of the substantive content, the course was concerned with ideas and theories about how the law and lawyers work, and the contribution of law films to their understanding of this process. This centred upon issues such as ethics, locating the courtroom, myths and images and tried to draw out what legal films might tell us about law and the legal process. A further outcome that had not originally been envisaged was that the course could be empowering to participants. It was strongly argued that students find films 'less threatening' than traditional texts and are more open to critical comment and discussion:

> This of course is the joy of using film; it is accessible and allows the students to perceive the films on a number of different levels without having to feel that their own answer is in some way peripheral to the traditional academic perspective. A crucial factor that has emerged, as the course has developed, is the ability of students to draw upon their own store of knowledge ... This enables the less assured students to gain confidence and feel able to make important contributions.[61]

Their aims of the module were helped by the fact that their film and the law course ran in the first year of legal study and that the students do not bring with them baggage that may have been acquired through prior legal study. However, changes brought about during the reorganisation of the degree meant that rather than being offered in the first semester the module now runs in the second semester thus lessening in some ways its impact as originally intended. This has been identified by Hunt as a problem of placing theoretical law options at the end of a degree, a 'finishing school syndrome' that means that students have already adopted immutable ideas that effectively have to be 'unlearnt' before theory can be tackled.[62] This point about the consequential effect of law teaching and being taught to think 'like lawyers' is made by Meyer, who argues that 'story senses' are important to lawyers:

> That upper-level law students rediscover their creative and imaginative story senses is imperative. They must learn to listen to and trust their instincts and their emotions in addition to categorical analytical functions.[63]

It is also important to note that there may well be a number of different educative functions that a film and the law course may have. Dunlop puts it thus in terms of research: that there is a crucial difference between research *in* law and research *about* law. The latter allows an appreciation of a subject by utilising the tools and experience of a different discipline, whilst the former 'consists of doctrinal analysis of texts ... tends not to involve empirical study of the actual workings of

---

[60] Greenfield, S and Osborn, G (1995a).
[61] Greenfield, S and Osborn, G (1995b: 6).
[62] Hunt, A (1987).
[63] Meyer, P (1992: 895).

the legal order or of its economic or social consequences ... It apparently has a coherence and an autonomy enabling one to call it a discipline'.[64]

The difference between the two is that research about law allows the law to be discussed, interrogated and critiqued. Dunlop has refined this categorisation to explain the difference between the competing, but arguably complementary approaches of 'law *in* literature' and 'law *as* literature'. Here, the former looks at representations within the field of literature, whilst the latter adopts some of the tools of literary criticism to assist in the analysis of legal texts. Our approach has generally been to utilise the first model (law *in* film) in order that it might tell us something *about* the law.

Meyer's argument for the use of film offers a distinct variation to many of the other versions of teaching law and film and is in part more about providing necessary legal-practice-based skills. There is, though, some comparison with the skills aim of the Film and the Law course taught at the University of Westminster. Meyer describes the use of film as part of a law and literature course entitled Law and Popular Storytelling. He persuasively argues that trial attorneys are 'fact-based storytellers' and draws a comparison with movie makers:

> Like the movie-maker the trial attorney is an oral cultural storyteller who tells fact-based narratives that convey a story and a particular vision of the world. The principles of narrative ordination for a trial storyteller are like the aesthetic structures that compel movie directors to craft stories along a tightly ordered narrative spine. Severe constraints are placed on narrative subjectivity by certain storytelling conventions, such as the rules of evidence.[65]

This is an interesting notion. First that trial attorneys are storytellers, and secondly that there is a close relationship with film directors and scriptwriters in terms of the structuring of the story. No doubt many lawyers would be surprised and some, perhaps, appalled to be described as storytellers and this view in part reflects a legal training described by Meyer as 'analytical indoctrination'. Again, this links to some of the criticisms of the rather limited aims of legal education, and the presence of the vocational alongside the academic. As the Film and the Law course has developed at Westminster themes or groups of films have been used to provide integrated links. For example, miscarriages of justice are well represented and can provide an excellent focus for detailed discussion of whole questions of innocence, guilt and the criminal justice system. Films can also be used to explore more involved issues. Robson's course has as one of its goals the use of film to provide a comprehensible introduction to concepts which impact on, but are outwith traditional legal theory, like feminism and postmodernism. Again the possibility of this developing a critique of the legal process and its operation is by no means automatic. Whilst the concepts within feminism and postmodernism may not be subjected to a rigorous critical analysis this approach

---

[64] Dunlop, C (1991: 67).
[65] Meyer, P (1992: 896–97).

makes space for the development of theoretical perspectives. We can see a wide range of approaches to the use of film in both general scholarship and the vital link to teaching. Different strands of work are continually being developed both nationally and internationally. Similarly some empirical work has been initiated to consider how law students perceive the whole justice system and the role of popular culture and the media in the forming of those perceptions. This in turn may lead us to reconsider the aims of our teaching and scholarship.

3

Theoretical underpinnings and physical boundaries—defining the territory

Members of a profession once eyed with suspicion by the film and TV community are now beginning new careers in the entertainment industry. Lawyers are everywhere in Hollywood—they're writing scripts, producing television shows and running film studios.[1]

Andrew Beckett proclaims in *Philadelphia* (1993) that he loves the law. As Moran notes, Beckett's love of law is manifested in a number of ways. First, in terms of the homosocial context of the law firm. Secondly, love of law is played out within the context of the 'buddy relationship'. Both Beckett and Miller love the law and can arguably be placed within a homoerotic dynamic.[2] We do not deal in this work with erotics of law or desire, which are beyond our remit.[3] What Beckett encapsulates for us is a shared love of law; shared by actors, directors and audiences, and a love that has a number of diverse roots. For example, the list of major 'stars' who have played lawyers is impressive, with Spencer Tracy (*Adam's Rib*; *Inherit the Wind*) James Stewart and George C Scott (*Anatomy of a Murder*); Paul Newman (*The Young Philadelphians*; *The Verdict*); Henry Fonda (*Young Mr Lincoln*); Denzel Washington and Tom Hanks (*Philadelphia*); Gregory Peck (*To Kill a Mockingbird* and *Cape Fear*); Marlon Brando (*A Dry White Season*); Tom Cruise (*The Firm* and *A Few Good Men*); Orson Welles (*Compulsion*); Al Pacino (*... And Justice for All*; *Devil's Advocate*); Richard Gere (*Primal Fear*); Sean Connery (*Just Cause*); Albert Finney (*Erin Brockovich*); Morgan Freeman (*High Crimes*); Alan Bates (*Evelyn*); Pierce Brosnan (*Laws of Attraction*) and George Clooney (*Intolerable Cruelty*; *Michael Clayton*). The later entry into the lists of women lawyers has produced a similar, if smaller, roll call including Glenn Close (*Jagged Edge*), Cher (*Suspect*), Jessica Lange (*Music Box*), Michelle Pfeiffer (*I am Sam*), Sandra Bullock (*Two Weeks Notice*), Julianne Moore (*Laws of Attraction*) and Laura Linney (*Primal Fear* and *The Exorcism of Emily Rose*).

---

[1] Natale, R (1987: 3).
[2] Moran, L (1998).
[3] Redhead, S (1995).

This Chapter draws out some of the issues surrounding why law is important, and some of the key thematic aspects that lend themselves so readily to film makers. It first explores why law and legal proceedings are perceived to be an attractive topic for film. There is, for example, a strong dramatic edge to law that can be successfully explored through films. The Chapter then engages with some of the issues around the nature of law: its imagery, its language, its visuality, orality and dress, which lend themselves to cinematic depiction. It then examines some theoretical issues through an analysis of the notion of 'courtroom drama'. Whether this is the most apposite descriptor will be examined in more depth in the following Chapter. As we have argued previously, law appears in a whole range of films that go beyond, and indeed exclude, the courtroom entirely.[4] Sometimes the films raise questions about the very nature of what a courtroom drama is. This is a fundamental issue encapsulated in the question 'What is a law film?'. This is a crucial, if unanswered, question for those working in the area who wish to push the subject beyond the limits of a narrow analysis of solely 'courtroom drama'. This, to us, appears an artificial, if easy, boundary to draw and consequently, we bring together some ideas around the notion of genre. This is the area where film theory is most useful in terms of trying to determine the limits to our enquiry.

Beyond the courtroom drama we explore the concept of law and justice within film, a topic which demonstrates the versatility of law as a subject, but which also blurs the boundary between law films, and films which naturally fall into other genres such as prison films and cop movies.[5] This is further expanded by examining how law films have dealt with wider moral and social issues, and provides a means to explore a number of social concerns.

The backdrop to the interaction between law and society often centres on important contemporary moral issues that develop into a two-sided 'legal' dispute. Law is shown as a means of formally settling these immediate questions in the short term. Interestingly the failure of law as a means of settling disputes is rare and offset by a just end result, a point well illustrated by *The Verdict* (1982). This is not necessarily the case with miscarriage of justice films such as *In the Name of the Father* (1993) and *Let Him Have It* (1991), although in the former law is shown as the tool to free the wrongly convicted. This overlooks the fact that it was deficiencies in the legal process that led to the original incarceration. The central question is which side, or whose side, is the law on? The portrayals of law are intimately connected with those who represent law, the lawyers. The characteristics of screen lawyers are examined later in the text when we attempt to draw common threads through the chronology of legal films. The relationship of the lawyers to these great moral points is also important and may affect their status within the community. As the very nature of legal films has changed, the question is whether the screen lawyers have changed with it. As we have identified, there

---

[4] Greenfield, S, Osborn, G and Robson, P (2001).
[5] Reiner, R (1978).

are certain themes that are particularly popular and constant in law films. These may tell us a number of things about the law and the legal process; indeed, this may be the prime way in which the public obtain their idea of what the law is, and how it operates, so the depictions may take on an important hue. There is also the question of the law, and how individual court cases might be used to debate wider moral questions and society's treatment of certain groups, for example *Philadelphia* (1983) and *To Kill a Mockingbird* (1962).

The Dramatic Dimension of Law

First and foremost, legal proceedings are inherently dramatic, not necessarily in the sense that we will be spellbound by the proceedings of the court, but in terms of the common threads that exist between drama and the law. As Carlen explains:

> Traditionally and situationally judicial proceedings are dramatic. Aristotle noted the importance of forensic oratory as a special device of legal rhetoric; playwrights have always appreciated the dramatic value of the trial scene; lawyers have always been cognisant of rhetorical presentations.[6]

The relationship between law and drama is a strong one; indeed, the dramaturgical aspects of the law might be seen to be part of law's artifice and gives support to a debate about which has provenance—the court providing the stage or the drama being the focus for the courtroom itself? This dialectic is one that is without easy resolution—perhaps it is safest to posit that there are two competing functions. The relationship becomes even more pronounced when we consider courtroom dramas, as these provide a number of spatial advantages in terms of presenting the law. Certainly, before motion pictures, the stage could easily recreate a courtroom scene, a particular bonus being the need for little change of scenery or location, as much of the action takes place within the confines of the court itself. The courtroom can be used to great effect by film makers who wish to utilise the architectural and symbolic qualities it embodies which appear ideally suited for filmic depiction.[7] The courtroom may be seen as a highly symbolic and charged environment, outside of any architectural or acoustic elements:

> Aside from the purely physical environment the courtroom contains a mythical and mystical quality: the setting for an ordeal steeped in historical pageantry. In the English courts this is more obviously exhibited with the almost exotic dress of the participants; at the same time, however, there is a corresponding aridity and solemnity attached to the proceedings.[8]

---

[6] Carlen, P (1976: 19).
[7] Goodrich, P (1990).
[8] Greenfield, S and Osborn, G (1995b: 110).

34

The courtroom has obvious attributes that have been utilised by playwrights and film makers. However, as we argue throughout, law films are much more than solely courtroom dramas, and it may be difficult, although not impossible, to sustain a complete film within the confines of the courtroom.[9]

So, why the law in the first place? First, the public appear to enjoy a fascination with aspects of the law. This is evidenced on a number of fronts and has increased with lawyers becoming media figures and the law occupying a prominent position both in print media and on television. A popular teaching device with new or prospective law students is to 'deconstruct' a newspaper by circling all the stories that have legal elements to them. Both students and teachers are usually surprised by the very high incidence of law-related items. In addition to Court TV (now called *truTV*), there is now a specialist law cable channel in Britain called *Legal TV*. Television programming has played upon this fascination with both factual and fictional portrayals being developed. There is a wide range of television drama based around law firms or lawyers.[10] The televising of trials perhaps reached its apotheosis with the trial of OJ Simpson in 1995. Secondly, in much the same way that courtroom proceedings are dramatic, the law is a marvellous vehicle for a diverse range of stories. At this juncture it is important to observe that the law has central characteristics and contradictions that make it such an attractive and useful vehicle for storytelling: 'The essence of the law movie is that it offers the writer and director a chance to explore the potential for the clash of two opposing forces which may be portrayed as good/evil, right/ wrong, moral/immoral.'[11]

Films, however, tend to concentrate upon the criminal arena, often because in the USA this may focus on a life or death outcome that lends an additional dramatic edge. This focus is at the expense of civil areas of litigation, although there are some notable exceptions to this such as *The Verdict* (1982), *Class Action* (1991), *A Civil Action* (1999) and *Erin Brockovich* (2000). It is trite to note that not all legal issues are inherently dramatic or interesting and consequently there are certain aspects that will not normally be as suited to cinematic portrayal, although there are of course exceptions to this. Detective films tend to concentrate on murders, as not having a victim who can give evidence helps to intensify the plot. Legal films continue this process. There needs to be a dramatic element, and this can be produced through a serious crime that draws in the viewer and captures the imagination. In addition to this, outside of any legal niceties, a film about the law may in fact be a vehicle for something else. Essentially, a law film may merely be a peg that the film is hung upon, while the film centres upon something rather different, such as racism, homophobia or environmental issues.

---

[9] Whilst it is a documentary, *Tenth District Court* (2006) is set solely within a French courtroom.
[10] Jarvis, R and Joseph, P (1998); Rapping, E (2003); Robson, P (2007a).
[11] Greenfield, S and Osborn, G (1995b: 112).

Visuality and Image

Law is visual. This can partly be seen in aphorisms such as 'law being seen to be done' and 'equality in the eye of the law', and partly by the visual spectacle of the process itself. Jay, for example, notes that while early iconographical depictions of justice were often presented with 'eyes uncovered' and with the sub-text that legal judgments could be based upon recourse to visual evidence, by the 15th century this vision began to become occluded, with, for example, the goddess Justitia having a blindfold placed over her eyes. Initially seen as a negative implication of imbalance:

> By 1530, however, this image seems to have lost its satirical implication and the blind-fold was transformed into a positive emblem of impartiality and equality before the law. Perhaps because of traditions transmitted by Plutarch and Diodore of Sicily from Ancient Egypt that had depicted judges as blind or handless, the blindfold, like the scales, came to imply neutrality rather than helplessness.[12]

This argument, supplemented by a series of historical images highlighting the visual, illustrates a shift away from the visual method in which law had been presented, towards a delivery based on rhetoric and language. As part of this process, judges' robes became more sober, and illustrations were removed from law books and the courts, and the privileging of the word over the image became apparent. Interestingly, more recently the use of traditional garb has been moderated with the abandonment of wigs in civil and family cases, though not in criminal hearings. Another contemporary manifestation of the dominance of the word is the prohibition of cameras in court within England. This analysis is firmly based upon a suspicion of the danger of the image set against the rationality of the word. Though as Douzinas and Nead note when commenting on Jay's work, 'alongside this distrust of the visual there is also a critical investment in the image, according to which sight ensures freedom'.[13] This creates a tension that Jay suggests requires a reappraisal of the visual aspects of law. There is much useful material on the aesthetics of law, and the role of the image or the visual, in this book.[14] In addition Jay offers much further food for thought in terms of 'ocularcentric discourse'.[15]

One aspect of visuality of law was, initially, seen in the sense of punishment and particularly in the meting out of corporal or capital punishment. However, as Foucault comments, this 'gloomy festival' of punishment was on the wane by the start of the 19th century, and punishment was beginning to be less conspicuous:

> While the chain-gang, which had dragged convicts across the whole of France, as far as Brest and Toulon, was replaced in 1837 by inconspicuous black-painted cell-carts. Punishment had gradually ceased to be a spectacle. And whatever theatrical elements it still retained were now downgraded, as if the functions of the penal ceremony were

---

[12] Jay, M (1999: 20–21).
[13] Douzinas, C and Nead, L (1999b: 12).
[14] Haldar, P (1999) and Taylor, K (1999).
[15] Jay, M (1993).

gradually ceasing to be understood, as if this rite that 'concluded the crime' was sus-
pected of being in some undesirable way linked with it.[16]

There is a vivid depiction of the chain gang in *I Am a Fugitive from a Chain Gang*
(1932) and such depiction is most obviously found within the genre of prison
movies. There are examples of inhumane prison conditions and the application
of the death penalty, for example.[17]

Foucault charts the history and practice of punishment, and graphically details
the methods used and the purposes to which punishment was put. These included
using the punishment to 'theatrically recreate' the crime for the execution of
the guilty party. Foucault charts the case of a girl from Cambrai, condemned
to be seated in the chair in which she killed her mistress and have parts of her
body removed with the same cleaver used in the murder, before having her head
mounted on a pole, exhibited outside the city gates. Here we see the visuality of
the law in tandem with a stark deterrence function. Once this highly visual element of punishment began to be eroded, as part of a shift towards a more humane
treatment, the punishment itself became more private and less based on torture
or conspicuous suffering. With the move away from public executions, and the
shift toward the private (no longer in public spaces) and more humane (no longer based on torture and visible deterrent), the great spectacle of punishment
began to disappear. However, it might be argued that the spectacle merely shifted
from gallows to the courtroom itself. Newman has noted that the law has always
provided entertainment, both in terms of the trial process and their sequels—the
hangings. Of course, the courtroom has natural visual and spatial qualities that
lend themselves to filmic portrayal.[18] Goodrich notes the gladiatorial and adversarial nature of criminal court proceedings, and how this self contained arena
exhibits theatrical qualities:

> In the court below, in those designed for jury trials, a certain symmetry prevails in which
> the dock, itself an elevated and enclosed space, faces the bench, and to either side rise tiers
> of seats to accommodate the jury and on the other side reporters and other official court
> observers. Prosecution and defence counsel take their place on either side of the open well
> of the court and conduct the combative game of trial directly in front of the bench'.[19]

Apart from the obvious 'combative' aspects, the ceremony of the court is also an
attractive feature for film makers. Sociologists have noted this ceremonial function of the courtroom and, in particular, its place as part of a degradation ceremony.[20] Bankowski and Mungham note that the perspective of a court (and in
particular a Magistrates' Court) of having a function of degradation, may seem to
the public at large a strange notion. For the public, the view of the court is more
likely to exist on a level of idealisation rather than reality, and certainly while the

[16] Foucault, M (1975: 9).
[17] Crowther, B (1989).
[18] Newman, K (1993).
[19] Goodrich, P (1990: 192–93).
[20] Garfinkel, H (1956).

courts are not televised and the public idea of how the courtroom appears may be distilled from the mass media:

> Those who depend upon certain media stereotypes of the court in process will be steeped in the mythology of courtroom encounters: an arcadian sketch which draws together the imagery of skilled and articulate advocates, of the protection of the meek by the strong, of open and vigorous debate, of a contest of principled and orderly minds—where the prize is the definition of truth itself.[21]

This raises a further point concerning the importance of law films and television law dramas on our understanding of the workings of the legal process, and our feelings about the legal profession and other personnel within the English legal system, an area we discuss later.

The Cult of the Robe: Dress and Appearance in Film

The dress of lawyers in England and Wales has been a source of debate for many years.[22] To some, its very existence is seen as an unwelcome throwback to a long-forgotten past, to others a symbol of gravitas worthy of preservation. The use of ceremonial dress within the law does have a long and distinguished history, with the use of robes in particular said to produce an effect of 'detached dignity'. In addition, one of the rationales for its use is that a consistency of colour and dress leads to an outward impression of uniformity of justice, and aids the idea that law is being seen to be done fairly. Other arguments have been raised in favour of preserving legal dress. These have included the potential for lawyer anonymity and that the use of such costume may balance opposing lawyers by removing idiosyncrasies. At the same time there have been a number of critiques of its use: these include the grounds that it perpetuates exclusivity and oppressiveness, in particular by dehumanising the participants and divorces them from humanity, is intimidating, expensive and out of date. The issue about intimidation, in particular, is an interesting one as the use of formal legal dress is part of the wider symbolism of justice that have as their purpose the reification of the law and the process via which the law is administered. Goodrich takes this argument further when looking at the process of 'keeping terms', still a key constituent of becoming a barrister in England and Wales:

> The order of dining—of arrival, dress, seating, service, food, speech, argument, exposition, dance, revelry and masques—is the order of a lawful world, a symbolic order in which Justice, Rule and Law are to be understood as being expressed together …[23]

---

[21] Bankowski, Z and Mungham, G (1976: 88).

[22] Lord Chancellor's Department consultation paper *Court working dress in England and Wales* May 2003 and the Ministry of Justice Response *Court working dress in England and Wales: consultation response* (4 June 2007).

[23] Goodrich, P (1991: 248).

This symbolic order is further celebrated in terms of court layout, architecture, language and dress. Dress has a crucial purpose in identifying the main players in the courtroom and accordingly the use of dress has been a device utilised by filmmakers both to set the lawyers apart and to help in their reification. In films based upon the English legal system there is rarely any difficulty in setting the lawyers apart from the participants. In *Brothers in Law* (1957) the robes and dress contribute to comedic moments such as when one barrister, Henry Marshall (Richard Attenborough) loses his wig as it is blown off the window sill into the street and onto a hearse travelling below. This provides the opportunity for the central character, Thursby (Ian Carmichael), to take his place in court and win the 'unwinnable' case. Thursby fiddling with his wig is also used to show his unfamiliarity with the dress and hence his greenness. One of the most impressive moments of formality shows the opening of the assizes and the entry into the court by the splendidly dressed legal personnel. This gaudy display provides a nice contrast with the solemnity and seriousness of the proceedings.

Films that are set within the American courtroom also use items of dress to make points about the central characters and *Young Mr Lincoln* (1939) is a good example of this. It is an important film on a number of different levels and clearly illustrates the point that stylistic devices can be utilised to set him apart from other participants in the film. One aspect of this is the use of dialogue and cinematographer techniques: '[T]he film's stylistic elements complement its dialogue in emphasising Lincoln's distance from mainstream legal practices. Lincoln, for example, rarely appears in the center of the courtroom scenes; usually, he is found roaming the edges of the film's frame.'[24] Lincoln's portrayal is of someone who is almost oblivious to, or detached from, the events. His dress throughout the film helps preserve this detachment, with his trademark stovepipe hat and austere black suit clearly demarcating him from the other lawyers in the process and allowing the viewers a clear signposting of his relevance. Atticus Finch in *To Kill a Mockingbird* (1957) shares many of Lincoln's characteristics, and he has indeed been described by some commentators as being a 'modern Abraham Lincoln'. Certainly there are clear resonances to be seen in the film—the lynch mob scene has the Lincoln lynch mob scene as its reference point and some of Finch's mannerisms are reminiscent of Lincoln and he is subject to a similar deification:

> [H]is coiffure is as resonant as the wig of a British judge. His forelock only falls out of place and onto his forehead at significant moments, such as when he must take off his reading glasses to shoot a rabid dog, or when he's assaulted by the film's white-trash villain, or when he finds that character murdered. The flopping forelock is like a TILT sign on a pinball machine, indicating somebody's trying to make the game go crooked and the system just won't stand for it.[25]

---

[24] Rosenberg, N (1991: 222).
[25] Appelo, T (1992: 175).

Finch's dress and demeanour are just as striking as that of Lincoln, perhaps even more so given the decision of Mulligan to dress Finch in white to place him apart. As well as portraying Finch as 'different' from the others, this device also further deifies him with the connotations of purity and plays on themes of good and evil, right and wrong and saint and sinner very overtly. This device has been utilised in a number of other films, notably by Sidney Lumet in *Twelve Angry Men* (1957) and by Rob Reiner in *A Few Good Men* (1992), in the respective anointment of Henry Fonda and Tom Cruise. Not all the contrasts are in this form, although often by showing 'difference' the same effect can be seen. For example, Vinny Gambini (Joe Pesci) in *My Cousin Vinny* (1992) is just as identifiable as Lincoln and Finch, notwithstanding the informality of his dress. Vinny's clothing is allied to his background as a town lawyer venturing into a different geography and sense of formality. Similarly his girlfriend, Mona Lisa Vito (Marisa Tomei) is also marked out not just because of her gender but also through her clothing. She is far more than the lawyer's girlfriend: she has a crucial role appearing as an expert witness offering an in-depth knowledge of motor mechanics. Vinny offers an alternative to the strict, rule-bound, formally dressed lawyers in the South. He is informally dressed, casual and undeterred by the formal procedures of the application of the law. There are clearly physical limitations to what may be achieved purely through dress, although an interesting futuristic example is provided by *Judge Dredd* (1995). Once again costume plays a part. Indeed, as the opening credits inform us, the costume was designed by Versace. Whilst it perhaps does not at first glance have the same gravitas as robes 'trimmed with ermine' and a wig, Dredd is just as clearly signposted as a legal player and his ceremonial dress marks him and the other 'judges' out. Dress may well be a minor point when compared to aspects of the personality and the behaviour but it is a means of drawing differences between characters and showing us who is important.

We would argue that our point of entry from the legal world into film presents us with a different view of what law and lawyers are concerned with, and consequently how filmic portrayals could be legitimately organised. Only a very traditional black-letter lawyer would lay claim to law merely being concerned with the application of cases and statutes, and there is a growing realisation that the practice of law, and indeed the importance of law, spreads widely throughout society. Our attempt to decide what is within the law film parameters is influenced by this belief that there is a great deal more to law than the study of both its rules and the application of those rules through the adversarial system.

Put into film terms, then, there is far more to law than a courtroom drama, and this Chapter seeks to begin to develop the concept of what the subject of our inquiry really is. In order to do this we first review some of the approaches to categorisation that have been taken by scholars working on law and film.

Defining the Parameters of Law and Film: Academic Approaches

There has then been a difference of approach as to how broadly scholars should cast their net in looking at films about law when engaged in law and film as an area of intellectual inquiry. These range from a suggestion that there is a need for a strict specification of the field, to an analysis in which the field of inquiry covers all fiction films.[26] For this latter approach nothing is off limits. One can contrast the difference in quantitative coverage by contrasting Harris's use of eight films with our own inclusive approach. At the far end of the scale the Tarlton Law Library Film Collection is exhaustive and eclectic with over 700 films on the shelves.[27] Much has changed since Harris's observations on 'courtroom cinema'. A growing and vibrant literature has emerged around the area of law and film that has addressed a whole range of distinct issues and has been part of the wider concern with law and popular culture. The precise object of these inquiries has not, however, always been made clear.

Writing on law and film has proceeded from an initial concern to describe the general portrayal of justice within a legal construct. Hence, much of the initial work of scholars has been to indicate the range of situations where the legal process has featured as a dominant factor. This descriptive work continues to be a significant feature as scholars seek to consider the nature of law's portrayal in film. This process is, however, not without its own problems of definition. The question of the breadth of the films under analysis, and perhaps more importantly the rationale for their selection, is often problematic. The starting point has been a shared understanding between writer and audience of the 'legal film'. This is sometimes referred to as the 'courtroom drama' or 'trial movie'. Harris refers to *Anatomy of a Murder* (1959) and notes that it features:

> many of the 'classic' elements of courtroom drama evidenced in countless previous efforts, both major and minor: the humble country lawyer versus the city slicker, with the former defeating the latter by virtue of his essential honesty; the drunken sidekick who risks his life for one last chance at fighting for justice; the witty unpaid secretary of the hero; the last-minute 'surprise'.[28]

Although Harris suggests that these are familiar elements in courtroom dramas it is not clear exactly what films he has in mind. He mentions, for example, America's love affair with certain kinds of court rituals as found in *Madame X* (1929), *Counsellor at Law* (1933) and *The Life of Emile Zola* (1937).[29] This is a somewhat unusual choice since the chaotic French courtroom scenes are more reminiscent of farce than the model Harris worked from: 'a muted atmosphere of

---

[26] For an example of the former approach see Robson, P (1996a) and the latter Black, D (1999).
[27] Harris, T (1987).
[28] *Ibid*, 107.
[29] Michigan Supreme Court Justice John D Voelker, author of *Anatomy of a Murder* cited in *ibid*, xi.

41

hushed ritual and controlled decorum … awash with ancient rites and Latinised antiquities'. It is, however, worth noting that none of the other films cited by Harris in his collection of films representing the finest hour of the courtroom cinema in America includes these 'classic' elements. Interestingly, Harris does not include *To Kill a Mockingbird* (1962) in his collection, nor is there any mention of that treatment in his book. His selection numbers only eight, and ranges between the mid-1950s and mid-1960s. They seem, according to Harris, to '… provide the greatest opportunity for examining social problems of the past and present and for making statements about the validity of the judicial process'.[30]

Other early writers tended to take a similar line to that of Harris and start from a shared body of experience. Thus we find Greenfield and Osborn talking of the 'cinematic portrayal of the law', 'films with a legal theme' and 'films with a strong legal content'. Their initial selection might seem random both in terms of time, nature and style and they did not specify their criteria in detail. They argued that they were starting out with little in the way of established literature and started their film collection for the Film and the Law course from scratch. They attempted to make use of literature where it relates to film, though this has generally been concerned with films based on 'true' stories. The accessibility of material and over-dependence on American films were two practical problems. At the outset it was perhaps inevitable that the net would be cast wide and their collection includes superb examples of the genre such as *The Trial of the Incredible Hulk* (1989), which not only starred but also was directed by Bill Bixby.[31] They also hint, in their later work, of notions of a sub-genre.[32] They suggest that legal films come within the same penumbra as police dramas and private detective stories. Their selection stems from a wide range of concerns, from the courtroom and the portrayal of justice, to lawyers as deliverers of this precious commodity and their overall demeanour and dress. They were generally concerned with the 'filmic portrayal of lawyers and the legal system'. Their initial analysis was based on some 25 films representative of this portrayal over the past 60 years, both British and American.

Rennard Strickland, in the early 1990s, talked of selecting films and including a film from 'the half-dozen or so classic lawyer movies from the late fifties and early sixties'.[33] He commented on the different motivations and skills shown by 'Hollywood lawyers' in a range of films from *Inherit the Wind* (1960) through *To Kill a Mockingbird* (1962) and *Cape Fear* (1961) to *The Young Philadelphians* (1959).

The contribution of Bergman and Asimow was also conceived in very broad terms. As they point out in their introduction, their book is written for everyone, not just lawyers.[34] They explain that their book selects 69 'trial movies' of the present and the past and this selection includes the 'great classics of the genre'.

---

[30] *Ibid*, xii.
[31] Greenfield, S and Osborn, G (1995a).
[32] Greenfield, S and Osborn, G (1995b).
[33] Strickland, R (1993: 50).
[34] Bergman, P and Asimow, M (1996).

They have also included some not-so-great movies that present interesting legal and ethical issues. The analysis incorporates a rating system from four gavels to one, ranging from classics through good to OK and finally 'ask for a new trial'. As indicated, they do not specifically define 'trial movies' although they do describe them as a 'genre'. Their goals then are diverse and conform to the notion of a shared understanding of the legal film. They use the phrase 'trial movie' although, of the films that they look at, some 25 have only a limited courtroom focus. Their criteria for trial movies' popularity, however, contain elements for identifying a genre with its stress on routine conventions:

the drama of one-on-one confrontations—attorney versus witness, attorney versus opposing counsel, attorney versus judge, attorney versus client;

the built-in suspense factor of wondering what judgment the jury (or in some cases the judge) will decide about the fate of the defendants;

movie makers select eternally fascinating themes such as murder, treachery and sex rather than day-to-day grind from the courts of speeding tickets or slip-and-fall cases;

controversial legal and moral issues are presented in a sugar-coated way. They can present the clash between good and evil such as the movie lawyer fighting for Morality and Justice.[35]

In one sense this plays down the importance of law in legal films, and makes the point that even courtroom dramas are far more about other things than they are about the law. Social issues are often more significant within the overall film and narrow legal issues may be confined to the periphery. The courtroom scenes can provide 'dramatic' moments or elements. These demonstrate climactic innocent or guilty flashes, but the very constituents, such as the architecture and the structure of the proceedings, also provide the limitations. Often the dramatic elements are created by the hero stepping outside of the formal limits, such as Frank Galvin in *The Verdict* (1982). The amount of leeway, though, is necessarily very confined otherwise the law film may lose its shape and recognition. These restrictions in terms of space, people, and conduct, thus require that the drama must extend beyond the confines of the court. For example the classic *Twelve Angry Men* (1957) is not just about the deliberations of the jury in a movie trial, as Cunningham has noted:

Treating typical Lumet concerns, such as the necessity for personal responsibility if democratic processes are to survive, and the tendency for humanity's illusions, guilts, and prejudices to endanger its legal systems *Twelve Angry Men* (1957) goes beyond the well-intentioned 'message picture' to make a remarkable cinematic statement about the nature of the limitations of the American jury system and of the American democratic process itself.[36]

---

[35] *Ibid*, xvi.
[36] Cunningham, F (1991: 109).

The subtleties and nuances in the work provide the depth that such dramatic works need, and go far beyond the built-in suspense factor. Yet it is possible to argue, taking a very narrow view, that *Twelve Angry Men* (1957) is not a law film on the basis that it is not really a courtroom drama. This film encapsulates some of the problems of making rigid classifications. Rafter's work deals in considerable depth with crime films and confronts the problem of genre head on:

> Crime films do not constitute a genre (a group of films with similar themes, settings and characters) as Westerns and war films do. Rather, they constitute a *category* that encompasses a number of genres—caper films, detective movies, gangster films, cop and prison movies, courtroom dramas, and the many offerings for which there may be no better generic label than, simply, crime stories. Like the terms *dramas* and *romances, crime films* is an umbrella term that covers several smaller and more coherent groupings.[37]

Rafter includes courtroom dramas within her crime film 'umbrella', and points out the changing nature of the genre, arguing that contemporary courtroom dramas 'increasingly embed a short trial scene in a longer adventure story'. Rafter's solution to this tricky problem is to divide crime films chronologically into three periods, the 1930s to the mid 1950s, the mid 1950s through the 1960s and the 1970s to the present. Rafter's analysis does quite neatly skirt around some of these seemingly unworkable dilemmas and concurs with some previous work that identified aspects of courtroom films. Perhaps almost inevitably it raises further questions, most notably where the issue at stake is not a criminal offence but relates to a civil dispute. Rafter acknowledges at the outset that her focus is crime, and that she is excluding films that have a civil core.

As we have observed, the prime focus of law films is generally a serious criminal offence, although there are a number of prominent civil examples such as *The Verdict* (1982), *Class Action* (1990) and *A Civil Action* (1998). There are other less obvious 'law films' that deal with other aspects of the function and purpose of law such as *Devil's Advocate* (1997) and *Cape Fear* (1991). In neither of these two latter examples is there a sufficient length of courtroom scene to merit the description of a courtroom drama, but both are strongly concerned with the role and function of law and, in *Cape Fear* (1991), achieving justice. In essence those writers pursuing a general theme have adopted an individual approach that fits in with their chosen methodology. The lines are not neat and tidy and much categorisation is subjective; in the absence of any clear conventions about relevance this is perhaps inevitable. As we noted above, there were a number of essay collections published in the 1990s and these seem to hint at the notion of a genre or at least a shared body of reference that emerges, albeit obliquely. We start by looking at the centrepiece of much of the early focus, the courtroom, in this Chapter, before expanding our coverage of what law and film scholars have also been working on, by looking more directly at the issues of genre in later chapters.

---

[37] Rafter, N (2006: 6).

Inside the Courtroom

As Goodrich has noted, '[t]he visual metaphor of justice as something that must be visible and seen enacted has a striking poignancy, in that it well captures the paramount symbolic presence of law as a façade, a drama that rolls before the eyes of those subject to it. Any attempt to depict the nature of a legal hearing does well to begin by examining that visibility, the physical structure and architecture of a peculiar auditory space.'[38] Thus, the most obvious classification for legal film has been to ring-fence courtroom drama, and this has emerged as a traditionally accepted type.[39] Here we see the legal process in action with (often) the full range of personnel, although as we note later, judges have often been given a limited role.

Films that fall into the category of courtroom drama could include, for example, *Inherit the Wind* (1960). The film is based upon the 1925 'Monkey Trial' in which John Scopes, a teacher, was charged under a state law prohibiting the teaching of Darwinian theory. The trial heralded Clarence Darrow's only *pro bono* appearance in court for the defence, with William Jennings Bryan, a former presidential candidate, acting for the prosecution, and the case was seen as a wider touchstone for issues facing American society. Although the names and some of the details in the film are changed, the script draws heavily upon the events and the transcript of the case. One key divergence is the treatment and potential punishment of Cates/Scopes, played by Dick York. In reality he only faced a small fine if the prosecution was successful as the case was a 'set-up' test case financed by the ACLU. Undoubtedly, Kramer added this punitive element to provide an extra dramatic edge. The film is memorable for a number of trial scenes, perhaps in particular the cross-examination of prosecutor Matt Brady, when called as a witness, to explain the meaning of the Bible.

Similarly, *Witness for the Prosecution* (1957) is perhaps the best example of a courtroom drama, and is centred upon the legal system in England and Wales. Directed by Billy Wilder and based on the Agatha Christie play, the film starred Tyrone Power, Marlene Dietrich and Charles Laughton. Laughton is memorable as the barrister, Sir Wilfred Robards, who takes on the defence, against medical advice, of a man accused of murdering a rich widow. A neat storyline twist creates real tension and the performances of Laughton and Dietrich in particular are excellent. Indeed, the film neatly illustrates the dramaturgical potential of the courtroom and the way actors can utilise powerful rhetoric within this context and the film takes place primarily within the courtroom or legal chambers.

Thus a film that 'revolves' around, and usually leads up to a trial, would attract classification as a 'courtroom drama'. The law, however, is often a vehicle for the telling of a substantial moral tale. In a sense, then, the courtroom element is the spatial focus, but does this make it a law movie? *A Fish Called Wanda* (1988) has

---

[38] Goodrich, P (1990: 16).
[39] Silbey, J (2001).

some significant courtroom scenes, as does *Brothers in Law* (1957), yet neither is a courtroom drama. Both are essentially comedies and not even explicitly courtroom comedies. Courtroom drama for this more tangential type of film would be a misnomer. These refer really to dramas that have an attachment to an *element* of the courtroom, not necessarily with the courtroom itself as its fulcrum.

Whilst the examples above may be termed traditional courtroom dramas, hemmed in by the use of the court as the central focal point for the action, there are a number of other films that could be said to fall more tangentially within this definition. For example, *12 Angry Men* (1957) shows virtually nothing of the courtroom itself, the action is almost exclusively played out in the jury room. However, it can be argued that many of the traits of the traditional courtroom drama are in evidence within this jury room, including members of the jury adopting the persona of defence and prosecution lawyers:

> ... it could be said that the courtroom is merely the theatre in which the substance is aired—much in the same way that the courtroom is the space in which law is delivered. That is, however, not to detract from the point that all these films *Witness for the Prosecution, Young Mr Lincoln, Inherit the Wind, Philadelphia* use the courtroom as the prime focus for the action and much feet of film that is expended is based within a court. The definition of courtroom can be stretched to include films such as *Twelve Angry Men* which is centred on the jury room, with Henry Fonda effectively performing the role of defence counsel.[40]

On this basis, the question of what a courtroom drama actually is becomes more contentious as it is possible to argue that portrayals that do not appear to fall within a 'traditional' definition can be seen as encompassing such features although some of the trappings and legal finery may not be so apparent at first glance. *Cape Fear* (1991) provides a good example of how it is possible to construct an argument that the boat at the end of the film takes the place of the courtroom, and that the film as a whole is concerned with the law. Outside of such debates concerning the spatial definitions of the courtroom itself, there have been a number of portrayals utilising different forms of the 'traditional' courtroom. In some ways this has been mirrored in professional practice with a move towards specific tribunals and courts, or extra-legal means of resolving disputes including the use of alternative dispute resolution (ADR). ADR certainly affects the view people have of the law and some of the traditional tenets of law and legal practice (justice being seen to be done, win at all costs, there must be a loser etc) may be exploded by such means. Law films must be more than mere courtroom located drama, otherwise films such as *The Firm* (1993) and *12 Angry Men* (1957) are outside of the established category. The latter film is probably one of the most memorable films concerning the legal process and to exclude it would seem perverse. Before we go on in the next chapter to deal with issues of genre, it is useful at this juncture to detail

---

[40] Greenfield, S and Osborn, G (1999: 37).

a further possibility of classification that we have identified running through these films that could prove of use in classificatory terms, the *phases* of law.

The Phases of Law

We have identified three distinct phases in which law appears in films concentrated on the criminal justice system. First there is the question of the *apprehension* of the alleged wrongdoer that will ordinarily involve the police in some way. The obvious link here is to the genre of 'cop films' such as *The Offence* (1972), *Prince of the City* (1981) and *Night Falls on Manhattan* (1996). Second there is the *deliberation* phase, which equates to the trial that may, or may not, feature prominently. Finally we have the *disposition*, whereby the convicted prisoner is sentenced. Normally this relates more closely to 'pure' prison films such as *The Green Mile* (1999), *The Shawshank Redemption* (1994) and *Dead Man Walking* (1995). Prison films may feature an element of wrongful conviction that leads us back to flaws in the disposition stage. The innocent man incarcerated lends a further dimension and features in numerous films. Interestingly there is a line of films around the rogue cop, the vigilante and future law enforcement where the three are merged both within one individual and in a short space of time.

These three phases are traditionally dealt with quite separately within cinematic culture with police, trial and prison films having only limited overlap. Only in the television series *Law and Order* do we have a very clear connection made, although this was prefigured to an extent in *Hill Street Blues* in the 1980s, with Joyce Davenport's expanding role. Thus it is reasonable to consider each of these phases separately.

In simple terms, the deliberation phase featuring lawyers does not arise in the vast majority of police or prison dramas and there is no sense, from popular culture, that the various phases inter-relate. Unrealistic and unhelpful though this is, it is worthy of a separate study that is beyond the scope of our current inquiry. This would explore the connections between the various phases of what comes under the umbrella of the 'justice system' and the portrayal of institutional isolation encountered in popular culture. This separation between police work and the trial process is a consistent feature of a considerable body of films in Britain, as well as the United States, under the umbrella of courtroom drama or trial films.

The problem of defining a law film is an issue that has caused some measure of debate amongst many working in the area. It draws upon the notion of genre and sets out some ideas and concepts about where the boundary may be drawn and what can legitimately be included within the compass of a 'law' film. The establishment of the boundaries to an area of academic analysis is certainly a concept that legal scholars are familiar with. In a sense the traditional compartmentalisation of law into discrete subjects of study is somewhat artificial and a result of the historical development of textbooks amongst other factors. For example, with respect to the common law the division between tort and contract is often artificial, with claims made for a common law of obligations encompassing the two areas, and even suggestions of a wider concept embracing other areas. Similarly new areas such as labour law and sports law have developed as it becomes apparent that there is a body of legal principles that apply to a distinct area. On one level this might be a fragmenting of different types or areas of law that might impinge upon a new or emerging area. An analogy here might be made with colour theory, and in particular the links between primary, secondary and tertiary colours—emerging subjects might build upon or blur the traditional primary colours (the core subjects perhaps) and in fact be coalitions or fragmentations of these core subjects (secondary or tertiary subjects).

This is further complicated by the field of enquiry moving outside of 'law'. This involves a move to embrace subjects such as psychology, literature, sociology, or even film studies. However, whilst we may be accustomed to shifting ideas concerning the order of the law curriculum, delving into the exotic world of film studies, and applying the concept of genre as a means of classifying our subject matter, is a rather different proposition.

Conclusion

An examination of the academic output on legal films reveals many different approaches to analysis but there is one compelling conclusion that we can reach. There is no identifiable consensus over methodology or the range of material studied and furthermore that examination of the same raw material produces alternative results. For example, as we note elsewhere, there is some widespread agreement about the heroic nature of lawyers in early portrayals. Yet much depends on the parameters of the investigation—heroic to whom? And judged by what moral standards, those of the day or contemporary ethics? Are modern-day lawyers any less heroic merely because they are burdened in some shape with human frailties? In short, we come to different conclusions about what legal films mean, and offer us, about law, lawyers and justice. Confusion abounds, although there is nothing unique about an approach to the study of law that is fundamentally concerned with interpretation. Primary sources of law, cases and statutes have to be deciphered and on more than one occasion. Previous decisions may assist or obfuscate the process. Any first-year law student will have experienced the problem of deciding what a case 'really means' and how it relates to other cases. In order to aid our understanding of judicial pronouncements, research has been developed to analyse the processes and mechanisms of reasoning.

We try to develop some ideas concerning the function and operation of law making. These are not narrow theoretical debates but attempts to discover more, not just about the boundaries of law's empire, but also the methods of construction. Unfortunately much theoretical work on the conception and utilisation of law is itself as shrouded in mystery as the subject it seeks to deconstruct. The failure to provide broadly accessible work contributes to the maintenance of an anaesthetic legal education. This is a wider problem and we outline below how theoretical work in this field might proceed but we suggest that are two routes of practical research that may enable film and the law to move forwards rather than sideways.

First we need to engage with the elements of the construction of film and, more specifically, legal film. A starting point is to incorporate ideas and theories that have been developed in cultural studies generally and more specifically film studies. As we note below, there is an increasing interest in the law and culture relationship and this needs to be directed by law and film scholars into those other areas that may prove fruitful. What we are proposing is taking the film out of law and film and interrogating the essential features of film theory. This is no trifling task. Redhead has previously noted some of the practical problems of mixing or rather mastering different disciplines.[41] It seems to us that we could, as a minimum, isolate a number of areas that could fruitfully complement current work. In particular we need to engage with theories of both construction and consumption of film. With respect to the former, the task is to work more broadly on the creation of genre. This needs to be supplemented with a deeper analysis of how legal films fit in to ideas of genre. We outline how problematic, yet important, fixing definitions of legal film without the framework of genre theory, is. All too often legal academics brush over or skirt around this issue rather than engaging it head on, though there are some notable exceptions. It may well be the case that this process cannot develop until we identify characteristics of legal film that constitute the elements of a genre. It is then perhaps work that needs to be carried out in parallel with interpretative work of groups of films or individual films. In addition to considering the classification of legal film we need to look more closely at other parts of production and at ideas of the auteur, something we touch upon only briefly in this text.

Similarly the role of the star may be significant in determining the status of the central legal character. The link between law (or at least the courtroom) and, as noted at the start of the Chapter, drama means many star actors have stepped into the lawyer's shoes. Making the lawyer the pivotal figure, and an attractive proposition to a major actor, may then involve writing the character in a particular fashion.[42] Apart from considering the theoretical angle of film making it is also worth thinking about extending the analysis to the creative process itself. Much as we spend time examining the work of practitioners of law, perhaps it would be worth examining the practice of making movies. This could be on a general level or more specifically concentrated on legal film. An examination of the whole process from writing to post production would give law and film scholars an idea of the dimension that determines the shape of our primary material. A cursory audit of deleted scenes from a number of DVDs demonstrates the type of material that may be left on the cutting room floor and the feelings of the director on the

---

[41] Redhead, S (1995).
[42] Goldman, W (1983).

shape of the film. Both Steven Soderbergh in *Erin Brockovich* (2000), and Norman Jewison in *The Hurricane* (1999), have explained why certain scenes were cut and the editing process clearly affects the final product in a number of ways.

We feel it would be profitable for us to engage more deeply with the production of film from both a practical and a theoretical standpoint. This also applies to the question of the consumption of film. Having outlined the rationale for the choice of law and some academic responses to how we try to categorise films as courtroom dramas, it is necessary to turn to the more specific and troubling area of genre.

4

Strictly Courtroom? Law Film
and Genre

Assuming law films include more than just courtroom drama, the issue becomes one of identification. Applying concepts of genre identification and analysis may help in providing an answer. The role and function of genre has been a hotly debated issue within film studies for a significant period, and is a theoretical 'problem' that needs to be confronted by film and law scholars. The flexibility of genre allows the enquirer to set his or her own boundary to the limits of the enquiry, without necessarily delving into any ideological morass. At the same time, it does offer the opportunity to break free from a purely descriptive, if interesting, dimension and explore the meaning and effect of film. There are of course dangers, voiced by some academics, such as that film and law scholarship can simply involve description without offering anything theoretical or applied.[1] Genre is indeed a double-edged sword. This Chapter builds upon the previous one, and focuses more explicitly upon genre theory and whether this is a useful way to examine films within this area.

It is important to recognise that the entire debate over genre arose as a direct result of a desire to engage with the products of Hollywood cinema as part of a high/low culture debate:

> As Gledhill indicates, there were two main reasons for the appearance of genre and genres on the agenda of theorists, critics and teachers of film at this time. One was a desire to engage in a serious and positive way with popular cinema in general and with Hollywood in particular. The other was a desire to complement, temper or displace altogether the dominant critical approach used hitherto—auteurism.[2]

This introduces a further problem. If the rationale was to engage with popular Hollywood products what is the effect on, and relationship to, the products of a national cinema industry? We consider the case of the British film industry in the following Chapter. As we have noted above, the introduction of the idea of genre as a tool of classification and analysis was developed to help understand the importance of the popular cinema created by Hollywood. We would argue that it is vital for film and law scholars to engage with contemporary debates around genre in order to develop new aspects within the scholarship. The concept of genre in relation to film may be used in two distinct ways.

---

[1] Black, D (1999).
[2] Neale, S (2000: 10).

The first is to classify films into particular categories through film analysis, identifying those components that make a 'cowboy film' a 'Western', and so on. This is in itself problematic, as Tudor observes:

> To take a genre such as a 'Western', analyse it, and list its principal characteristics is to beg the question that we must first isolate the body of films which are 'Westerns'. But they can only be isolated on the basis of the 'principal characteristics' which can only be discovered from the films themselves after they have been isolated. That is, we are caught in a circle which first requires that the films are isolated, for which purpose a criterion is necessary, but the criterion is, in turn, meant to emerge from the empirically established common characteristics of the films.[3]

This dichotomy has exercised many of those working in the area of law and film, who have had to start from scratch in trying to build up those characteristics that represent the taxonomy of the law film. This explains why one approach is to adopt film analysis that pulls out common threads, drawing attention to similarities and differences between films. This work is vital in trying to determine what the components of such a film might be. Some of this work has been extremely broad and ambitious in its outlook, seeking to show law and/or lawyers as a dominant force within a wide range of films that at first analysis might seem to belong within a different area of classification.[4]

Others have sought to delineate the border through a specific geographic or spatial boundary by using the term 'courtroom drama'.[5] This in itself can be just as problematic in terms of potential coverage as applying the broad brush of 'law as justice', given that the courtroom clearly extends to a military tribunal, and arguably the jury room. If we did not, could we really accept that *12 Angry Men* (1957) is not a law film because the action takes place almost completely within the confines of the jury room with an absence of lawyers? Though interestingly enough, and to add to the confusion, Lumet himself was concerned with issues beyond the justice system: 'As is so frequent in his films, Lumet here is far more interested in human character, in the nuances of the ways that people make up their minds about things (or think they do), than in the more obvious spectacle of such legal melodramas as *Kramer vs. Kramer* (1979) or … *And Justice For All* (1979)'.[6] Before discussing the value of genre theory, we need to delve deeper into the attributes and characteristics of courtroom drama.

Critical Aspects of the Courtroom Drama

A range of writers on law and film have talked of constituting a genre or sub-genre—namely 'trial movies'.[7] Here the action resolves in the courtroom and the

---

[3] Tudor, A (1974: 137–38).
[4] Greenfield, S and Osborn, G (1999).
[5] Black, D (1999); Rafter, N (2000); Rafter, N (2006).
[6] Cunningham, F (1991: 109); Robson, P (2006).
[7] Bergman, P and Asimow, M (1996).

trial is the crucial feature of the film. The outcome is what the jury in the film and we, the audience as jury, are there to determine. Some films that intuitively sound like courtroom dramas—*Kramer vs. Kramer* (1979)—turn out to be only concerned with the courtroom for a limited part of the film. Here the time spent in court occupies only a fifth of the screen time, and is much less central to the conflict between Ted and Joanna over the custody of their young son, Billy, than the title might suggest. It would be perfectly feasible to miss out the courtroom scenes and retain the core meaning of the film, effectively a plea that, if necessary, men can demonstrate appropriate child-rearing skills. There are examples of films that appear to be heading towards a 'courtroom drama' but, in fact, develop into purely a thriller. *Wild Things* (1998), for example, builds for the first 38 minutes until the opening of the trial, but this is completed in nine minutes and serves only as a prologue to a *Body Heat* (1981) type thriller with several unexpected twists and turns. Other films merely feature a court sequence as part of the narrative, and in such instances the focus is not on whether or not there will be a successful outcome.[8]

Genre may also have certain attractions as an explanation for factors that drive production, a basis for industry programming decisions, and a way of relating film to audience expectations. It is not difficult to discern visual and plot conventions that are shared by a sufficiently large number of films over time to allow us to delineate what we expect to find in a 'courtroom film' or 'trial movie'. It is possible to look at how these features have altered over time and make some sort of assessment of law and lawyer portrayal. Focusing upon 'courtroom dramas', a term often used interchangeably with trial movies, rather than law films more generally, there are positive reasons for separating out these films for distinct analysis. We recognise, however, that there are a whole host of films of interest to ourselves and other scholars in the field where we do not venture inside a courtroom and where no trial takes place or is even an issue. Genre as we know has certain attractions as a way of:

> (p)roviding the formula that drives production; constituting the structures that define individual texts; programming decisions are based primarily on generic criteria; the interpretation of generic films depends entirely on the audience's generic expectations.[9]

Plot Conventions

There are visual and plot conventions, shared by a sufficiently large number of films over time, to allow one to delineate what can be expected in a 'courtroom drama'. It is possible to go on to look at how these features have altered historically and see the contribution this roster of films makes to our assessment of the portrayal of law and lawyers. Courtroom dramas have certain identifiable features.

---

[8] *A Fish Called Wanda* (1990); *Vera Drake* (2004).
[9] Altman, R (1999: 14).

These involve visual, oral and narrative elements. There is also a recognition of it being a tangible entity in itself—and one that can be used as a counterpoint to knowing spoofs, references, and even tributes in comedy and futuristic films.

The visual conventions include a signalling of a courtroom phase, typically by an external establishing shot of the exterior of the court building. We then have further images of the interior of the courtroom, which often occur at an early point in the film.[10] For example, in *12 Angry Men* (1957), *Class Action* (1995) and *Philadelphia* (1993), the opening shots establish us in a court setting. In the former there is slow pan up from the ground of the columns of justice of the New York City Court ending in the inspiring motto 'Protect the children of the poor'. In both *Class Action* (1995) and *Philadelphia* (1993) we see the splendid dome of a courtroom and then cut to counsel arguing a case. The scene may also be set later on in the action, an example of which would be *8 O'Clock Walk* (1953). Here we see a reverse, with a pan down from the statue of Iustitia to reveal that this is the Central Criminal Court. The next shot takes us into a courtroom, in preparation for a trial, which is revealed as Court Number One. The same kind of juxtaposition, of external and internal shots, is encountered in many films with trial sequences, such as *Brothers in Law* (1957). The symbols of justice range from ornate marble stairways and interiors to sombre wood panelling.

Oral conventions include how the portrayal of the taking of evidence is shown. Inevitably concessions are made with this in a standard-length commercial film. Even though the trial is the centrepiece of a courtroom drama, the portrayal is, of course, a truncated version of the principal issues at stake. In addition to compressing time, the format and language are stylised. Perhaps the most compelling device is the collapse of the witness, Marlene Dietrich's character Christine Helm in *Witness for the Prosecution* (1957) being a great example of this. The witness is shown as trapped, her credibility destroyed and she flees the courtroom a broken woman.

The approach may be histrionic, or may be more subtle. *Guilty as Sin* (1993) opens with Jennifer Haines (Rebecca De Mornay) shown quietly but ruthlessly destroying what appears at the outset to be a sound prosecution case in her role as a defence attorney. The final submission to the jury is not always so measured. Jed Ward (Gene Hackman) in *Class Action* (1995) invokes the world of Alice in Wonderland when seeking to defend his client's actions against a polluting factory complex. The contrast is between his exuberant rhetorical flourishes, intercut with the presentation of his daughter in another case. She is shown arguing quietly and dispassionately that society should be guided by the law, not subjective notions of justice. Eddie Dodd (James L Woods) in *True Believer* (1989) is seen walking away from the courtroom with his drug-dealing client after ranting at the jury, to great effect:

> Despise my client … I do. But are we going to allow his vile trade to rob us of our constitutional rights? Are we going to allow the pursuit of this little white powder destroy the Constitution of the United States?

[10] Silbey, J (2001).

Jake Brigance (Matthew McConaughey) in *A Time to Kill* (1996) seems to subvert the slickness of this process when he stands almost penitent before the jury admitting his own lack of experience. In a similar vein, the world-weary resignation of Paul Newman in *The Verdict* (1982) sums up the way in which film lawyers appeal specifically to emotions, and to justice. He asks the jury to take power into their own hands and rise above the mundane day-to-day constraints of life. By comparison, British courtroom dramas may appear very restrained. For example, counsel address their questions to witnesses and address the jury from a static standing position, limiting theatrical movement. Despite this, films do feature witnesses being confused and tongue-tied, and falling into the well-laid traps of their inquisitors, neatly exemplified by the final courtroom appearance in *Brothers in Law* (1957). Here, in his third attempt to conduct proceedings in court, *ingénu* barrister Roger Thursby (Ian Carmichael) manages, with the assistance of the well-disposed judge, to succeed in his witness examination. The same kind of climax occurs at the end of *In the Name of the Father* (1993) when, with the incriminating note written by the prosecution, 'Not to be shown to the defence', at her disposal, Gareth Peirce (Emma Thompson) is able to bring down the witness and indulge in a grand flourish condemning the system. Of course, cinematic witnesses tend not to remain as bound stoically to their stories as may happen in real life.[11]

Additionally there are a range of narrative conventions applied. Thus the background and build-up phase allows us to glean some context for the issues at trial before we get into court. In *Adam's Rib* (1949), *The Accused* (1989), *Jagged Edge* (1985) and *Primal Fear* (1996), the crime or aftermath of the crime with which the trial will be concerned is outlined at the outset. The framing device of 'the extended flashback' from the courtroom is also used on occasion. In *Presumed Innocent* (1992) the prosecutor introduces the majestic Chicago courtroom. Similarly, the start of *North Country* (2005) intercuts the evidence of a female witness being asked questions about her life as a mother with the experience of her suffering from and then fleeing domestic abuse. Following the use of such a device, the main issues of the case are then narrated. This may be in the office with the arrival of the tentative client having been referred as having no money,[12] or with no other option.[13] Occasionally the lawyer comes calling when either justice or publicity is at stake.[14]

The way the trial is set up may often obey certain conventions, particularly the 'David versus Goliath' approach. It is a *sine qua non* of courtroom dramas that main protagonists should not have the support of a wealthy well-resourced law firm at their disposal. They are either up against the implicitly limitless resources of the state in criminal trials, or face a well-heeled adversary in civil litigation. Interestingly, in one instance where the accused is financially secure, *Jagged Edge* (1985),

---

[11] See *inter alia* the real trials shown in *Boston Law* (2001) BBC (aka *Real Justice* (PBS)).
[12] *To Kill a Mockingbird* (1962); *Suspect* (1987); *Losing Isaiah* (1995); *Erin Brockovich* (2000).
[13] *Philadelphia* (1993).
[14] *Adam's Rib* (1949); *Just Cause* (1995); *A Time to Kill* (1996); *Primal Fear* (1996).

the lawyer chooses to present his defence single-handed to create a good impression to the jury.

Prominent examples of the 'David versus Goliath' approach include Frank Galvin (Paul Newman), the down-at-heel sole practitioner, who faces no less than 10 lawyers acting on behalf of the Diocese of Boston in *The Verdict* (1982). Similarly, in *Class Action* (1995), Jed Ward (Gene Hackman) has only a small team of dedicated lawyers seeking to take on the might of Meridian. Jan Schlichtmann (John Travolta) faces equally formidable odds in *A Civil Action* (1999), as does Ed Masry (Albert Finney) in *Erin Brockovich* (2000).

Another typical approach may involve different ways of dealing with the problem, particularly by adding some drama by way of seeing either an absence, or a subversion. Courtroom dramas obviously require 'drama'. In other genres these dramas are often engendered through various misunderstandings. Part of the convention of the romantic comedy requires our mismatched couple to fall in love and, eventually, recognise each other's true worth. There has to be a misunderstanding in which he or she becomes convinced either of the worthlessness of the other party or discovers that there is someone else—who will, of course, not really be a significant other. In the same way in the courtroom drama there is an incursion into the flow of events. The evidence or witness on whom the case depends goes missing. The witness may be bought off as in *The Verdict* (1982), or an accident may befall them as in *The Exorcism of Emily Rose* (2005). Evidence may be ruled inadmissible by an unsympathetic judge, or it may not even come to light or be delayed as in *In the Name of the Father* (1993).

In a courtroom drama, whatever the problem, events will not progress smoothly from complaint through to trial. Just as in the romantic comedy, where the path of the two lovers is interrupted, so too in the courtroom drama things go wrong. The neat twist in *The Life of David Gale* (2003) is the last-minute reprieve from execution. At the beginning of the film a car breaks down and later it transpires that this is the car containing the vital evidence that will show that David Gale (Kevin Spacey) did not murder former colleague and death penalty abolition campaigner, Constance Harraway (Laura Linney). The evidence has been deliberately concealed long enough to prevent it being revealed before the execution. The key point is to show that the system does not always work, and that it is possible for an innocent person to be executed.

A well-used device for the courtroom drama is 'the unexpected resolution'. There are dramatic films where the evidence is never obtained or it is destroyed. For example, in *The Shawshank Redemption* (1994), the *deus ex machina*, Tommy Williams, who can provide the evidence that Andy (Tim Robbins) is innocent, is shot while trying to escape, on the orders of the prison governor. This is not, however, a standard feature of the courtroom drama. Pieces of paper are often crucial elements in the courtroom drama, where concealed evidence comes to light, often by accident or good fortune. Witnesses whom one doubted had the courage to come forward and testify appear. Ken, the roommate of one of the rapists in *The Accused* (1989), places his faith in the truth, and his abhorrence at what happened, above his friendship. The nurse who has originally been frightened off by the Catholic Church is prepared to risk all to give her evidence as to how the doctor's error was hushed up in *The Verdict* (1982). Maggie Ward (Mary Elizabeth Mastrantonio) has a crisis of conscience in *Class Action* (1995) and reveals the existence of a secret memorandum to the other side in the case. The vacillating workmates of Josey Ames (Charlize Theron) come up trumps in *North Country* (2005) in a Spartacus-like demonstration of solidarity at a crucial juncture in the case thus allowing the action to proceed with enough complainants.

The vast majority of trial movies have a coda. These come in three forms. First, there is the 'twist' that involves a subversion of the legal process. Essentially it shows how people can operate without lawyers, courts and strict rules. It seems to suggest that the legal process, by its very nature, cannot really provide a proper just solution. Thus in *Kramer vs. Kramer* (1979), Joanna (Meryl Streep), having won in court, returns Billy to Ted (Dustin Hoffman). Similarly, in *Losing Isaiah* (1995) Khaila Richards (Halle Berry), having won the right to rescind the adoption of Isaiah, brings him back to Margaret Lewin (Jessica Lange). The end is enigmatic. The camera pans back as Isaiah is left playing happily on the floor of the Lewin house between his natural mother and his adoptive mother. The courts and the legal system can only provide winners and losers. Life can provide draws and justice. We see this exemplified in the ending to *I am Sam* (2002). Having lost the battle for custody of his daughter, Sam Dawson (Sean Penn) gets access because his daughter is so unhappy in her new home without him. At the end of the film, Lucy Diamond Dawson (Dakota Fanning) is shown back with her father in the new home.

There is also the reflective coda. This provides an opportunity for the characters to reflect on what we have learned and what the future may hold. Father and daughter are reconciled in *Class Action* (1995). The fight for justice never stops so that, even after the great success against Pacific Oil and Gas, Erin Brockovich is back on the doorstep seeking out more victims of injustice in *Erin Brockovich* (2000). In some we have learned that racial tolerance is a by-product of the defence of the vigilante in *A Time to Kill* (1996), with the barbecue at the home of Carl Lee Hailey (Samuel L Jackson) being attended by white lawyer Jake Brigance (Matthew McConaughey). The film ends as their two daughters play happily unaware of their skin colour.

Sometimes there is the simple coda of context. For example, in *The Accused* (1989), the audience is informed in stark terms, on a plain black background with no music, about rape cases. In *North Country* (2005) immediately following the victory in the final courtroom scene the 'long march' towards equality in the iron mines is laid out. There appears to be only one courtroom drama in which the judicial decision is the final shot of the film with neither twist, reflection, or context. This occurs in the British film *The Boys* (1962), a worthy piece of social comment in itself, with some young men accused of a murder just because of their age, and stereotyped as dangerous. The whole issue of capital punishment permeates the film, where it looks as if someone will hang as a result of nothing much more than prejudice. A crusading barrister, Victor Webster (Richard Todd), is determined to save them from the law's injustice only to discover in court that one of them did actually commit the murder.

Laughing at the Law

The coverage of comedies has now become standard since the issues revealed in these are outweighed by the limitations as models for practice. Comedies are able to subvert the genre precisely because an expectation has been created. The joy of watching some films, and indeed their comedic content, is often informed by the accuracy with which they spoof recognised elements in a genre. Thus *Young Frankenstein* (1974), *Blazing Saddles* (1974) and *Airplane* (1980) derive their success from the fun they poke at the clichéd and hackneyed visual and narrative effects of horror films, the Western and disaster movies respectively. The use of courtroom dramas in this way can be seen in a number of films. The point is that we enjoy seeing familiar routines presented tongue in cheek. The seriousness and solemnity of the proceedings are clearly established so when, for example, Archie Leach (John Cleese) becomes bemused and lost for words during his cross-examination in *A Fish Called Wanda* (1988) it is drawing on our knowledge of what a cross-examination should be that contributes to the comedic effect. Similarly the courtroom scene in *Bananas* (1971) is funny because it critiques all the normal courtroom drama conventions. The jurors are shown smoking dope, a witness sings and the defendant who is representing himself is bound and gagged. It is so far removed from our understanding (through previous film portrayals) of what happens that it becomes amusing.

The references may be light or quite dark in tone. In *Trial and Error* (1962), for instance, the whole development of the film is towards Morgan Hall's demonstration of his forensic skills. He is shown standing up in court and dropping his papers, with the subsequent acquittal of his client on the grounds of inadequate defence. What is promised, and what fails to materialise, is the cut and thrust of the courtroom drama. It is our knowledge of what is expected to occur in the missing phase that provides the impetus to the film. Without the existence of that knowledge our experience of the film would be an empty one.

The ideas of witness credibility and jury prejudice are neatly highlighted in the black comedy *Serial Mom* (1994). This spoofs the whole notion of celebrity status and justice well before the trials of OJ Simpson, Michael Jackson and Phil Spector.[15] Beverly Sutphin (Kathleen Turner) is attempting to cast doubt on the reliability of her friend Rosemary Ackerman (Mary Jo Catlett), who has important information in relation to a murder. She asks a number of serious questions calling into question the motive and opportunity of the witness to have

---

[15] Rapping, E (2003).

committed the murder herself and then in a tension-building moment asks the 'key' question:

Mrs Ackerman, Do you recycle?

A hush falls over the courtroom. The jurors lean forward. The friends and relatives lean forward. The prosecutor leans forward. The judge perks up. Then comes the flustered reply from the witness/accused:

No. I don't have time.

There is an audible gasp around the courtroom and the jurors exchange meaningful looks. The credibility of the witness has been destroyed. Just as in a 'proper' courtroom drama. This time, though, the torpedo question is patently nonsense, the recycling question clearly does not inform their likely culpability or even credibility.

In a slightly different way the success against all the odds of the lone attorney is parodied in *My Cousin Vinny* (1992).[16] This is more 'realistic' than *Serial Mom* (1994), but it still involves a high degree of exaggeration, including the behaviour and dress of the serial exam-failing Vinny and his girlfriend, to the casual yet pernickety judge, and the spectacularly incompetent Public Defender. Here we have the eyeglasses trick, with Vinny destroying the credibility of a witness by showing the severe limitations of her eyesight. The *pièce de résistance* is the use of the specialist automobile knowledge of his girlfriend to discredit the remaining circumstantial evidence tying the accused to the commission of the murder and robbery.

In a subtle way, too, we see the trial *shtick* of Ricky Rietti (Michael Richards) as an actor forced to impersonate his drink-incapacitated lawyer friend in *Trial and Error* (1997). He uses television as his medium of instruction. Unable to contain himself from cross-examining a witness he asks a series of blindingly stupid questions in relation to his client's character and the judge duly accepts the prosecution's motion to strike the testimony derived from the following exchange:

Did my client look shifty?

I don't know.

You don't know?

I've never met your client.

Then you can't say he looked shifty.

No.

Thank you.

---

[16] The director of *My Cousin Vinny*, Jonathan Lynn is the cousin of Norman Naftalin, of Naftalin Duncan, a firm of Glasgow solicitors specialising in housing law.

As one of the courtroom guards passes him on the stairs, as he is being admonished by his now sober lawyer friend for this piece of folly, the guard observes: 'Nice work in there, man.' It may be nonsense but it is what the public want, and expect, from crafty lawyers.

The trial sequence in *Legally Blonde* (2001) is a tribute to the normal rules of a courtroom drama. The fluffy rom-com, which the film appears at the outset to be, transmogrifies into an improbable but standard courtroom drama. With a first-year law student taking over the defence of a woman charged with murder we see the demolition of not just one, but two witnesses, and the revelation of the real murderer in the process. After failing to elicit any worthwhile responses from the crucial eye-witness, Elle asks what the witness did earlier that day prior to leaving the shower and finding the accused crouched over her father's body with the murder weapon in her hand covered in the victim's blood. It transpires the witness had visited the hairdresser and had her hair permed. Elle notes that the 'first cardinal rule of perm maintanence' is not too wet the hair and thus the witness is destroyed.

We also have *Wild Things* (1998), which appears to be an absolutely standard courtroom drama but where the whole set-up, prosecution and trial scene, with vindication through witness collapse, are completed inside 50 minutes. The standard elements are again all present and it is only in this coda phase that we discover that things are not as they seem. We think we are watching a courtroom drama but in reality we are not. The protagonists have used their knowledge of the courtroom drama to create a set-up that relies on the conventions of the courtroom drama to provide the narrative impulse for the subsequent mazy thriller. Only as the credits roll do we discover what has actually been happening and how the fake courtroom drama fits into the overall schema. The film makes sense because we think we know where it is going and how it is likely to play out. We have been fooled by our own excessive knowledge of the generic features of a courtroom drama.

Whilst we have outlined some of the key attributes of the courtroom drama, there are, of course, many films that are concerned with the operation of the justice system which have little or nothing to do with the drama of the courtroom. The location of these in any taxonomy is another interesting point. Indeed, commentators within law and film scholarship have always regarded the true object of their inquiry as going well outside the courtroom and have analysed films as diverse as *Casablanca* (1942),[17] *It's A Wonderful Life* (1946),[18] and *The Man Who Shot Liberty Valance* (1962).[19] We are not suggesting that there is anything flawed in such an approach, and indeed celebrate the diversity and eclecticism. It is, however, our contention that it is worth seeking to make a distinction between law films and non-law films for heuristic purposes. Just as the concept of what amounts to a British film may produce occasional 'misfits' as we argue below,

---

[17] Almog, S and Reichman, A (2004).
[18] Denvir, J (1996a).
[19] Ryan, C (1996a).

nonetheless the categories can be of some value. By having a set of criteria for determining the category of 'law film' it allows analysis of changes in representations of issues within this body of film over periods of time. If one is serious about discussing the portrayal of women in the legal system, or the role of minority ethnic lawyers, as issues, then the range of material which is relevant to such a discussion must surely be restricted to those films where these matters have the potential to arise. A discussion, for instance, of *Casablanca* (1942) or *It's A Wonderful Life* (1946) is not germane in these debates. They are able to be part of different debates concerning the notion of law as a separate self-contained system, and the notion of community welfare as a guiding social principle. The fate of a working class woman operating her own code of morality in defiance of the system's proscriptions on abortion in *Vera Drake* (2004) is different as it fits within our definition of what we previously termed a 'law film'.[20] Whether categorising films as such is a germane or useful taxonomy is a different matter, and something this Chapter seeks to analyse.

Genre Theory

Beyond this initial task of providing a taxonomy, genre has a second important purpose. It offers us the potential to explore the construction and reception of different kinds of film. This second use of genre has a far greater theoretical significance as it draws within its compass a broad range of (potentially) interlinking factors. Tudor suggests that 'the genre concept is indispensable in more strictly social and psychological terms as a way of formulating the interplay between culture, audience, films and film makers'.[21] In this way, genre is an analytical tool that can be used to explain the creation, reception and effect of a film or group of films. We have already been involved in this type of work within law and film scholarship, as we detailed briefly in Chapter 1.

This point has found resonance with the professional bodies who have claimed that the 'poor' visual image of lawyers has damaged the public perception of the profession.[22] A recent example is the furore caused by the five-part series *Criminal Justice* shown on the BBC in summer 2008 where some barristers were shown to be less than ethical. There are, however, problems with ascribing public perception to cinematic portrayal on a simple level not least because of the difficulty in establishing exactly what 'message' is being received. Indeed, a related question might be 'what is the subjective view of the writer or director, and, indeed, does it matter to audience perception?' An example of the academic debate on the understanding of the nature of the portrayal of lawyers is an indicator of the problems faced.[23]

---

[20] Greenfield, S, Osborn, G and Robson, P (2001).
[21] Tudor, A (1974: 145).
[22] Haddad, T (2000).
[23] Asimow, M (2000a); Rafter, N (2000); Rafter, N (2006); Greenfield, S (2001).

One way to avoid the seeming impasse of the question of the characteristic of the law film, and the vexed question of genre, is to find a different theoretical framework and apply it to a central core of films. Of course this argument might, at first blush, appear somewhat circular, as it returns us to the question of which films to utilise. This, in turn, requires some sort of initial classification. It does, however, at least provide us with a point of departure and an opportunity to explore the benefits of taxonomy from a different perspective. There seems to be general agreement amongst those writing in the area that 'courtroom dramas', or 'trial movies', are within an accepted variety of 'law film genre' and the central question is how far it extends from the courtroom. As we note above, there are visual, oral and plot conventions shared by a sufficiently large number of films to allow one to delineate what can be expected in a 'courtroom film' or 'trial movie'. This has value in that it allows for analysis of how these features have altered over time and make some sorts of assessments of law and lawyers as they are here portrayed. When considering the whole issue of legal film and genre it is worth bearing in mind the important differentiation in terminology drawn by Schatz:

> Because it is essentially a narrative system, a film genre can be examined in terms of its fundamental structural components: plot, character, setting, thematics, style, and so on. We should be careful, though, to maintain a distinction between the film genre and the genre film. Whereas the genre exists as a sort of tacit 'contract' between filmmakers and the audience, the genre film is an actual event that honors such a contract. To discuss the Western genre is to address neither a single Western film nor even all Westerns, but rather that system of conventions which identifies Western films as such.[24]

At this point our primary focus of analysis is with what Schatz has labelled film genre: the description of the category. We have outlined above some of the problems of organising definitions of legal film once we stray beyond the courtroom, and there does seem to be a common consensus regarding the problems that arise around this descriptive tag. It appears to be an accepted category of a *type* of legal film, regardless of what exists beyond this line, and wherever this line may be drawn. We argue throughout this book that it is very difficult to draw clear boundaries. At one end we have those who claim that the crucial feature of law films is 'justice', and at the other those who take a very narrow interpretation using the courtroom drama label. This is the wider debate that is at the core of the book, but it is worth starting with the more accepted condensed definition.

As we argue above and in the previous Chapter, there are good reasons why the courtroom drama has been categorised and recognised as a distinct type: the setting, the pageantry, the uniform, etc. Thus the physical environment is a limited and known quantity and cannot be altered, trials cannot take place elsewhere though there are other tribunals such as courts-martial that need not take place in courtrooms, but will generally still adopt the same formal set-up. Thus law governs the type of building rather than the other way round and the style is

[24] Schatz, T (1981: 642).

also fixed. We know the rules of engagement and these must follow their course. The participants cannot shift to any degree from the pre-determined path. Of course individual eccentricities are permitted, even encouraged, as are moral and ethical defects that are capable of rectification. The whole point of trials is that they are formulaic. They are, after all, based on procedure, and films must follow this or else the courtroom becomes unrecognisable. Films will sometimes stress the importance of the procedure; for example in *My Cousin Vinny* (1992) when the judge is checking the credentials of the defendants' newly arrived lawyer, the solemnity and procedural dogmatism of his court is stressed, and the point forcefully made that the system of criminal justice in place in Alabama is as highly sophisticated as that of states such as New York.

This is the beauty of the courtroom scene—it is fixed; it has to be, otherwise the law does not work. Of course the director can throw in a biased or corrupt judge, lawyer or juror, but the framework remains. Similarly the plot is constant, with two parties taking opposing sides over a serious issue. Trials do not take place over minor incidents, though lawsuits involving mistakes are acceptable, especially when wrongful convictions result. There is little room for humour. Courtrooms are serious places, especially where the defendant may be on trial for his or her life. Behaviour must necessarily be grave and solemn. We cannot joke about a person's possible execution, although humour may be used tactically, as in *Young Mr Lincoln* (1939). Thus it is possible to see that courtroom actions are by definition limited, instantly recognisable, and easily attributable to the idea of a genre. However, this does not tell us much about law and legal films that must be more than the strictly defined courtroom drama/trial movie.

It has been argued that one solution to this debate is to take a broader perspective on what is meant by courtroom, and that the places and spaces of 'justice' might be a way out of the genre problem. This would involve, for example, including films such as *Judge Dredd* (1995) that portray instant, street-level justice:

> Dredd is as much the master of his 'courtroom' as any previous cinema judge, the change is the arena not the authority, his judicial robes are signposted as clearly as those historically trimmed with ermine. When Dredd indicates his judicial supremacy by declaring 'I am the Law' he is still acknowledging the legal process albeit it one vested within him.[25]

This is, perhaps, the other end of the spectrum from the limitations of the traditional courtroom drama. It cannot fit into the more rigid structures enjoyed by films such as *Inherit the Wind* (1960). Similarly, the jury room in *12 Angry Men* (1957) could be viewed as the courtroom. An alternative approach is to adopt the classification of 'trial movies', to cover all those films that have some element of a trial or trial process. In many ways, however, this has the same fault line, with much of the action taking place outside of the trial. The development of the concept of courtroom drama, or trial movies, undoubtedly reflects influence from outside the legal world and offers a view that this is what law and lawyering are all about.

---

[25] Greenfield, S and Osborn, G (1999: 33).

If law films are more than mere courtroom drama the question is how and why do we adopt the definition(s) we choose? One possibility is to take a broader approach and consider what the role and function of law are within society and how this is translated into film. The key concept is probably the relationship between law and justice, and a recurring theme through law films is the delivery of justice at the expense of formal legal rules. Law is often portrayed as a barrier to justice, and lawyers have to step outside of legal procedures to ensure the end result is just. In *Suspect* (1987), public defender Kathleen Riley develops an improper relationship with a juror to try and solve the mystery that is inevitably leading her client towards a wrongful conviction. Again, in *Young Mr Lincoln* (1939) procedure and legal niceties are warped somewhat in the search for truth.

If justice is the key concept how can we devise a category or genre that has sufficient meaning to make it a workable and useful tool? We suggest that law films are always concerned with the enforcement of justice in some shape or form and that this is a crucial starting point. Films may then be divided into a number of sub-categories of films that share the relevant characteristics—rookie lawyer wins through; lawyer on the skids redeems himself; last-minute evidence or witness saves the day; unpopular cause or defendant is proved to be meritorious. There are then two factors that may be applied to the question of justice, formal and informal enforcement, though these may exist separately or co-terminously. For example, with vigilante films the emphasis is solely on an informal subjective method and system of the enforcement of justice. At the other end of the scale is the formal process of law, though often there will be an element of informal or improper justice such as in *Suspect* (1987).

We would argue that in order to qualify as a law film the following characteristic(s) must be present in some shape or form: the geography of law; the language and dress of law; legal personnel; and the authority of law. This excludes films where 'justice' is enforced outside of any legal framework, for example war films, social dramas and family sagas. This book further develops this definition of law films through analysis of each area to determine the operational characteristics. To academics operating outwith its borders, film studies seems to offer a very different terrain. A central feature is the ability to find a means of analysing films and finding common ground to develop that analysis. Genre is a way of fulfilling this need to classify film, so that theoretical and descriptive analysis may be developed:

> Genres are formal systems for transforming the world in which we actually live into self contained, coherent and controllable structures of meaning. Genres can thus be considered to function in a way that a language system does—offering a vocabulary and a set of rules which allow us to 'shape' reality, thus making it appear less random and disordered.[26]

When considered in this way, the use of genre ought to be well within the compass of lawyers. After all, the common law is heavily reliant upon the classification of

[26] Phillips, P (1996: 127).

cases through the doctrine of precedent. The theoretical point of the doctrine of *stare decisis* is to find common ground and make future decisions on the basis of this original case. So in a sense we might usefully compare the process of the classification of films with the classification of cases, and an essential part of this action is finding out the meaning in both.

Although cases have the benefit of written statements, the reason for a decision is often unclear, particularly when judicial creativity in distinguishing cases is taken into account. Comparing a judge with a film director may, on the face of it, seem a little bizarre, yet, if we move more towards a consideration of auteur theory, the link becomes, perhaps, more obvious. For example, Lord Denning operated in a very distinctive manner both with respect to his approach to the substantive law and his written style. See, for example, his innovative attempt to create a principle of inequality of bargaining power in *Lloyds Bank v Bundy* [1975] QB 326, a view firmly rejected by the House of Lords in *National Westminster Bank v Morgan* [1985] AC 686. His judgments have a distinctive mark, as recognisable in their own way as the films by directors such as Sidney Lumet.[27] That judges develop their own styles is well chronicled and, indeed, the whole issue of whether the function of the judiciary is creative or interpretative has been subject to academic scrutiny and the differences between judges such as Blackburn, Denning and Goff, with their more creative and realist approaches, are in stark contrast to approaches by those such as Keith.[28] Phillips posts a warning on treating the boundaries of a genre too rigidly, and that classification can become self-fulfilling. Furthermore, he argues that the creation of genres can be counter-productive to analysis:

> Ultimately we need to be alert to the possibility that in constructing an argument around a particular genre, auteur or star, we may be producing a very neatly organised over-view—but we may also be constructing a fiction every bit as credible but every bit as contrived as the narratives of the films themselves ... [t]he temptation to force the film into the framework we have constructed, by the most convoluted of means if necessary, is great. Neatness will have been prioritised over genuine complexity and truth.[29]

We have argued consistently that if law and film is to develop as an area of critical inquiry then efforts will have to be made to determine the legitimate framework to the subject. We are also conscious that there is another dimension to genre that may illuminate our understanding of film. Hunter suggests that:

> [m]ost Hollywood films are 'hyphenates' these days, opportunistic fusions of successful formulae. Thus *Under Siege* is *Die Hard*-on-a-boat, *Waterworld* is *Mad Max*-on-water, and so on ... genericity ... is signified by glancing allusions to famous movies.[30]

---

27 Robson, P and Watchman, P (1981).
28 Adams, J and Brownsword, R (1987); Pannick, D (1987); Osborn, G and Sutton, T (1996).
29 Phillips, P (1996: 125).
30 Hunter, IQ (1996: 115)—*Under Siege* (1992), *Die Hard* (1988), *Waterworld* (1995), *Mad Max* (1979).

This point may have some relevance for law films that maintain the key elements but then expand other, perhaps more significant, issues. Genre as a method of classification within film studies has also been criticised because of the problem of 'isolating intentions', and the related issue that any classification is only useful in terms of what it is designed to achieve; that is that the classification should have some *point*. This dilemma can be solved in one of two ways. First, by classifying on the basis of the critical purpose of the inquiry, genre as a specific term becomes redundant as the classifier can determine his own 'genre'. The second way to solve the dilemma is to attempt to reach a common consensus as to what a 'Western', or 'law film' is and then establish relevant conventions to go with this.

However, we would argue that there are a number of other significant factors at work here and minor criminal or civil disputes are unlikely to offer sufficient depth of story line. Thus it is not the rules of law that provide the fascination essential for maintaining audience attention but rather the human and social context to the dispute. Often the key element is the larger social or moral issue that is being debated through the medium of law. For example the rules relating to the submission of evidence in a trial are unlikely to quicken the beat of many hearts, but in *The Verdict* (1982) they become a vital feature of the case. The crucial part of the plaintiff's claim is struck out by the judge, as it falls foul of the procedural rules. The issue then switches to the morality of the plaintiff's claim and the ability of the jury to deliver justice as they see it regardless of the paper evidence. Frank Galvin (Paul Newman) implores the jury to find the right result. His summation in *The Verdict* (1982) runs thus:

> Well you know so much of the time we're just lost, we say 'Please God tell us what is right, tell us what is true.' And there is no justice, the rich win, the poor are powerless, we become tired of hearing people lie. And after a time we become dead, a little dead—we think of ourselves as victims and we become victims. We become, we become weak, we doubt ourselves, we doubt our beliefs, we doubt our institutions and we doubt the law. But today you are the law.

> (Galvin walks towards the jury box.)

> You are the law. Not some book, not the lawyers. Not a marble statue or the trappings of the court, those are just symbols of our desire to be just. They are, they are in fact a prayer, a fervent and a frightened prayer. In my religion they say 'Act as if ye have faith, faith will be given to you'. If we are to have faith in justice we need only to believe in ourselves and act with justice. I believe there is justice in our hearts.

The rules of law here are being shown as a barrier to the pursuit of a just cause and the issue at stake is not the narrow one of whether the evidence should be admitted, but a broader one of achieving justice in spite of the rules. This idea of the legal rules operating as a barrier to justice is a theme that we explore in greater depth elsewhere in the text. Our point here is that the rules are a side issue compared to the wider moral point. A good example of law being the means to debate great moral questions can be seen in the Scopes trial. The issue is the relationship between science and religion examined through a state law that prohibited the teaching of Darwinian evolution theory in public schools. Law in this instance provides the means to address social dilemmas of the era in the same way that *To Kill a Mockingbird* (1962) considered race relations in the USA in the 1950s.

Law, then, has little to offer intrinsically. What matters is the moral point at stake, for example racism (*To Kill a Mockingbird* (1962)), homophobia (*Philadelphia* (1993)), and the death penalty (*Let Him Have It* (1991)), *Dead Man Walking* (1995)). The crux of the film is generally the wider social problem or moral issue and the legal dimension is how the law can be used to resolve such questions. A further dimension can be explored through the range of legal roles that can be introduced and such things as character defects and development can be addressed via the lead role. This may relate to a great public figure such as the emergence of Abraham Lincoln (*Young Mr Lincoln* (1939)), where his background in law allows him to emerge as a figure within the community. In *Suspect* (1987) and *The Verdict* (1982) the storyline is concerned with redemption in personal terms and, in the latter film, also professional rehabilitation. Indeed, as we argue later, this element of personal redemption is often a key feature in a number of legal films. Law films are, then, not really about what might be described as the substance of law or the detail of law, rather they are concerned with the penumbra of law, the places of law and the people of law. If this is right and law itself is largely peripheral, two linked questions are immediately pertinent. First, what can we classify as a law film, and what characteristics apply, and, secondly, if films are not directly about law, what can they tell us about law and indeed the other subjects they cover?

5

The British Law Film:
From Genre to Iconography

As we have acknowledged, there is now a huge range of work to be found in the area of law and film, but one thing that is marked within the research is the centrality, initially at least, of work emanating from the United States. This is undoubtedly a reflection, in part, of the significance of Hollywood to the global film audience. Historically little attention has been devoted to material produced 'locally', whether within Europe or beyond. Such has been the dominance of Hollywood that academic work within the field has tended to concentrate on products of American cinema.[1] As scholars we must come clean at this point—much of the work we ourselves have previously conducted has focused largely upon American cinema and output. As we observed in 2001:

> It needs to be noted at the outset that the focus is entirely on films originally made for the cinema, rather than television movies, and is dominated by American made films. In a sense this latter point reflects the cultural hegemony achieved by the American film industry. Within Europe it is Britain that has found its market most saturated with American films.[2]

There have, however, been moves in recent years, particularly with scholars such as those engaged with the European film network 'Images et Justice', to redress the balance somewhat by considering the output of national cinema within our own native jurisdictions.[3] At the same time there has been much debate about the role of American culture more generally, outside of just film:

> There is a purely economic rhetoric, mainly on the American side, which presents the issue as solely one of free markets and consumer choice. And there is a culturalist rhetoric, mainly on the European side, which talks of cultural identities, of language as the

---

[1] See, eg, Bergman, P and Asimow, M (1996); Greenfield, S, Osborn, G, and Robson, P (2001); Chase, A (2002); Levi, RD (2005); Strickland, R, Foster, T and Banks, T (2006) for instances of this US-centric tendency.

[2] Greenfield, S, Osborn, G, and Robson, P (2001: 1). See also here Nowell-Smith, G and Ricci, S (1998).

[3] Images et Justice/Images of Justice started as a primarily European network with representatives from England, France, Germany, Italy and Scotland at initial meetings. Its scope has already broadened to include other countries, extending as far as Israel.

soul of a nation, of the right to national self-expression, of resistance to alien cultural hegemony, and so on.[4]

This Chapter uses the categorisation of 'Britishness' to identify the canon of somewhat neglected British law films, and chart the attempts that have been made to encourage and protect the British film industry. In addition, this Chapter will use the British law film as a way to engage with the genre debate, by offering a different perspective that draws upon this Britishness. This approach is one based upon the notion of iconography, rather than the content and flow of the narrative. It does this against the backdrop of both the British film industry generally and its law film product, and illustrates that the British law film, or at least the images and objects it deals with, has a perhaps hitherto under acknowledged importance.

Britishness and Film: Protection and Representations

British cinema is a broad term which could be seen to encompass the network of production, distribution and exhibition of films in Britain. But we immediately come up against a problem here in that, just as films made in Britain are not shown only in Britain, films that are distributed and exhibited in Britain are clearly not just British films.[5]

With a first public cinema exhibition in 1896,[6] and a British manufacturer inventing the first film projector to be placed on the open market in the same year, Britain can be seen as being a crucial part of the birth of cinema.[7] With the embryonic film industry focused around music halls, Britain produced a large number of short films, some of very high quality and importance.[8] However, at the start of the 20th century British producers were unable to keep pace with the cheap and plentiful supply of film that was emanating from the United States. In addition, British film began to be seen as a lesser cousin of other more film-focused cultures in other parts of the world. As Napper notes:

From the 1920s to the 1970s the paramount tendency was to judge British films not in terms of British culture, but in the light of international movements stemming from Europe and America. Internationalism on the part of critics led them to bemoan British cinema partly because it was so very British, because it retained the popular culture

---

[4] Nowell-Smith, G and Ricci, S (1998: 2).
[5] Cooke, L (1996) in Nelmes, J (1996a: 295).
[6] This was on 21 February 1896, at what is now the University of Westminster. For some of the history see the University's Compton Club project, details at www.wmin.ac.uk/law/page-772 (last accessed 23 April 2009).
[7] Street, S (1997): in particular see ch 1, 'The Fiscal Politics of Film'.
[8] See Street, S (1997).

of Britain as its inspiration rather than aspiring to the cinematic culture of Russia, Germany or America.[9]

Notwithstanding this early importance and influence, only a small percentage of early films were denoted as British, and the British market was undoubtedly affected by critical approaches to its output. Hollywood's approach was bold and very successful, and this led to attempts being made to protect the British market against this American 'imperialism'. Grantham notes some examples of a number of countries attempting to regulate film production, distribution and exhibition; here our focus is British film policy.[10] The Cinematograph Films Act 1927 had as its focus an aim of encouraging the production of British films, primarily by establishing an obligation to show a specified quota of British films. A British film was defined as one made by a British subject or company, and that all studio scenes needed to be filmed in studios within the empire, but the Act did not stipulate that the company need be actually in British hands. The Act was part of general protectionism as competition from Germany and the United States displaced Britain's share of the world export trade from the level of 35.8 per cent in 1890 to 23.8 per cent in 1921–25.[11] This strategy achieved some success in the 1930s with the share of British films distributed rising from 4.4 per cent in 1927 to 24 per cent in 1932. Britain was, during the 1930s, the most lucrative external market for the United States with some 30 per cent of the income of Hollywood coming from Britain.[12] In addition, there were signs of moral panic around the subject matter and portrayals in American films, Street arguing that '[c]oncern over the propaganda value of film and anti-Americanism therefore played a large part in securing the passage of the Cinematograph Films Act 1927'.[13]

Following the findings of the Moyne Committee,[14] the 1927 Act was replaced by the Cinematograph Films Act 1938 which made a number of changes designed to attempt to ensure that the policy of protectionism was successful. The Act continued the quota approach for a further 10 years, although based around a lower figure of 15 per cent. Short films were protected as well as features, and the 'quota' films had to cost a certain minimum amount. This latter point was designed to circumvent the problem of producing 'quickies' to get round the quota formula, although the Moyne proposal of a 'quality test' was not adopted. Film production during the 1940s was limited by war and austerity.[15] These years also saw the emergence of the 'second feature' in Britain—short films of about 60 minutes

---

[9] Napper, L (1997: 37–38) in Murphy (1997).
[10] See Grantham B (2004) in Moran L *et al* (2004).
[11] Street, S (1997).
[12] This figure was contributed to by the virtual exclusion of US films from Germany Italy and Russia for simple political motives.
[13] Street, S (1997: 8).
[14] Cmnd 5320, 1936.
[15] See the following figures of film production during these years. 1940: 41 films; 1941: 47 films; 1942: 45 films; 1943: 50 films; 1944: 36 films; 1945: 42 films; 1946: 39 films; 1947: 58 films; 1948: 77 films (inc 24 B features); 1949: 96 (inc 45 B features); 1950: 82 (inc 32 B features).

with low production values. They would be shot in less than two weeks and often at night to get maximum use of studio space using actors from the theatre who had completed their 'day's work'. During the 1940s, film policy began to change, in part because of wider world events and in part because of the vexed issue of film financing more generally. Government policy shifted to a more open approach to foreign films and statutory quotas were replaced initially by a tax on imported films, and then by limited government financial support from the National Film Finance Corporation.[16] There were further challenges to the British film industry in the 1950s with the increase in television ownership. There was extensive American investment in British films in the 1960s, and the notion of a national cinema became somewhat problematic with 'British films' including the 'Bond' series. Indeed the issue of America's link with British cinema market became more explicit after the Second World War:

> [b]etween 1948 and 1950 the five Hollywood majors spent nearly £6 million of frozen sterling on production activities [reference omitted]. American investment in Britain increased, however, to unprecedented levels later on in the 1950s and 1960s as the trend of runaway production in Europe became an essential part of Hollywood's overseas operations.[17]

The quotas for renters under the 1938 Act were eventually removed as a result of US pressure under GATT talks. This was replaced by an exhibitor's quota under the Cinematograph Films Act 1948, which was initially set at 45 per cent, later reduced to 30 per cent, and finally abolished in 1983. The post-war Labour government did attempt to assist film producers in a number of other ways, including creating the National Film Finance Corporation in 1949 and the Eady Levy in 1950. The former was a short-term idea designed to help ailing British film producers, specifically British Lion, which provided a limited amount money to film companies. The Eady Levy was a scheme which was to hive off a proportion of income from cinema takings at the box office to create a production fund. Both schemes were partially successful, but the broader context of the film industry in that period was of a continued decline in admissions. Even the vibrant 'new wave' of British cinema between 1958 and 1966 did not halt the decline. Films dealing with life as lived in Britain such as *Room at the Top* (1958), *Saturday Night and Sunday Morning* (1960), *This Sporting Life* (1963) and *Darling* (1965) garnered critical acclaim and Oscars but were unable, it seemed, to compete with either the onward expansion of television or the continued flow of glamorous Hollywood films.

The UK Film Council, initially the British Film Commission, was constituted to attempt to stimulate British film industry and film culture. Part of its remit is to 'encourage and support inward investment feature films' and 'promoting UK talent'. In Britain in the 21st century, in order to be eligible for UK Film Council

---

[16] Porter, V (2001).
[17] Street, S (1997: 15).

funding, or to obtain tax relief for film production, a project needs to be wholly or substantially capable of qualification as a British film under the terms of the Films Act 1985.

The Department for Culture, Media and Sport (DCMS) considers applications for certification as a British Film; this is either done under Schedule 1 of the Films Act or alternatively as part of a co-production. Schedule 1 provides that there are three specific criteria: (i) the nationality of the film maker must be UK, EU or EEA; (ii) 70 per cent of the production costs must be spent within the UK, and (iii) 70 per cent of labour costs must be spent on citizens of the UK, the EU or the EEA. The co-production qualification effectively revolves around situations where the film is produced under a bi-lateral co-production treaty. After a consultation process in 2005, the DCMS published a document detailing a new test to establish criteria and enable identification of 'culturally British' films that might attract tax relief.[18]

As a result of all these factors, the number of British films produced between 1970 and 2006 has varied wildly. It went from 40 in 1978 to as low as 24 in 1981. The numbers have always been very variable, with 100 in 1999. The figures for the 21st century have been a little higher. The collapse and subsequent recovery of film attendance has not helped as one might have imagined since what we now have is a narrow range of products from the major distributors—with over 80 per cent of films coming by way of American production companies.

Apart from the administrative task for funders of assessing whether a project qualifies, cultural analysts are faced with complex judgments. The mixed reality of production can be seen in two British-based, American-made, courtroom dramas. In *The Paradine Case* (1947) we have a film with a major American star in Gregory Peck, based on a novel by Robert Hichens. The director, Alfred Hitchcock, was British—although from 1940 the next 40 years of his life was spent working in the United States.[19] Is this a British or an American product? In *Witness for the Prosecution* (1957) the whole enterprise is an American concoction, financed and shot in Hollywood. Two of its major protagonists, Marlene Dietrich and Tyrone Power, were big Hollywood names. The director, Billy Wilder, had worked for over 20 years in the United States after fleeing Germany. The Britishness stems from the location of the action in the British courts. This in turn is a product of the original play by the quintessentially English Agatha Christie. There are also British stars in the form of Charles Laughton and Elsa Lanchester. The fact that it might feel like an ersatz Hollywood product would seem to be a feature of the original writing rather than any excessive 'Hollywoodisation'. The original play has the same narrative and much the same conclusion. Hence it would be misleading to attribute the denouement to the Hollywood system. That said, the original play concludes with Leonard Vole lying dead on the floor of the courtroom and his

---

[18] Cultural Test for British Films DCMS. Creative Industries, Film Branch November 2005.
[19] Taylor, J (1978).

ex-wife receives no promise of assistance from Sir Wilfred, but rather she intones to the empty Bench, 'Guilty My Lord'.[20]

If the emblematic films to represent American justice through the decades are *12 Angry Men* (1980), *To Kill a Mockingbird* (1960s), *And Justice for All* (1970s), *The Verdict* (1980s) and the whole Grisham 'trope' (1990s), then the search for British equivalents would produce *Brothers in Law* (1950s), *The Boys* (1960s) *10 Rillington Place* (1970s), *Dance with a Stranger* (1980s) and *In the Name of the Father* (1990s). Perspectives on British cinematic justice draw on a much smaller pool of films as well as providing a much narrower portrayal of lawyers within British film. The number of films produced is not huge, but this has to be seen within the context of the British film industry, and the issues that it has historically faced.[21] What is does share with the dominant worldview of justice that emerges from Hollywood is an increase in the scepticism over the ability of the justice system to work effectively.

British Law Films

As we have previously argued, we are of the view that there is a benefit to be derived from having a working definition of a law film in order to set boundaries for assessing shifts in themes and personnel. We would stress that this does not in any way delimit the films which scholars may wish to analyse for other purposes. Hence, anyone concerned with the ways in which ethnicity, gender or class have been covered in popular culture will be looking far beyond narrowly legal-centric films. It all depends on which questions scholars are seeking to ask. When we are focusing on how the adjudicative part of the justice system operates it makes sense to limit ourselves to those films which are concerned with that realm. Hence cop films and prison films receive little attention from us since they relate to the apprehension and disposition phases of the justice system rather than our focus, adjudication. With all these caveats, we would adhere to our claim of 2001, noted in Chapter 4 above, that:

> [i]n order to qualify as a law film the following characteristic(s) must be present in some shape or form, the geography of law, the language and dress of law, legal personnel and the authority of law. This excludes films where 'justice' is enforced outside of any legal framework e.g. war films, social dramas and family sagas.[22]

There are some 25 British films produced in the past 65 years which are centred on either a trial or the formal legal process. Whilst this is a limited output from which to analyse trends, nonetheless it is possible to note that most of these

---

[20] Christie, A (1954).
[21] Robson, P (2007a).
[22] Greenfield, S, Osborn, G and Robson, P (2001: 24).

films meet the criteria of being 'courtroom dramas'. That is to say they share the narrative, visual and speech conventions identified as comprising the basis for the sub-genre. The overwhelming majority of these films, then, come broadly within the description of 'courtroom dramas'; 22 out of the 25 law films have as their centrepiece a courtroom trial. *The Paradine Case* (1947) and *Witness for the Prosecution* (1957) follow the 'classic' courtroom drama narrative conventions. Most have the same straightforward structure with a background and build-up phase. There is a trial set-up of varying length, inevitably a problem encountered by the main protagonist and often an absence of evidence or witnesses. The matter is almost always resolved through some *deus ex machina*. There is then a short period of reflection on the meaning of the trial and what the future holds, for those involved, before the credits.

In some instances such as *The Winslow Boy* (1948) and *Trial and Error* (1962) the trial takes place offscreen. The actual courtroom sequence can occasionally appear as a very minor part of the action as in *Dance with a Stranger* (1984) and *Vera Drake* (2004). There are also a few films which contain a courtroom sequence but which have a focus away from the law and legal system. Thus, for instance, *A Fish Called Wanda* (1988) incorporates a courtroom sequence as a comic device and involves one of the main protagonists, barrister Archie Leech (John Cleese). It is, however, not concerned with the legal process but is a farce centring on the escapades of a disparate group involved in a jewel theft caper and is not covered in our analysis. In addition, films such as *Bridget Jones's Diary* (2001) may contain legal personnel but are not focused upon the law, and we merely note them here.

British law films split neatly into two types. First we have films, principally based on fictional events which were encountered from the 1940s through to 1970. In the first fictional *tranche* we find a range of films including courtroom dramas. They exhibit the characteristics of the genre. It is, however, worth refining the classification of the films a little further. In addition to noting that the basis of the material shifts between fiction and reality, the content and style of the films are worth observing. Thus it is possible to discern further elements in terms of the extent to which the films were thrillers (*The Girl in the News* (1940), *The Blind Goddess* (1947), whilst others were concerned with social issues (*The Boys* (1962), *Oscar Wilde* (1960). Some have involved a combination of the two (*Eight O'Clock Walk* (1953), *The Winslow Boy* (1948). In addition we have a small number of light-hearted comedies (*A Pair of Briefs* (1961), *Brothers in Law* (1957)), which are neither thrillers nor involve weighty social policy matters.

Thereafter, the overwhelmingly dominant theme for law films has been miscarriages of justice based on real events. The concern with miscarriages of justice from 1970 onwards was presaged in the military justice film *King and Country* (1964). Here we have a situation not where the system has got the wrong man but rather where the legal test is distorted and wrongheaded. There is a sense in which the system fails to do justice towards the accused. In the film, an upper-class officer in the British Army of the First World War changes from casual disdain to despair as he defends the hopeless cause of a shell-shocked private who is being sacrificed to maintain discipline in the trenches.

The distinction is not entirely watertight but it does broadly cover the style and themes encountered in British law films.[23] Furthermore, some of the films from the earlier period were concerned with serious social issues rather than merely being cheap-to-produce courtroom 'whodunnits' which had dominated British law films of the 1930s. The point, though, is the contrast between modern ways of seeing matters and the prevailing orthodoxy. The miscarriages of justice which concerned British films from the 1970s were more concerned with the inadequacies of the legal system as a method of uncovering the truth. These might have dire consequences as in *10 Rillington Place* (1971). This was the story of a multiple domestic killer from Britain in the 1940s, whose evidence helped convict the (probably) innocent husband of one of his victims, and provided ammunition for capital punishment campaigners.

Rather more oblique was the dramatisation of the trial of Ruth Ellis, the last woman to be hanged in the United Kingdom. She was convicted of the killing of her violent and unfaithful lover. The film, *Dance with a Stranger* (1985), implies that her failure to provide any kind of defence was a result of her suffering from battered women's syndrome. The killing was carried out apparently with the connivance and encouragement of another jealous man. The audience is aware of the unsympathetic figure cut by a woman who defied social and moral conventions and who 'got what she deserved'. Here was a hanging which would not have taken place if a defence had been mounted. The related notion of a public mood for revenge had tragic consequences in *Let Him Have It* (1991). This was based on the case of a killing of a police officer after a failed robbery in 1952. The 16 year old who fired the shot was jailed for life, being below the age for capital punishment. His 19-year-old accomplice, who had a mental age of nine was, however, hanged. In a poor run for the British legal system's image we also find the public mood figuring in the trial of a young Irishman, Gerry Conlon, in *In the Name of the Father* (1993). This took place during the IRA campaign against the British occupation of Ireland, and in the wake of the bombing of a public house popular with soldiers of the British army in Guildford. Conlon (Daniel Day Lewis) was convicted on the basis of his own confession, despite having sought to provide an alibi. This was verified, but then hidden from the defence team, resulting in his conviction. The only difference in this portrayal of the justice system is the presence of a committed lawyer, solicitor Gareth Peirce (Emma Thompson).

We have here, then, a whole range of British films concerned with the British justice system. This identification of national law films is important in itself

---

[23] Thus *Dr Crippen* (1962) tells the story of the trial of the murderous dentist and his efforts to flee with his secretary. Since the Crippen story is factual, well known, involves no obvious socially redeeming features and it is told in flashback, this falls outwith the standard distinction.

for reasons of cultural identity in a hegemonic world. It is also thought worth considering what distinctive features and aspects of a national cinema might bring to wider debates about law and film. We suggest that by going back and re-examining debates about genre and law films we can provide a richer under-standing of differences and similarities within the area. By focusing not simply on narrative aspects but also upon the iconography, we can illustrate the potential of the British legal system and the British law film to add to the global debates on the significance of law films.

The Iconography of Law

One possible alternative way to examine these films, outside of the traditional approach to genre dealt with in Chapter 4, is to focus upon the visual dimen-sion of conventions rather than the narrative. The rationale is twofold. First, law has a wide range of distinctive imagery and visuality is imperative to the law.[24] Outside the architecture of the law, and concerns over legal spaces and places, we have aphorisms that concern its very visuality, of the law being 'blind', of 'justice is seen to be done' and images such as the Goddess *Justitia*, displayed blindfolded at the Old Bailey. Indeed, the very issue of punishment itself has historically had a spectacular, and visual, resonance.[25] Secondly, outside the legal system itself the concept of iconography has an established place within genre theory. Originating in art history, Alloway[26] applied the idea to cinema and in particular to genre theory, in the 1960s:

> The concept of iconography was widely used by genre theorists and critics during the course of the next decade. There were two main reasons for this. One was the extent to which, in Alloway's formulation at least, it dovetailed with a sympathetic interest in popular films. The other was the extent to which it could be used to stress the visual aspects of popular films (in keeping with the stress placed on style and *mise-en-scène* by auteurism, and in contrast to the emphasis placed on character, plot and theme by more literary-minded theorists and critics).[27]

Visual conventions are crucial within film, and iconography focuses in particular upon three basic aspects of imagery according to McArthur: (1) imagery sur-rounding the physical aspects of actors and characters; (2) images emanating from the milieu within which the characters are constructed; and (3) images con-nected with the technology at the actor's disposal. Whilst McArthur applied this to gangster films, if we apply this scheme to the law film it may provide us with

---

[24] Jay, M (1993) and Jay, M (1999).
[25] Foucault, M (1975).
[26] Alloway, L (1963), cited in Neale, S (2000).
[27] Neale, S (2000: 15).

some interesting material.[28] It seems to us that we can adapt these three categories for our purposes as follows:

(1) The imagery surrounding the physical aspects of the principal actors and characters; this includes dress, physical presence, poise, attitude to other characters. The relationships between the key non-legal personnel and the legal personnel.

Within the British law films noted herein, there are some classic examples of this. The barrister's wig left casually on the passenger seat of Gareth Peirce's car in *In the Name of the Father* (1993), and lingered upon by the camera. Indeed dress can be seen as a key element within the British law film given the particular uniform prescribed for advocates. This can be seen in *Witness for the Prosecution* (1957) and *Brothers in Law* (1957), where the regalia of the law are used to good effect. Thus, Roger Thursby gets his chance to appear in court in *Brothers in Law* only because his colleague has lost his wig and would not be 'recognised' in court by the judge. Without this trivial sartorial detail a barrister is invisible. This notion of dress, which we have discussed elsewhere, ties into the second category as the milieu of the law itself is riven with iconographic imagery.

(2) Images emanating from the milieu within which the characters are constructed. The courtroom itself and any allied surroundings such as law offices, judges' chambers and the jury room.

The tradition of the opening shot and subsequent establishing shots involving the majesty of the courtroom setting either at the outset, or during the film, is present in a number of films, both British and American. It is perhaps harder to think of films where such shots are absent.[29] From the 1950s and 1960s with *12 Angry Men* (1957); *8 O'Clock Walk* (1953); *Brothers in Law* (1957) through the 1980s and 1990s with *Jagged Edge* (1985), *Class Action* (1990), *Philadelphia* (1993) and *A Civil Action* (1998) and finally in the new millennium with *Legally Blonde* (2001), *Evelyn* (2002), *North Country* (2005) and *The Exorcism of Emily Rose* (2003) we know when we are in a courtroom drama. Trial mode is always established visually. Conventions also influence the ways in which the substance of trials is presented—the tentative jury arrival; the view from the jury; counsel looming near the witness under pressure; the closing speeches usually close to the jury; the empty courtroom while the jury is out.

From the 'scales of justice' to the occlusion of the law (justice blindfolded), from the pomp and pageantry that surround the legal process and the legal players, legal imagery is forcefully used by film makers. This may take the form of establishing shots of the court building, close-ups of legal images, all designed to

---

[28] Neale makes the point that it is not clear whether McArthur intended his scheme to be applied to other genres, but we would argue that a number of common resonances between the gangster and the law film make this a line worth pursuing.

[29] Silbey, J (2001).

illustrate the solemnity of the law and the seriousness of the business taking place in the hallowed courtrooms. This is especially clear in British law films given the traditional focus on ceremony within legal procedures in Britain, and can be seen in many of the films. Certainly *Brothers in Law* (1957) utilises these at the assizes and elsewhere, although often the pomp and ceremony is 'pricked' by the humour or incompetence of the lawyers.

(3) In replacement of McArthur's technology we have identified the use of, and relationship to, the process of law itself. This seems to be the right comparison given that it is application of law that is the 'tool' at the lawyer's disposal.

'Technology' for the lawyer presumably equates to legal process, and how the lawyer uses the tools of his trade within his job. In particular here we might see the misuse, or abuse, of legal process. We have previously looked at this in terms of going beyond the law to achieve justice; notably we have used Fonda's portrayal of *Young Mr Lincoln* (1939) as an example of this. However, we can see it too in the British trope—especially in *In the Name of the Father* (1993) with Emma Thompson (Gareth Peirce) seemingly using evidence obtained outside of the traditional legal process and using the High Court as a vehicle to voice her concerns in breach of any number of legal protocols.

We can also expect the witness to be subject to cunning examination on the witness stand. It is here that cases are won and lost. The collapse of the witness and the fatally damning admission are the stuff of the courtroom drama. This is what law in trial movies is about, whether it be in criminal issues—*Witness for the Prosecution* (1957) and *Let Him Have It* (1991)—or civil matters—*The Blind Goddess* (1947) or *Evelyn* (2002). The style may be dramatic or it may be low-key. The central role of the lawyer cross-examining and the limited role of the judiciary in this process are a constant.

Conclusion

Because of sheer weight of numbers, and dominant position in the marketplace, it is undoubtedly the case that the portrayal of the American justice system dominates. We have demonstrated here that there are important national alternatives that are worthy of excavation and analysis. That in itself is a worthwhile project. By adding these to the oeuvre, the entire body of law films becomes wider and more reflective, and allows a more measured and sophisticated analysis. This is intimately connected to the first dimension of genre theory, further delineating the field of study. Identification of national films brings new ideas about the genre of the law film into consideration. The second thread of genre theory, the deliberate construction of the law film by the filmmaker, can also be investigated with a new perspective. This opens up opportunities to consider the relationship between audience and legal film, something that looks at the effects of such media and that has already been attempted on a small scale and which warrants further analysis.

Conclusion

This then brings us back to a central contention in our work and, on a micro level, a key issue within this specific chapter. Part of what we have illustrated above shows a paradox. On the one hand we see a limited number of British films, and British law films, and the attempts made to protect and safeguard these very artefacts. At the same time, we see the importance of the iconography of the British law film, both in terms of the 'British', but also its wider relevance and use in other law films, particularly from the United States. Indeed, this very iconography becomes a staple of the US film and often 'the British' is used as a signifier within the avowedly Hollywood law film. This goes beyond the narrative and concentrates on the visual, so whilst the British law film might appear as a minor footnote to the catalogue of law films, in fact its importance is far greater than perhaps expected and its trajectory can be charted through a specific application of a line within genre theory.

6

Military Justice on Screen

Previous chapters have covered in some detail the cinematic portrayal of law within those places where formal justice is delivered. By looking specifically at the archetypal form, the courtroom drama, we outlined the reasons why the courtroom has been used as a vehicle for filmmakers, and has become synonymous with the idea of legal films. This Chapter takes these mechanisms further, initially by examining another area of formal adjudication, the courts martial. This is another arena that has been used as a forum for the administration of formal justice that provides interesting material to aid understanding of many of the issues raised in earlier Chapters. Courts martial have quite distinct procedures that make them unhelpful as models for those using law films with a primarily training purpose in mind if concentrating on procedure, although there are some examples of advocacy and cross-examination eg (*A Few Good Men* (1992)) that could be used to illustrate the legal skills concerned.

There are other reasons for making a distinction between these kinds of films and standard legal films. This is irrespective of whether this is based on the thriller model (*Jagged Edge* (1985), *Suspect* (1987), *Physical Evidence* (1988), *Primal Fear* (1996), *The Firm* (1993), *The Client* (1994)) or the procedural model (*... And Justice for All* (1979), *The Rainmaker* (1997), *A Civil Action* (1998), *Erin Brockovich* (2000)). In addition, the context of dispute generally centres on concepts of military discipline that involve a very distinctive culture. The goals are quite specific. They involve the protection of national defence, which is rather different from the standard fare of the criminal courts in which a contrast between the community and the aberrant individual is determined with reference to breach of rules, rather than being subject to an overarching ethos. Sometimes, however, this distinction may be more apparent than real. This section begins by exploring the specific approach to the nature of the legal system found in a range of films where the military authorities are involved. The analysis looks at the different ways in which abstract concepts of fairness and justice are constructed in this alternative setting. As we have noted, the major focus for legal scholars has been the 'naturalistic portrayals' of lawyers and the legal process. There is, however, one area of film where there is a strong legal focus but where the distinctive nature of the area has important implications and dictates that they be considered separately. The cultural context means that in terms of a direct impact on legal practice they are of limited value.[1] Courts martial operate in a quite distinctive way that is unlikely to be mistaken for anything like a mainstream court. There are none of the establishing shots of the exteriors of courts or the steps/pillars of justice that are conventional fare in almost all law films.[2] They are generally located in unimpressive military rooms rudely adapted for the purposes of rapid justice.[3] Interestingly, the opening shot in *The Rising—the Ballad of Mangal Pandey* (2005) is of an execution with much ceremony and formality with the red uniforms providing colour. Courts martial have their own procedures; writing in 1969, Borrie noted:

> How does court martial procedure differ from that of assizes or quarter sessions? The vital differences are (a) the accused is not tried by his peers, there being no jury; (b) the court consists of a number of officers none of whom are legally qualified but who determine both guilt and sentence; (c) the court's verdict may be by a simple majority; (d) the defence may be conducted without legal assistance; and (e) the role of the Judge Advocate.[4]

The administrative procedure of the courts martial system was challenged after the enactment of the Human Rights Act 1998 on the question of both the internal structure of the courts martial system, and the relationship with the ordinary criminal court system.[5] Given the differences from civilian justice, little would be gained in practical/procedural terms by studying images from film depictions, although technique and stylistic elements might still be useful. However, as we have noted elsewhere, where the remit of enquiry is conceived rather more broadly than looking solely at the purposes of technique training, then going beyond the strict boundaries of the standard courtroom can be of value. Similarly, whilst branching out into a consideration of how justice can be achieved within conflict situations, the courts martial offers interesting possibilities.

Paradoxically, although they offer less of a model for court personnel behaviour, they seem to have more to say on the broader theme of the role of justice within the legal process. They take place in the context of a highly formalistic hierarchical structure of command and obedience. The very strictures on what kind of defence may be used in such a set-up means that the courts martial can be seen as a metaphor for the operation of the law itself. The rigid rules under which soldiers serve, and their need to adhere to these, provide a version of inflexible law against which the interests of the individual can be counterposed. Further, the proceedings enable the viewer to see the political nature of law. The idea of pure disinterested pursuit of truth can be contrasted with the broader policy concerns of the state, the military or similar.

---

[1] Whilst taken from a TV series, the court martial scene in Blackadder from the episode Corporal Punishment (Season IV, Episode 2) has been used with first-year students at Westminster to identify elements of procedural injustice.

[2] Silbey, J (2001).

[3] With the exception of *Paths of Glory* (1957) held in the supremely inappropriate surroundings of the grand salon of a French chateau and more recently *A Few Good Men* (1992).

[4] Borrie, G (1969: 44–45).

[5] See *R v Spear and another; R v Boyd; R v Saunby and other appeals* [2002] 3 All ER 1074.

There are some caveats, however, which must be considered. Disputes centred on concepts of military discipline involve a quite distinct culture. The goals are quite different. They involve the notions of protection of national integrity. This is rather different from the standard fare of the criminal courts in which a contrast between the community and the aberrant individual is determined with reference to a breach of rules. In the military setting the test represents an overarching ethos. Thus we see trials centring on elusive concepts such as 'conduct prejudicial to military discipline', and this next section explores whether this distinction may be more apparent than real.

Filming Military Justice

There are good reasons for pointing out the different kinds of issues that may be raised in military settings. Whilst it would be unhelpful to simply exclude these types of confrontations from our consideration of the representation of law, a number of important caveats must be made. There is a developing group of films that can be analysed as courts martial, and the concept has featured in a little over a dozen films since the 1950s. The general narrative approach that recurs is the contrast between the inflexibility and higher purpose of the state, as expressed in the panel of military men, and the challenge of justice in the form of the soldier/sailor/airman. From the narrower perspective of the law/justice dichotomy, it is possible to trace this opposition chiefly between the protagonist 'victim' of military rules and the implacable enforcers of the rules in the form of the judge/jury that is the courts martial. This relatively straightforward pattern holds true for most of the films examined in this section from *Carrington V.C.* (1954) to *Breaker Morant* (1980), by way of *The Court Martial of Billy Mitchell* (1955), *Paths of Glory* (1957) and *King and Country* (1964). The matter emerges in slightly different form in *The Caine Mutiny* (1954) and *A Few Good Men* (1992). The more recent examples have been thrillers centring on disputes as to what did or did not occur in a given fact set-up; *High Crimes* (2002) and *Rules of Engagement* (2002). Interestingly we also have two recent Indian films, *The Rising: the Ballad of Mangal Pandey* (2005) and *Shaurya* (2008), which contribute some interesting and new material. Shaurya was criticised for 'copying' the plot of *A Few Good Men* (1992), earning the name 'A Few Hindoo'd Men'. The context for *The Rising: the Ballad of Mangal Pandey* (2005) is India's First War of Independence of 1857 and the role of the infamous Honourable East India Company. It introduces a host of issues around politics, class and race in addition to the requirement for military discipline.

Looking at the films as a group there are a number of important themes that emerge. Kuzina lists no less than seven 'well-established configurations, storylines and motifs' that are encountered in courts martial films. We note three major themes in the portrayal of military justice below. These broad approaches have also been affected by other factors. There have been class, political and racial elements as well as gender. Thus the arrival of soldiers before the firing squad is portrayed as directly related to their class position in *Paths of Glory* (1957) and *King and Country* (1964). Rather less final solutions are visited on non-conformists to social mores in *Carrington V.C.* (1954) and *The Winslow Boy* (1948)—their social positions are affected. The racial status of the defendants in *Sergeant Rutledge* (1960), *Breaker Morant* (1980) and *The Court-Martial of Jackie Robinson* (1990) similarly effectively determines their presence as accused, if not the outcome. The personality and personal politics of the counsel involved have ramifications in *The Caine Mutiny* (1954) and *A Few Good Men* (1992). In *Rules of Engagement* (2000) and *High Crimes* (2002), the identification of a renegade spy and the disputed actions of a veteran soldier are at issue. In fact, it is only in *The Court Martial of Billy Mitchell* (1955) that we actually see the military judicial process as a process unmediated by other social factors. Here, however, like the other courts martial, the nature of the event calls to the fore the purpose of the military as a collective rather than the rights of the individual. In order to see how and why we have come to these conclusions we want to provide a little more background. Beyond the general 'public good/private interest sacrifice' theme there are other important factors which account for the persistence of this sub-group of legal films.

The strongest and most enduring images from all these films come from the earliest and one of the more recent of the films. For example, the sweating, twitching Humphrey Bogart as the alleged coward, Captain Queeg, in *The Caine Mutiny* (1954) breaking down in court is compelling viewing. By way of contrast, the explosion of self-righteous rage of Jack Nicholson's Colonel Jessep in *A Few Good Men* (1992) has entered popular culture with the line 'You can't handle the truth!' In *The Rising: the Ballad of Mangal Pandey* (2005) we see the emergence of the heroic revolutionary figure prepared to give his life for the noble cause of Indian independence. Beyond these driven characters there are more extensive examinations of the actual system of judgment.

In *The Caine Mutiny* (1954), for instance, the interest, beyond Queeg's psyche, lies in the very different motives of the principal protagonists in the court. We have the young Executive Officer, Lieutenant Steve Maryk (Van Johnson), who relieved Queeg of his command and stands accused of mutiny. Maryk has exercised the right under Article 184 of the Navy Code to relieve his captain of command of their minesweeper during a typhoon. The incident follows a number of instances of misjudgments and possible cowardice by the captain, Commander Phillip Queeg. In one action he orders the ship to turn back from the beach, when supporting landing vessels, much too early, insisting they are within 1,000 yards of their target The captain has also demonstrated an attention to detail and concern with minor matters which show him to be either a martinet or on the edge of sanity. Tom Keefer (Fred McMurray) suggests he is paranoid and Maryk starts to keep a diary of 'incidents', such as the banning of film shows, after the

Captain was not invited to a showing. In another incident he orders a full inquiry into a small amount of strawberries that have been given as a present to the officers from those of another ship. Although these are not finished at the meal, the remaining strawberries have been eaten by the next day. This trivial incident is blown up into a major breach of discipline and only the solidarity of the crew prevents Queeg exacting indiscriminate revenge. Finally, his actions in refusing to alter course during the typhoon seem as though they will cause the ship to founder. His Executive Officer, Maryk, relieves him of command and with the support of Junior Lieutenant Keith (Robert Francis) takes command. A court martial ensues.

The defence makes little headway with its version of events. Queeg's record and his interpretation of events as taking necessary steps to reinstate discipline in the ship are entirely plausible. When Queeg takes the witness stand he is entirely plausible, at least initially. His account is, however, later contradicted by his own written assessments of his officers. He breaks down and demonstrates that his years of service have taken a toll on his mental health. Although the officer charged is acquitted, we can see how the rigid command structure would have in all probability resulted in a conviction for Maryk had Queeg retained his demeanour on the witness stand. Although Barry Greenwald (Jose Ferrer), as defence counsel, was the man to secure the crucial breakdown of the witness, he blames the officers for failing to rally to their captain when he sought their support after the beach landing incident. He knows that the ethic of solidarity is more important than legal niceties and would have preferred to prosecute than defend. The person whom he blames for instigating the whole affair is, in fact, the outsider, Tom Keefer. He planted the seed of mutiny in Maryk's brain and drew his attention to Article 184. As a cool observer of the Navy rather than someone committed to its values, Keefer undermined the trust essential between captain, officers and men. He, with his civilian values, is the villain of the piece rather than Queeg, who has been 'doing his duty' and could have been saved by a more supportive officer corps. The film was remade with a screenplay by the original author, Herman Wouk, and directed by Robert Altman as *The Caine Mutiny Court Martial* (1988). It is worth noting that in this version the blame of Keefer (Kevin O'Connor) is even more pointed with the Jewish lawyer, Greenwald (Eric Bogosian) explaining that Queeg (Brad Davis) was fighting the anti-semitism of the Nazis more effectively than Keefer's amused critique of the absurdities of naval life.

In these films we have particularly arresting representations of the playing out of core themes that run through legal philosophy and legal practice. What control do the populace have on those applying and enforcing the law? How does the 'rule of law' operate when those in charge of the rules determine what those rules mean? What happens when there is abuse of their position by those 'on high'? These issues emerge not only in the 'man in command' trope but also in a rather different way, as detailed below.

The Scapegoat

In the rash of mid-1950s court martial-centred films we also have the central factor of the courts martial as the location for dealing with a 'scapegoat'. First, in *Carrington V.C.* (1954), alternatively known as *Court Martial*, we have an unconventional officer, Charles Carrington (David Niven), who is proceeded against by his jealous superior officer. The charge is one of 'fraudulent misappropriation of funds'. He had, indeed, taken the sums charged to pay off debts incurred as a result of the frequent moves he has had to undergo at the behest of the Army. There are, though, complicating factors. The Army admits to owing him various removal payments for dislocation but is slow to pay and the matter has been dragging on for many months. The temporary borrowing of funds is, however, prompted by a suicide threat by his mentally unstable wife. He opts to defend himself and runs into problems through the discovery, by his wife, of his liaison with a woman officer. His senior officer denies he has ever been told of Carrington's threat to take what is rightly his from the Army funds in his keeping. This lie is compounded by his wife's evidence. Feeling understandably vindictive on discovering the liaison, she denies him the evidence that would substantiate his account of events. He is found guilty and dismissed from service, only for a post-trial witness to emerge in the shape of the nosy telephone operator. The latter overheard the suicide threat phone-call. As the credits roll, the audience know that Carrington will be vindicated.

If Major Carrington is a victim of a prudish morality and the jealousy of his superior, then the true-life film based on the life of General Billy Mitchell shows the conflict between the official policy and Mitchell's own view of US inter-war air strategy. *The Court Martial of Billy Mitchell* (1955) shows the development of Mitchell's conviction that the air service is being seriously under-funded. His career is sidelined and he is hounded off to an administrative post in deepest Texas after his attempts to persuade his superiors to change their view of the potential of aerial bombardment in the 1920s. When young officers, whom he has trained, are killed, Mitchell (Gary Cooper) denounces the authorities. In effect, he seeks a court martial to get his day in court. Such is the nature of the offence he is charged with, however, that he is unable to introduce his evidence into the official record of the court. He is, nonetheless, found guilty, partly it seems because he insists that there is a serious future threat from the Japanese at a base in Hawaii—the base is Pearl Harbour.

Whilst the motives of the authorities are put down to lack of foresight and imagination in *Billy Mitchell*, there is evidence of sheer malice in the pursuit of deserters in *Paths of Glory* (1957). Colonel Dax (Kirk Douglas) defends three men who are to be sacrificed to cover the failure of the strategy of General Broulard (Adolphe Menjou). Broulard's strategy is intended to put an end to the stalemate into which the war has fallen. He has used the temptation of promotion to turn the head of General Mireau (George Macready) and get him to undertake command of an attack on a heavily fortified enemy position. Mireau expresses concern to avoid the senseless slaughter of his troops and initially turns down the chance to earn the glory of taking the impregnable 'Anthill'. With the carrot of a further promotion dangled in front of him, however, he accepts this task. As forecast by himself and his line commander, Colonel Dax, the attack is a fiasco. An enraged Mireau, committed to the success of the attack for his own personal promotion, even orders his artillery to shell their own soldiers to get them out of their trenches into attacking the German positions. This order is disobeyed and the attack peters out.

Mireau decides, in his rage, that there must be scapegoats for this cowardice. Initially he plans to have 100 men from each company shot. He is persuaded that one from each, chosen at random, will suffice, since as General Broulard explains: 'All we want to do is to set an example.' Three men are chosen from each company and charged with 'cowardice in the face of the enemy'. The trial is a farce with the President taking his cue from above that the purpose is to set an example. By returning to their trenches under heavy fire they have duly exhibited cowardice and they are shot in what the man behind the original morale-boosting plan to take the German position describes as a 'tasteful ceremony'. General Broulard has achieved a long-term strategic aim of boosting fear. The judicial intervention of the courts martial has added a dimension of legality and justice to what are no more than strategic issues.

On a small scale, and reflecting its origins in a stage play, *King and Country* (1964) has the rather unsympathetic Captain Hargreaves (Dirk Bogarde) initially going through the motions of defending Tom Courtney's naïve young deserter, Private Hamp. Clearly suffering from what became accepted as the syndrome of shell shock, Hamp trusts that the authorities will treat him humanely. Hargreaves recognises the reality and that the procedure has only one aim—to scare the frightened out of the trenches to act as cannon fodder so that the military strategy of victory through attrition can be played out. The whole set-up is an exercise in class control with the rules being laid down by the privileged and their adherence being determined by denizens of the same social group. This notion of the insignificance and dispensability of the individual in the great sweep of history and the cruelty of such a perspective, when put into practice, is the central theme. The courts martial, whilst not prepared to accept the defence of medical unfitness, is nonetheless minded to recommend mercy. This evaporates, however, in the face of a new push, for which High Command believes that the question of the troops' morale is crucial. In order to encourage the maintenance of morale, Hamp has to be shot. It serves the higher purpose and the long-term ends of the war effort. His lack of blameworthiness is not the issue. Here again we have community purposes triumphing over concepts of individualised justice. It is this same issue that is also briefly touched on in Sidney Lumet's *The Hill* (1965). Whilst the main part of the film deals with the treatment meted out to Joe Roberts (Sean Connery) and his comrades at the hands of Ian Bannen's sadistic NCO, Harris, we see the perfunctory treatment of Roberts that resulted in his arrival at his North African army prison.

The simple solution to military problems as seen in *Paths of Glory* (1957) is to draw a line in the sand by sacrificing one individual, or in that instance, three individuals. Much the same trope appears to be on the minds of the military hierarchy in *Rules of Engagement* (2000). Here under the command of Colonel Terry Childers (Samuel L Jackson), a crowd of civilian demonstrators is fired upon. Childers claims the crowd was armed; witnesses say otherwise. Making a crude calculation of the likely external backlash, the authorities court-martial him for his actions. He asks a washed-out fellow veteran and lawyer, Hayes Hodges (Tommy Lee Jones) to defend him. It turns out that the innocent crowd was, in fact, full of gunmen.

A further scapegoat film is *High Crimes* (2002). Here, lawyer Claire Kubik (Ashley Judd) suffers a robbery attempt at the family home. She and her husband are accosted by the FBI, who arrest her husband, Tom (James Caviezel). He is charged with the murder of Salvadorian civilians under his previous identity of Ronald Chapman. Chapman was a covert military operative serving in the US Marines, who has been on the run for 12 years. Tom does not deny his involvement in an operation that resulted in the loss of civilians, for which he was blamed. He maintains, however, that he was made a scapegoat as only he could identify the men who did carry out the killings. Assisted by Charles Grimes (Morgan Freeman), a cynical former military lawyer, Claire Kubik defends her husband in what appears to be a variant on the 'scapegoat' theme. Whilst there is a twist in the tale we recognise the scenario with which we are familiar from earlier films with the juggernaut of military justice flattening everything in its path.

In *The Rising: the Ballad of Mangal Pandey* (2005) we find two scapegoated characters. The first is Mangal (Aamir Khan) himself, who must be made an example of in order to preserve the reign of the East India Company for 'a further hundred years'. His trial and execution are required to show the power of the company and the futility of revolt. Alongside him is William Gordon (Toby Stephens), who has the temerity to befriend Pandey and treat him like an equal. Gordon's relationship with a native girl and his 'common' background single him out as someone not to be trusted and who can be used to lie to the Sepoys and further the interests of the company.

In addition, one of the classic films in this vein is *The Winslow Boy* (1948), which involves a variant on standard portrayals of military justice. The central thrust of Arthur Winslow's (Cedic Hardwicke) struggle for justice is a challenge to the way in which the naval authorities treated his son Ronnie (Neil North). Ronnie had been expelled from the Naval Academy, where he was enrolled as a 13 year old, owing to a finding that he cashed a five-shilling postal order belonging to a fellow cadet. The decision to expel him is taken following internal investigation at which the young boy is not allowed any counsel or adult support. Unlike other military justice films there are no scenes set in the courtroom. We hear of the events as the family seek to have the matter raised in Parliament and dealt with in the open. They enlist the support of a prominent QC and the film traces the decline in the family's fortunes as the pursuit for justice becomes the central feature in their lives leaving Arthur a broken invalid at the end.

The film was remade in 1999 with a script by David Mamet which opens up the action a little, but which is not dramatically different in content from the original version co-written by Terence Rattigan and based on his own play. What Arthur Winslow (Nigel Hawthorne) pursues so relentlessly is the concept that the operation of legal rules must not be part of some arcane process. The criteria must be made clear and this goes to the very heart of notions of procedural justice. It is a metaphor for the emergence of democracy and the point is buttressed by two sub-themes. We have the suffocating pressure of class, and the need to be the 'right sort', which impedes the marriage prospects of daughter Catherine (Rebecca Pidgeon) into a 'good' military family. In addition there is her own impotence as a woman, fighting an apparently doomed battle for political recognition. Far from being a golden age, this Edwardian England is a land of social prejudice and class bigotry. It is a place where a challenge to the upper reaches of the Establishment even by a member of the solid ranks of the bourgeoisie can lead to social ruin and in which only the voices of a few carry weight. The film depicts a land of deference to the established order and shows the problems involved in daring to question on what basis this order is constructed and whose interests it serves. In this social context, challenges to class power, embodied in the Edwardian military establishment, result in their own form of scapegoating.

The Courtroom Drama in Uniform

There are instances where the courts martial more precisely resembles the standard courtroom drama. What is at stake here is not the greater public good, however defined, but the actual rights of the individual charged. *Sergeant Rutledge* (1960) contains both the traditional trope of a weighing up of the common good and individual responsibility and a more standard courtroom 'search for truth'. This provides an exception to the 'normal' type of courts martial. Here we have the more traditional truth-seeking procedure, in relation to the heroic Sergeant Rutledge, within the trial. It is prior to the hearing that we have the conflict between the individual and the common good. Here the individual's responsibility for deserting is, in the field, weighed against his selfless actions in returning and helping to save a patrol from ambush. *Sergeant Rutledge* (1960) is mainly noted for its presentation of an African American actor, Woody Strode, in a leading role. *A Soldier's Story* (1984) is also worth a short mention in that it covers that area between a thriller and a court martial. The film addresses the theme of race in the army and in Southern society generally. A black attorney investigates the death of a black sergeant and encounters both overt and casual racism. This is mediated, however, within the hierarchical context of the Army by his rank as a Captain.

Conduct Unbecoming (1975) is a mixture of the traditional courts martial 'greater good' concept mixed in with straightforward evidence and fact finding of the courtroom drama. Here we have the notion of revenge but of a private kind. This concerns the theme of resentment of the second-class role of women in the military and a resultant accusation of assault. At a regimental function an attractive widow, Mrs Marjorie Scarlett (Susannah York), is pestered by the disillusioned young Lieutenant (James Faulkner) keen to be discharged from the regiment. He hopes that her complaint about his behaviour will result in this; however, it merely provokes annoyance. A person unknown subsequently attacks Scarlett. Fed up with the male chauvinist culture of the regiment, and seeking revenge, she accuses the young Lieutenant of the assault. To avoid matters being brought into the public domain the matter is dealt with by an unofficial procedure. The appropriate mechanism is a Subaltern's courts martial, which consists of four young officers, members of the regiment and Subalterns themselves. Evidence is taken as in a general courts martial and the hearing is presided over by Captain Harper (Stacey Keach). Harper determines both the relevance of evidence and the procedure. It is clear that the overarching goal of the process is the protection of the honour of the regiment, which is why the Subaltern's courts martial is chosen as the way of dealing with the assault complaint. A young officer, Lieutenant Arthur Drake (Michael York), is deputed to defend. However, he misunderstands his role and attempts to insert formal justice criteria. He does not appreciate that he is not supposed to introduce such external standards. He does, however, become convinced of the importance of the individual in the face of the common good and after investigation he secures an acquittal.

The culprit, Major Roach (Richard Attenborough), it transpires, has been transformed by his military experiences into a Jekyll and Hyde character and it is while in the Hyde phase that he has attacked Mrs Scarlett. His suicide resolves the matter and the honour of the regiment; the universally agreed greater good has been preserved. The legal mechanism and its procedures have been set up specifically to achieve this rather than any notion of procedural fairness or evaluation of the truth. The justice which this represents is, however, based on the notion of mutuality and trust and the crucial requirement to be able to place absolute faith in the word of a fellow officer. This could be seen as a veneration of the value of truth rather than the kind of empty blind faith which has been communicated to Private Downey in *A Few Good Men* (1992). Again we have juxtaposed a goal centred on justice in terms of truth against a higher order interest. It provides another metaphor for the juxtaposition of legality and fairness.

A novel twist on the whole concept of the military justice and the courtroom drama is encountered, finally, in *Hart's War* (2002). Here a POW Camp Kommandant is keen to see a trial for murder of one prisoner, apparently by a fellow prisoner 'just like in the American movies'. This echoes the point made by Kuzinas that the court martial was a topic in 34 American films from 1931 to 1940.[6] Here, two lawyer soldiers are selected to battle it out over the evidence

---

[6] Kuzina, M (2005: 161), quoting the AFI Catalog of Motion Pictures Produced in the United States 1931–1940, Berkeley, 1993.

implicating one Negro officer in the death of a racist white soldier who has shown him disrespect. Hart (Colin Farrell) is aghast when he discovers that the trial has been a sham engineered to distract the German authorities from the escape attempt that is being made from underneath the hut where the trial is taking place. The African-American officer is to be left to his fate once the Presiding Officer at the courts martial fails to return to deliver the court's verdict as he will have made good his escape. Hart is aghast that the principles of individual responsibility should be subverted by this application of the 'good of the whole'. In a messy ending this is what occurs, but with Hart seeking to take the blame himself in order to maintain the ideals of individualist justice and preventing the death of a man who did not cause the death for which he is to be shot.

Mangal Pandey strikes a disinterested figure at his trial, aware that his martyrdom is an essential part of the move towards rebellion. He is aware of the need to sacrifice himself at the hands of the British, having failed to take his own life on the parade ground. Gordon, however, demands that justice be done and that the tribunal consider the context to Pandey's actions, and the betrayal of the Seepoy's religious beliefs. Part of Gordon's rage is due to the way he has himself been treated and how he feels used against the Seepoys by the company. Gordon is unwilling to see his friend sacrificed as an example and attempts to provide Pandey with a defence. However, both the court and Pandey are uninterested, moving inexorably together towards the predestined conclusion.

Justice and Legality in the Military Context

In *Paths of Glory* (1957) and *King and Country* (1964), Corporal Paris and Arthur Hamp lose their lives with the authorities satisfied that they had failed to conform to the greater plan. The common theme is the fate of those who fail to or refuse to blindly obey. Although given a military setting, these films are essentially about class, whilst *Breaker Morant* (1980) adds the twist of colonial hierarchy. Based on a true story from the Boer War at the start of the 20th century, this involves the activities of a mobile force, the Veld Carbineers, operating an unofficially sanctioned 'no prisoners' policy in their anti-guerrilla campaign. In pursuit of peace, before Germany joins the fray on the side of the Dutch Boer farmers, Britain is seeking to demonstrate its civilisation and that infractions are treated seriously. When a German Minister is shot, alongside some captured Boer guerrillas, the British authorities are happy to put on a show trial to achieve this goal given that it involves Australian recruits to the Carbineers. The outcome is more or less a foregone conclusion with the defence penalised by having only a day to prepare their case from receipt of the relevant papers. In addition the defence attorney is a country solicitor with experience only of conveyancing and wills. The instigator of the 'no prisoners' policy, Lord Kitchener, explains that 'If these three Australians have to be sacrificed to secure a Peace Conference then it's a small price to pay'.[7] Colonialism is at the heart of *The Rising: the Ballad of Mangal Pandey* (2005), with the Honourable East India Company shown as a corrupt and exploitative body peddling opium to the Chinese and waging war when the trade is rejected. The Indians are mere cannon fodder in the attempt to govern trade through monopolistic practices. Immorality is also a key theme with young women sold as slaves to become the playthings of the officers.

In addition to class and colonialism the issue of ethnicity has been discussed in one courts martial film. Confronting the strictures of the military leads to a race-based courts martial set during the Second World War. In seeking to challenge the racism of a superior officer an all-American baseball player finds himself unable to break through the policy, within a hierarchical set-up. There is no appeal on the merits of the case. The concept of justice and injustice is absent from the military mindset. *The Court-Martial of Jackie Robinson* (1990) is based on a true story of an incident in the army life of the man who became the first African-American major league baseball player. Robinson (Andre Braugher) starts off with the problem of simply being allowed to be recruited onto the officer training programme. His Colonel consistently refuses to permit his entry as he has done for other African-American soldiers. Robinson overcomes this initial hurdle only to find that his officer status is secondary to the colour of his skin. When a driver refuses to allow Lieutenant Robinson to sit away from the back of the bus leaving the camp, Robinson is escorted away by the military police. He is subsequently interviewed and when he complains he is charged with abuse of a superior officer. The assigned defending officer's services are dispensed with on the basis that he does not believe in integration and claims to be a traditional 'good ol' boy'. Here the courts martial not only shows the conflict between the individual and the regiment but also the way in which the trial is engineered. The baseless charges are dismissed by Robinson's Colonel. There are other forces at work, however, and Robinson is re-assigned to another unit whose Colonel has a more traditional view of the place of African-American soldiers in society. When matters eventually reach court, a young radical lawyer officer, William Cline (Daniel Stern), is able to expose the evidence of the racist officers who were unable to accept the notion of African-American officers.

The role of the lawyer, which figured as a sub-theme in *The Caine Mutiny* (1954), also provides a central focus in *A Few Good Men* (1992). Here we have a neat contrast between two distinct approaches to the law. On the one hand we have a lazy self-centred young lawyer, Daniel Kaffee (Tom Cruise) serving out his time in the military avoiding conflict and (more importantly) work by pleading out the cases in which he is detailed to act as defence counsel. Also assigned to the case is the keen, but inexperienced, Jo Anne Calloway (Demi Moore), who is desperate to get to the truth. A pair of young marines, are to appear before a general

---

[7] This was based on the book *The Breaker* by Kit Denton and the ensuing play *Breaker Morant: A Play in Two Acts* by Kenneth Ross.

court martial. They are accused of having caused the death of a fellow marine. One of their colleagues, has written to the authorities complaining of a breach of the rules. However, by going outside the Corps he has broken the unwritten rule of the marines. A Code Red had been ordered, which was the informal procedure for internal discipline within the Corps. The defence is simple, they were simply following orders in carrying out the Code Red. Furthermore, the orders had their source in their commanding officer.

The question for the defence was whether they can establish this. The clue comes from the intermediary between the Colonel and the men who have gone to ground. There are few chances for them establishing that there was indeed a chain of command linking the actions. The conflict between the ethos of the Marines as a body and the right of individuals to stand up to this kind of communitarianism is the underlying theme. It is Colonel Jessep who is unable to accept this external interference with the core value system of the marines. The audience, and ultimately the offending Marines, can see how the logical conclusion of this conflict between these competing notions is that the individual is ultimately worthless before the group's interests. Jessep, unable or unwilling to grasp this with his view of the greater public good dominant, is revealed, like Commander Queeg, as a man for combat.

Whilst there is a consistent representation of the personnel and rules of the courts martial as rigid and inflexible it is clear that here in these films, more than anywhere in the world of the law film, the nature of rules is explored. The underlying political purpose of the order, which is buttressed by the rules, is an aspect that occurs throughout this sub-group of law films. It is against this that the protagonist battles in these portrayals of justice. The sense is that, despite protestations to the contrary, it is the 'bigger picture' that really counts. There is, however, an ambivalence concerning the nature and operation of the process. The President of the Court in *Carrington V.C.* (1954) stresses the legality that is at odds with the approaches of the members of the court:

> Listen to this from the Manual. 'The members of Courts Martial must remember that their findings must be based on the evidence given before them'... Now a Letter that's not produced is not evidence and I am sure that any court of law, and a Courts Martial is a court of law, which decided that the accused could have proved his case but didn't and yet acquitted him is on dangerous ground.

Conclusion

Courts martial films have the advantage of being a small manageable group with a clear set of identifiable themes. There are clear links to the traditional courtroom drama although the military dimension requires a precise level of formality. There is less room for histrionics or sharp practices and the moral dimension is often drawn between duty and justice. We expect to see some conflict with innocence being sacrificed for some higher outcome, normally the preservation of the state. Individual characteristics and foibles may come through this more formal justice system but unlike the usual trial films where justice is the ultimate requirement regardless of procedural impropriety, here the system is everything as the administrative system of the courts martial is designed to uphold the military and the state itself.

7

Assessing Cinematic Lawyers (I): Heroes and Villains

One issue that has exercised much of the academic writing, and attracted the concern of the professions in both the UK and the USA, is the nature and substance of the portrayal of lawyers both in individual films and television programmes and in general. For the former group the interest is primarily to look at theoretical aspects. The legal profession, however, is more concerned with the public image and perception of lawyers, and the effect of 'negative' portrayals both with respect to individual films and collectively across a longer time frame. There are a number of issues that require exploration within the broad parameters of 'lawyer portrayal'.

The question as to how lawyers are portrayed, and the effect on public confidence, seems at first sight straightforward. A consistent image of sleazy, unethical, greedy lawyers with little in the way of 'heroic' alternatives will affect public opinion as to the worth of lawyers. However, within this broad statement are a number of complicated factors that require detailed analysis. First, on what basis can we determine whether the portrayal is good, bad or indifferent? A seemingly obvious example is Paul Newman's characterisation of Frank Galvin in *The Verdict* (1982). However, as we argue later in this Chapter, Galvin is a diverse and complicated character, and whilst there are negative elements these are not consistently so. In that case, how are we to determine the overall nature of the portrayal? Furthermore, whose perception should we prefer, and is it a uniform perception? Filmgoers with a different set of real life and cinematic experiences, which itself takes us back to ideas of genre and reception, may well leave the film with different impressions and ideas about the characters. This ties in to ideas from film theory concerning the reading and understanding of films and the role of the audience. In short, we don't believe that the answer is a straightforward good or bad, or ethical or unethical.

To that end we have split our assessment of cinematic lawyers into two halves. First, in this Chapter, we consider the more traditional reading of lawyers from a binary good/bad perspective. We consider a number of films to examine this method of categorisation. We then, in Chapter 8, consider some alternative methods of categorisation that present the issue in terms of a more nuanced reading recognising the complex and complicated nature of many of the portrayals.

The Heroic Lawyer: When Atticus Met Lincoln

Asimow argues for a golden age or period of the portrayal of lawyers:

> In years past, film and television presented us with a set of lawyers who were decent people and honest, competent professionals—sometimes even heroes. In film, Atticus Finch, Paul Biegler, Clarence Darrow, Amanda Bonner, or Judge Dan Haywood served as wonderful role models for everyone in the profession from law students up to grizzled veterans.[1]

This is supported by Appelo, who claims that contemporary screen lawyers, and indeed those of the last 30 or so years, are vastly different from some of the earlier portrayals: 'Wisdom has rotted into calculation, justice into deal-making. The lawyer today is forced to face all manner of complex problems confusing his moral authority: matters economic, racial, sexual, political. The magic circle is broken.'[2] This might be described as the 'what has happened to Atticus Finch?' question. Finch, played by Gregory Peck, is the heroic defender of the innocent black Tom Robinson in *To Kill a Mockingbird* (1962). However, first it needs to be established that the great lawyer heroes, generally accepted as both Atticus Finch and the portrayals of lawyer and President Abraham Lincoln, did indeed have these 'heroic' qualities. Only then can we answer the question as to what has replaced them, and whether the 'magic circle' has indeed been broken. First, then, what made these two in particular the great screen lawyers and, more pertinently, what, if any, faults do they have? Appelo offers the following description of Finch who, he argues, even supersedes Perry Mason as the infallible screen lawyer:

> As Finch, Peck is crowned with the white fedora of truth and walks with a stately asymmetry, the result of an actual back injury but put to immortal use. His gait emphasizes his gravity, the essence of the law. It doesn't come across as a limp; it makes him seem to be striding straight from Mount Olympus. Arguably the most physically beautiful male product in Hollywood, Peck makes an even better symbol of incorruptibility than Burr.[3]

The question is whether this view of Atticus Finch is a shared, or correct one. On the question of 'shared' perspective, one additional factor that we need to consider is the contemporary influence of both of these characters. Films on Lincoln, of which there are many, may have been standard fare for a long period and indeed continuing. There is a host of cinematic and TV offerings on Lincoln reflecting his status ranging from *The Dramatic Life of Abraham Lincoln* in 1924 through DW Griffiths' (1930) offering *Abraham Lincoln* to Spielberg's scheduled 2011 release of *Lincoln*. Interestingly Spielberg's biopic will compete against another Lincoln-based film, *The Conspirator* (2010) directed by Robert Redford. The well is apparently not yet dry for Lincoln as a source for film. Commenting on the

---

[1] Asimow, M (1996: 72).
[2] Appelo, T (1992: 177).
[3] *Ibid*, 175.

competition from *The Conspirator*, Spielberg noted: 'It is completely different from what our DreamWorks Lincoln movie will be, and we believe that it will add to the commercial potential of our film. Lincoln as a subject is inexhaustible.'[4] For our purposes, we utilise *Young Mr Lincoln* (1939) as this film spends considerable time on Lincoln's career as a lawyer. However, an important point is the extent to which the portrayal of both Lincoln and Finch pervade the contemporary popular consciousness.

Certainly our experience of teaching film is that many students are reluctant to engage, at least in the same way, with older black and white films that are not such a natural medium. The coverage of important law films such as *To Kill a Mockingbird* (1962) and *12 Angry Men* (1957) may be diminishing by generation, and thus affecting the overall perception of the viewing group. Even within an audience familiar with the film, we need to consider the level of integrity attributed to Finch. Much depends on how the film itself is viewed and to what we attribute Finch's role, and his function. As we have observed earlier, the film is also a vehicle to discuss the wider question of racism within American society. John Jay Osborn offers an interesting perspective:

> Although the film *is* about natural law values in confrontation with transactional positivist values, the genius of the film lies in its willingness to take a traditional law figure to the edge, to the point where he must accept transactionalist values in order to succeed.[5]

Atticus defends the legal system and the right to a trial even though it is apparent that the outcome will be a conviction. His moral stand is, in fact, a limited one. He agrees to take the case and defends the courthouse so he is firmly and formally on the side of 'law and order'. The question is, though, what law and order—a defective legal system that permits a wrongful conviction of the innocent Tom Robinson? Does it really matter whether Finch supports and defends an imperfect system as he tries his very best to provide justice within the fatally flawed process? There are three fundamental scenes that demonstrate his relationship to the hegemony of law within this small community. First, there is the point where he accepts the case from the court and agrees to represent Tom Robinson, who has been accused of rape. This takes place in a very informal manner with little discussion or thought. It is clear that Finch has to represent Robinson, as there is no alternative. No alternative either for him as the custodian of the morality of the community and the ethics of (Finch's) law and legal practice. Asimow explains the importance of the assignment:

> The task required him to challenge the comfortable myths of rural southern life. At a minimum, this made him and his children highly unpopular. In fact, it placed his family in mortal danger. To his children, Atticus explains that if he refused the assignment he could never hold his head up in town again. This simple explanation says it all.[6]

---

[4] Child, B (2009).
[5] Osborn, J (1996: 1140).
[6] Asimow, M (1996: 1135).

Along with the promulgation of ethical practice is the upholding of the rule of law through the physical defence of the defendant who is imprisoned in the town's gaol. Robinson has originally been held outside the town for his own protection but is then returned to the town by the Sheriff the day before the trial. The Sheriff goes to see Finch in the evening and passes on his concerns that there may be some trouble, as people are aware that Robinson has been brought back. Finch goes over to the gaol to protect his client, the children realise he has left the house and, inquisitively, follow him. At this point the film is viewed through the children's perspective and they become the most important characters, both in terms of character activity and viewpoint. They approach the building and see him sitting outside on the veranda reading a book. They are about to leave when they see a number of cars draw up, and men armed with rifles get out and approach Finch. The children run through the lynch party to Atticus, who tells them to go home. When they refuse, one of the protesters grabs Atticus's son, Jem, his daughter Scout kicks the man and they join Atticus outside the door. While Atticus is talking to Jem, Scout scans the crowd and, seeing a face she recognises, speaks to him, initially eliciting no response, but eventually her rhetoric leads to the crowd dispersing.

So, the key figure in this physical defence of the defendant is not Finch, but the storyteller, his young daughter Scout. Her recognition of Mr Cunningham and attempts to engage him draw out the notion of humanity, but more than this there is a link to law and to her father. Scout refers to Cunningham's 'entail-ment', his debt to Atticus for legal services provided that Cunningham is repaying through produce. The hickory nuts she refers to are part of this payment. During this original scene, at the start of the film, Cunningham is embarrassed by both the situation and Finch's thanks. Finch's contribution to the crowd dispersal is limited to a clear determination not to move from the building and his attempts to send the children home.

The second important scene is at the end of the film, and the killing of Mr Ewell by Boo Radley. Ewell attacks the two Finch children, Jem and Scout, as they are walking through a wooded part of the town. Suddenly in the midst of the attack a shadowy figure emerges, grabs Ewell and rescues Jem, who has been knocked unconscious. Scout struggles out of her 'ham' costume and runs home to find Jem in bed injured. Finch telephones the Doctor and the Sheriff. After investigating the scene of the incident Tate reports that Ewell is lying dead with a kitchen knife in his back. Boo Radley appears from behind the door and it becomes apparent to the two men that it is Radley who has rescued the two children and killed Ewell. This raises a significant problem for Finch, who has defended the legal system throughout. For example, when he is told of Robinson's death, for trying to escape he goes to the family and stresses the importance of the proposed appeal. Finch thinks through the course of action, but Tate immediately takes a far more prag-matic approach and Finch is content to allow Radley to escape any investigation and accept Tate's view of rough justice. John Jay Osborn concludes that there is a line to be drawn in the film between the heroic and the ridiculous:

The issue presented by the film is not merely the heroic struggle of a man of values in a valueless society. The film's real power comes from posing the more difficult question: When does holding onto traditional values in a valueless world become not heroic but absurd? Atticus Finch is as childlike as his daughter Scout. His vision of law is as unrealistic and yet as touching as her vision of childhood. Both hold views that are more eccentric than the town's identifiable eccentric, Boo Radley.[7]

This provides an interesting perspective, and offers a critique of Finch the lawyer and, to a lesser extent, Finch the man. What is absolutely clear is that Finch is prepared to subvert the process of law in the wider interests of justice, or rather his subjective perception of justice. Yet according to commentators such as Strickland, he presents an image that is:

the idealized portrayal of a lawyer as guardian of society. He is the dream that young lawyers hope to achieve and that old lawyers regret having lost. He is, in so many ways, like a modern Abraham Lincoln, who is the favorite American dream of the country lawyer.[8]

Thus those who revere the image of Finch as the idealist moral and ethical cinematic lawyer face a challenge on two fronts, his pragmatic approach to due process and his apparent acceptance of a racist legal system. This latter point has already developed into a lively debate.[9] Radical criticisms of Atticus Finch appeared in an article in the *Legal Times* in 1992.[10] There has been further comment on the relationship between Finch the man, and Finch the lawyer.[11] There are a number of different points of interest here, not least by which standards of morality should the behaviour of Finch be judged, that of the era or by more contemporary beliefs. Freedman takes an unequivocal stance:

So let me declare myself. I do believe that there are prima facie principles of right and wrong (which can be called Natural Law), which each of us is capable of recognizing by the use of experience, intellect and conscience. There may not be many such principles of right and wrong, but the terrorizing of the Levy family, the attempted lynching of Tom Robinson, and the apartheid that Atticus Finch practised every day of his life—those things are wrong today, and they were wrong in Maycomb, Alabama, in the 1930s.[12]

What is important is that the accepted wisdom of Finch, the hero lawyer, is becoming subject to more detailed analysis, and the rather one-dimensional perspective of the character is being challenged. It neatly illustrates the tensions and stresses at the heart of the hero and villain debate. One of the clear perspectives arising from this is the apparent lineage of the heroic lawyer from Lincoln through to Finch. It is worth a closer examination of Lincoln in *Young Mr Lincoln* (1939) to see whether and how he conforms to the 'heroic' type, and how he links to Finch.

---

[7] Osborn, J (1996: 1142).
[8] Strickland, R (1997: 17).
[9] See, eg, Crespino, J (2000).
[10] Freedman, M (1992).
[11] Freedman, M (1994).
[12] *Ibid*, 473.

Law, and the practice of law, are important features of the film that single out this Lincoln film from the others. There are four particularly crucial scenes. First, his initial relationship with the law through the handing to him of law books by the mother, Abigail Clay, and his reading of the law books under the tree and his subsequent decision to engage with the law. Second is his first case, the settling of a grievance between two farmers. Third is the physical defence of the court-room from the attempted lynch mob and finally the trial itself. The first of these shows Lincoln accepting books from a newly arrived family. In return for goods he accepts the books without knowing the subject matter, but swiftly reduces law to a simple matter of 'right and wrong'. Here we see a deconstruction of colossal proportions—a deconstruction that later allows Lincoln to see things firmly in terms of black and white and right and wrong. Gallagher makes an interesting observation concerning the portrayal of Lincoln's initial relationship with the law and the association with nature:

> Lincoln in seeking what is in him, would expect to find guidance in Nature herself. Truth exists, within oneself and in the natural world consubstantially; the only 'mystery' is the fog that blinds us to it. And Ford *does* tell us about Truth, for as Lincoln wonders, 'Law!', gawking at the book, and then repeats, 'Law!,' the medium shot dissolves, nay slowly explodes into an immense riverbent landscape, wherein Lincoln lies against a big tree reading the book. Thus we know that Law and Nature are one. 'Why gee,' he says, 'that's all there is to it, right and wrong!'—and thus we know that Law and innate intuitive knowledge are one with Nature, too.[13]

The second scene is after he has started his legal practice, in Springfield in 1837. He is approached by two farmers who are in dispute, and who have previously fought. His response is to propose an equitable settlement that ensures that he gets paid, that relies on a barely veiled threat to knock the two protagonists' heads together. Here we see a pragmatism of approach and a willingness to both go beyond the law where necessary and also to utilise force if 'justice' were to be achieved by so doing. Lincoln shows, at a number of points, that he is not beyond cheating. Even at the fair he cheats during the tug of war, but it appears he considers the wider picture of his actions, and is almost utilitarian in his approach.

The third legal scene involves the murder of Scrub White and prosecution of the two Clay brothers. Lincoln volunteers his services to Mrs Clay and then moves to physically prevent the lynching of his clients (the scene replicated by Finch). Finally we see the behaviour of Lincoln during the trial: he ridicules the pros-ecutor, the drunken juror and aggressively questions Jack Cass. Lincoln is often physically removed from the action and the process of law moving in at times to interact with the course of the trial:

> The film's stylistic elements complement its dialogue in emphasizing Lincoln's distance from mainstream legal practices. Lincoln, for example, rarely appears in the center of the courtroom scenes; usually, he is found roaming the edges of the film's frame. At one point

---

[13] Gallagher, T (1986: 167).

in the trial, he wanders toward a law book; but rather than finally using textual authority to make 'legal' argument Lincoln continues to clown, seemingly all to no point.[14]

It is clear from the ridiculing of Jack Cass that this is Lincoln's courtroom and not the judge's. The late understanding, by the judge, of Lincoln's mockery of Cass's name places the judge within Lincoln's ambit and he does little to control Lincoln's frequent interruptions of the prosecuting counsel. The real problem in determining Lincoln as the foremost hero lawyer is separating out the myth from the man. The problem is that we all know the course his life will take and cannot divorce this knowledge of Lincoln as 'good' from his behaviour that might otherwise be viewed more critically. A further side issue is the question of relationships and this dimension of the heroic lawyer. Rafter has observed that 'good personal relationships parallel good legal relationships: Everyone eventually recognises and happily accepts the rule of a wise father/judge.'[15]

However, both Lincoln and Atticus Finch have problematic and unsettled personal lives. Finch is a widower bringing up his children alone, and they frequently disobey him. Lincoln is confused by the death of Ann Rutledge and his later relationship with Mary Todd and is clearly uneasy. If we conclude that the 'heroic' picture, apart from Lincoln's dress, is not purely black and white as some would argue, we can now consider what the nature of the 'post heroic' portrayals look like.

Flawed Characters?

A number of writers have talked about the periods of decline in the kind of image found in lawyer films. This has been linked to broader social issues, as well as filmmakers relying on stock characters and situations.[16] Nevins suggests that after the first 'golden age of juris cinema', there is a gap to the second 'golden age' of the 1960s:

> The source of the motifs that link most of the law-related films of the second golden age was the idealism of the Warren Court and early civil rights era, reflected in *12 Angry Men, Inherit the Wind, Judgment at Nuremberg, To Kill a Mockingbird, Man in the Middle,* and others.[17]

For him the way in which legal institutions are portrayed is part of what he describes, we assume ironically, as a 'third Golden Age', free from the censorship of the Production Code:

> The radical cynicism of the Vietnam and Watergate era offered newly liberated filmmakers the leitmotifs for a third golden age. Most of the key works of this period are marked

---

[14] Rosenberg, N (1991: 222).
[15] Rafter, N (2006: 137).
[16] Rafter, N (2001: 21), referring to the reliance on 'camera tricks, manipulative scripts and recycled plots'.
[17] Nevins, F (2004: 954).

by a contempt for law, lawyers, lawyering and justice—and for just about everything else in American society to boot—far deeper and darker than the 1920s-style cynicism of the early talkies ... *Dirty Harry*, ... *And Justice for All, Criminal Law, Presumed Innocent*, Martin Scorsese's version of *Cape Fear*, the list goes on and on through the closing years of the twentieth century and the opening years of the twenty-first.[18]

Rafter, writing specifically in relation to criminal trial movies, talks of the 'heroic tradition' from the mid 1950s to the 1960s in which men laboured 'heroically within the system to ensure that man-made law coincides with the justice ideal'.[19] This was followed by a period in which there was a 'tendency to portray women lawyers as flying pigs, creatures that were not meant to be'[20]—a less than heroic set of images for sure.[21] More recently, she has suggested that courtroom dramas have been replaced by law films that raise issues of justice, and responsibility, in 'non court settings'.[22] Kamir locates her account of Hollywood's hero lawyers with her division of cultures between those based on honour and those on dignity. The heroic lawyer figure is drawn from the Western:

> ... Hollywood's influential image of the hero-lawyer is modeled on the western genre's hero. *Anatomy*'s hero-lawyer features significant western hero characteristics, including extraordinary, professional fighting skills and 'true manhood', which entails a commitment to justice and natural law, as well as inherent honor. In its construction of its lawyer as a western-hero, *Anatomy* embraces the Old West's mythological honor code, introducing it into the new hero-lawyer film genre. This results in an uncritical adoption of honor-based attitudes, such as the suspicious scrutiny of women's sexual conduct, and the glorification of men's violent assertion of their traditional masculine honor rights (including over their wives' sexuality).[23]

Asimow is one of the leading proponents of the view that contemporary portrayals of lawyers are negative ones. He makes the claim that:

> In the majority of films involving law, lawyers and the legal system since the 1970s, the lawyer characters and their law firms were pretty bad. This generalization holds whether the film fits the standard lawyer/courtroom genre, whether it involves legal issues, whether the film is a comedy (black or otherwise) or a drama, or whether it falls into other genres such as romances, mystery stories, or thrillers that just happen to have lawyer roles.[24]

He supports this contention with a detailed analysis of some 284 films between 1929 and 1999. He commences his argument with a 'rogues gallery' of recent portrayals. He includes within this bunch *Body Heat* (1981) ('lazy greedy, incompetent'), *Carlito's Way* (1993) ('an utter scumbag'), *The Firm* (1993) (vicious killers), *Liar Liar* (1997) (perjurer) and *Devil's Advocate* (1997) (lawyer as the devil).

---

[18] *Ibid*, 954–55.
[19] Rafter, N (2001: 15).
[20] *Ibid*, 21.
[21] See, eg, the discussion in Chapter 8.
[22] Rafter, N (2006: 152).
[23] Kamir, O (2005a: 39).
[24] Asimow, M (2000a: 533–34).

Asimow and Mader retain this simple division between lawyer as hero and lawyer as villain in their Law and Popular Culture course book, selecting Atticus Finch for the former and Frank Galvin for the latter.[25] There are other writers who suggest that there is more to this than a fairly one-dimensional question as to whether the lawyer is shown to be good or bad, and that there have been a number of constant factors that cut across different eras. Whether or not we accept the heroic lawyer image of Finch and Lincoln, the second part of the argument revolves around the idea that contemporary portrayals are, to use Asimow's term, 'pretty bad'.

Assessing the Good/Bad Categories

It is worth looking at some of these in more depth and we have selected the legal characters from the following films, with Asimow's criteria in brackets: *A Civil Action* (1998, negative), *Cape Fear* (1991, negative), *The Client* (1994, mixed), *Devil's Advocate* (1997, negative), *The Firm* (1993, mixed), *Just Cause* (1995, positive), *Suspect* (1987, mixed), and *The Verdict* (1982, negative). He would add to this list the lawyers in *Changing Lanes* (2002), *Chicago* (2002), *Michael Clayton* (2007),[26] and we have given a view of these films' lawyers in order to provide an overview of this method of categorisation.

A Civil Action (1998)

The film is based on the book of the same name by Jonathan Harr.[27] Its coverage is the environmental pollution that led to the litigation in *Anderson v Cryovac, Inc.* Outside its relevance as a film depicting real life events, it is useful to consider it in terms of the ways in which lawyers are presented. Our analysis in this section is based purely on the cinematic version and does not draw any contrasts with the real events. The film has one central legal character, Jan Schlichtmann (John Travolta), and several others on the periphery (Schlichtmann's partners, the two defence lawyers and the judge). The firm has taken the case because one of the partners is very sympathetic to the situation of the families and saddened by the deaths of the children. Schlichtmann is shown as having no such sympathy and the opening of the film indicates his cynical perceptions on the legal system and specifically personal injury litigation. He applies his rigid criteria to the Woburn case and is initially not keen to proceed on the basis that there is a lack of a 'deep-pocketed' potential defendant. He only becomes enthused once it becomes apparent that there is a potential defendant of such financial worth that the case

---

[25] Asimow, M and Mader, S (2004: chs 3 and 4).
[26] Correspondence between Michael Asimow and the authors, August 2008. 'By my criteria, the lawyers in *Changing Lanes*, *Chicago* and *Michael Clayton* are bad.'
[27] Harr, J (1996).

has some prospects. The whole thrust of Schlichtmann and the firm's raison d'être is the gathering of sufficient evidence for leverage to press for a settlement. The case proceeds on this basis until there is a realisation, by Schlichtmann, that the case is not just about money, but justice for the Woburn families. He almost sabotages the chances of a settlement by asking for so much and is eventually forcefully persuaded by his partners to accept the settlement that is on offer.

Schlichtmann is a very complex character and defies the good/bad classification. Whilst initially concerned purely with financial advancement for himself and his clients, by the end of the film he has altered radically, financially ruined and having no material possessions left. Thus the end portrayal is a very sympathetic one and we have a figure that has become obsessed with finding the truth. Even after the settlement he continues to investigate how the poisoning might have occurred and gathers further evidence that he submits to the Environmental Protection Agency (EPA). He is handicapped by a lack of funds and the conclusion we are left with is of a small firm trying to fight for justice against large corporations with greater resources. Schlichtmann is transformed from the heartless to the caring and thoughtful lawyer who cares little for his own status. His early arrogance dissipates and he transforms into a humble figure who apologises to the families. The other lawyers are not shown in the same light. Schlichtmann's partners, whilst making financial sacrifices to pursue the case, do not share his zeal but are more concerned with obtaining a sufficient settlement to cover their costs and fees. They are so disenchanted with Schlichtmann's crusading approach that they split up the firm and exclude him.

The defendants' lawyers are more insignificant figures though they have some important characteristics. Jerome Facher (Robert Duvall) is shown as a slightly eccentric albeit disinterested figure, although at times this borders on rudeness. Duval has little to say in the film and has a detached air about him. This is, though, more than he says in *To Kill a Mockingbird*, where he plays the eccentric and silent Boo Radley. When talking to either Schlichtmann or Cheeseman (Bruce Norris) he seems indifferent to the case or the people involved in it. He is on the periphery and rarely makes a positive step. At the settlement meeting he is more concerned with the hotel's complimentary pen and the food on the table. He makes no contribution whatsoever having arrived late and signals his intention by leaving after Schlichtmann has made his opening bid. He is given a semi-intellectual air and a prophetic knowledge of what will happen. Cheeseman is shown as an efficient, thorough attorney prepared to do what is needed for his clients. Overall he is a fairly nondescript figure, neither particularly likeable nor offensive. We have thus an interesting range of characters.

Cape Fear (1991)

The re-make of *Cape Fear* has a number of interesting legal elements, though it does indicate some of the problems inherent within classifying 'legal' films. In terms of a critical comparison between the two, Halliwell offers the following description of the 1961 film: 'Unpleasant and drawn-out suspenser with characters of cardboard and situations from stock.'[28] The 1991 film gets a better critical reading: 'A remake superior to the original, a grimly effective thriller, filled with a sense of brooding menace.'[29] Indeed the 1991 Martin Scorsese version alters some of the plot of the original J Lee Thompson version. The re-make is certainly more brutal and sexually explicit, and has attracted some criticism. For example, Cook argues that:

> The real horror in *Cape Fear* is feminisation: the contamination of positive 'masculine' values (heroism, integrity, honour and so forth) by 'feminine' values of weakness, prevarication and moral laxity, typified by the ambivalent figure of anti-hero Sam Bowden. Scorsese has produced his most overtly feminophobic movie. We can hardly admire him for that.[30]

Interestingly, the two principal actors in the original, Gregory Peck and Robert Mitchum, are both given cameo roles in the second film. There are two leading figures set up in opposition and divided by the law. One is the client, Max Cady, played by Robert De Niro, and the other his lawyer, Sam Bowden, played by Nick Nolte. Whilst in prison serving a 14-year sentence for a brutal sexual attack, Cady discovers that his lawyer had concealed evidence, a report on the victim that revealed that she was sexually promiscuous. The report would have devalued the testimony of the victim and increased Cady's changes of an acquittal. After his release Cady sets out to achieve retribution against Bowden (and his family). He starts a campaign of psychological and physical harassment and Bowden explains what happened, in the original case, to his colleague:

Sam: '... I buried it, I mean I didn't show it to the client, I didn't show it to the prosecution ... but if you had seen what this guy had done to this girl ...'

Tom: 'In every criminal prosecution the accused shall have the assistance of counsel for his defence.'

Sam: 'Hell I know the sixth amendment, I believe in the sixth amendment. I mean that's why I left the Public Defender's Office; there was no way to serve the law in that capacity.'

Tom: 'Some folks just don't deserve the best defence eh Sam?'

Sam: 'No of course they deserve the best defence but if you had seen what he did to this girl ...'

Tom: 'Buried the report ...'

Sam: 'I mean if it was your own daughter Tom ... I mean ...'

Tom: 'Buried the report ... Jesus Sam.'

---

[28] Halliwell, L (2008: 192).
[29] *Ibid*, 192–93.
[30] Cook, P (1993: 137).

Despite the horror of crime, Tom has little sympathy for Sam's position. Overall Bowden is shown as a morally weak individual, cheating on his wife and breaking his duty to his client. Yet there was no personal gain for Bowden in concealing the report, essentially he had everything to lose. Little is made of Bowden's apparent sacrifice, even though he was clearly acting for what he perceived to be a subjective, higher notion of justice. The idea that the legal system was likely to free Cady when he, Bowden, knew what he had done and was capable of triggers a protective trait, towards society, and an attempt to impose justice. This can clearly be attacked from a perspective of lawyer–client duty, but criticism ought also to be levelled at the legal system that would allow Cady to walk free, not just the individual who is enmeshed helplessly within the system. There is a nice contrast between Bowden the man, weak and immoral, and Bowden the lawyer, someone who seems primarily concerned with the question of justice over and above the legal rules. This comes out in a number of ways, not just over the buried report. Perhaps his most pertinent comment relates to his response in the public defender's office when he explains his departure: 'That's why I left the Public Defender's Office, there was no way to serve the law in that capacity.' His concern seems to be justice and he realises that the rules of law cannot always serve the best interests of justice.

He is also prepared to go beyond the law when hiring thugs to attack Cady as the law is proving an ineffective vehicle to restrain Cady as he has actually done little (legally) wrong. He may appear a threatening figure but this is not enough for any legal action. This adds to Bowden's portrayal as someone not law-abiding, though he is initially reluctant to countenance direct action. We may not like Bowden's personal (im)morality, and we may not like or agree with the treatment of his client (Cady), but we can, perhaps, appreciate his motives even if we do not approve of his action. It is precisely his own flaws that make his personal stand so surprising.

The Client (1994)

The Client (1994), the third cinematic offering from John Grisham, has several prominent legal characters: the two opposing lawyers, Reggie Love (Susan Sarandon) and the District Attorney, Roy Foltrigg (Tommy Lee Jones), in addition to an interesting judge, Harry Roosevelt (Ossie Davis). It is perhaps a mistake to consider Love and Foltrigg as being on opposing sides given that both are trying to ensure that justice is delivered. The real fight is over how the testimony of Mark Sway, the 11-year-old child who witnessed the suicide of the mob attorney Jerome R Clifford, should be dealt with. Clifford had been working for Barry 'the blade' Muldano and was aware of the location of one of Muldano's prominent victims, a Senator.

Foltrigg is seeking to prosecute Muldano to enhance his credentials and improve his political status as he is supposedly seeking election as State Governor. Much is made of Foltrigg's naked political ambition and it is stressed throughout that he is pursuing this case for exactly these reasons. However, he frequently protests that he is on the side of the law: 'My real interest is to see justice done.' Whilst there may well be some idea of political advancement it is apparent that Foltrigg is prepared to track down the killer vigorously and pursue the mob. He is certainly prepared to bend the rules to do so, notably when trying to gather a witness statement from Mark, but throughout he is also concerned about the threat, posed by the mob, to Mark's physical safety. It is a mistake to cast him as motivated purely by political considerations. For example, when discussing how his press conference should appear, the scene is so overstated to reduce it to a level of ironic criticism. Foltrigg often retains his humour and develops an almost flirtatious relationship with Love. What is also interesting is that they both express distaste with lawyers, a perception shared, with some vehemence, by young Mark, who has a totally negative perception based on his personal experience. Foltrigg attempts to question Mark without his mother or Reggie Love being present; they are in a room along with four other men who are part of the entourage of lawyers and FBI officers:

Mark: 'Do I need a lawyer?'

Man: 'What for?'

Mark: 'To protect my rights?'

Foltrigg: 'No.'

McThune: 'You've been watching too much TV.'

Trumann: 'We just want to ask you some questions, you can trust us. Lawyers just get in the way, you gotta pay em and they object to everything.'

Foltrigg then proffers the view that 'lawyers are a pain in the arse' and Sway pointedly asks him: 'Aren't you are a lawyer?'[31] Reggie Love also criticises lawyers, and refers to the one who represented her husband in the divorce as a 'fancy lawyer'. Similarly Mark has a very sceptical view of the profession and despises the lawyer who represented his mother in her divorce hearing. In all the three central characters, two lawyers and one who often represents himself, have little affection for the profession. The other peripheral lawyers are shown in fairly stereotypical fashion.[32] Reggie Love is heroic in her defence and support of Mark and shown as prepared to break the law, as Foltrigg points out to her at the end of the film. Foltrigg's view of Love alters radically: he starts off by referring to her as an amateur, who is out of her depth, yet by the end of the film he asks her whether or not she wants a job when he becomes Governor of Louisiana. Love of course declines, pointing out that she already has one. The two adult figures start off as fighting

---

[31] This line is returned to at the end of the film when Mark Sway tells Roy Foltrigg that he has been a pain in the arse, to which he responds 'and I can assure that you have been an even bigger pain in the arse'.

[32] In addition to the District Attorney's entourage, Sway encounters two lawyers before he stumbles upon Reggie including ambulance-chasing Gill Teal.

over Mark, Reggie to protect and naturally mother him and Foltrigg to advance his career. However, as the film moves on, both are seeking to exercise a protective function and Reggie Love is prepared to let him leave and Foltrigg to offer him a new life with his mother and brother. Once they are aware of the realities of the situation, and what Mark actually knows, both pull together to achieve the same overall objective, the discovery of the body and the safety of the family. This drawing together of the two opposing sides can only happen because of the presence of the third party, the mob. The inherent dangers of the mob to the safety of Mark and his family provide a rationale for Love and Foltrigg to join together; they are no longer at odds but able to reach a solution acceptable to all sides. Thus we end up with the acceptable happy ending and perhaps even a hint of a possible romantic liaison between the two leading players.

Devil's Advocate (1997)

If we are able to identify only one film that offers an extremely negative portrayal of lawyers, surely *Devil's Advocate* (1997) must be towards the top of the bill. The film is awash with lawyers with several of them literally satanic. The film commences with a young Florida lawyer, Kevin Lomax (Keanu Reeves), a very successful trial attorney, being presented with an ethical dilemma. Does he carry on his defence of a schoolteacher accused of molesting one of his pupils once Lomax privately discovers he is culpable? A journalist confronts him in the washroom with the view that everyone has to lose sometime, as the evidence appears overwhelming. Professionally stung, Lomax goes back into court and browbeats the young child in the witness box into submission by using information no-one could have known, showing almost superhuman powers. Following this victory, he is invited to New York to help with choosing a jury. He is successful once again and is seduced to join the firm owned by John Milton (Al Pacino). He proves extraordinarily successful, but is plagued by self-doubt and the illness of his wife, with a number of inexplicable and bizarre events taking place. The film reaches its denouement once Lomax's mother reveals that Milton is in fact his father, and it becomes apparent that Milton is, in fact, Satan. Summoned to Milton's penthouse lair, Milton indicates what he can offer and deliver for him:

Milton: 'How about the thing you love the most, a smile from a jury? That cold courtroom just giving itself over, bending to your strength.'

Lomax: 'I get that on my own'.

Milton: 'Not like this. I take the bricks out of the briefcase. I give you pleasure, no strings. Freedom baby, is never having to say you're sorry. This is revolution, Kevin.'

(breaks into song, *It happened in Monterrey*)

Lomax: 'Why law? Cut the shit dad, why lawyers? Why the law?'

Milton: 'Because the law, my boy, puts us into everything. It's the ultimate backstage pass, it's the new priesthood baby. Do you know there are more students in Law School than there are lawyers walking the earth? We're coming out! Guns blazing. The two of you (Lomax and his 'sister'), all of us, acquittal after acquittal after acquittal until the stench of it reaches so high and far into heaven that it chokes the whole fucking lot of them.'

Lomax: 'In the bible you lose. We're destined to lose, Dad.'

Milton: 'Consider the source.'

Milton's plan is for Lomax to have a child with his own sister; however, Lomax resists his sister's advances and shoots himself through the temple, making his own ultimate sacrifice, despite his own vanity. The film cuts back to the original courtroom scene, before he has defended the schoolteacher. This time he withdraws from the case and is threatened with disbarment. When asked what he is doing, he replies: 'the right thing'. In the final scene, the original journalist re-appears and offers to cover his story and ultimate fame. Kevin agrees and as he walks away, reunited with his wife, the journalist's face morphs into that of Milton, who merely looks to camera saying: 'Vanity, definitely my favourite sin.' Here we see the ultimate flaw, that of vanity. This ties in to Lomax's belief that he couldn't lose—after all, he was a lawyer, and lawyers do not lose. This in fact presents a somewhat ambiguous perspective on lawyers—on one level we see the legal profession as conduit of evil via Satanic appropriation, on the other we see a man, a lawyer, making the ultimate sacrifice to save a man with all its own obvious religious resonance. Perhaps *Devil's Advocate* is not a negative lawyer movie after all?

The Firm (1993)

A film that has the potential for a negative portrayal, as it seemingly contains a fairly disreputable bunch of lawyers, is the very first of the six John Grisham adaptations of the 1990s, *The Firm* (1993). It starts with the soon-to-graduate, high-flying Harvard law student Mitch McDeere (Tom Cruise) considering a variety of offers from leading law firms. McDeere's motivation for accepting the offer from Bendini, Lambert and Locke is apparent from the outset. It is the highest financially. The salary is 20 per cent higher than the next best offer and there are numerous perks. It becomes apparent at his interview that there has been a degree of subterfuge in his recruitment as the Managing Partner admits to bribing a clerk to find out what he had been offered. The financial package sways McDeere and when his sceptical wife, Abby (Jeanne Tripplehorn) indicates some uncertainty he chides her with the comment 'You're used to it'. That he is concerned with financial security and protection is drawn out at lunch on his first day with Avery Tolar (Gene Hackman):

Tolar: 'What led you to law school?'

McDeere: 'I can't remember?'

Tolar: 'Sure you can Counsellor.'

McDeere: 'I was a delivery boy for a pizza parlour and one day the owner got a notice from the IRS. He was an immigrant, didn't know much English, even less about withholding tax. He went bankrupt, lost his store. It was the first time I thought of being a lawyer.'

Tolar: 'In other words you're an idealist?'

McDeere: 'I don't know any tax lawyer who's an idealist. When he lost his store I lost my job. It scared me.'

Tolar: 'Being out of work?'

McDeere: 'No what the Government can do ... to anybody.'

Thus the backdrop is established with a young lawyer anxious to impress and earn the rewards that have been dangled in front of him. McDeere's relationship with his wife alters almost immediately he gets the job, as he throws himself headlong into his work. He says that he is trying to repay her sacrifices in getting him through law school. The question of money and his background is a vital difference between them from the outset:

Abby: 'You don't even know what moves me about you do you? You don't know what you want but it's not for me it's not even for you and you know it.'

McDeere: 'It's easy for somebody rich to talk about being poor like it's some fly that's bothering you just wave it away.'

Abby: 'This isn't about rich or poor. This isn't about trying to fix something that won't get fixed with ten Mercedes.'

McDeere: 'Hey that's not fair Abby. That's not fair.'

Abby: , 'This is about a mother in a trailer park and a brother you pretend you don't have. Have a nice trip.'

The odd part of this portrayal is that clearly McDeere has not significantly altered in this short space of time. There was clearly some attraction, in his personality, to her at the outset. The clear message he is giving out is that he wants to be free, from the poverty of his family. For Abby she loses her control over him once he becomes liberated by the financial rewards. He is no longer dependent on her and resents her trying to prevent him aspiring to her own background. In retrospect we view her as a wiser figure who sees through the initial advancements of the 'firm' whilst McDeere is plainly greedy. This greed blinds him to the obvious flaws in the company make-up. Early on Abby complains sarcastically that the offer is ok because the firm will 'let her work and encourages children'. Her sagacity is born out of her freedom, and desire not to pursue material rewards, whilst McDeere is driven by the need to rise above his family's poverty. The message of the film is clear; that the relentless pursuit of money blinds us to the realities in front of us.

McDeere only 'comes to his senses' once he has been unfaithful to his wife in the Cayman Islands; his guilt leads him to visit his brother in prison and question what is happening at the firm. His adultery on the beach is his cathartic moment. From that point onwards McDeere is both liberated and handicapped and must search for the truth in both the relationship with his wife and the activities of the 'firm' and deliver an element of subjective justice for both Abby and his brother Ray, who remains in prison. Of course on one level *The Firm* (1993) is a story of corrupt lawyers, they are after all lawyers for the mob. Once McDeere is on course to extract himself from the crossfire between the FBI and the firm a new conflict emerges. The FBI wish to 'nail' the firm, at any cost, including a threat to swing Ray McDeere's parole hearing unfavourably. McDeere is concerned with his and of course his wife's personal safety but also his professional position as he sees himself as a victim, without much of a sense of justice. His concerns are made explicitly to an FBI agent:

McDeere: 'Let me get this straight. I steal files from the firm, turn them over to the FBI, testify against my colleagues, send them to jail.'

FBI Agent: 'They suckered you into this.'

McDeere: 'Reveal privileged information that violates attorney client confidences get me disbarred and testify in open court against the mafia.'

Agent: 'Well unfortunately Mitch ...'

McDeere: 'Let me ask you something? Are you out of your fucking mind?'

McDeere is not happy to work with the FBI on their terms but needs to find a resolution to the problems of his professional and personal life. He must somehow leave the firm to maintain his relationship with Abby but he is still anxious to protect his much-sought-after professional status. The murder of Eddie Lomax (Gary Busey) disturbed McDeere and pushed him towards ditching the firm. From this point the film is about McDeere and how he can manage to achieve the solution he wants. This involves persuading the Mob that they are protected from his knowledge by the lawyer–client relationship. The firm are guilty of skimming the accounts of their clients, a federal offence since they used the US Postal Service. His personal safety is guaranteed by his continued existence since the details of the money laundering will be made available to the Federal authorities if he dies. The confused viewer may wonder where this leaves Mitch's legal career. The answer is to gift the money he has extracted from the operation to his brother so he can sail through and leave corporate law behind. He and Abby set off to set up small firm in Boston. So from his reflection on his relationship with his brother and his wife, Mitch realises that what in the end appeals is the well-being of others.

This Chapter has dealt in some depth with how films might be categorised on the good/bad spectrum, and has identified some problems with this rather narrow conception. The following Chapter details some other typical attributes that might be used to frame a categorisation, and some concluding points about categorisation are made.

8

Assessing Cinematic Lawyers (II): Alternative Categorisations

Introduction

Irrespective of whether or not our doubts about the value of Asimow's gradings, as detailed in Chapter 7, are deemed convincing, it would be hard to deny that the screen lawyers in the 21st century legal dramas are distinctly nuanced. The range of situations and portrayals is quite wide. We have a young man, Gavin Banek, coming to the full realisation that he lost his moral compass in *Changing Lanes* (2002). Similarly, a related type of realisation of the shallowness of success, compared with the value of children, is shown by Rita Harrison, in *I Am Sam* (2002). As a contrast, the portrayal of a man who appears to be focused solely on personal material gain, irrespective of justice, is seen in Billy Flynn in *Chicago* (2002). Within one film, *The Exorcism of Emily Rose* (2005), there are contrasting versions of the responsibility of the lawyer to the client, and to the community, from Erin Bruner and Ethan Thomas. The core of *Michael Clayton* (2007) centres on how Clayton will resolve the various personal and professional pressures exerted on him during a difficult time in his life. None of these lawyers is an obvious successor to the mantle of Atticus Finch, and yet each of them in their own way show degrees of compassion, and action, which put them beyond a simple classification of good or bad lawyer. Outside of the good/bad duality, this Chapter looks at some other potential categories into which lawyers could be placed. To do this, it first looks at some specific film examples of portrayals that do not fit neatly into the traditional schemata, before suggesting some other potential categorisations.

Changing Lanes (2002)

There is an element of the classic redemption trope in this legally centred thriller in which we encounter the smug, self-centred Gavin Banek as a lawyer with a clear sense of his own importance as a representative of the power of law and lawyers. He does not need to conform to the norms of mere mortals and can solve problems by a wave of the cheque-book. When the accidental loss of a crucial legal document presents him with a problem, he changes into a vengeful wielder of

serious institutional power. He is prepared to wreck another man's life to preserve
his own position as a would-be partner in a law firm. He descends further into
moral turpitude in conjunction with his bosses in agreeing to falsify documents to
retain his gilded position. It is not until he has the opportunity to speak with his
wife, Cynthia (Amanda Peet), that he begins to realise what kind of compromised
person he has become:

> Cynthia: 'She decided it would be hypocritical for leaving a man for cheating at home
> when the expensive life she enjoyed so much was paid for by a man whose
> job was based on finding ways to cheat.'
>
> Gav: 'Is that your opinion of the law?'
>
> Cynthia: 'What do think the law is Gav at this level of the game, at my father's level
> of the game, at your level? It is a big vicious rumble Gavin. The people who
> founded this law firm and the people who sustain it, understand the way the
> world works. If you want to continue to live the way we've been living ...'
>
> Gav: '... you have to steal.'
>
> Cynthia: 'I could have married an honest man. I could have lived with a Professor
> of Middle English, for example, if he was a moral man and had tenure at
> Princeton. But I didn't. I married a Wall Street lawyer. Which means I mar-
> ried a man who lives in a world where when a man comes to the edge of
> things he has to commit to staying there and living there. Can you live there
> Gavin? Can you live there with me?'

Her advice is that Gavin should be complicit in creating a fake new Power of
Appointment that will allow the firm to continue administering the lucrative
charitable Foundation of Simon Dunne, which the partners have been overcharg-
ing for years against the wishes of his niece, Mina Dunne. Her father, his boss in
the law firm, Stephen Delano (Sidney Pollack) points out to him that the money
made by the 'great philanthropist' came from the exploitation of child labour in
the developing world, and is itself already tainted.

This recognition of where he has come to as an individual, and the type of
world he lives in, leads him to rediscover his human essence. We see this in the
answers of the young job applicant as to why he wants to become a lawyer. Tyler
Cohen (Kevin Sussman), who has spent the day awaiting interview, explains the
rationale for being a lawyer. This almost banal formulaic mantra is counter-posed
to the primeval revenge battle we have seen Banek spending the day waging with
Doyle Gipson (Samuel L Jackson):

> I believe in the law. I believe in order and justice. I believe that people are by nature good.
> I believe that historical forces push us into conflict. Without the law as a buffer between
> people, we would have a world of vendetta, a world of violence, a world of chaos. The
> law keeps us civilised.

By the end of the film we get an inkling as to why he probably entered the legal
profession. The ending, though, is ambivalent. Gavin is not leaving the corruption

of the world to work in a leper colony. He is, however, doing his bit to rescue some ideals. He rejects his father-in-law's suggestion that, with the forgery accepted by the court, the 'unpleasantness' is behind them:

> I was thinking about what you said to me about doing more good than harm. That's what you said to me … can you imagine how unpleasant it would be if the judge got hold of this file? … I am going to hold onto this file. I am going to keep it in a very safe place. But I'm not going to Texas. I am going to come back into work on Monday and I am going to start doing that pro bono work that you recommended that I do. But I am going to do it from our office. First thing we're going to do is help a man buy a house … then I would like to be the one to call Mina Dunne to tell her that you and Walter are going to give back the $3 million you stole from her grandfather's Foundation.

This, then, is man who has been offered a simple way out of his dilemma, but who opts to take a position that is less secure, but which offers a possibility of redressing the moral balance in his professional life as a Wall Street lawyer.

Chicago (2002)

The wonderful irony of Billy Flynn's opening song identifies him as a man who is in the legal profession for the things he ostensibly rejects—fancy clothes, shiny cars, big cigars. He is only interested in securing justice for his clients. His goal is to pocket as large a cheque—or preferably cash—as the client can scrape together. Without this he is not interested. Unless, of course, there is an even bigger pay-off in terms of publicity. What is so refreshing is the complete contrast between the worthy words of Billy Flynn when we first meet him and the reality of his legal practice. By counter-posing the myth and the reality we are able to fully appreciate a world in which money provides people with an escape plan from the wheels of justice. By being portrayed in cartoon style we know that the values of a true lawyer are indeed how Billy describes them. Switching between his true fancy suit, big car reality and his fantasy poor boy look we hear his fine selfless credo interspersed with his visit to his paying clients:

I don't care about expensive things,

Cashmere coats, diamond rings,

Don't mean a thing

All I care about is love

That's what I'm here for

I don't care for wearing silk cravats,

Ruby studs, satin spats

Don't mean a thing

All I care about is love

Give me two eyes of blue

Softly saying I need you

Let me see her standing there

And honest Mister I'm a millionaire

I don't care for any fine attire

Vanderbilt might admire

No, no not me

All I care about is love

Show me long raven hair

Flowing down, 'bout to there

When I see her running free

Keep your money

That's enough for me

I don't care for driving Packard cars

Or smokin' long buck cigars

No, no not me

All I care about is doing a guy in

Who's picking on you

Twisting the wrist

That's turning the screw

All I care about is love.[1]

Roxie asks if he would represent her. His immediate response is 'Do you have $5,000?'. Despite the lascivious words of the song he is not interested in proffered sexual favours: 'You mean just one thing to me. You call me when you got $5,000.' Billy, though, is not blinkered in making financial calculations and so is able to readily appreciate that Roxie has the potential for good income-generating publicity. This contrast between the words and the actions we see in the courtroom scene where Billy outlines his methods of mesmerising the jury with tricks, explaining to Roxie that 'It's all a circus. A three ring circus. That's all. These trials. The whole world. It's all show business.'

That lawyers may be presented with some judicial assistance is hinted at when Billy leaps to his feet to object. The judge sustains the objection only to

---

[1] Screenplay Bill Condon, Book of Musical Play Bob Fossey & Fred Ebb.

be reminded by the District Attorney that he has not even asked his question. Yet beneath his shameless pursuit of money, Billy is the one who recognises the fragility of celebrity and dissects it best when Roxie discovers that within seconds of being acquitted and being 'the famous Roxie Hart' there is a new even more sensational case around the corner when a woman outside the court shoots her husband and then her lawyer:

> This is Chicago, kid. You can't beat fresh blood on the walls.

By being so shamelessly immoral Billy effectively shows us what the path to being a just lawyer should be.

I Am Sam (2002)

The central thrust of this film is the way in which society is able to adjust to those who do not meet social norms. In *I Am Sam* (2002), Sam (Sean Penn) has the intellectual capacity of a seven year old and sustains supported employment with Starbucks. Faced with his daughter being taken from him due to his inability to look after her he is advised to seek a lawyer. His friends decide the advert of Rothman, Glenn Harrison and Williams in the yellow pages is attractive. Thus he encounters Rita Harrison (Michelle Pfeiffer), a hard-nosed professional with too little time for interaction with her clients, workmates and family. Sam comes to her office in person. She is frank in explaining that Sam cannot afford her rates. We see her immensely stressed and unable to communicate with her son or her therapist. She initially tries to brush off Sam, promising to get someone to act for him. She is not even sufficiently empathetic to do this and it is only the idea of being mocked for not being the kind of person who would contemplate doing *pro bono* that gets her involved in Sam's case. When Sam turns up in at a reception where she is entertaining, she wants to look good in front of her colleagues. Accordingly through Rita's pride, Sam gets a lawyer. She is prepared to fight dirty in court for Sam causing a witness to break down into tears. She uses the concept of 'manipulating the truth' but is unable to get Sam to take this on board.

She interviews a range of Sam's friends with their various emotional and learning problems and comes to appreciate that a person's ability to love has no relationship to their intellectual capacity. When Sam suggests that people like Rita do not feel anything she is moved to a fiery response revealing her insecurities stemming from her unseen errant husband and unresponsive son:

> People like me feel lost, and little and ugly and dispensable. People like me have husbands screwing people more perfect than me. People like me have sons who hate them ... it's like every morning I wake up and I fail.

It would be hard to accuse this film of having a low saccharine count and, of course, Rita is redeemed through her encounter with Sam and his friends. She changes from being single-minded and efficient to being caring and—as far as we can see—still effective. She learns to care less about material success and more about her family—apart from her husband, who moves out. She ultimately becomes a soccer mom, perhaps the ultimate mothering role in North American culture.

The Exorcism of Emily Rose (2005)

When Emily Rose dies after a series of exorcisms the priest involved is charged with negligence resulting in her death. The principal legal figure in this genre offering is Father Richard Moore's lawyer, Erin Bruner (Laura Linney). In order to entice her to take the case, her boss has to dangle the promise of a partnership in front of her. She does not seem, by nature, one with ethical scruples. As she is described at the film's outset as she sits apart from the crowd at the bar finishing some notes: 'There's ambition. She never stops. She even works when she drinks.' Her boss knows how to appeal to her when he asks her to take a difficult case of defending the man whose conduct has led to the death of Emily Rose:

Karl: 'Erin, the Van Hopper case got you back on the fast track. Once again you're a rising star ... I'm saying you do this for me and the rising star keeps rising.'

Erin: 'Just how high do I get to rise this time? I've been junior partner for too long Karl ... I want my name on the door, right next to yours.'

Under no circumstances is the priest to testify, as it is felt by the Church authorities that he could be an embarrassment. Father Moore, on the other hand, is desperate that the world should know what happened to Emily Rose and why. Erin, though, is sufficiently self-confident and morally centred that she agrees to let him testify and works tirelessly on his behalf without being committed to a belief in exorcism. By contrast her adversary, Ethan Thomas (Campbell Scott), differs from the traditional ambitious and even vindictive prosecutors, anxious for conviction and with little concern with the community. He appears to take a simple moral line. He sees his job as simply representing the 'interests of the people'. Although a churchgoer he is prepared to prosecute because the priest broke the law and would make no plea bargain offer of reckless endangerment. Here then are two lawyers who are far from perfect but who embody objectivity and empathy.

Michael Clayton (2007)

The fixer for the New York law firm Michael Clayton is a lawyer with a number of aspects. We know early on that he has a gambling problem, and we learn that he is the 'fixer' in a large, up-market, New York law firm. He knows people. He has contacts. He stops things getting in the papers. We gather from the way he deals with his first assignment that he is sharp and streetwise. He is described by one of the partners as a 'miracle worker'. His own description of himself is self-deprecating:

I am a fixer. I am a bagman. I do everything from shoplifting housewives to bent congressmen ... what do you want? You want a carry permit? A heads-up on an insider trading subpoena?'

Clayton's first appearance is low-key. He advises an important business client who has left the scene of a traffic accident that he would be better off with a local firm representing him. He takes a realistic line indicating the strength of the police case in a hit and run. He describes himself rather as a janitor. The smaller the mess, the easier it is to clean up.

The next assignment we see him undertaking some four days earlier is to sort out the mess caused when the litigator of the firm, Arthur Edens (Tom Wilkinson), suffers some kind of breakdown in the middle of taking evidence. This happens, as we discover, when he finds the opponents have been knowingly poisoning people with their agricultural pesticides and Michael is dispatched to sort this out. In between his assignments we see Michael as a man meeting his obligations in a responsible way. He takes his son to school and is shown having a much more positive relationship than Rita and Billy Williams start off with in *I Am Sam* (2002). He meets the debts of his brother, Timmy Clayton's (David Landsbury), failed restaurant. The character is shown with sufficient depth for us to be less than sure as to what his final play will be. Is he so fed up with what the world has done to his friend Arthur Edens (Tom Wilkinson) and the way his skills have been exploited by lawyers in their firm like Marty Bach (Sidney Pollack) that he will throw it all up and walk away? The audience is unsure of the depth of Michael's commitment to doing the right thing. There is still an element of ambivalence after we discover Clayton has not been seeking to be bought. Instead he is setting up the U-North lawyer to agree to bribe him for his silence. Where does this leave him in his life as he takes off for a taxi-ride to nowhere with no purpose? All we know is that he is, basically, a moral man.

The contrast between Michael and U-North's in-house lawyer, Karen Crowder (Tilda Swinton), is stark. She is a cold professional whose natural manner disguises a ruthless preparation. This in itself merely makes her less than loveable, but does not make her a bad person. It is as a lawyer, though, that we encounter a woman with no apparent redeeming features. She is prepared to sanction the murder of someone who threatens her employer's interests as well as agree to a $10 million bribe to buy Michael Clayton's silence. We would see these as the redeemed and the unredeemed. Michael, though, was living a life in which he accepted responsibility as well as acted in more traditional 'mouthpiece for the mob' style.

Alternative Categorisations

Determining whether the portrayals of lawyers or an individual lawyer is good, bad or indifferent may ultimately merely be a question of surprising subjectivity. What we would argue is that often the portrayal is neither clear, nor obvious, but a far more complex question that involves a host of value judgments. What we can see is a number of common threads or issues that contribute to the portrayal. One important point is that such features are often repeated for a number of reasons, which leads us back to the idea of genre, not least being that the reliance on a formula is a Hollywood tradition. There are a number of law films that often show the central roles with flaws of character or personal unhappiness. Certainly with respect to women, few are shown as happy in their personal lives. The men are also largely unsettled: even Finch is a widower with a less than traditional relationship with his children. Below we explore some of the other potential categorisations.

The Rookie

One of the most obvious dramatic elements, particularly when there is the potential for execution, is the rookie lawyer. This is part of the notion that he must succeed against all odds. Of course coming out of the ordeal will bless him with an even greater knowledge and standing; in this sense many films contain a rite of passage element. In *Young Mr Lincoln* (1939) he (Lincoln) stresses his greenness, and the paucity of Lincoln's legal knowledge is pointed out by his opponent. In *A Time To Kill* (1996), the defence of Carl Lee Hailey is the lawyer's first murder trial, a similar situation to that in *My Cousin Vinny* (1992). Here the defence lawyer, Vinny, is a rookie who has only just passed his exams at the sixth attempt. Jenny Hudson has only ever done traffic law and minor matters before her big murder trial in *Physical Evidence* (1988) and both Kaffee and Gallacher have minimal court experience in *A Few Good Men* (1992). We also have the involvement of non-'qualified' figures such as law students (*The Pelican Brief* (1993), *Legally Blonde* (2001)), a law professor (*Just Cause* 1995) and, perhaps most interestingly, in *Erin Brockovich* (2000), where the leading figure is a 'mere' paralegal. In *Hart's War* (2002) we have a young man with only two years of law school as his background defending a fellow soldier on a murder charge. This perhaps raises an interesting genre point as to whether films without professionally qualified 'lawyers' are law films? We take the view that they conform in all significant respects to our model. In a sense, the lower the status and experience, the greater the end achievement.

Personal Jesus

The lines between domestic and professional lives are often blurred, and the personal problems and angst carried into the case to provide an added dimension that can be explored. As noted above, *Cape Fear*'s Sam Bowden's adultery is in contrast with his protective approach of the original victim. The woman with whom he is having a relationship becomes another area in which Cady can exert pressure as he also does with both mother and daughter. Kathleen Riley (*Suspect*, 1987) castigates herself for not having a relationship outside of her attachment to the law, a problem naturally solved by the case. Galvin (*The Verdict*, 1982) is consumed by alcoholism, barely able to function, and his decline as both a lawyer and a person is noted. There is a sense in which the word 'troubled' is a *sine qua non* for modern lawyers. Some have problems with their children: Sam Bowden (*Cape Fear*, 1991); Rita Harrison (*I Am Sam*, 2002). Problems in relationships are also a common feature from Arthur Kirkland (... *And Justice For All*, 1979) to Rita Harrison (*I Am Sam*, 2002) and Gavin Banek (*Changing Lanes*, 2002).

The Ethical Dilemma

The essence of the cinematic lawyer, as opposed to, for instance, small-screen counterparts like Perry Mason and Ben Matlock, is the ever present issue of their ethical duties. In TV neither Mason nor Matlock was concerned with anything more vital than identifying the real killer in order to free their client. How would the good lawyer act? In some instances the question is simple. An ethical Gavin Banek (*Changing Lanes*, 2002) would not even consider lying to the court. We know that Wendell Rohr (Dustin Hoffman) is a moral man with not only a conscience but ethical standards when he has the opportunity to 'buy' the jury in *Runaway Jury* (2003) and does not do so. Others from Frank Galvin onwards have more problems. Although in *The Verdict* (1982) he ultimately wins, he is rightly upbraided for taking a decision without consulting his client when there was neither pressure of time, nor any other reason, not to put the Church's compensation offer to his clients. Jan Schlichtmann operates in the same way in *A Civil Action* (1998).

Courtroom demeanour and behaviour

An issue which ties into the debate around ethical conduct is the behaviour we see from lawyers both inside and beyond the courtroom. Professional conduct lines may become blurred as the cinematic lawyers seek to achieve a just result and are apt to use a number of devices to advance their cause. In *Suspect* (1987) we see both sides utilising visual devices in their arguments. Charlie Stella (Joe Mantegna) begins the prosecution by walking slowly along in front of the jury tapping a money clip on the front of their seating area. The point he is making concerns the amount of money in the clip – it was the amount of money found on the corpse allegedly murdered by the defendant and Stella asks the jury whether that is all a life is worth today. Kathleen Riley (Cher), too, is not above using such tricks.

When the evidence shows the slit on the corpse's throat, she makes a great play of demonstrating how this would have been conducted, acting this out on the expert witness. Having completed this analysis, at the end of her questioning she throws a ball directly to her client. He instinctively catches this with his left hand—the previous argument had just established that the cut was made by someone holding the blade in the right hand. This scene draws directly upon a similar event in *To Kill a Mockingbird* (1962), when Atticus Finch attempts to draw the jury's attention to the fact that Tom Robinson is unable to use his left hand. The rape victim was also alleging that Tom Robinson had tried to strangle her with his hands around her neck and Finch was indicating that it could not possibly be Robinson as one hand was useless. The odd thing about the way he does this is that he throws the water glass to Robinson, who catches it right handed, and then asks him what would happen if he tried to catch it with his left hand. He does not demonstrate that Robinson could not have caught it left-handed.

These devices are typical in film, and often heavily melodramatic.[2] Occasionally they may be tinged with irony such as when Lincoln produces the evidence, in the form of the Farmer's almanac, magician-like, out of his stovepipe hat. Indeed, Lincoln is perhaps the best example of devious courtroom behaviour. This has a number of effects, including abstracting him from the wider process and illustrating that his intuition, his mythical status, will allow him to ensure that justice is done.[3] He treats the law with something approaching disdain, and is patronising and dismissive of many of the other players in the scenes. That he is prepared to resort to other means to achieve what he wants is illustrated outside the courtroom when he cheats during the tug of war. Inside the courtroom his tactics include ridiculing witnesses and casting aspersions on others. For example, the following exchange takes place during the cross-examination of J Palmer Cass:

Lincoln: 'You say your name's J Palmer Cass?'

Cass: 'Yeah.'

Lincoln: 'What's the J stand for?'

Cass: 'John.'

Lincoln: 'Anybody ever call you Jack?'

Cass: 'Yeah.'

Lincoln: 'Why J Palmer Cass? Why not John P Cass? Anything the matter with John P?'

Cass: 'No.'

Lincoln: 'Has J. Palmer Cass anything to conceal?'

Cass: 'No.'

Lincoln: 'Then what do you part your name in the middle for?'

Cass: 'Well, I got a right to call myself anything I please so long as its my own name.'

Lincoln: 'If it's all the same to you, I'll just call you Jack(c)ass.'

---

[2] Bergman, P (1996a).
[3] Böhnke, M (2001).

On the one hand an aside that many of the people in the courtroom (and the audience) find highly amusing, on the other the sort of bullying and intimidatory tactic that legal procedure would outlaw as unfair to someone appearing as a witness in court. Perhaps, though, our screen lawyers cannot win. We condemn Lincoln for bullying a witness whilst Finch may be criticised for not pursuing Mayella Ewell with sufficient vigour and hostility. We may admire Kathleen Riley (Cher) in *Suspect* (1987) and Vinny Gambini (Joe Pesci) in *My Cousin Vinny* (1992) for their courtroom tactics even though these may be beyond the strict rules of procedure. Perhaps this sums up the problem of classifying our lawyers as good, bad or indifferent; it depends on our subjective view of the character in front of us. This perspective is created for us and we are likely to be conditioned to know which characters we are attached to.

All the above provide other potential categorisations, but we would argue that the good/bad split is the ascendant one, and in fact allows for the nuances of the tension between the seemingly binary poles to be drawn out.

Conclusion

> Lose? I don't lose, I win. I win. I'm a lawyer, that's my job, that's what I do. (Lomax (Keanu Reeves) in *Devil's Advocate* (1997) responding to his father's (Al Pacino) taunt that perhaps it was his time to lose.)

What are we to draw from the different portrayals of lawyers that appear in legal films, and that have been outlined in this and the preceding Chapter? Outside of the problems in determining what law films actually are, the problem is exacerbated by trying to analyse lawyers' characteristics, and how they are shown. There have been some attempts to draw out generalisations concerning a number of films and also how different portrayals have altered during different chronological periods. There is a great danger in trying to search for the definitive screen lawyer. Many have their own attractive cinematic features whether as positive attributes or by displaying human weaknesses. Lincoln and Finch seem lofty and detached when contrasted with the gritty realism of the lives of Erin Brockovich or Frank Galvin. The latter are not less attractive for having to struggle. Similarly when we see the developing relationship between Reggie Love and Dianne Sway we relate to the loss of her children and the void that this has left in her life. The personal dimension draws on our feelings for her as a mother and lawyer.

In many ways it is the blemishes and flaws that give the characters depth and allow them to develop. This struggle within their own lives is mirrored with a struggle with law. Some films may portray blemishes more overtly, such as Galvin (Paul Newman) as the alcoholic ambulance chaser at the beginning of *The Verdict* (1982) and Henry Turner (Harrison Ford) in *Regarding Henry* (1991) and Rusty Sabich (Harrison Ford) in *Presumed Innocent* (1990), who are portrayed as arrogant, selfish and insensitive. Galvin is shown at the beginning of the film sitting in a bar unable to raise his glass to his lips because he is shaking so much. He is scouring the local paper for news of accident deaths so that he can tout for business. Interestingly, the films show a marked shift in their portrayals towards their denouements.

For example, by the end of *The Verdict* (1982), Newman is effectively rehabilitated, drinking coffee and resisting the advances of Charlotte Rampling, his morality and sobriety restored. In *Regarding Henry* (1991) Turner can no longer stomach the idea of being a lawyer and Sabich is moving on to simply be a good father. Turner has discovered that one's identity does not stem solely from one's occupation. Even success against corporate greed and cheating law firms are not enough to keep Rudy Baylor in the legal profession and *The Rainmaker* (1997) ends with him heading off to rural America, probably to teach rather than practise law.

Can we draw any firm conclusions from the films we have viewed about how lawyers are portrayed? Is there any commonality, or can we find different perspectives? There does seem to be a fairly common acceptance that we started with good portrayals and moved into eras of generally darker and more malevolent cinematic lawyers. Much depends on the depth of analysis applied and the standards we apply. Can we expect Atticus Finch to disregard the community and make a more vigorous stand against racism? Is his acceptance of a flawed system of justice a serious personal flaw? What we can say with some certainty is there are some heroic acts performed by lawyers in defence of their clients. Risking disbarment to move the case towards a just conclusion is a common feature and this unselfishness is certainly not a feature of either Finch or Lincoln: neither make much in the way of personal sacrifice nor take risks with their careers. This professional risk taking can be seen in a number of ways: Vinny Gambini lies to the judge about his qualifications whilst Kathryn Murphy goes out on a professional limb in *The Accused* (1988). Kathleen Riley risks her entire career, as do Frank Galvin, Sam Bowden and Reggie Love. Perhaps this is the key to the whole debate: the stakes are higher and the portrayals more realistic in terms of the depth and flaws in the characters. Of course this does not make them truer to the real world but perhaps this is the most fundamental mistake. There is no real point in comparing John Milton (Al Pacino) in *Devil's Advocate* (1997), the satanic lawyer, to the storefront, mall or high street practitioner or indeed any other lawyer. If we are dealing with fictional dramatic characters is there any reason to assume they ought to resemble the real thing? Perhaps we should acknowledge that the law is not largely about capital cases but is about 'parking tickets':

> Popular culture ... is involved with law; and some of the more obvious aspects of law are exceedingly prominent in popular culture. But of course not all of law. No songs have been composed about the Robinson-Pateman Act, no movies about capital gains tax.[4]

---

[4] Friedman, L (1989: 1588).

There is the impossible and arguably an almost pointless task of matching the fictional portrayal of lawyers to the reality and trying to decide whether lawyers are good, bad or indifferent. Importantly they are rarely indifferent, the conventions of legal film require that they are substantial characters even when weak and flawed. Too much work on legal film and the criticism of the professions is concerned with why we have a negative image. This point is itself by no means certain but in any event it really doesn't matter, in terms of relationship to reality, whether lawyers are shown in a good light or not. We, the audience, know that screen lawyers do not exist in the way they are shown; a significant test might be whether we believe *Erin Brockovich* (2000) reflects reality. We certainly don't believe that Joe Pesci in *My Cousin Vinny* (1992) is real, or rooted in reality. What matters for the audience is the contrast between the screen portrayal and the mythical qualities and idealism of law and lawyers as reflected in films. Because of the absence of real-life encounters the benchmark is our popular culture experience in what law should stand for and what we would wish lawyers to be like. It is a contemporary screen presentation married against the history of the representation in popular culture.

It therefore does not matter that we know the cultural construction is false, as it is more about what we believe law and lawyers should be, the ideal of law. This explains why Finch, for example, becomes a role model not because law students can expect to be like the great Atticus Finch but because he is a symbol of the idealism of law. The myth and ideals of law have led to the creation of screen conventions that need to be followed hence the elements of sacrifice by the 'bad' lawyers such as Lomax in *The Devil's Advocate* (1997). Similarly Joe Pesci has to win, otherwise the construction of screen lawyers starts to fail. There is so much more to the cinematic portrayal of lawyers than just good or bad and such categorising only serves to reflect subjective perspectives on what lawyers ought to be like, for example Atticus Finch. The cinema audience is more sophisticated: schooled by genre conventions, lawyers must deliver the myth of law, not the reality, even if it means subverting the negative image they have with some citizens. After all, motivation can be complex, and even neo-Freudian. As one of the most morally driven of the crop of new young lawyers explained at the start of his filmic quest for justice:

> My father hated lawyers. All his life. He wasn't a great guy, my old man. He beat up my mother. He beat me up too. So, you might think I became a lawyer just to piss him off. But you'd be wrong. I wanted to be a lawyer ever since I read about the Civil Rights lawyers in the 50s and 60s and the amazing uses they found for the law. They did what a lot of people thought was the impossible. They gave lawyers a good name.[5]

---

[5] Rudy Baylor at the start of *The Rainmaker* (1997).

9

Missing in Action (I): Judges

This chapter is concerned with something of a mystery. As we have noted in the preceding Chapters, the general thrust of interest in law films has been the criminal trial. Within this we have a concentration on murder trials within the American system. This helps to explain why one of the principal focuses of legal scholarship, the judge, has only a limited role in law films. The judiciary and their doctrinal work, interpreting and developing the meaning of rules, continue to be a focus of much legal scholarship yet this focus has not been meaningfully translated onto film. As we note in the next Chapter the jury are also under-represented, though one reason for the limited role of both can be the role of the audience: the cinematic audience are the effective judge and jury. In terms of cinematic devices, this is manifested in the use of framing patterns, and the relationship between the camera and the viewer-subject:

> The viewer-subject is in the jury box when counsel makes closing remarks, for example, or he is on the witness stand when counsel asks questions that are crucial for the revelation of the truth of the case. In this way, the trial's promise as a cohesive and satisfying process lies in the confluence of these positions as inhabited by the viewer-subject.[1]

It is undoubtedly the case that other actors in the legal process have dominated the cinematic portrayals. Apart from the courtroom personnel, the investigative process has been the subject of detailed treatment by Hollywood and this extends beyond the police to the private eye and amateur sleuths, which we consider in later Chapters.

In terms of the trial movie it is the role of the advocates, and his, or occasionally her, struggle to convince the jury, which has been the central issue in the vast majority of law films. The law film has tended to concentrate on the work of the defence and prosecution lawyer in the murder trial. From *Anatomy of a Murder* (1959) and *Witness for the Prosecution* (1957) to *Presumed Innocent* (1990) through *A Time to Kill* (1996) to *The Exorcism of Emily Rose* (2005), the focus has been remarkably consistent. Judges have received similar treatment to juries, but without even their own *12 Angry Men* (1957) to provide an account of what might be going on behind closed doors. Erin Brockovich provides a brief, enigmatic exception to this practice with the crucial role played by the local district court judge, Leroy J Simmons, in striking out the delaying tactics of the Pacific Gas and Electric Company. He does not, however, explain his decision. He does express

---

[1] Silbey, J (2001: 106–107).

concern on a personal level as a local resident that, far from warning people about the dangers of the toxins being produced, the company positively claimed they were good for people's health.

In this Chapter we look at the limited number of films where judges have been central. In addition, we offer a perspective on what aspects of the judicial role appear in film. The judge is a largely passive observer of the process over which he, and it is almost always he, has limited control, and to which his filmic input is minimal. We examine not only those few films that have detailed coverage of the judge but also a number of films where he has a more minor role. It is possible to look at the peripheral portrayals of the judge, and in the next Chapter the jury, to see whether we can build up some meaningful analysis of the portrayal and answer the question why they attract such little overall attention. Our starting point is the key judicial figure, the judge.

Predominantly, judges play a minor role in the majority of law films where they have an active appearance. They are seldom the focal point of the action. Their portrayal, nonetheless, is important in creating a sense of what potential they have to affect the lives of those before them. Levi suggests a slightly different approach from the one we have adopted, emphasising the style of the screen judge. He suggests that the judge in legal cinema 'goes about his or her duties in one of four distinct ways: strictly and sternly, with folksy charm, wearily or cynically, or sometimes corrupted by greed or other nefarious motivation'.[2] We prefer to look at the extent and nature of the portrayal, which for the most part shows them as rather passive spectators of the action around them.

The Invisible Judge

Although, as indicated above, the judicial role is limited to occasional interventions and to acting as part of the courtroom furniture, they do appear with sufficient frequency to allow for some kind of classification. It is possible to make a rough typology of the various guises in which judges appear in film about legal phenomena. Most of these involve the judge playing a very restrained role in the drama. There are both technical reasons as well as dramatic reasons for this. First, the role of the judge in criminal and civil matters is significantly different. In the absence of the jury, judges are the people who require to be convinced by argument made by counsel before them. They have an active role in clarification of points and intervene during submissions extensively. Theirs is no mere passive observance of the rules of hearsay or relevance, which is their criminal trial function. Yet despite this active function this is often reduced in film to minor points. Even when there are civil law issues under discussion and the judge might be expected to be even more proactive, the judicial input, on film, is almost

---

[2] Levi, RD (2005: 59).

non-existent. In *Erin Brockovich* (2000) we hear that the objections of the alleged polluters about prima facie liability are rejected though the reason why Judge Leroy J Simmons rejects the 84 motions of the Pacific Gas and Electric Company is not clear. They are specious but in what way we do not discover. However, in *A Civil Action* (1998) the judge takes an active role in the proceedings and interrupts the trial, after hearing the technical evidence, to put a number of questions to the jury to see which defendants are to be left in the action. The plaintiffs' counsel, Jan Schlichtmann, fiercely opposes this move and wants the plaintiffs' tragic evidence put before the jury. The judge is determined to proceed with his approach, and protests that it is his plan and not that of the defendants' lawyers. Consequently one of the defendants is ruled not to have contributed to the poisoning of the water supply and is removed from the proceedings. A parallel can be seen with the actions of the judge in *The Verdict* (1982), who is severely irritated by Galvin's failure to settle the action, leading him to become hostile to Galvin.

The essential lack of drama in debates before the bench has led filmmakers to alter the reality to inject an element of human agency into the forensic process. Thus, the changes to the story of *In the Name of the Father* (1993) are necessary to convert a technical 'behind the scenes' assessment of information into the British equivalent of the surprise witness. Since there has been a reticence to explore the judicial decision-making process, we are left with a vacuum that cannot be filled by the competition between different legal principles. This is largely a sterile notion unless duplicity can be introduced as in *Suspect* (1987), *Class Action* (1990) or *Erin Brockovich* (2000). There is even more difference between the role of the judge in the common law and civil law legal systems where the inquisitorial process in the latter militates against the drama of one version of the truth 'winning' and the other being rejected. There is also a limit on the dramatic possibilities of the internal decision-making which occur in a single judge's head. What is required here is the interplay between such decision makers. We do, in fairness, find occasional examples of this kind of ratiocination and these are discussed below. It is, however, very much the exception as for the most part the judge is a mere cipher. As Sundermann expresses it:

> In the pre-1970s era, Judges in films were usually faceless people sitting behind the bench who occasionally nodded sagely when an attorney would ask to approach a witness or introduce a piece of evidence.[3]

It is useful to note at this point the role of the judge in different cultures generally. In the common law tradition the judge is said to be concerned with matters of law rather than fact, although in civil trials the judge additionally takes on the jury function.[4] Civil law traditions differ in that the judge can have a more 'hands on' role, sometimes actually being actively involved in the investigative process.

---

[3] Sundermann, H (2002).

[4] There are examples of criminal trials without juries, such as the Diplock Courts in Northern Ireland, but more recently s44 of the Criminal Justice Act 2003 permits judge-only trials where there is evidence of a danger of jury tampering.

There are some examples of criminal dramas set in a civilian jurisdiction, such as *A Woman's Face* (1941), which again illustrates the issue of the role of the audience as jury.[5] The portrayal of this latter aspect can be seen, for example, in Costa Gavras's *Z* (1968). At the same time, within the common law, there is a debate as to the role that a judge should take within proceedings. Whilst a more traditional black-letter approach would stress the adjudicative role, where the judge must interpret the rules as presented to him, a more realist approach is to consider the role of the judge as being a proactive and creative one.[6] The most visible judge that we see is indeed a civil judge, Michele Bernard Requin, who appears as herself, in *10e chambre – Instants d'audience* (2004), although this is a documentary of the Paris courtroom so lacks any fictional input.

In terms of the traditional idea of judge being arbiter and often non-interventionist, *12 Angry Men* (1957) provides a prominent example, and illustrates the role of the judge as almost secondary or peripheral. He intones the instructions to the jury almost as if he has done this hundreds of times before and wishes he could be home before the thundery weather breaks. In *Witness for the Prosecution* (1957) the judge has a brief comic cameo near the end of the film that highlights the notion that judges may be worth toadying to. The film never makes explicit why this should be, since the only role we observe being undertaken is the introduction of the significant actors, the counsel and the witnesses. In *Inherit the Wind* (1960), the judge, Mel Coffey (Harry Morgan), is limited to overseeing the battle between the fictionalised titans of Matthew Brady, who occupies the William Jennings Bryan role, and Henry Drummond, who to all intents and purposes plays Clarence Darrow. Coffey occupies the sidelines and his most significant decision is to arrange for Drummond to be made a Tennessee Colonel, like his adversary, to prevent greater authority being invested in his opponent.

Perhaps surprisingly, the judicial contribution in *Kramer vs. Kramer* (1979) is restricted to a very occasional 'overruled' and the odd 'sustained'. Even as recently as *Philadelphia* (1993), Judge Garnett (Charles Napier) plays an almost silent part in the proceedings. From these films we could never divine why judges and their thinking might be of interest to legal scholars. They are presented as traffic policemen simply directing the forensic protagonists when to start and when to stop. This refereeing role is confirmed in the trope that emerged from the 1980s. The limited role has been supplemented by the convention that there should be a scene in chambers for the judge to warn the participants that he, or she, will not stand for any grandstanding in the courtroom. We find this in, for example, *Jagged Edge* (1985), *Suspect* (1987), *The Accused* (1988) and *Primal Fear* (1996). They can also be intolerant of delays, such as in *Changing Lanes* (2002).

---

[5] We are grateful to an anonymous reader for the reference to this film.
[6] See, eg, Osborn, G and Sutton, T (1996).

The Corrupt Judge

One issue which has caught the imagination of filmmakers, and screen writers to some degree, has been the notion of corruption at the core of the legal system. The rotten apple in the judicial process, guilty of previous unlawful or unethical actions prior to achieving judicial office, has been a feature of a handful of films in the past 20 years. Sundermann goes so far as to suggest that since the 1970s 'judges often now seem to be portrayed as lazy, corrupt, biased and arrogant'.[7]

In *Suspect* (1987), Judge Matthew Helms (John Mahoney) goes further, and provides the unexpected twist through a past indiscretion which catches up with him just as he has been offered the highest accolade, a position in the Supreme Court. It is the criminal activity of Judge Henry T Fleming (John Forsyth) which finally causes Arthur Kirkland (Al Pacino) to lose any semblance of control in ... *And Justice for All* (1979). Finally in *Presumed Innocent* (1990) it is the malpractice of Judge Larren Lyttle (Paul Winfield) when acting as a prosecutor in the past that provides the key to why the prosecution of Rusty Sabich (Harrison Ford) is pursued so diligently. Whilst, however, these malpractices provide the narrative key to the action and situation in which the main protagonists find themselves, the judges are still no more than ciphers. They have little/nothing to say and their characters are not sketched in.

The notion of a vigilante judiciary was taken up by the big budget *The Star Chamber* (1983). This involves Judge Steven R Hardin (Michael Douglas) joining a group of nine disillusioned judges who have had enough of the system being manipulated by the restrictions on the rules of evidence. They believe that over the years the system has been twisted into something incapable of delivering justice. Everyone looks the other way but the lawyers feel that they must stop the rot and decide to 'review cases' where the 'wrong' decision has been arrived at due to technicalities such as lack of evidence. This is leading to a breakdown of society: 'No-one wants to be held accountable. Well, we're accountable. We're the judges for Christ's sake. We're the law. We let it all happen.'

There is no discussion of the broader issues involved. What we see of the process of the court of last resort does not lend any confidence that their decisions are likely to be much better than those of the much disparaged ordinary courts. When they make a decision an anonymous contract killer carries out the sentence, the notion that death is the only appropriate penalty is not discussed. The film resolves into a race against time for Hardin to ensure that the execution, which has been ordered by the 'court', is not carried out on men who turn out to be innocent. It transpires that they are not the notorious serial child killers since the true perpetrator has been captured.

Subsequently, Judge Timothy Nash (Tom Selleck) in *Broken Trust* (1995) is persuaded to act as decoy for what the FBI suspect is a system of organised

---

[7] Sundermann, H (2002).

corruption within the judiciary. In this film adaptation of William Wood's Court of Honour the principal cause of this corruption centres on the practice of judicial election and the need to be able to finance this process as well as low judicial salaries. There is no question of the judicial process being explicated within the courtroom scenes since the issues that determine the judicial action are motivated by the main theme of financial corruption. We see the throwing out of cases in the absence of evidence that has been 'disappeared' by other corrupt actors in the scenario. Occupying a strange kind of unclear moral position is the judge in *Three Colours Red* (1999), who talks of his own failings and the moral dilemma that he faced when confronted with his wife's lover as an accused. Instead of excusing himself, because of conflict of interest, he explains that he chose to use his position to obtain his revenge.

The Troubled Judge

The judge does appear as a character with worries and concerns about the judicial process in a number of specialist portrayals. The problems of imposing fair and just retribution on a cowed people in *Judgment at Nuremberg* (1961) is essentially seen through the eyes of Dan Haywood (Spencer Tracy) as the judge brought in to preside over the trials of second-level state officials. Often there may be a dilemma that the judge has to attempt to resolve. In *Judgment at Nuremberg* (1961) the protagonist who has to deal with the problems of resolving difficult questions is Judge Haywood, a down to earth and thoughtful character placed in opposition to his antagonist, German judge Ernst Janning (Burt Lancaster). As Shale notes:

> Whether hero or anti-hero, if the movie is to succeed, the audience must find itself able to identify with the protagonist. How? The most compelling invitation to identify oneself with the screen character is offered when the protagonist is forced by the narrative to make hard choices and difficult decisions. This is the moment when the audience recalls the agony of minds we would rather not make up, and are generous with our sympathy for characters who cannot avoid doing so.[8]

Obviously, in cases of this nature, or one where the outcome is potentially severe (often in terms of it being a capital offence where those on trial may lose their lives), it is unsurprising that such deliberations will be pressing and troubling ones. The same device is borrowed in a later, similarly fact-based examination of the problems of the Cold War in *Judgment in Berlin* (1988). Here, we see a simple 'holiday' trip turning into a moral dilemma for a judge attempting to reconcile notions of human rights with his own government's *realpolitik*. It would be stretching meaning too much to describe the unbalanced Judge Rayford (Jack Warden) as a concerned judge. In his relationship with Arthur Kirkland

---

[8] Shale, S (1996: 1001).

(Al Pacino), however, in … *And Justice for All* (1979) we see a combination of personal loss and futility. This has produced neither cynicism nor corruption, in Kirkland's old mentor, but a death wish which he indulges in on a regular basis including flying a helicopter with the minimum of fuel to see whether he will make it back home. He has, however, inspired Arthur sufficiently that he is prepared to fight in the dispiriting trenches that is low-rent petty criminal legal practice.

Judge Dredd (1995) provides a different angle on the troubled judge. After Dredd (Sylvester Stallone) is placed on trial for murder, Chief Justice Fargo cannot believe that he has committed such a crime. In the face of apparently irrefutable forensic evidence, Fargo sits ashen-faced with head in hands. Here his mind is racked with guilt as he had spared Dredd some years ago when Dredd's 'brother' Rico was banished, but now it appears he should have banished Dredd too. Here we have not only the troubled judge, who feels responsible for the situation that has arisen, but also a judge who has the opportunity to make noble sacrifice for his principles. This is notwithstanding the evidence, he cannot believe that Dredd has committed the murder and he is able to save him by giving up his own life. The Long Walk involves a retiring judge walking off into the metaphorical sunset of the 'Cursed Earth', a walk outside of the city to take law to the lawless and certain death. What is apparent here is the seriousness nature of the judicial figure placing his life on the line to save another. This is not often the case, and rather than such a serious aspect of judicial intervention, we are more likely to be confronted by the judge as a figure for humorous exchanges.

The Comic Judge

Judges have adopted a 'larger than life verging on comic' persona on a number of occasions in film. In *First Monday in October* (1981), for instance, one could describe Dan Snow (Walter Matthau) and Ruth Loomis (Jill Clayburgh), portraying the Supreme Court, as a comic interlude. The decision-making range indicated as available to the protagonists in this portrayal is a simple political reductionism between libertarian liberalism and strong state conservatism. The issues in dispute are free speech and economic interventionism and unregulated market economics in relation to the environment. There is a sense of the pair of them lusting after a transformation into Adam and Amanda Bonner from *Adam's Rib* (1949). Even in comedies the judge may be played straight. Thus we find a small but kindly presentation of the judge in the Australian comedy property dispute, *The Castle* (1997). In similar vein Judge Chamberlain Haller (Fred Gwynne) appears as the stickler for procedural accuracy in *My Cousin Vinny* (1992), whilst giving no hint that he is concerned at the extreme thinness of the evidence presented in a contemporary capital murder case. Here the judge is comedic in a very ironic way; we laugh at the idea that the judicial system should be so concerned with the minutiae of information, and that apparently procedure might come before the truth. The judge's seriousness and of course the solemnity of the law in *My Cousin Vinny* (1992) provides the perfect foil for the comedy performance of Vinny (Joe Pesci). This provides a counterpoint to Lincoln's admonishment of prosecuting counsel in *Young Mr Lincoln* (1939) to the effect that he may not be knowledgeable about the intricacies of the law but, more importantly, he knows what is right and wrong.

Judge Haller could also, in some ways, be seen as akin to the British style with judges portrayed as doddering old fools whose wigs confer some kind of invincibility on them—*Witness for the Prosecution* (1957), *Brothers in Law* (1957) and *A Pair of Briefs* (1962). Being a judge is carte blanche to act in a rude and eccentric way; certainly the interchanges between Thursby (Ian Carmichael) and the various judges in *Brothers in Law* (1957) illustrate this comic interplay well. Initially he appears in a Chancery case before a judge whom he has previously encountered on the golf course. He is made to appear incompetent and is given no leeway by the judge; as a consequence he loses the easy case and is embarrassed in front of his prospective father-in-law. An interesting twist on the comedic judge theme is seen in the film made from the play by Rumpole's creator, John Mortimer, *Trial and Error* (1962). Here Morgenhall (Peter Sellers) persuades his client Fowle (Richard Attenborough), in a fantasy scene, to pretend to be the judge trying him. Fowle does this, and is cajoled into adopting the persona of the stern judge, ultimately allowing him to go free and 'sentencing' all the policemen in court to be reduced to the rank of Police Constable.

The Political Judge

There is of course one major exception to these fictional judges and that is the portrayal of the whole Supreme Court in the made-for-TV movie *Separate but Equal* (1991). Here, drawing on the *Brown v Board of Education* decision in 1954, we see the legal work of the court as a series of policy meetings with arm-twisting and politicking between the judges as the essence of the judicial work process. In its way *First Monday in October* (1981) hints at this with the discussion of the First Amendment between the fictional Supreme Court justices Ruth Loomis and Dan Snow, before it shifts into a romantic mystery. This debate between the advocate of community standards and of free speech lasts for some five minutes. It bears hallmarks of being a cut-down version of a full scene in the Broadway play on which it was based. In *Amistad* (1997), we see a judge chosen for political reasons, put forward as a pawn by Martin Van Buren (Nigel Hawthorne), the president of the USA, thinking that he would be sympathetic to the governmental line. This ploy stems from the perceived threats to Van Buren's re-election hopes. Here the ploy backfires as the judge is not as compliant as it was thought he would be. In *The Rainmaker* (1997) the spectre of judicial prejudice and partiality is raised by the actions of Judge Harvey Hale (Dean Stockwell). He is reputed to be a defenders' lawyer and in the pockets of the rich and powerful and their law firms. His precise impact can only be surmised since he dies before the trial and is replaced by a scrupulously fair new judge, Judge Tyrone Kippler (Danny Glover). Coming from the ranks of prosecuting authorities he is determined not to allow the size and prestige of the law firm determine the conduct of the litigation.

An interesting example of the link between judges and the wider political process can be seen with the closing scenes of *In the Name of the Father* (1993). The 'narrative' of the film is detailed elsewhere, but it is the final freeing of the wrongly imprisoned where we see some interaction between the Crown barristers, the Appeal Court judge and a shadowy figure who appears in the public gallery. The defendant's barrister has produced the 'smoking gun' evidence that appears to exonerate the imprisoned. The missing statement that Gareth Peirce (Emma Thompson) has discovered, which provides an alibi for Gerry Conlon, is taken to the shadowy figure in the public gallery who makes a decision not to pursue the Crown's case. This is conveyed through the barristers to the judge, who dismisses the case against each of the four in turn to tumultuous scenes. There is a clear link between the executive and the judiciary and the judge is clearly aware of the figure in the public gallery as he glances towards him when he reads the statement. However, he tries to reassert the independence of the court and save the battered reputation of the English legal system.

The link of the judge to politics also appears, briefly, in *The Client* (1994). Roy Foltrigg (Tommy Lee-Jones) is the ambitious political figure who expects to get his way even in the courtroom. Harry Roosevelt (Ossie Davis) clearly knows Reggie Love (Susan Sarandon) and makes it fundamentally clear who is in charge of the court proceedings that have been brought to force Mark Sway (Brad Renfro) to testify. Roosevelt dismisses an armed police officer and throws out a journalist who has been reporting the case in a sensationalist manner. He then lays down the rules to Foltrigg and his entourage.

The closing scenes of *The Hurricane* (1999) best illustrate the interplay between politics and judicial activities. There are a number of tactical problems facing the defence team when they have discovered new evidence that shows that Rubin Carter (Denzel Washington) is innocent of the murders for which he has served over 20 years. According to the procedural rules new evidence must be submitted to the original trial judge, no doubt on the basis that he is familiar with the case and it should then be treated expeditiously. Carter makes it clear to his legal team that he doesn't trust the legal system in the state of New Jersey and he wants to take the risk of going to the Federal Court. He is less concerned with procedure than justice, observing that it is time to 'transcend the law' and 'get back to humanity'. This argument is repeated in court when the judge makes it clear to Carter's legal team that they are pursuing a risky strategy is trying to introduce the material. As the argument about the admissibility of the evidence rages, the New Jersey prosecutors argue: 'Your Honor must, according to the law, drop his entire petition where it belongs, in the garbage.' As the debate draws to a close Carter rises to make a personal address to Sarokin (Rod Steiger):

> Don't turn away from the truth. Don't turn away from your conscience. Please don't ignore the law, embrace that higher principle for which the law was meant to serve, justice, all I ask for is justice.

Sarokin, after a recess, is prepared to overlook the strict legal procedures that require him to refuse to consider the evidence and remit the case to the state court in search of a higher ideal, to get Carter justice. Sarokin is an interesting judicial figure. His role, in terms of the time he takes up in the film, is extremely minimal, yet he is one of the most important characters. When we see how Carter has been treated by the legal system throughout it would not have been surprising if the judge had blindly followed the strict legal procedure and rejected the evidence. Sarokin is a quiet though determined figure who is shown as someone more concerned with justice than legal niceties. He doesn't impose himself on the proceedings—this is perhaps not possible given the length of his appearance—yet his calmness is reassuring. A quiet and small but monumental part in righting a terrible injustice.

Judges as Protagonists—the Judge under the Spotlight

Although the norm is that the judge has a limited role, there have been a few instances where, instead of simply the words and actions of the advocates, we get to see and more importantly hear the active participation of the judge in the process. There are a number of distinct approaches where the judge's role in the process has been portrayed. Again a range of styles emerges from this handful of attempts to essay a glimpse into the judicial mind. Thus we find the judge as pragmatic solver of problems in John Ford's *Judge Priest* (1934) (and its post-war remake *The Sun Shines Bright* (1953)) and as earnest seeker after the proper course of action in *Judgment at Nuremberg* (1961) and the subsequent sober *Judgment in Berlin* (1988). We also discuss an alternative to these two styles in *The Life and Times of Judge Roy Bean* (1972).

As we have noted above, in the vast majority of 'legal films' judges do little more than keep the action going and are seldom featured as crucial actors in the drama. It is essential that the plot flows steadily forwards and in this respect the traditional role of the judge is to direct the action from behind the scenes. More significantly we see almost nothing of the process of decision-making. This remains a mystery. The type of factors that might play a part in this process have been left largely unexplored. The legal process is presented as an essentially rhetorical process in which the most persuasive arguments on the day determine the outcome. Verbal forensic skill is the key factor. There is, perhaps unsurprisingly, little to guide one as to how decisions are reached. Whilst this is true looking at the evidence there are a small number of films where judges have occupied a foreground position. These allow one to examine the judge rather than the prosecutor, defence lawyer or accused. Here we examine five films where judges have played a more active role. The films span six decades and given their unusual nature no general trends or genre features obviously emerge. They include three comedy dramas and two more serious essays. The films are no mere quirks but feature three of the major directorial figures from Hollywood: John Ford (twice), Stanley Kramer and John Huston. Three distinct approaches have been identified in the films where judges have figured as protagonists.

The Judge as Pragmatic Solver of Problems

John Ford directed two films using a Southern Circuit court judge, William Pitman Priest, as the protagonist. The first, *Judge Priest* (1934), is part of a trilogy of Will Rogers vehicles directed by John Ford for Fox in the early 1930s. It was based on stories of Irvin S Cobb first published in 1920. The setting is Fairfield, Kentucky in 1890. The film is prefaced by a note from Cobb indicating that in his short stories he was seeking to evoke 'familiar ghosts of my own boyhood ... the tolerance of the day and the wisdom of that almost vanished generation'.

The publicity material suggested that in the film offering there were 'enough laughs to make your head spin'.[9] The film consists of personal and professional problems for the judge. Out of the court room he is keen that his sister-in-law's matrimonial plans for his young lawyer nephew, Jerome (known as Rome, played by Tom Brown) should not come to fruition. He is keen to support the claims of his next-door neighbour, a schoolteacher with no proper family background. He is also exercised by the question of being re-elected against prosecutor Maydew (Berton Churchill). In his day-to-day work he has two legal matters to look at. First there is the charge against a young black man, Jeff (Steppin Fetchit), who is new to the area. He has been charged with loitering and chicken stealing by Priest's officious political opponent, Maydew. Jeff is apparently acquitted of this charge since he and the judge are seen at the end of the trial going off fishing together. Billy Priest (Will Rogers) cuts an interesting figure as a judge seeking re-election. He reads the newspaper whilst being addressed by Maydew. He engages in irrelevant debates with old friends about half-remembered incidents from the Civil War with his cronies in the courtroom during court business. He appears to decide in favour of an accused on the basis that his unsupported alibi might well be correct because he has a novel method of catching catfish. It is not immediately clear why we should feel that anything is safe in his hands.

The personal and the political become intertwined in connection with his nephew's love life. The apparently comic romancing of Ellie May Gillespie (Anita Louise) turns rather darker or more sombre when her other suitor is wounded in a poolroom brawl. This leads to a trial of the mysterious recluse Bob Gillis (David Landau). Judge Priest's impartiality is challenged on the basis of his antipathy towards the injured suitor. He steps down from the bench for the trial and duly becomes co-counsel for the defence. The glowing character testimony for the

---

[9] Halliwell, L (2008).

accused from the local preacher saves the day. He is acquitted by a jury fuelled by the vigorous playing outside the court of Dixie. It transpires that the accused is none other than the father of the orphan Ellie May. As an insight into the judicial process, however, little can be gleaned. The film is principally of interest as an early example of the work of director, John Ford.

The Sun Shines Bright (1953) is a revisiting of the work of Cobb and the doughty character of Billy Priest (Charles Winninger). It is sometimes described, misleadingly, as a remake which is not entirely accurate. The main figures and the location are the same but much is different. The second version is based on three of Cobb's stories: 'The Sun Shines Bright', 'The Mob from Massac' and 'The Lord Provides'.[10] It is both more comic than Judge Priest and yet looks at much more serious issues. It was one of two or three John Ford pictures that Gallacher suggests are his finest. It was certainly one of which Ford was proud. He explained to Kennedy: 'Maybe there's one that I love to look at again and again. That's *The Sun Shines Bright*. That's really my favorite … it was just a good picture.'[11]

Denied a New York first run, its performance at the box office was poor and the studio cut it from 90 to 65 minutes after initial reviews.[12] Critically it received some kind words from Lindsay Anderson at the time for its 'passages of quite remarkable poetic feeling' and was described by him as being 'alive with affection and truthful observation'.[13] This time it is 1905, although the setting is still Fairfield, Kentucky, and we are presented with a town 'fraught with divisions'. There is a Southern faction holding on to the glories of the United Confederacy veterans who are counterposed with a Northern faction maintaining the traditions of the Grand Republican Army.

In this complex context Judge Priest has three major incidents calling for the judge's intervention. The courtroom is a scene for the divisions to be personal and institutional politics. The judge is a Southern Democrat whose morning routine is to have a reveille recalling his days as a bugler in the Civil War in the Kentucky regiment. His political opponent, Horace Maydew (Milburn Stone) is standing in the upcoming election as judge. He is the local public prosecutor, a member of the Republican Party. Billy Priest's first task is how to deal with an itinerant banjoist, US Grant Woodford (Elzie Emanuel), accused of vagrancy. Billy shows he is no casual racist and disposes of the case by recommending the young man follow his uncle's advice and get steady paid work in the cotton fields. Nor is Billy morally censorious of fellow citizens. In the same session Judge Priest treats the town madame, Mallie Cramp (Eve March), with dignity although the charge is not made clear, nor its resolution.

These decisions are reached, it seems, on grounds of a personal sense of what is right and wrong. Gallagher suggests that Billy is 'a Fordian hero who mediates

---

[10] Gallagher, T. (1986).
[11] 'Burt Kennedy Interviews Ford', *Action*, August 1968 quoted in Gallagher, T (1986: 284).
[12] The version available on video has been restored to its original length.
[13] Halliwell, L (2008).

community tensions, searching for a middle way between chaos and repression'.[14] However, it is possible to characterise these two forensic encounters as much more a search for a personalised, albeit pragmatic notion of justice. There is a contrast between the flowery and pompous blustering of the representative of the law, Maydew, and the pithy common sense of the representative of justice, Priest. The reasons for rejecting a custodial sentence seem to be the ability of the accused to play Dixie on his banjo. This is complemented by the judge's knowledge that there is work for idle hands picking cotton in the Tornado district. Interwoven with the legal business is the return of two crucial characters—a dying woman gets off the paddle steamer and asks to be directed to the local bordello before collapsing terminally ill. By the same transport Ashby Corwin (John Russell) arrives. He is an unspecified 'bad apple' of good family who develops a romantic attachment to Lucy Lee Lake (Arleen Whelan), the neighbour of Billy for whom Billy has an avuncular concern. He has a rival in love, the unsavoury Buck. The action is principally concerned outwith the courtroom with the election campaign and the meetings of the rival factions. This conflict is interrupted by a rape in the infamous Tornado District. Bloodhounds, the only animal whose 'evidence' is accepted in court in the United States, 'tree' the banjo player.

He is arrested and placed in custody in the town jail. A lynch mob is on its way. Borrowing from Ford's earlier *Young Mr Lincoln* (1939) and predating the similar scene in *To Kill a Mockingbird* (1962) Billy stands guard on his black prisoner, the luckless US Grant Woodford, in front of the jailhouse. He confronts a band of ignorant tough farmers from the Tornado District. They are bent on lynching the itinerant banjoist. Wisely Billy is armed and threatens the mob that whilst he may be overpowered, he can guarantee that their leader, Buck will go first. Buck loses his courage and the mob disperses. Despite dark muttering Billy's bravery is recognised and he is duly re-elected with the would-be lynch mob voting for him. Their placard reads 'He saved us from ourselves'.

There is a wealth of interesting detail in these two films about the culture of the South and how it faced up to reconstruction and beyond. There are also implications for those who are interested in the operation of an elected judiciary. The fictional work of Cobb and its representation in film provides the basic framework for Ford's work. Twenty years separate the two versions of the Judge Priest stories that contain Cobb's essential judicial character. The first is by a young contract director of the 1930s. His reputation had been cemented by films from the late 1930s such as *Stagecoach* (1939), *The Grapes of Wrath* (1940) and *How Green Was My Valley* (1941). By the time *The Sun Shines Bright* was released in 1953, he had become an independent and much respected figure although it has been suggested that by the mid-1950s his career was in decline.[15] It is not clear in what sense this can be said given the critical acclaim accorded to *She Wore a Yellow Ribbon* (1949), *Rio Grande* (1950) and *The Quiet Man* (1952) and the box

---

[14] Gallagher, T (1986: 287).
[15] Caughie, J (1981).

office figures of both these and his other films of the period like *What Price Glory* (1952) and *Mogambo* (1954).

The notion of judging and the function of the judge, espoused in the Ford films, sees the legal process as a way of getting people to rub along tolerably well together but with a moral basis. The canvas and scale are local. Law is seen as a living system serving the day-to-day needs of ordinary people—not just those who have the reins of law in their hands. This was very much the impression given in *Young Mr Lincoln* (1939). The credo is not, however, simply compromise for its own sake. Billy Priest is prepared to take the consequences of his notion of justice and even accept it philosophically when the formal legal process has been usefully superseded by action. When mountain man Brother Feeney (Francis Ford) shoots the escaping rapist, Priest comments philosophically 'Good Shootin! Saves the expense of a trial.'[16] This notion of the conflict between the source of law as being from some recognised lawgiver as opposed to emanating from the community and expressing community justice is a theme which has been further explored in the context myth across a range of John Ford's work.[17]

The Judge as Earnest Seeker after the Proper Course of Action

A much more serious kind of portrayal is encountered in two later political trial films set in Germany. Here we see judges embroiled in politically sensitive work that is of global import. We gain some sort of insight into their thinking about the issues confronting them.

Judgment at Nuremberg (1961) fits firmly into the serious film themes that Stanley Kramer tackled over his career. These ranged from moral bankruptcy and cowardice to racism and illiberal bigotry. The titles are a list of mainly serious issues alongside the occasional foray into comedy (*It's a Mad, Mad, Mad, Mad World* (1963), *The Secret of Santa Vittoria* (1969). They include early films he produced such as *Death of a Salesman* (1950), *High Noon* (1952) and *The Caine Mutiny* (1954) as well as those he both produced and directed like *On the Beach* (1959), *Inherit the Wind* (1960), *Ship of Fools* (1965) and *Guess Who's Coming to Dinner* (1967).

Kramer felt his work could be summed up in a single idea expressed by Spencer Tracy in the film and which he liked to think his films encouraged people to think about: 'This, then, is what we stand for: truth, justice, and the value of a single human being.'[18] In *Judgment at Nuremberg* (1961) Stanley Kramer has Dan Haywood as the 'everyman' figure confronting the moral issue of the defence of

---

[16] Gallagher, T (1986: 287).

[17] Böhnke, M (2001).

[18] The same notion of the judge being set up to provide a solution to a political problem is encountered in a TV movie in 1990. In *Incident in a Small Town* local judge Harry Morgan is disconcerted to discover that he has been assigned to hear a murder charge against German POWs because he is expected to be a pliant judge for the prosecution. There was a subsequent film with the defence attorney, Walter Matthau, and Morgan capitalising on their roles as two trusty old fighters for justice: *Justifiable Homicide* (1994).

superior orders. Here, interestingly, this debate is located within the role of the judiciary itself. Based on a screenplay by Abby Mann, it is very much a filmed play with the outdoor scenes of very limited significance. Although, at more than three hours running time, this is not a cursory glance at the question of superior orders, the contribution of the judiciary is restricted. Haywood, the War Crimes Panel Chairman, spends a great deal of time looking anguished and inwardly eaten up by the context of the trial in post-war Germany. Much of the film is given over to the presentation of the evidence of a number of 'star' witnesses. The accused German judges spend a limited amount of time in verbal communication before the camera. The principal judge whose role is most complex, Ernst Janning, does not actually speak until some two and a half hours of the film have passed. The very special circumstances of Nuremberg are familiar and most attention has been given to the trials of the major Nazi politicians and German military leaders. Kramer takes the treatment of lower-level state functionaries and examines their moral and legal responsibilities. This was based on a series of real trials of 10 judges, in 1947, by the United States Military Tribunal.[19]

Echoing themes in the fascinatingly prescient wartime film *None Shall Escape* (1944), the film explores the notion of personal responsibility within a bureaucratic hierarchy. What is interesting is that the film looks at the role of judges in enforcing laws. The film attempts to build a picture of one of three judges' arrival at Nuremberg and his reactions to the problematic social relations he sees around him. It seeks to contextualise his actions and decisions which he is called upon to judge. There is, however, surprisingly little actual articulation by Haywood of his ratiocinations. He does ask his other judges about the whole notion of absolution under the legal positivist notion of acting 'lawfully' under an immoral regime, and the role of the judge and some of the difficulties that may be encountered.

There is a link to the role of judges under the Nazi regime in a rather less powerful film, *Judgment in Berlin* (1988). Martin Sheen portrays an ambitious Jewish Federal US judge, Herbert Stern, with a moral dilemma. His problem is that at an early stage in a novel assignment to Berlin he realises that he has been selected to reach a politically convenient decision that will suit both the United States and East Germany. Placards outside the hearing cast doubt on whether he will judge by proper standards. His initial naive assumption was that this assignment would provide a brief chance to have a 'second honeymoon' with his wife, as well as being good for his chances of elevation to the Supreme Court. It soon becomes apparent, however, that he is a pawn in the backstairs political arrangements between the United States and East Germany to try people for escaping from East Germany. The complication is the recently signed International Convention on Hijacking of aeroplanes. To support such actions by not criminalising them is to encourage terrorism. This tale from the early 1970s is based on a book by the judge who had to decide the issue, Herbert J Stern. It stemmed from the

---

[19] Shale, S (1996).

skyjacking, to Berlin Tempelhof, of an aeroplane on an internal Polish flight. The conflict is between the individual and the state. Whilst for the most part the arguments are put in the mouths of the counsel in the case, Stern does discuss his dilemma with his wife and clerk:

> They want me to be a good little boy and follow the Fuhrer's orders and the rule that the defendants in my court are no more than an extension of foreign policy. They want me to be a goddamn Nazi judge.

Stern builds on this link back to the Nazi era by suggesting one effective way out of the impasse: 'I am going to do what those German judges should have done in 1934. I am going to resign. They can get someone else to do their dirty work.' Is justice, then, achieved by serving the higher good of the nation state? How does the notion of due process relate to the integral purpose of the law? The benefits to the larger community are weighed against those of the individual in this scenario. The subtle political problem is that as an occupying power the United States sends out a dangerous signal by allowing the conquered to judge themselves in divided Berlin. This theme is not explored at any length. It is reduced to the emotional symbolism of using a jury to supplement a professional judge.

Stern accepts the notion of an individual's fundamental constitutional right to a trial by a jury of his peers. Since this consists, in this instance, of 12 West Berliners, he is, in effect, opting to acquit the hijacker. The resolution of the issue between due process and the problem of international terrorism is not addressed except in the broadest terms and the privileging of due process is only baldly articulated. Stern's conclusion is to exalt the values of due process 'while this flag stands in the courtroom'...'My sole responsibility is to uphold my oath to the Constitution and not to any Government policies or personal causes.'

What animated this preference remains unclear, at least in the film version, given the finely weighted interests of individuals to both enjoy fair trials and be free from fear when travelling, although Stern does suggest that he has weighed these matters before coming to his decision. In carrying out his duty to honour their judgment that the hijacker was not guilty of the charges of hijacking, depriving persons of their liberty, doing bodily injury and illegal possession of a firearm, he was guilty of taking a hostage. He inveighed against the prosecuting counsel who sought a four-year sentence—which would be served, presumably, under the Treaty back in the communist bloc:

> They tried to tell this judge how he must rule. They placed themselves above the law and tried to turn this court into a charade ... I am left to wonder who would be here to protect [the accused]'s rights if I did give him four years because I believe it when you say he has no rights and there is no limit to your powers. I am also left to wonder if this city needs another judge who follows orders.

With that ringing rejection of the binding nature of the Treaty he opts to sentence the accused to 'time served' and he is freed. It is perhaps no coincidence that one other film where a judge plays a central role involved a real-life drama of equally profound political and social significance. In the TV movie *Judge Horton and the Scottsboro Boys* (1976) we see the judge dealing with an ethical dilemma of how to deal with information about the alleged victims of the accused. First there is the problem of controversial medical evidence that a doctor will not give in open court but discloses to the judge. Then there is the issue of what to do when the jury convict on the evidence they actually hear. He is prepared to sacrifice his career in granting the motion for a new trial.

The Judge as Enforcer of the Letter of the Law

By way of contrast to these comic and serious portrayals, John Huston's sprawling *The Life and Times of Judge Roy Bean* (1972) seems to offer a rather different perspective. This portrayal of the semi-reformed outlaw, Roy Bean (Paul Newman), provides an oblique critique of the political and social source of the judging function. Judge Roy Bean explains his law enforcement philosophy to the Reverend LaSalle (Anthony Perkins) early in the film thus: 'I want peace—and I don't care who I kill to get it.'[20] Almost hidden beneath layers of genre tribute and irony Huston makes telling points about the transience and temporal nature of something as solid and seemingly permanent as state power. In the settlement west of the Pecos where Roy Bean takes control there is no state. This is not unusual within the Western. The sheriff being called in from outside or the unwilling citizen being morally press-ganged into acting on behalf of civil society and paving the way for the local state is a staple in the diet of Westerns. There is a difference here, however. Huston's hero never really comes to terms with the notion that there is an external authority. The law and order he creates is autochthonous, as Bean explains when describing the personal source of his authority to the Reverend LaSalle:

Bean, Judge Roy Bean. I am the new law in this area.

What has qualified you as such?

I know the law since I have spent my entire life in its flagrant disregard.

In *Judge Roy Bean* (1972) Huston takes a chaotic-looking lengthy examination at the myth of the creation of the West. The film sees Bean bushwhacked by the occupants of an out-of-the way country saloon/bordello at the start of the film. They steal from him his goods, and subsequently seek to kill him by attaching him by a long rope behind a horse and sending this off into the countryside. This is a cruel rather than teasing ploy. Fate intervenes in the shape of the rope attaching him to horse breaking and Bean survives with the help of a Mexican woman, Maria Elena, played by a young Victoria Principal. His takes his revenge on his tormentors leaving a dozen corpses scattered around the saloon. Having disposed of the previous

[20] Quoted in Halliwell, L (2008).

owners of the saloon he takes to running it by his own rules. His attitude is one of strong 'order' aided by a dash of symbolic law in the form of a volume of the criminal statutes of Texas that he finds in the saloon. The source of his authority over the land, which the Mexican workers do not want, neatly subverts the convention of property ownership as the prize for physical occupation: 'You mean I own everything if I do all the getting shot at?' He is aided in this enterprise by a gang who offer their services as Deputies to help develop the effectiveness of Vinegaroon. They have come to the area after failing in their most recent attempts to rob the Three Rivers Flyer when the passengers shot back at them 'for sport'. Bean is pragmatic in his treatment of these outlaws and it seems doubtful initially whether he is serious in his plans to maintain a form of 'Law West of the Pecos' as the sign over the saloon reads: 'Ordinarily I'd take you in my court and try you and hang you. But if you've got money for whiskey we can dispense with those proceedings.'

When, however, asked whether he did much 'judging' he points out that he has 'a whole graveyard of previous cases'. We soon see this is more than an idle boast when a fugitive is brought in by the new Deputies: 'Do you have anything to say before we find you guilty?' In addition to the copy of the Texas Criminal Statutes mentioned above he and his Deputies swear allegiance to two ideals. One is the State of Texas, which is notable by its absence in any concrete form. The other which is at least present in picture form is the 'spirit of Lily Langtry', the actress mistress of Prince Edward with whom Bean is besotted.[21] With these as guides he is able to construct a quixotic form of justice. This is, however, not some kind of despotic Khadi justice. It is harsh but it is consistent. Huston portrays the task of applying the simple rules of living in Vinegaroon as involving elements of common-sense social engineering,[22] occasional personal whims,[23] and hints of venality as a process of social improvement without pretensions. To the suggestion that there is no formal provision covering a crime Bean explains the centrality of justice in his scheme: 'Trust in my judgment of the book. Besides you're going to get a hangin' whatever it says in that book because I am the law. And law is the handmaiden of justice.'

Once the town develops there is a challenge to Bean's simple approach to justice. This comes, however, from outside in the person of Roddy McDowall's weasel-like lawyer, Gass. Initially he is persuaded by the brute force of Newman's pet bear to abandon his formal legal claim to the town. He accepts the offer of a share in the profits of the legal enterprise that involves persuading criminals to offer up their ill-gotten gain as an alternative to the widespread death penalty.[24] He is able to take advantage of the rifts between Bean and the socially aspiring

---

[21] Like the State of Texas, Jersey Lily does make a fleeting appearance at the end of the film.

[22] Bean remarks that their success was partly attributable to the fact that outlaws arriving west of the Pecos mistakenly assume there is no law operating there—a fact they rapidly learn is not true.

[23] Snake River Rufus Kile is shot for drilling a bullet-hole in a large poster of Lily Langtry—and then fined for lying about the place as he lies a corpse on the floor.

[24] This had a policy pedigree in Saxon law in England in the 8th century. It is now a standard part of formal state practice in Britain and elsewhere with forfeiture of goods gained through crime and compensation to the victims.

wives of his Deputies when Bean's Mexican helpmeet becomes pregnant. When she dies in childbirth Bean ups and leaves and the way is open for the formal replacement of Bean's personally created legal fiefdom:

> Lawyer Gass—he took over and with a carpetbag full of papers he was able to steal the same land that the judge had wrested from the devil with a gun and a rope—civilisation.

With Bean gone the town develops into the kind of dystopian vision of the money-dominated society encountered in Bedford Falls (*It's a Wonderful Life* (1946) until challenged by Bean's daughter. The other memorable features of the film serve to give the film its rambling incoherent reputation—the pursuit of the Lily Langtry cult in the town; the parody of the 'raindrops sequence' from Newman's earlier film, *Butch Cassidy and the Sundance Kid* (1969) with a saccharine Andy Williams song; the magical realist moment when director Huston himself appears as an itinerant and dumps a bear in the town before heading off into the night. Nonetheless, overlaid as the first half of the film is by these other plot and stylistic developments, it remains a fascinating insight into the relationship between law and community and a telling illustration of the potential of Weber's ideal type of informal irrational justice.

All these films provide a refreshing opportunity for those concerned with explicating the legal process to consider law's fundamental purpose in very different historical contexts. They illustrate that, whilst the judicial role remains a cinematic 'cool zone', it has been possible to feature the judicial process in quite distinctive ways. By locating the decision making as the core of the film within its full social and political context it promises to reveal the triggers for decision-making. It seems, however, that exposing the final sacerdotal moment of judging from the mysterious world it has enjoyed in the past is a step too far for filmmakers. No doubt many lawyers are grateful for this restraint. There may have been a shift to providing fuller reasons for decisions in the 20th century with longer and longer judgments in Anglo-American jurisprudence and an expansion of socio-legal perspectives, but these remain post-hoc justifications. Thus we find that in the films examined here the context is supplied within which decisions can be located. The alternatives and dangers of various courses of action are sometimes explored. There is, however, little to distinguish how Billy Priest, Roy Bean and the judges in the German trials came to their decisions. They opt for what they opt for because that is what they opt for. It can be reduced to values such as 'truth, justice and the value of a single human being' or 'the Constitution'. These are so imprecise, however, that the decisions made in their name threaten to become indistinguishable from 'the public interest' or 'the common good'. On the evidence available, how such a choice is reached, significant or not, remains beyond the realm of the filmmaker. This may be inevitable as one eminent British judge claimed it was sometimes impossible for decision makers to do anything other than simply state their conclusion:

> in the very nature of things reasons, in the scientific sense, are not possible in such an instance [on fair rent fixing]. It is worth remembering that valuation is not a science: it is an art. There will be many, many cases where all the assessment panel can

do is to say, 'Doing our best with the information provided, we think the rent should be £x'.[25]

This seems to be where post-apocalyptic courts are heading in some versions of the future—certainly *Judge Dredd* (1995) shows how notions of the courtroom can be depicted in a different sense and the role of the judge is portrayed as far more wide-ranging and powerful.

---

[25] *Guppy's Properties v Knott (No 1)* [1978] EGD 255 at 259.

10

Missing in Action (II): Juries

A s with judges, juries have had limited cinematic exposure. However, one of the classic law films is *12 Angry Men* (1957), which is almost entirely set in the jury room. There are also a number of other films where juries, or sometimes individual jurors, have a prominent role to play. In terms of general characteristics, there are two broad issues within the jury film. First, the selection and process stage and, second, the deliberation phase. *12 Angry Men* (1957), for example, concentrates entirely on the latter deliberation phase, as the jury is already in place at the commencement of the film. Aside from these two themes it is possible to identify one further role for the cinematic jury that interestingly appears in those films based around civil law disputes with respect to the determination of damages. After *12 Angry Men* (1957) perhaps one of the high points of the cinematic jury is to be found in *The Verdict* (1982), although the role that the jury occupies is insignificant in terms of the period of time its deliberations occupy. A further example of a jury acting independently contrary to legal 'principles' can be seen in *A Time To Kill* (1996). Carl Lee admits to killing the two men who had assaulted his daughter, and seriously injuring a police officer, so his defence prospects are somewhat limited. The vast majority of law films concentrate on the criminal trial with a serious offence at the centre, though there are examples of civil disputes where the jury have a different role from determining innocence or guilt, termed the compensatory role.

The Importance of the Jury

The jury occupies a highly symbolic place at the centre of the criminal justice system, described by Lord Devlin as 'the lamp that shows that freedom lives'.[1] The principle of the determination of guilt by one's peers retains its allure despite the fact that some 90–95 per cent of criminal offences are dealt with by magistrates, without recourse to a jury. Thus the jury is of limited actual importance within the criminal justice system for the vast majority of trials, and juries have a very limited role for the civil justice system in the United Kingdom. This returns us to the idea of realism that courses through the film and law enterprise. Films

---

[1] Devlin, P (1956). The claims that are made for the jury system are not without critics. See, eg, Darbyshire, P (1991).

generally utilise a serious criminal offence, which brings with it an accompanying jury, thus elevating the role of the jury in film. Individual experience of the jury is restricted and part of the mysticism around the jury system is maintained by a lack of information about how it works in practice, which is reflected by the limited cinematic offerings. For those seeking a realist approach to law films there is little to contrast with films once the jury retires, although the restrictive approach in the United Kingdom is more relaxed in the United States, though televising trials is still forbidden in around a dozen states. Furthermore, even where televised trials are permitted, there may be restrictions in terms of the number of cameras and the type of shots permitted. One key point is not to reveal who the members of the jury are. A key question is whether a televised trial can adversely affect the nature and quality of the proceedings. Specifically there was a range of criticism of the theatrical aspects of the televised OJ Simpson trial.[2] Those who support the use of televised proceedings argue that it increases public awareness of the justice system. This contrasts with the severe restrictions that exist with respect to reporting jury deliberations in the United Kingdom. Given this secrecy, there is little primary information on which to base a screenplay. For example, the record of the deliberations that saw the convictions of Derek Bentley or the Guildford Four would provide a telling insight into the central issues of the case, and particularly the perceived veracity of the police evidence. It would add to the accuracy of the portrayal if this information could be included. Clearly it is possible to write fictional perspectives about what might occur in the jury room. However, it is not clear how 'entertaining' jury scenes might be, given that the role is to determine guilt or innocence on the story that has already been told. In one sense it is the climax to the drama that has been played out in front of it and the end decision is part of the process that either concludes the story or may link to a further phase of wrongful incarceration. Clover, for example, notes that the specificities of a jury trial are used for a considerable amount of television and film output.[3] So the jury decision is part of the story, but often a small and restricted part.

There are, though, a number of physical problems in trying to explore the jury system at length within a film given that the action takes place in one small room with a limited number of participants. However, as Lumet demonstrates in *12 Angry Men* (1957), it is possible to concentrate the film in one room. Indeed, he held out against pressure to jazz up the room:

> Somebody had the idea that we should explain that all the regular jury rooms are occupied and have this in the basement, where we could show the exposed pipes and maybe the furnace in order to provide pictorial contrast.[4]

However, the entire film need not be located in the jury room, as with courtroom films the whole trial sequence, let alone the jury deliberations, is often

---

[2] See, eg, Fiske, J and Glynn, K (1995).
[3] Clover, C (1998b).
[4] Cunningham, F (1991: 119).

just a smaller part of the action. The paradox of the jury is that it represents the community version of law's genesis and yet is almost entirely passive in film. The jury may also be spectators of the action that is recorded in the film. As Hambley notes:

> In most courtroom dramas, the jury is just another audience, sitting quietly in the corner of the courtroom; the jury exists in these movies simply because legal accuracy requires there be a jury during a trial.[5]

Thus a favoured shot of the camera is over the shoulder of the jury so that counsel addresses both camera and jury simultaneously.[6] The audience are themselves sometimes cast as the jury, as in *None Shall Escape* (1944). This involves a court-room-based examination of the conduct of a fictional leading Nazi during the occupation of Poland. At the end, the presiding judge addresses the jury about the deliberations and what approach should be taken. The camera then zooms in on the presiding judge and it becomes clear that his remarks are addressed to the viewing public. It is to be an audience decision, we are the jury. Given that this film was made during the war, this is a real decision over which the viewing public did have some sort of input. The same kind of device was adopted in another war-inspired film, Powell and Pressburger's *A Matter of Life and Death* (1946). Whoever the jury may be, the first issue that can be explored and used for dramatic effect is the selection.

Jury Selection

In terms of legal practice, jury selection is an important consideration for lawyers within some jurisdictions. However, in the UK, the ability to challenge jurors is strictly limited and has been reduced in recent times. In the US, the construction of the jury is something of a science to achieve a jury sympathetic to the plaintiff or defendant:

> The next step is to develop a checklist of critical desirable and undesirable characteristics accessible to scrutiny in prospective jurors (blue collar workers, former policemen, participants in two defense verdicts in the past etc). We can then construct the hypothetical ideal composite juror for the case at hand, eg, cigar-smoking male chauvinist with classy address, expensively dressed, middle-aged Republican, carrying *US News and World Report*, has many children most of whom are beginning professional careers; or welfare mother carrying old, tattered *New Republic*, splinter party registration, and emitting warm, possibly seductive smile at attorney.[7]

Blinder notes a number of key factors that ought to be examined to decide on whether the juror is suitable or not, including occupation, age, sex, religion and

---

5 Hambley, G (1992: 173).
6 Silbey J (2001); Clover, C (1998a).
7 Blinder, M (1984: 84).

ethnic group. Jury selection will inevitably only be a small part of any courtroom drama and indeed in many films with a trial sequence it is ignored altogether. The process of jury selection occurs as a minor theme in a number of films. In *To Kill a Mockingbird* (1961) there is the natural assumption of an all-white male jury whose determinations are unguided by evidence.[8] Even in *A Time to Kill* (1996) with its tale of a father killing the white racists who had raped his 10-year-old daughter, there is only a brief section of peremptory challenges with the prosecution seeking to keep African-American men off the jury. Similarly the defence's limited approach is to challenge the selection of white women. In *The Rainmaker* (1997), with the suit against the recalcitrant insurance company, the jury list is unlawfully made available to the plaintiffs. It is used to provide misinformation to the other side knowing that any challenge will reveal that the lawyers have tapped their phones. In *Midnight in the Garden of Good and Evil* (1997) the process is adverted in the appearance as jury foreman of a seriously eccentric Savannah resident who is kept on the jury for no obvious reason.

Occasionally, however, selection issues contribute more fundamentally to the film. For example in *Suspect* (1987) one prospective juror, Mr Davis, is rejected by the defence after it is revealed that, without qualms, he handles foreclosures as part of his job as a loans officer. Eddie Sanger (Dennis Quaid) is also questioned after it has become apparent that he is very keen to avoid his civic duty. Charlie Stella (Joe Mategna), the prosecuting counsel, attempts to discover his views on capital punishment, something that Riley (Cher) strongly objects to. After the judge intervenes, Riley ascertains that he is a lobbyist and accordingly must be a very persuasive figure, though Sanger is surprised to find out that he has been retained. Interestingly, Riley uses this seemingly innocuous procedural challenge as an opportunity to try and begin the process of jury persuasion. Sanger becomes part of the investigative team and enters into a relationship with Riley in order to achieve justice for the (innocent) homeless defendant. The relationship between the juror and the lawyer, both going way beyond their assigned roles, is the fulcrum of the story. Their partnership is formed during the selection process and is fundamental to the outcome.

Similarly, in *Brothers in Law* (1957) the turning point in the court case for the green Roger Thursby (Ian Carmichael) occurs during the selection phase. Unaware of the correct procedure, fearfully nervous and appearing before a crusty fussy judge, Thursby realises his mother is about to be sworn in as a member of the jury. It is a civil case of defamation with a jury present. He hesitates, but is urged to get up by his instructing solicitor, but each time he does so is waved back down by the judge, who appears increasingly irritated by Thursby's persistence. Finally Thursby blurts out: ' I object to the next juror, she's my mother.' Thursby has an agonising wait as the judge considers his position, heightened by the judge's tapping pencil. Finally the judge peers benevolently

---

[8] See also the jury in *Mississippi Burning* (1988), who return a verdict on race lines.

at Thursby and congratulates him on his courtroom etiquette. From that point on, Thursby has the judge on his side, and he triumphs in the case that had been considered unwinnable.

The skill in jury selection is explored in the early stages of *The Devil's Advocate* (1997). Lomax (Keanu Reeves) is a young lawyer from Florida who is incredibly successful. He is approached in a bar after he has successfully defended a school-teacher from charges of child molestation despite the fact that Lomax realises he is guilty. He is invited to go to New York to assist with the jury selection on behalf of a powerful law firm. The courtroom scene shows counsel interviewing the potential jurors. He is called over by Lomax:

Lomax:	Lose number four and number six, and I'd say lose number 12 except the prosecution is going to fuck up and do it for us.
Counsel:	Number six? You're kidding right? She's my first pick.
Lomax:	She's my first pass.
Counsel:	And four?... the dreadlocks, that's crazy. That's a defendant's juror if ever I saw one.
Lomax:	Did you see his shoes ...
Counsel:	Er, look kid. Maybe down in Florida you are the next big thing, this is New York, Manhattan, we're not squeezing oranges here.
Lomax:	He polishes his shoes every night, he makes his own clothes, he may look like a brother with an attitude to you, but I see a man with a shotgun under his bed, and woe betide the creature that steps into his garden. And your favourite, she's damaged goods ...
Counsel:	She's a Catholic schoolteacher, believes in human frailty ...
Lomax:	No, there's something missing from her, she's wronged. She wants on this jury, somebody hurt her and she wants revenge.
Counsel:	How the hell do you know that?
Lomax:	I dunno.
Counsel	(to Lomax's 'superior') Look, are you gonna put a stop to this shit or do I walk?
'Superior':	(looking at Lomax) Walk.
Counsel:	Alright, here's the deal. I lose with your jury, you do the explaining.

Lomax is the possessor of a 'gift' that allows him to interpret people's minds which obviously gives him a strong advantage in terms of picking a sympathetic jury. Lomax also raises an interesting point about who the jury actually are, stressing to Cullen, a high-profile property developer accused of a triple murder, that the 'jury' may be wider than the 12 people sitting in the court.

Jury selection with a twist is encountered in *Runaway Jury* (2003), an adaptation from John Grisham's book; in one alteration the defendants are changed from the tobacco industry to gun manufacturer. One of the jurors manages to get selected for the jury with the purpose of extracting as much money as he can from either the plaintiffs or defendants. This film is interesting in two ways in relation to jury selection. Rather than merely being a tactic for knowing who one wants on the jury and what will appeal to them in their decision making, the jury consultant Finch (Gene Hackman) is prepared to threaten jurors with revelations about their families and events in their own murky past. Nick Easter (John Cusack), the character who has inserted himself onto the jury, relies solely on his use of psychology. He is not charismatic like juror number eight (Fonda, *12 Angry Men* (1957)) but rather a manipulator for the 21st century. Like Fonda's role, though, what it says about juries in the modern age is open to interpretation.

In *We, the Jury* (1996), there is a portrayal that appears initially to be an exception to the *12 Angry Men* (1957) holdout trope. Here, jury analysis is carried out by both the prosecution and the defence. It is deemed crucial to determine the kind of decision that the jury is likely to reach in a scenario involving the shooting of an unfaithful husband by his TV celebrity wife. Thus we have the defence team seeking to have as many women as possible on the jury and the prosecution trying to counter the celebrity sympathy that is evident from some from the jury pool. This is, however, dealt with fairly perfunctorily and we set off with a jury of seven women and five men and the panel includes three jurors from ethnic minorities. Kelly McGillis is the sensible sympathetic Alyce Bell and herein lies the link with *12 Angry Men* (1957). The conflict within the jury opens up broadly along gender lines. The wife, a TV talk show host, claims to have suffered psychological abuse during the marriage so that she is rendered an automaton unable to control her murderous actions. The conflict is, however, between levels of culpability. The wife admits killing her husband and the question for the jury is whether she is guilty of premeditated homicide ('murder one'), unpremeditated homicide ('murder two') or involuntary homicide ('manslaughter').

Like *12 Angry Men* (1957) the first discussion reveals a split in the jury. The split is, however, between the seven women jurors who opt for manslaughter and three male jurors who opt for murder one. The foreman is undecided and one man sides with the women. Discussion takes place and the remaining men are brought round to opt for manslaughter. This leaves only one man as a 'standout' for murder one. Unlike Henry Fonda, however, this juror appears to be merely a prejudiced misogynist unwilling to engage in rational debate about the evidence. Before there is stalemate, however, the reticence of the foreman in explaining his position is exposed as stemming from his extensive notes, which he is making in order to cash in on the notoriety of the case. He is duly replaced by an alternate juror, a self-confident man who accidentally opens up the case for reconsideration. According to the wife she had taken her husband's gun from a closet and in a trance gone to see him at his mistress's apartment. One of the quiet women

149

jurors, however, recalls that she took the gun from her own closet. The husband had moved out some time before. The new, worldly, juror with expertise in marital conflict casts doubt on whether one would leave one's gun after moving to the guest room. Everyone reconsiders and most change their minds. Reminiscent of the psychologically damaged juror number three (Lee J Cobb) in *12 Angry Men* (1957), one of the women has herself been cuckolded by her late husband—a fact she only discovers at the funeral service with the appearance of his mistress. She confesses this has motivated her rather than the evidence. Like the racist juror number 10 (Ed Begley) in *12 Angry Men* (1957), having purged herself, she switches. One of the women jurors believes that this decision is a political case sending out a message about wife abuse. There remains, however, a single 'standout' for not guilty. Again the same quiet juror recalls that the doctor who testified to the mental state of the accused based her work on that of someone who had been a guest on the TV show of the accused. They all suddenly realise they have been lied to and everyone is prepared to opt for murder one.

Strangely, the film, like *12 Angry Men* (1957), does not actually consider whether the ultimate decision is actually correct. In the classic film this was equally significant as death was the result of a guilty verdict. The flimsy 'evidence' which results in convincing the jury in *We the Jury* (1996) casts doubt on the version of events of the accused. Whether it establishes the prosecution version 'beyond reasonable doubt' is another matter. Of course the drama of the jury situation is considerably less where there are different versions of the jury. In England and Wales, for instance, a majority of 10 is sufficient to convict. In Scotland there are three alternatives—see *Madeleine* (1950) on the notorious Madeleine Smith trial—guilty, not guilty and the finding of 'not proven' (the Scottish or Scotch verdict). This third alternative provides a halfway house between guilty and not guilty where evidence does not permit a conviction though there is doubt over the innocence of the defendant. Cases such as the acquittal of OJ Simpson led to discussion of the introduction of a third verdict.[9] The significance of the jury trial in films is made more crucial by the fact that the home of these films, the United States, remains one of the few developed countries where capital punishment is still a punishment providing a more significant outcome. Jury selection and its manipulation are the central focus of *A Runaway Jury* (2004). The story is a Grisham thriller in which one of the jurors has somehow managed to get selected for the jury with the purpose of delivering some indirect justice. What is demonstrated is both how legitimate jury selection operates as well as how the process can be subverted in the same way as we saw in *The Juror* (1994) and *Trial by Jury* (1996). Having failed to get people excluded, the jury consultant, Rankin Fitch (Gene Hackman), seeks to neutralise their antagonism to his client by blackmailing them. The twist is that Easter inexplicably is able to win over these people to the side of decency.

[9] Bray, S (2005).

Jury Deliberation

12 Angry Men (1957) was the first and almost the only film that has concentrated on the deliberations of the legal 'audience'. The jury are judging the forensic performances of the lawyers who are seen as the moulders of truth and reality and effectively determining what the law amounts to. They are also judging the characters who appear before them. This is an ensemble piece that assembles a range of different social types and abstracts them from their normal daily activities. They are allowed to expose their own values and methods of deciding matters. The jurors comprise a cross-section of attitudes rather than purely ethnic or class backgrounds. The discussion which they are involved in provides the sole action in the film. There is the desire by the architect juror, number eight (Henry Fonda), for some discussion of the case before sending an 18 year old to the electric chair brings out a range of character traits. The jurors have to explain why they voted to convict in order to convince juror number eight, who is isolated after the first vote. He wins support from the 'old man' juror number nine (Joseph Sweeney). Juror number nine resents the racist reasoning behind the push for conviction by juror number 10 (Ed Begley). He has 'lived among them' and regards both racial minorities and slum dwellers as lesser humans. Similarly outspoken against slum dwellers is the blustering bully, juror number three, a small businessman (Lee J Cobb). He alienates quiet juror number five (Jack Klugman) and immigrant juror number 11 (George Voskovec).

A combination of the underlying prejudices, and emergence of rational reasons to doubt the conviction, start to win over other jurors. Some are slower to change their minds. Juror number 12 (Robert Webber) is not really giving the process much attention, thinking instead about his advertising agency work. Juror number seven (Jack Warden) is a cynical salesman whose initial concern is to get away quickly so he can attend a baseball game. He even changes his mind on the basis that this is the ways things are going and by changing sides he will still get to the game. The plain working man juror number six (Edward Binns) resents the bullying of the old man. Finally, juror number four (EG Marshall) is convinced by the evidence cast on the eye-witness evidence on which he had been so reliant. When it is pointed out by the old man that the woman who witnessed the murder wore eyeglasses but would not have been wearing these in bed, from where she claimed to see the murder, across a railway line, after midnight, he is satisfied that there is a reasonable doubt. What we have is a mixture of rational evaluation of evidence and prejudice. Jurors change their minds both as a reaction to the evidence and as a reaction to their fellow jurors. Even though the jury is split nine–three at the time, it is clear from his final vitriolic outburst that juror number 10 is no mere thoughtless racist. He is a fully developed, conscious bigot which none of his colleagues can stomach. Their own ambivalence on this issue is rooted and overcome and symbolically they all turn their backs on him. This may be seen as celebration of the core common sense of the jury system and of the innate decency of humanity. It can also be read as an indictment of the lazy stereotyping and lack of commitment that sullies the whole process of justice.[10]

Its shadow has been long enough to inspire awe, but almost no other stories centring on jury deliberations other than a comedy 'tribute' have resulted. This latter film had as its central trope the desire of the protagonist to keep the process going as long as possible in order to enjoy food and accommodation at public expense (*Jury Duty* (1995)).[11] Not surprisingly, perhaps, given the mythical status of the jury as a bulwark against despotism in all subsequent 'jury'-centred films, the decision which is finally reached in the film, whether by the jury itself or the through the actions of the protagonist, does not question the concept of the jury. *12 Angry Men* was remade for cable in 1997 with Jack Lemmon, George C Scott and Ossie Davis. William Friedkin, the director of *The French Connection* (1971) and *The Exorcist* (1973), acted as director. The screenplay was left totally unaltered from that of the original author of the 1957 film screenplay and the stage play on which it was based, Reginald Rose. The judge is now a woman and the time is moved forward from the 1950s to an unspecified future. In keeping with the title of the work the jurors remain all male, though their ethnic composition has been radically altered. Now instead of one European immigrant and 11 white men all native-born and speaking unaccented English, we have one European immigrant and three African-Americans. The foreman of the jury is an African-American, and the role of the racist is played by an African-American. His views on race are so extreme that he has been ejected from the Nation of Islam and he has a strong negative view of Hispanic immigrants. Despite the changes, the conclusion of the film is true to the original.

The other jury pictures, which appeared in the 1990s, took the unlikely, but fascinating, notion of the lone juror suborned to produce a 'not guilty' verdict. In *Trial by Jury* (1994), Valerie Alston (Joanne Whalley-Kilmer) is a young woman whose family is threatened by a vicious gangster and she is tasked with single-handedly changing the mind of the jury and obtaining an acquittal. Single-handedly. Annie Laird (Demi Moore) in *The Juror* (1996), based on the novel by George Dawes Green, performs a similar function. In both these instances the jury process is shown as involving people whose perspectives are easily swayed. There is an assumption of a high level of plasticity. In fairness the central drive of these two films is on whether the trapped victim of blackmail will somehow deliver justice for the 'evil gangster'. Rather less focus is on the problem of achieving an outcome that satisfies the individual moral commitment to family and general duty to the community to assist in the punishment of crime. Nonetheless the basic premise seems to have been inspired more by Henry Fonda's courageous

---

[10] The *Chicago/Kent Law Review* (2007) devotes 350 pages to the film on its 50th anniversary.

[11] Described in *Variety* as 'one of the worst major studio releases of recent memory'. A much more satisfactory comedy version appeared in 1959 on British TV: *Hancock's Half Hour*.

stance in *12 Angry Men* (1957) than in any grounded knowledge of the jury system's operation. The research that has been carried out in relation to the notion of the 'standout' juror suggests that outcomes like this one almost never occur in real life.[12]

The Compensatory Jury

As civil law films are few, there is not much material to work with, though the jury may have a significant role that is different from the normal acquit/convict in the traditional criminal justice film. This may not be the life or death decision but can be used to judge the quality of the work carried out by the lawyers. In *Runaway Jury* (2003), after much deliberation the jury punish the gun manufacturers with an award of damages of $111 million, of which $110 million were punitive. As with Carter's plea to the judge in *The Hurricane* (1999) to give him justice, Frank Galvin in *The Verdict* (1982) makes a last-ditch appeal to the jury to save his case. He has little admissible evidence or useful expert testimony to rely on so it is left to bare emotion. The decision of the jury flies in the face of the evidence that Galvin has presented but there is obvious sympathy for the dire position of the plaintiff. This is acutely demonstrated when the jury returns to deliver its verdict:

Judge: Have you reached a verdict?

Jury Foreman: We have your honour. Your honour we've agreed to hold for the plaintiff Deborah Ann Kaye and against St Catherine's ... and Doctors Towler and Marks but your honour are we limited on the size of the award? What I mean sir ... are we permitted to award an amount greater than the amount the plaintiff asked for?

Judge: You are. You are not bound by anything other than your good judgement based on the evidence.

Whilst we don't find out the extent of the award, it is clear that the jury is acting out of sympathy rather than an objective cold decision on the evidence presented. In *Erin Brockovich* (2000) the whole concept of a jury trial is important for the injured plaintiffs to establish the truth behind their illnesses and have to be persuaded by Erin to go to arbitration. She manages through the power of her personal relationship to convince them that this is the best course of action and they duly succeed and are compensated to their surprise. *North Country* (2005), which is based on the landmark sexual harassment case of *Jenson v Eveleth Mines*, avoids the importance of the ultimate jury trial despite the fact that the threat of the trial by jury corrects the previous wrongs in the legal processes. In *Philadelphia* (1993) the jury is sympathetic to the plaintiff Andrew Beckett (Tom Hanks), and after he collapses in court and is hospitalised the jury find in his favour, awarding

---

[12] Johnson, SL (1985); Marder, N (1997); Fukurai, H (1999).

damages including punitive damages to punish the conduct of the law firm. There are other examples of juries being involved not in individual issues but of moral or ethical decisions that are reflected in individual cases, for example the question of freedom of speech and obscenity in *The People vs. Larry Flynt* (1996).

Conclusion

Both the judiciary and juries have been examined in sociology of law and socio-legal studies, but there have been limited comments on the cinematic versions of these institutions. Judges may have been particularly ill-served, but juries have fared little better.[13] Despite being, as Clover suggests, central to the construction of the popular legal process:

> Tocqueville was right: we are a nation of jurors, and we have created an entertainment system that has us see everything that matters—from corporate greed to child custody—from precisely that vantage point and in those structural terms.[14]

The dearth of actual scholarship can be attributed, at least partly, to the relatively limited material available to examine. The limited extent of coverage and the way in which juries are filmed has been linked to the significance of the cinema audience.[15] Clover concludes that the limited visual coverage of the jury and of their discussions stems from the assumed fact that the 'real' jury is us, the audience:

> It must be the film's presumption of an extradiagetic jury that explains why diagetic juries are so little seen and the process of deliberation so consistently avoided in Anglo-American cinema; we are the jury, and any sustained representation of an opposite number within the diagesis would interfere with our habitual relation to the text.[16]

The focus of this kind of scholarly analysis has been on the broader picture such as the trial itself,[17] and the differences between the reality of this civic institution, and how it is portrayed within popular culture.[18] Abramson suggests that, despite the limited coverage of juries in popular culture, the characters used in relation to civil issues do embody the great debates in American society about blame and responsibility.[19]

There has been an understandable concentration on *12 Angry Men* (1957) despite the fact that it is atypical of the portrayals of the jury in popular culture.[20] Nichols compared the film with 'the real thing' in the form of a television

---

[13] Levi, RD (2005).
[14] Clover, C (1998c: 272).
[15] Clover, C (1998a).
[16] *Ibid*, 404.
[17] Papke, D (1999a).
[18] Papke, D (1999b).
[19] Abramson, J (2000 & 2007).
[20] Papke, D (2007).

documentary from Milwaukee, *Inside the Jury Room* (1986), concluding that juries work within a framework of justice which they can articulate.[21] The significance of *12 Angry Men* (1957) has also been examined in the context of empirical studies on the operation of the jury, both within the United States and elsewhere.[22] It has been seen as a religious allegory,[23] and a beacon of hope in brutalising,[24] or careless world.[25] The quality of the discussion has been doubted,[26] as well as the conclusions reached by Fonda and his colleagues.[27] The whole notion of the 'standout' juror, which has entered popular consciousness via the film, has been examined by a number of writers. The conclusions seem to be a little mixed. Valerie Hans' review of the evidence leads her to suppose that 'Henry Fonda, or someone like him, sits today on an American jury'.[28] There are also other reports that such behaviour does take place,[29] although fewer accused deny factual as opposed to moral guilt than we might suppose.[30] Rather less encouraging is the conclusion of Jeffrey Abramson that jurors tend to vote with their race rather than the evidence.[31] Efforts, too, to increase citizen participation across all racial and ethnic groups have run into difficulties.[32]

The perspective from scholars in continental Europe has varied. There has been from Spain a focus on how juries are presented in American films and to look at the implications of the jury selection process in the context of a modern Spanish practitioner.[33] From France we have a focus on the way the jury film *12 Angry Men* (1957) reveals the difference between the Anglo-Saxon oral scheme, and the reliance on written pleadings in France.[34]

The countless hours of law films have, for a range of reasons, not focused on the less dramatic actors. These individuals are passive. They are spectators. They are us, the viewing subject.[35] Quite how one interprets this depends on how you view the evidence. Clover suggests that this notion of the viewer's role elevates the jury box of the cinemagoer into prime place:

> the American legal imagination, as it plays itself out among the 'common people', inhabits first and foremost not the judge's bench, not the attorney's chair, not the witness stand, not even the jail cell or the electric chair, but the jury box.[36]

---

[21] Nichols, B (1996).
[22] Jimeno-Bulnes, M (2007b); Machura, S (2007); Thaman, S (2007).
[23] Hay, B (2007).
[24] Sarat, A (2007).
[25] Marder, N (2007b).
[26] Weisselberg, C (2007).
[27] Asimow, M (2007).
[28] Hans, V (2007: 589).
[29] Babcock, B and Sassoubre, T (2007).
[30] Hoffman, M (2007).
[31] Abramson, J (2007).
[32] Gertner, N (2007).
[33] Colomer, JL (2003).
[34] Guery, C (2007).
[35] Silbey, J (2001).
[36] Clover, C (2000: 258).

We do not agree with this. Our principal problem is that, for a range of reasons, we have few cinematic glimpses into the jury's possible inner workings. Whilst we may in thrillers be weighing the evidence, at the end of the process we actually are identifying much more with defence lawyers than anyone else. As we have noted, there has been some work contrasting real juries such as that in *Inside the Jury Room* (1986) and the film *12 Angry Men* (1957),[37] and discussion of the effectiveness of juries as a result of the influence of popular culture. In addition, we get few glimpses of how prosecutors work. There is of course Katheryn Murphy (Kelly McGillis) plea-bargaining in *The Accused* (1988). We see a young woman Assistant DA seeking proper recognition of her qualities by being assigned a murder prosecution before she gets involved with the accused in *Physical Evidence* (1989). We hear the inner thoughts of Senior Assistant DA Rusty Sabich in *Presumed Innocent* (1992) about how he sees his job before the story veers off to concentrate on his new role as the accused in another murder mystery. Public defender work, a staple of the TV screen, has despite Cher's sterling effort in *Suspect* (1987), scarcely made an impact in film. What we get is a partial view of the system centred on the craft of defence lawyers. They range from the noble, such as Gregory Peck in *Cape Fear* (1961) and the redeemed (Paul Newman, *The Verdict* (1982)), to the cheated (Richard Gere, *Primal Fear* (1996)) and the gullible (Glen Close, *Jagged Edge* (1985)). Identification with the oppressed victims of the legal process has been a trope that has captured the imagination of filmmakers rather more than the more prosaic processing of those apprehended by the forces of law and order. The exciting work has already been done by the likes of Harry Callahan and the predominant cinematic concern has been with ensuring that they have not got 'the wrong man'.

---

[37] Nichols, B (1996: 1055).

11

Fact, Fiction and the Cinema of Justice (I): Presumed Accurate?

In the Courtroom, whoever tells the best story wins
(John Quincy Adams, in *Amistad* (1997)).

WHILE films that are products of the imagination, involving law and lawyers, are themselves a well-used construct, a further heavily utilised vehicle is the film based upon a true story. Historic events, which may be adapted or interpreted from pre-existing text(s), are a productive source for the cinema generally. This can be seen in a number of arenas. War has been an obvious base for cinematic transformation—witness the plethora of films based upon the First World War and the Second World War—centred on both the military campaigns and other military aspects, such as prisons and prisoners of war. In terms of legal film, the events of the Second World War led to *Judgment at Nuremberg* (1961). Previously the Russian Revolution was the subject of Eisenstein's *October* (1928), described as 'a propaganda masterpiece whose images have all too often been mistaken and used for genuine newsreel'.[1] This provokos an interesting discussion that life becomes art, and often which is the 'true' depiction becomes blurred. For the purposes of this Chapter we look at where these two issues intersect, the portrayal of true life 'legal stories' through the medium of film. This type of true life legal film may take a number of forms, for example Crowther analyses prison movies, a subject that 'captured the imagination of movie makers and audiences from the earliest days of popular cinema'.[2] Indeed, Crowther devotes one chapter of his text to 'Factual Fiction: True Prison Movies', citing numerous films under this umbrella ranging from *The Prisoner of Shark Island* (1936), through *Unchained* (1955), to films such as *Papillon* (1973), *McVicar* (1980) and *Midnight Express* (1978).

We have generally not considered prison movies within this work, although some of the films analysed, such as *In the Name of the Father* (1993), *The Hurricane* (1999) and *The Green Mile* (1999), have important prison scenes. In a sense, prison is a very important part of the cinematic criminal legal system, particularly where

---

[1] Halliwell, L (2008: 866).
[2] Crowther, B (1989: 3).

there is a link to miscarriages of justice. We made this point explicitly when we discussed the phases of cinematic justice in Chapter 3. However, in the same way that 'cop' films may have a relationship to law films, prison films do not necessarily contain those other 'legal' elements that specifically interest us. This of course brings us back round to the issues of genre and the problems of typology outlined previously.

Perhaps one of the earliest examples of a 'law' film based upon a true story is one of the most famous within the canon of law films generally: *Inherit the Wind* (1960). The film was based upon the 1925 'monkey trial' of John Scopes, a teacher who was charged with teaching Darwin's theory of evolution to high-school children in defiance of state law. The film has been analysed many times and from a number of angles.[3] Uelmen illustrates two contrasting views of the film, what might be termed those of the 'layperson' and the 'lawyer', which illustrate some of the problems of portraying or adapting real-life events:

> I saw *Inherit the Wind* for the first time thirty-five years ago, before I became a lawyer, and I loved it. In some respects, becoming a lawyer ruined the film for me. Not much that goes on in the film resembles a real trial, and some of the theatrics now seem hokey. Also, in the course of writing a one-man play about the life of William Jennings Bryan, I spent considerable time reading accounts and transcripts from the actual trial the film is supposed to depict. That ruined the film even more, realizing how many liberties were taken with actual events.[4]

In terms of portraying events that actually took place, this can be done through fictionalising the actual circumstances, as occurred with the Scopes case, so that they form the basis of the film. This allows the creator leeway to introduce his own particular perspective, and not to be rigidly constrained by allegations of inaccuracy. He can, in effect, exercise artistic licence. Other examples of this include two of the films discussed elsewhere, *Paths of Glory* (1957) and *King and Country* (1964), which are based on events that took place in the First World War. Following revolts in the French Army, individuals were shot '*pour encourager les autres*' on the Allied side. The screenplays are, however, based on amalgams of events and characters rather than being the precise individual stories. Whilst this version of the *roman à clef* may weaken the impact of the politics of the denunciation of injustice it permits a degree of latitude to the filmmaker; charges of inaccuracy are less easy to level at a work that does not claim to be that person's encounter.

There can, of course, be problems where the author of a real-life account in fact conveys the flavour of events rather than the specific incidents. Thus, there has been a wave of criticism of two best-selling authors in the depictions of their struggles against poverty and oppression. Winner of the 1992 Nobel Peace Prize, Rigoberta Menchu, was forced to admit that some of the passages in her

---

[3] See, eg, the analysis of Minow, N (1996).
[4] Uelmen, G (1996: 1221).

autobiography, *I Rigoberta*,[5] had been cobbled together from disparate events,[6] although this did not amount to lying. The story was, however, illustrative of the treatment meted out by the Guatemalan Government to the indigenous people. It was not so much an 'autobiography' as a 'testimony'. The same kind of defence was mounted against charges of inaccuracy and invention levelled at Frank McCourt in the book *Angela's Ashes* by locals and contemporaries in Limerick, including actor Richard Harris. To compound matters, this controversial version was faithfully reproduced on screen in 1999, under Alan Parker's direction, with a strong emphasis on the nature of the poverty and the contributory role of the Church to this misery.

There are a number of examples of legal films that use real events as their basis, but which do not seek to avoid problems of exact accuracy. They do, for example, retain details such as the names and the form of the original narratives. These include *The Court Martial of Billy Mitchell* (1955), *Reversal of Fortune* (1990), *Breaker Morant* (1980), *The Court Martial of Jackie Robinson* (1990), *A Civil Action* (1998) and *Erin Brockovich* (2000) amongst others.

In addition to films that are acknowledged as firmly based on real events, there are also films that 'draw' upon real life. For example *Philadelphia* (1993) provoked a lawsuit from the family of a lawyer who had AIDS. The case was settled and the film now acknowledges that 'This motion picture was inspired in part by Geoffrey Bowers' AIDS discrimination lawsuit' (from Philadelphia credits). All these films have had to deal with a central problem—how to translate these real events into a couple of hours of celluloid print. Apart from the general problems of fitting an often detailed sequence of events into such a short time frame, other problems encountered have centred upon issues of accuracy and authenticity. Goldman's description of the writing of *All The President's Men* (1976) indicates some of the problems and tensions in transferring real life to the screen. Goldman listed six particular problems with writing the screenplay, one of which related to the fact that it was to be based on factual circumstances:

> Great liberties could not be taken with the material. Not just for legal reasons, which were potentially enormous. But if there ever was a movie that had to be authentic, it was this one. The importance of the subject matter obviously demanded that. More crucially was this: We were dealing here with probably the greatest triumph of the print media in many years, and every media person would see the film ... and if we 'hollywooded' it up—i.e. put in dancing girls—there was no way they would take it kindly. We had to be dead on, or we were dead.[7]

The other five problems he noted were: overexposure of the subject matter; it was a political story; the book had little structure; the names were difficult; and one

---

[5] Originally based on interviews with Venezuelan anthropologist, Elizabeth Burgos Debray, *Me Llamo Rigoberta Mencho y asi nacio la conciencia* (1982) and released as *I Rigoberta* in English in 1984.

[6] Stoll, D (1999).

[7] Goldman, W (1983: 233).

of the two stars, Robert Redford, was the producer. Goldman produced a script that was sent to *The Washington Post* as well as the two reporters, Woodward and Bernstein, for comment. He then notes that a new version of the screenplay was produced by Bernstein and his girlfriend, a writer. Goldman records that one of the 'new' scenes appeared in the final version of the film, though according to Goldman it wasn't based on fact, and that he would not have used such a 'made-up' scene in a film concerning the downfall of the President of the United States.

Often films based on historical events have proved easy targets, with critics all too willing to admonish a film or its director for filmed events that do not tally with the official story. This is not confined to film but applies to all interpretations of historical episodes that invoke political disputes. In the 1990s the BBC commissioned a drama series, *Rebel Heart*, on the history of the partition of Ireland and selected Ronan Bennett to write the screenplay. This produced a critical response from David Trimble, the First Minister of Northern Ireland, who claimed that Bennett was a most unsuitable person as his work was 'hopelessly one sided'.[8] Work that deals with the 'Irish question' often attracts political controversy and demonstrates that historical events and film making do not always fit well together.[9] Even if there is not a question mark over political bias, other issues may affect the subsequent interpretation of events. As Crowther notes:

> Real life tales, of course, have one strike against them in Hollywood. Acting against the intentions of film-makers who drew their inspiration from biographical accounts or newspaper reports was the film community's general inability to tell a true story without a great deal of inaccurate embroidery. It is justifiable to paint a true story with a thin layer of fictionalisation in order to improve its dramatic structure, but there is no excuse for the frequent appearance of movies so changed from reality as to make one wonder why they pretended to be true stories—unless, perish the thought, the makers of movies concerned were motivated by just plain greed.[10]

Studios will clearly exert commercial pressures in a number of areas, and there are examples of endings being altered to improve ratings. Halliwell notes with respect to *The Long Kiss Goodnight* (1996) that 'Samuel L Jackson's character originally died at the end of the film, which upset preview audiences. As a result the ending was re-shot so that he lived.'[11] In addition to political and commercial pressures there may also be practical problems in recreating original events. Goldman indicates this type of problem with the film *A Bridge Too Far* (1977), which detailed attempts by Allied soldiers to cross a river and attack German soldiers who were defending the bridge.[12] There were two different waves of soldiers involved, the second group having witnessed the carnage of the first body, as the German

---

[8] See Johnston, P (2000).
[9] For example, on Ireland and the media generally see Curtis, L (1984). Another film that attracted some media criticism for its treatment of Irish issues was Neil Jordan's *The Crying Game* (1992).
[10] Crowther, B (1989: 41).
[11] Halliwell, L (2008: 706).
[12] Goldman, W (1983).

soldiers were ready for the attack, as the smoke screen cover proved ineffective. The film shows the first attack but not the second, as it proved too difficult to portray realistically:

> I tried as hard as I knew to use the second wave, but I failed. The single most heroic action of the war, and I couldn't figure out how to include it. The moral I guess is this: Truth is terrific, reality is even better, but believability is best of all.

Because without it, truth and reality go right out the window ....[13]

This raises an interesting point. The crucial factor in terms of deciding how to film an event may be whether the audience will accept the portrayals of the issues and the characters, regardless of any adherence to the factual base. As Norman Jewison, Director of *The Hurricane* (1999) observes: 'Believability is what film making is all about. If you believe what is happening on the screen is real and believable then you stay linked in to the film.'

An important question that arises throughout this Chapter is whether it matters if events are bent or moulded in some way to fit either contemporary tastes or commercial requirements. One of the problems with producing work that outlines historic events is that the film may itself, because of its popularity, become a significant source of reference. This is especially the case where the film is seen by generations that have not lived through the period, and see the film as the initial point of information. An obvious example of the problems of filming history is Hollywood's portrayal of the Holocaust. This is naturally a subject of extreme sensitivity and there is a real problem in trying to convey the historical events within the physical constraints of film making. Apart from limitations over time, there is the sheer enormity of what happened and the related difficulty of potentially trivialising the events by committing it to such a depiction.

There may also be problems of 'authenticity', even with respect to the casting of certain actors. Referring to *The Boys from Brazil* (1978), Insdorf asks whether we can 'really believe that upstanding Gregory Peck with his Lincolnesque gravity is the man responsible for killing two and a half million prisoners in Auschwitz'.[14] Similarly, the question of who would be able to direct *Schindler's List* (1993) was a sensitive one. The fact that Spielberg took on the director's role was seen as crucial, by virtue of his background and empathetic stance, in terms of the film's authenticity. Apart from the actors playing the roles, style and content are also both important. Should events like the Holocaust be subjected to the full Hollywood 'big film' treatment or be more underplayed? Crowther makes a valid point about the magnitude of the task: 'Once again, the sheer size and scale of the depravations caused most of the problems for film-makers ... How can a film-maker depict six million deaths? And at what point does the exercise so de-sensitize an

---

[13] Goldman, W (1983: 145).
[14] This became a more serious point with the casting of Vanessa Redgrave as Fania Fenelon in the TV film *Playing for Time*. Fenelon objected to Redgrave on the grounds of her political activism. Insdorf, A (1983: 12).

audience that it ceases to have any further effect?'[15] Perhaps the answer is to downplay such scenes and treat them with due reverence as Insdorf suggests: 'Intensity does not necessarily mean sweeping drama: given the emotion inherent in the subject matter, perhaps the Holocaust requires restraint and a hushed voice—a whisper rather than a shout—as evidenced by the effective understatement of films like Lilienthal's *David* or Markus Imhoof's *The Boat Is Full*.'[16]

In a sense, any attempt to portray the Holocaust is going to be criticised from one perspective or another. Some of the arguments about accuracy that are repeated with respect to other films, such as those outlined in Chapter 12, are likely to be intensified with an issue such as the Holocaust. There is also the initial debate about whether it is a topic suitable for 'entertainment' as opposed to a more factual documentary analysis such as that by the television programme *Holocaust* (1978). Insdorf points out that there were problems with this account:

> The television programme *Holocaust* (1978) heightened awareness of both the historical facts and the problems of how to dramatize them on film. This mini-series took Nazi atrocities out of the province of specialized study and made them a 'prime-time' phenomenon—with both the benefits of exposure and the drawbacks of distortion. Its case illustrates the rewards and tendencies inherent in films made for mass audiences—from the power of sensitizing, to the danger of romanticizing and trivializing. Indeed *Holocaust* must be appreciated for its stimulation of concern, both in America and Europe, but questioned for its manner of presentation—including commercials (for example, it packaged devastating gas chamber scenes into neat 15-minute segments separated by commercials for an air deodorizer and panty shields).[17]

Films may inform our view not just of events, but also of individuals and their contribution to history. This is a crucial constituent of conventions regarding the active nature of the audience role, which engages with the material in terms of predicting outcomes and maintaining a critical distance from the film. Such a convention is constructed to help in our own reading and response to a film that we deal with below. In terms of historical figures, our reading of the film and its own conventions are largely pre-figured or constrained. Significant historical figures are inevitably attractive to film makers because of their achievements and links to great moments. Thus Abraham Lincoln has been the prime subject of at least three serious biographical accounts. First, *Abraham Lincoln* (1930), described by Halliwell as 'rather boring even at the time, this straightforward biopic has the virtues of sincerity and comparative fidelity to the facts'.[18] Second, *Young Mr Lincoln* (1939), an offering from John Ford and described by the *New York Times* as 'a film which indisputably has the right to be called Americana'.[19] The third film, *Abe Lincoln in Illinois* (1940), was based on the Broadway play

---

[15] Crowther, B (1984: 144).
[16] Insdorf A (1983: 6).
[17] *Ibid*, 4.
[18] Halliwell, L (2008: 4).
[19] *Ibid*, 1350.

written by Robert E Sherwood. It is *Young Mr Lincoln* (1939) that has attracted the greatest critical acclaim although it was not a huge box office success. There is, according to Gallagher, some conformity between the three portrayals:

> The character of Ford's Lincoln is quite consistent with the Lincoln of the Robert Sherwood/John Cromwell *Abe Lincoln in Illinois* (Raymond Massey, 1939) and the Lincoln of DW Griffith's *Abraham Lincoln* (1930). But the latter does offer contrasts. Walter Huston's sprawling, declamatory, loutish Lincoln splits logs while Ann reads him law; Fonda's Lincoln, tidy, self-conscious, lies lazily on his back reading when Ann comes by. Both associate woman-law-nature, but Griffith concentrates on the axe: his Lincoln is the North's hammer, a man of perseverance in a dark psychodrama.[20]

Crowther agrees that whilst the film is generally accurate, the construction of the narrative by John Ford alters the perceptions of Lincoln, without any detailed exploration of the character:

> The historical accuracy of the Ford–Fonda portrait of the Great Emancipator's early life does nothing that is noticeably unfaithful (dare any film-maker, even in the iconoclastic 1980s, tamper with this particular giant?), but the historical veracity of the film is undermined by the degree to which the film-maker has assumed the audience's knowledge of the main character's life, both at the times depicted and in later years. It is in this second assumption that the audience knows what is to become of Lincoln, that the film is most unsettling.[21]

Gallagher makes the important point that the portrayal of the Lincoln characters are themselves constrained not just by historical fact, but also by previous representations. The expansion of the character is constrained by the previous limits that have been self-imposed by the script writers, of stage or screen, and the 'onerous tradition' that had grown up around the myth of Abraham Lincoln. The only way to break out of this straightjacket is to reinvent the character or to present a new slant. The link between real-life characters and the screen portrayals is clearly more difficult, in terms of accuracy, if the individual has long since died. Interestingly, though, Iris Bentley explains that she lent the actor playing Derek Bentley, Chris Ecclestone, Derek's lighter and watch and that according to Ecclestone they 'sparked his imagination'.[22] Clearly as more historical details become available perspectives on historical events may change. The cinematic examination of the Vietnam War is one example as *The Green Berets* (1968) offers a completely different account, and political perspective, of the war than later films such as *Apocalypse Now* (1979) and *Born on the Fourth of July* (1989). Different political persuasions may provide the rationale for alternative accounts of the same events and history is open to divergent versions. But as Gallagher points out, above, there are internal constraints that may affect characterisations as well as any box office considerations.

---

[20] Gallagher, T (1986: 171).
[21] Crowther, B (1984: 38).
[22] Bentley, I and Dening, P (1995).

As can be seen in Chapter 12, a number of themes can be identified within these real-life films. These range from the miscarriages of justice cases of *Let Him Have It* (1991), *In the Name of the Father* (1993) and *The Hurricane* (1999) via films depicting famous and important historical events (*Amistad* (1997)) and community stories (*Erin Brockovich* (2000) and *A Civil Action* (1998)) to social commentaries in the vein of *Inherit the Wind* (1960) or *Vera Drake* (2004).[23] Many of these films, their coverage and plot devices, are detailed in Chapter 12.

Facts, Cases and Lawyers

We have previously identified that law films need a serious issue to be tried, or some interesting characters for us to engage with. Whilst *In the Name of the Father* (1993) seems to lack any really distinctive individuals, in cinematic terms, and *Amistad* (1997) is primarily concerned with an important social matter, the other films we have examined in this section all contain significant characters. These individuals—Derek Bentley, Erin Brockovich and Jan Schlichtmann—all have characteristics, or a story about them, that lends itself to film audiences. Bentley is very much a victim, and consequently great sympathy can be engendered through the portrayal. The link is made between the horrific punishment, death, and Bentley as an individual and with his family all impotent in the face of the criminal justice system. The film is about miscarriages of justice and the death penalty but also about the life of Derek Bentley; the two events are interlinked and it is his character and aptitude that feed into the wider issue of the nature of the legal system and capital punishment. In essence the film would not have worked had Bentley or the end result been different.

There are also elements of being a 'casualty of life' in *Erin Brockovich* (2000), notably in the early stages of the film. One of the edited scenes shows Erin 'stealing' medicine for her children from a drug store and she confirms that this event occurred. Schlichtmann is not portrayed in the same way, though at the end of the film his life is shown to have altered irrevocably with the end of his existing legal practice. Both *A Civil Action* (1998) and *Erin Brockovich* (2000) are about the metamorphosis of the two lawyers through the medium of the two cases. There are then two parallel themes telling the stories of both the plaintiffs and the two lawyers. The two stories intersect and are largely interdependent. Because of the eventual closeness between the lawyers and the group they represent, both to a large extent stand or fall together. Whilst Erin Brockovich is shown from the outset as empathising strongly with the poisoned community, Schlichtmann is initially highly sceptical of becoming involved despite the personal tragedies of the families themselves. This was shown through the way he gets the case, after being reminded about it by a caller to a radio show, and his original opinion that

---

[23] These categories may, evidently, overlap.

the case was unlikely to succeed. Travolta realised that he would have to play the character with all his blemishes and that even if he was to be a hero, he would be flawed.

All these films tell us something different about the nature of portrayals, the link between the real and the unreal, and questions of subjectivity, balance and audience perception. The inaccuracies in *Let Him Have It* (1991) undoubtedly caused upset to some of those involved, largely because the constructions of the characters and dialogue did not tally with what they (principally Iris Bentley) 'knew' to be true. However, when these negative aspects were balanced with the wider effect upon the campaign for a pardon, we would argue that the wider picture justified the inconsistencies. *Let Him Have It* (1991) also provides a useful counterpoint to many of the other films, as this is a film where the upshot is that the law ultimately fails Derek Bentley, and the ending is bleak. *In the Name of the Father* (1993) created a whole new set of problems. Unlike *Let Him Have It* (1991), the film portrays the law as ultimately the tool by which the Guildford Four are freed, although there is of course an ambivalence in the law, in that, effectively, the law was only the tool via which the law's earlier mistake was rectified. The rectification for Bentley came after both his death and the film.[24] In addition, a further aspect of *In the Name of the Father* (1993) was that some commentators felt that mistakes in the portrayal might be seen as an admission that mistakes were made when the Four were freed, giving fuel to those who maintained that they were still guilty. Our own experience of this in terms of student responses to the film over the years does not support this notion.

The Hurricane (1999) takes this a stage further. The film shows all parties involved in the film prepared to make concessions and appreciative of the needs and purpose of the film itself. However, a key difference is that here the law is shown as being bent in order to free Carter, whereas in *In the Name of the Father* (1993) the legal process is seen as being the means by which the appeal is phrased. *Amistad* (1997) creates a different problem in terms of our understanding of history, with the role of the 'real' being diminished via the use of composite characters and the like, so detracting from what we understand of history. However, as we noted above, sometimes the end is more important than the means, and if something that has been occluded becomes visible because of such a treatment then it serves a valid purpose in terms of awareness.

Having discussed the difficulties and criticisms that can be encountered when dealing with real-life events, we now turn to some other factors that may affect such depictions. First, even the traditional way of portraying 'the real', the documentary, may itself be beset with difficulties. Secondly, we analyse whether the law of copyright may have some impact upon the protection and ownership of events or their depictions. Thirdly, we place the issue of storytelling within its broader context and argue that all stories, in all their forms, are essentially subjective.

---

[24] Derek Bentley received a Royal Pardon in 1995 and on 30 July 1998, the Court of Appeal set aside his conviction.

Documentary Films[25]

The term 'documentary' was first coined as a way to describe how film could visually document a set of events.[26] These films have, certainly until recently, rarely been seen as commercial vehicles and often were funded by sponsorship rather than a studio.[27] To some viewers, documentaries may appear as dry and unappealing. Whilst motion pictures funded by commercial studios utilise fantasy or escapism, with big stars as the box office draw, documentaries eschew this in favour of attempting to convey the truth, or the real. In fact, Wheale notes that some of the early documentaries were, in fact, scripted.[28]

One of the chief advantages of the documentary is that, at first sight, it might be perceived to present what actually happened, the real life events, and so provide a means of avoiding some of the criticisms that have been made of 'faction' films. This is of course not always the case. In a different but related sense, the achingly poignant depiction of 'the walk into the heart of darkness' of James Bulger in 1993 via CCTV image is illustrative of this. Here this image was reproduced, forensically examined, and technologically enhanced and became our prime way of connecting with the tragedy: 'The technologization of the images of James Bulger's abduction is the product of … anxiety. The images must be technologized to be incorporated into modernity, to be owned as ourselves. In the responses to the event of James Bulger's killing, we are attempting to own our sense of horror, to make ourselves into versions of the oppositions that structure the event.'[29] However, it is important to note that documentary is only a *representation* of reality and that whilst real footage might be used, it is still *authored* and subjected to the whims of the creator. The documentary film is still constructed:

> It is often the case that documentary is believed to be the recording of 'actuality'—raw footage of real events as they happen, real people as they speak, real life as it occurs, spontaneous and unmediated. While this is often the case in producing the material *for* a documentary, it rarely constitutes a documentary in itself, because such material has to be ordered, reshaped and placed in sequential form.[30]

As an adjunct to this, the more manipulated the footage becomes, the less real it appears to be. In addition images of themselves may be mute or without meaning and need to be interpreted; this interpretation itself may lead to manipulation and distortion. One of the prime attractions of documentaries was initially that

---

[25] A full analysis of the role of documentary film is beyond the scope of this book. Useful texts on documentary film and its convention can be found, apart from the texts referred to explicitly in this chapter, in Barnouw, E (1974), Corner, J (1986), Sussex, E (1976).

[26] Wells, P (1996: 169).

[27] This, of course, may have an impact upon the slant of the finished product just as issues such as film conventions may create a similar effect.

[28] Wheale, N (1995b).

[29] Young, A (1996: 137).

[30] Wells, P (1996: 168).

they should provide a means to communicate an argument with great clarity and conviction. However, as Wheale notes, whilst the technological equipment should allow a direct transcription, it is in fact subject to a number of complex conventions and all claims to authenticity have to be seen within this context.[31]

Trinh Minh-ha has argued that documentaries may be illusory and has heavily criticised the idea that they may be able to provide 'the truth'. Her arguments have a number of strands. First, that documentary practice is in itself misleading. Whilst it claims to offer a view of the real, it actually presents the subjective as if it were objective. Secondly, the styles and techniques that are commonly utilised are themselves only conventions, and the documentary might in fact only become a style, or an aesthetic in itself. Minh-ha also gives the example of documentaries based on third world situations and shows how in these contexts the documentary can itself be misleading in that it may perpetuate false values by ignoring wider issues. All these arguments point to the fact that while the documentary might claim to portray real-life events, it is in fact heavily affected by the gauze of camera and creator. As Alexander Kluge has noted:

> A documentary film is shot with three cameras: (1) the camera in the technical sense; (2) the filmmaker's mind; and (3) the generic patterns of the documentary film, which are founded on the expectations of the audience that patronizes it. For this reason one cannot simply say that the documentary film portrays facts. It photographs isolated facts and assembles from them a coherent set of facts according to three divergent schemata. All remaining possible facts and factual contexts are excluded. The naïve treatment of documentation therefore provides a unique opportunity to concoct fables. In and of itself, the documentary is no more realistic than the feature film.[32]

Apart from its authorship, the effectiveness and relevance of documentary in the context of justice can be major. Richard Sherwin has written of the power of the documentary in both filmic and political terms.[33] Discussing the film *The Thin Blue Line* (1988), by Errol Morris, he points out that the way in which the film maker operates can have an impact on events.

Two Dallas police officers stopped a car back in November 1976. One officer, Robert Wood, approached the car which had not, apparently been showing any lights. He was shot dead even though it had only been a routine stop to advise the driver to turn his lights on. David Harris, a youth who had fled his home town of Vidor in a stolen car, was arrested after boasting about the murder. He put the blame on a hitch-hiker he had picked up, Randall Adams. At a subsequent date three witnesses appeared who claimed to have seen Adams in the car just before Officer Wood was shot. They were driving past, two in one car going the other way and one person going in the same direction. Adams was tried and sentenced to death. This was later commuted to life.

---

[31] Wheale, N (1995b).
[32] Kluge, A (1988). Quoted in Minh-ha, T (1995, 268).
[33] Sherwin, R (1994).

Some 12 years later, the documentary film maker Errol Morris produced *The Thin Blue Line* (1988). The film consisted of interviews and reconstruction of the events. The evidence of those who had convicted Adams appeared thin in the extreme. It came both from his alleged companion, David Harris, as well as the three independent witnesses. By the time of the film Harris was serving a life sentence for another killing. Two of the other witnesses were in serious financial difficulties and the reward of $21,000 they received for their testimony was crucial. The doubts raised by the film were serious. It includes Harris explaining that if Adams had been able to provide him with accommodation on the night of the murder he would not have ended up in the situation he was in. This, combined with the other interviews, provided such a likely picture of miscarriage of justice that there was a re-trial and Adams was finally released after spending over a decade in prison. Its wider impact on documentary film making has been such that it:

> ... also led to a new line of documentaries about prison life and the cases of specific prisoners including *Through the Wire* (1990), *The Execution Protocol* (1993), *Aileen Wuornos: The Selling of a Serial Killer* (1992), *Aileen: Life and Death of a Serial Killer* (2003) and the quasi-documentary *Dead Man Walking*.[34]

Even documentaries have problems in determining what the 'truth' is, or was, and this relates to a wider question about determining historical information and translating it onto film.

Developments in the 21st Century

In more recent times, documentaries have achieved significant prominence in cinemas, both in art house venues and multiplexes. Major box office successes have been recorded by Michael Moore with *Bowling for Columbine* (2002), *Fahrenheit 9/11* (2004), and *Sicko* (2007) for example. In addition, he also achieved both commercial and critical success in the form of an Oscar for *Bowling for Columbine* (2002). This same mix of box office and awards came to Al Gore with his environmental powerpoint lecture tour *An Inconvenient Truth* (2006), which saw the ex Vice President pick up an Oscar and a Nobel Peace Prize in the same year.

In amongst this new enthusiasm for the documentary form in cinemas has been a handful of examples that continue the fascination with the imprecision of the legal system, and the possibility of miscarriages of justice. The strange video diaries which form the core of *Capturing the Friedmans* (2003) provide the most oblique commentary on a modern case. Defying the standard notion of the point of view, these consist of a mélange of home videos by one of the three sons, David Friedman, and contemporary interviews with the Friedman family and

---

[34] Rafter, N (2006: 180).

other players in their drama. The father, Arnold, and one of the sons, Jesse, in this seemingly conventional middle-class family are charged out of the blue in 1984 with various offences of sexual molestation arising from the father's computer home tutoring classes. For some reason David Friedman started to video the family as they coped with the lead-up to the trials of Arnold and Jesse. At the end of the film audiences are left to ponder with a very limited steer on how to evaluate the evidence available. Some critics have found it disturbing with its 'gloomy and ambiguous conclusion',[35] whilst others have railed against the irresponsibility of the film's maker, Andrew Jarecki, for opting to make a piece of fascinating art rather than following obvious lines of questioning and leaving out relevant details in pursuit of a box office success.[36]

Equally disturbing is the portrait of the French lawyer Jacques Vergès in *L'Avocat du Diable,* aka *Terror's Advocate* (2007) which garnered a number of critical awards. It depicted a lawyer employed by those ranging from the revolutionary left—Algeria's FLN, Palestine's FPLP and leading members of the Khmer Rouge—to Carlos the Jackal, the Nazi war criminal Klaus Barbie, Slobodan Milosevic and other notorious figures. This draws attention to an issue on the international stage which is found more normally at the domestic level. Namely, the ethical questions raised where legal wiles are employed in defence of the apparently indefensible as well as the freedom fighter/terrorist dichotomy. These are questions to which there are no easy answers but which Schroeder's documentary, like his filming of *Reversal of Fortune* (1990), leaves the audience uncertain and uneasy.

The eye of Erroll Morris has turned most recently to the conduct of the American state in its failures to meet the Geneva Convention in *Standard Operating Procedure* (2008). This details the abuses at the Abu Ghraib prison in Iraq and is a fierce indictment of some of the saddest collateral effects of that murderous adventure. Given the emerging popularity of the documentary amongst the public, veterans like Morris, Moore and Bloomfield can expect to be joined by others switching between the styles of film and perhaps changing their dynamic. In addition to Schroeder we have Jonathan Demme, the director of *Silence of the Lambs* (1991) and *Philadelphia* (1993) describing his latest documentary project, *Jimmy Carter: Man from Plains* (2007) within a clear Hollywood Western framework:

> The more I thought about Carter, the more I started thinking about High Noon. The idea of the ageing peacemaker who should be in retirement, having once again to strap on is guns—in Jimmy Carter's case, he's strapping on his heart and soul—and coming forth into town, one last time, to confront his adversaries, those who would perpetuate violence. It's Gary Cooper, striding down the street, all alone: no one's stronger than the really old guy who takes on a good mission when he should be allowed to be on the porch in his rocking chair.[37]

---

[35] Haviland, D (2004).
[36] Edelstein, D (2003).
[37] Burkeman, O (2008).

With this in mind, Demme's documentary manages a slightly different kind of confrontation when Brandeis University initially refuse Carter's offer to speak there but rescind, so there is what Demme calls the final gunfight:

> He'll waltz on to this fiercely pro-Israeli campus, and confront the students, and his views will be tested to the maximum. And then he jumps in the car to the airport, and he's off to Darfur. Fantastic! It's like, 'Who *was* that masked orator'.[38]

Who Owns History?

Amistad (1997) provides a neat example of how issues of ownership have been played out with respect to historical facts. The film was broadly based upon the Amistad revolt and Supreme Court case of 1839 and 1841 respectively. Whilst the story was not particularly well known before the film, at least in populist terms, there had been a number of various documented analyses of the events. One of these was a book by Chase-Riboud entitled *Echoes of Lions*. Before *Amistad* (1997) was released in December 1997, a case was launched against Dreamworks alleging that the film infringed copyright in *Echoes of Lions*. Her argument was based upon two chief limbs, first that there were similarities between her book and the film and secondly that people at Dreamworks had come into contact with her book in a number of ways. On the issue of similarity, Chase-Riboud alleged 40 similarities, including the crucial one of the creation of Joadson, the black abolitionist as a central character.[39] There were a number of alleged links between Dreamworks and the book that Chase-Riboud utilised to reduce the chances that any such similarities might have been incidental. These included allegations that the screenwriter for *Amistad* (1997) had, previously, been contracted by a different production company to write a screenplay, of *Echoes of Lions* in 1993, and that Jacqueline Kennedy Onassis had given a copy of the manuscript of *Echoes of Lions* to Spielberg's production company in 1988.

For their part, Dreamworks had two chief arguments to rebut the case: first, that no one owns copyright in a historical event or facts, and secondly that *Echoes of Lions* itself was derivative and contained copied elements.[40] In the event the case was settled:

> On Monday February 9 (1998), plaintiff Barbara Chase-Riboud settled with Steven Spielberg and Dreamworks SKG. Chase-Riboud complimented Dreamworks for their film, Amistad and, as part of the settlement, dropped her plagiarism suit against the studio.[41]

---

[38] *Ibid.*

[39] Other similarities included the friendship shown between Cinque and Adams in the film. This was also in the book but was not backed up by historical evidence.

[40] An earlier work, *Black Mutiny* by William Owens, was alleged to have been 'copied' by Chase-Riboud.

[41] See www.cornell.edu/background/amistad, last accessed 3 October 2009.

The issues raised here do, however, provide interesting food for thought and another slant on issues of ownership and authenticity. The UK position is encapsulated by the case of *Ravenscroft v Herbert* [1980] RPC 193. The plaintiff in this case wrote a non-fiction book entitled *Spear of Destiny* centring upon the history of a spear which forms part of the Hapsburg treasure, and argued in the book that it in fact had a very important place in history. The defendant read the plaintiff's work and used it as the basis for a novel, and argued that, while he used the work as a source, he did not copy a substantial part of the work. Brightman J, the judge in the case, made clear that no monopoly could be claimed in historical facts and that:

> The law of copyright does not preclude another author from writing upon the same theme. It is perfectly legitimate for another person to contrive a novel about the Hofburg spear, even about its supposed ancestry and supernatural powers. Otherwise one would be driven to the conclusion that the plaintiff has a monopoly of the facts. Members of the public are entitled to use *The Spear of Destiny* as a historical work of reference.[42]

Notwithstanding that, the judge found that substantial copying had taken place with large elements of the language copied and incidents and occurrences copied wholesale, primarily as a labour-saving device. The issue of ownership of historical events was summed up by Irving Kaufman, Chief Judge in *Hoehling v Universal City Studios, Inc*:

> A grant of copyright in a published work secures for its author a limited monopoly over the expression it contains. The copyright provides a financial incentive to those who would add to the corpus of existing knowledge by creating original works. Nevertheless, the protection afforded the copyright holder has never been extended to history, be it documented fact or explanatory hypothesis. The rationale for this doctrine is that the cause of knowledge is best served when history of the common property of all, and each generation remains free to draw upon the discoveries and insights of the past. Accordingly, the scope of copyright in historical accounts is narrow indeed, embracing no more than the author's original expression of particular facts and theories already in the public domain.[43]

Similar issues are discussed in *Miller v Universal City Studios, Inc*[44] and *Nash v CBS, Inc*,[45] so drawing upon familiar copyright philosophy that the expression of an idea can be subject to copyright protection, but not the underlying idea (or in this case the facts) itself. However, whilst this is useful in terms of documented and protected material, it does not help us with the crucial question of how conflicting stories are resolved.

---

[42] Ravenscroft (1980: 208).
[43] 618 F 2d 972 (2d Cir 1980).
[44] 650 F.2d 1365 (5th Cir 1981) No. 78-3772.
[45] 899 F.2d 1537 (7th Cir 1990) No. 89-1823.

Whose Story?

The law is based upon stories. The law reports are full of stories, of documented histories of people's lives and aspirations and how the judicial system has resolved conflicting evidence (stories). Within the story of the law report itself lies layer upon layer of other stories (evidence and testimony) which are woven together to provide the official story. In many situations future cases are decided, in common law countries at least, by having recourse to previous 'stories' via the doctrine of precedent. The law of evidence and the adversarial system of justice allow certain stories to be disregarded, and for certain ones to be given more weight. Ultimately, a subjective judgment must be made, perhaps under the gauze of objectivity, by the arbiter in the court. This is done by the fiction of whether the underlying principle or rule contained in case A, as modified and glossed in case B or those in case C and D, are more appropriate to decide the conflict in case E. When it all comes down to dust, the role of the judge is to decide whose story is most credible as a solution. Frequently the parties will invoke the 'what if' scenarios. If this line of authority is applied then the result could be a slippery slope, whilst this alternative line leads elsewhere. A simple example was the conflict of lines of authority that built up in relation to the question of ouster injunctions in English law during the 1970s and early 1980s. The ouster injunction allows one party to have the other partner evicted from the matrimonial property. There were two alternative guiding principles that had guided the courts up until *Richards v Richards*.[46] One indicated that the matter should be determined by reference solely to the welfare of the children whilst the other suggested that all matters should be covered including these interests. The arguments in rejecting the former were of this consequentialist type stressing the potential injustice.

It is obvious that in many situations stories compete for ascendancy and may be heavily contradictory. In film terms, films may be based upon stories, however loosely, that are themselves highly subjective. Even the transformation of a work of fiction into film may cause problems in that the representations do not match what the original author intended, or that the 'consumers' feel some hold over the original, and feel that it should not be defiled.

Judge Dredd (1995) provided a useful example of this. Highly successful as a comic launched in the UK in 1977, rumours of a film adaptation abounded almost from its inception. Fan conventions would ask questions such as who could play Dredd, what should Mega City One look like, and so on and the makers of the film struggled through a number of scriptwriters and revisions out of fear that a celluloid representation of what initially at least was a counter-cultural and subversive

---

[46] (1984) AC 174.

comic 'might end up a fascist film'.[47] There are a number of other films that have had to confront similar issues, especially when classic or cult texts are transformed for the first time. This is compounded by the fact that the director's vision of the story, or his interpretation of the facts, creates in itself another story. Auteur theory posits that films are identifiable by stylistic or thematic 'signatures' which can be attributed to a particular director:

> In other words, an auteur possesses a *sign(ature)* marking out his own individuality which is legible in a film over which he has enjoyed sufficient creative control for that sign(ature) to permeate the film. In practice the auteur sign, like the star sign, can be approached as a structure made up of a set of paradigms working in distinctive rules of combination.[48]

The auteur is as much of a persona as the a star who appears in the film itself— while the auteur will not usually appear in the film his mark may be just as indelible. Crowther argues that there are certain conventions that are followed, some of which are fixed by the nature of the medium. The restrictions of time are very real, particularly when book adaptations are made; for example Jonathan Harr's book has over 500 detailed pages that need to be compressed into around 110 minutes of celluloid. Characters cannot be developed in the same way and there is a need to keep the story moving forwards. The audience may not have prior knowledge of the surrounding events though with the Lincoln films discussed above the audience knowledge affects the viewing of the film. It is also very much a question of interpretation, but of what? As Crowther puts it:

> Seldom, however, do they [filmmakers] appear overawed by the need for historical accuracy. Perhaps they are subconsciously acknowledging that there is no guarantee that any aspect of history is accurate. Every historical account, whether on film, in a book, a newspaper report, or an oral statement, is adjusted and amended and altered by the reporter, or by the recorder, or by both.[49]

Essentially the issue here is one of innate subjectivity. Whatever, or whoever is the basis for the story, the way in which this story is told will be constructed by the framework (ideological or otherwise) of the person who frames the text, or tells the story. When stories are retold, or told in different settings, perhaps by players with a different agenda, what may have seemed crucial to one storyteller becomes peripheral to another. It is these inconsistencies that further create difficulties for the film maker attempting to portray real-life factual events— someone has to have told the facts in the first place, and often the film maker will rely on a composite framework even before he places the story within his own agenda.

---

[47] Barker, M and Brooks, K (1998: 17).
[48] Phillips, P (1996: 150).
[49] Crowther, B (1984: 10).

Conclusion

If something is inaccurate, one should ask what's the effect of the inaccuracy? Smaller inaccuracies can serve larger truths. Clearly it's good to get things right, but people who complain about inaccuracies normally have an agenda. They argue 'facts speak for themselves'—but those tend to be conservative claims—the facts are conservative until proved otherwise.[50]

But are there dangers in inaccuracies? Logan argues that with respect to *In the Name of the Father* (1993) the 'facts' did not need to be misrepresented and that the story was powerful without the film's inaccuracies and omissions.[51] Further, he argues that such misrepresentation actually plays into the hands of those who still question the innocence of the Guildford Four and Maguire Seven:

> The co-producers of the film reject criticisms of its factual inaccuracies by suggesting that these will give succour and comfort to those who seek still to say that the Guildford Four and the Maguire Seven were guilty of the offences they were charged with in 1974. The truth of the matter is that a factually inaccurate film which does not 'come clean' about its inaccuracies and poses as a dramatic documentary will be used by those in the police service, on the bench, in the temple and in Parliament who still whisper that the Guildford Four and the Maguire Seven are guilty, as evidence that lies are being peddled as fact to justify the assertion that these were miscarriages of justice.[52]

Logan also pointed out that the Guildford Four were in fact freed because of a great deal of work and effort by a number of people rather than just because of the work of Gareth Peirce, as the film tends to suggest. Michael Mansfield actually argued that the film version in fact presented a crucial truth that was neglected in the 'real' story—the alibi that proves so crucial in the film, but which was not relied upon at the Court of Appeal. As, fundamentally, the convictions were quashed because of the findings of the Somerset and Avon police during their inquiry, the prosecution chose not to resist the appeal. Because of this, Mansfield argues, 'they were cheated of their appeal'.[53] Gareth Peirce is a solicitor who is not keen on media attention and scrutiny, and in fact asked the film's producers to not portray her.[54] When asked about the film, she was quick to point out the fact that the story, for all its perceived faults and inaccuracies, was providing a crucial function in disseminating information about a terrible miscarriage throughout the world:

> All societies have traditions of relating history through drama. There is value in giving an account, however impressionistic and subjective, of a truly appalling story.[55]

---

[50] Michael Wood, Professor of English, Princeton University, quoted in Jeffries, S and Hattenstone, S (1998).

[51] Logan, A (1994).

[52] *Ibid.*

[53] Bawdon, F (1994).

[54] 'Yet her portrayal, against her wishes, in *In the Name of the Father*, has meant that Gareth Peirce has become public property. She has even become the focus, in some quarters, of the attendant criticism over the film's many deviations from the facts'. *Ibid.*

[55] Peirce, quoted in Bawdon, F (1994).

In fact, given the whispering campaign that persisted after their release, it could be argued that the film, with its telling of the story not told at court, provides a crucial function in stressing their innocence. Jim Sheridan, the director, would go further, arguing that the distortion is justified by the rationale of his project—to show the corruption of the British police and the justice system. However, as Jenkins notes, 'he puts facts that he knows to be untrue. He doctors evidence, makes up scenes and implies that Emma Thompson stood alone against the might of British justice ... Sheridan decided on his verdict and headed for it by the shortest route available. That is precisely what he accuses the Guildford police of doing. He has fallen into the same trap as them.'[56] Michael Mansfield, however, felt that such alterations were permissible given the purpose that the director wanted to achieve: 'Although the distortions may become hostages to fortune for those who are unwilling to accept the basic truth, such sacrifices were necessary to ensure a compelling presentation.'[57] The only alternative was to present 'real testimony', something that Mansfield felt had already been done in the various books that had been written, although the impact these had had was negligible compared with the effect a film might have:

> All creative works are interpretive. By omission you lead people to believe some things and lead them away from believing others. It is a hugely arrogant assumption I suppose that by interpreting the truth you have as good a chance of remaining close to it as you do by trying to honour every detail. But I don't believe that any of what might be considered the misleading details of the film are dangerously misleading.[58]

In discussing *Amistad* (1997) Hadden noted: 'What has happened here is the same phenomena we have read about with other movies based on historicized fiction: the average American has not read or is not interested in reading history crafted by professional historians, but will devour works that have some historical gloss to them when presented as novels.'[59]

One of the key points with films is the audience it reaches as opposed to other sources of record and therefore the story the film tells may quickly become embedded as 'fact'. It may then be very difficult to counter the story in the film. Interestingly there is information on a website (www.civil-action.com) that 'explores new information and offers many important facts about Woburn, beyond what is portrayed in either the book or the movie'. This refers to the background for the book and the film *A Civil Action*. The site is sponsored by one of the companies involved, WR Grace & Co. The film gathered a large amount of publicity and the danger, for the defendants in the action, is that this account becomes the accepted truth. The website seeks to provide a significant amount of information for those interested in the environmental issues and to draw attention to a number of other factual reports that have been published.

---

[56] Jenkins, S (1994: 16).
[57] Mansfield, M (1994: 3).
[58] Daniel Day Lewis, talking to *The Guardian*, cited in *ibid*.
[59] Hadden, S (1998: 6).

The power of film to draw attention to issues has a potential to effect social change and individualised justice. This may be done, as is more common in the cinema of the imagination like the abortion issue in *The Cider House Rules* (2000) and *Vera Drake* (2004), or through fictionalising true events. This has been evidenced over the years from the early talkies like *I Am a Fugitive from the Chain Gang* from 1932 right up to the 1980s and *The Thin Blue Line* (1988) and the 1990s with *Dead Man Walking* (1995).

The first of these films had the effect of drawing attention to the inhuman conditions within the Georgia penal system. Certainly the media and public campaign that grew around the Derek Bentley case contributed greatly to changing the public's perception of criminal justice, and in particular the question of the death penalty. In terms of filmic depictions, the question of authenticity and accuracy this is perhaps best summed up by Iris Bentley's approach to the film *Let Him Have It* (1991). Once it became clear to her that the film would be made in any event, she acceded to take a role as consultant in the film. While she was disappointed in some of the aspects of the film as we have detailed above,[60] she made clear to the authors in interview that for all its faults, the film portrayed a useful purpose. For the first time in almost a generation, people were reconsidering the Bentley case and people who were not even alive at the time were taking an interest in the events surrounding his execution. As Greenfield and Osborn point out:

> In the months following the film's release Iris Bentley received over 10,000 extra letters of support, and in terms of increasing awareness of the injustice that had been perpetrated, she believed the film was a great success. She also saw how important it was that the case was discussed in as many arenas as possible.[61]

There is a balance to be struck with such films and they are often an uneasy compromise between the 'truth' and the cinematic equivalent. They cannot, for numerous reasons that we have outlined above, be completely accurate. All the events are subject to interpretation by the casting directors, the scriptwriters, directors and the actors themselves, not to mention the viewer subject. The following Chapter examines some more of these films in depth.

---

[60] See generally her own account: Bentley, I (1995).
[61] Greenfield, S and Osborn, G (1996: 1196).

12

Fact, Fiction and the Cinema of Justice (II): Specificities

Common Themes

This chapter seeks to examine some of the common themes and issues that have prevailed in filming true stories. This is, effectively, a sister Chapter to the preceding one, in that it explores some of these issues by looking in depth at these real-life films as a series of case studies. These issues are explored by utilising a number of specific legal films that are based, to a large degree, on historical events. A number of films are selected for analysis as part of this section, all of which provide interesting and relevant material. This breadth of coverage, and the detail on the films, is, we feel, justified by their individual nuances. Our analysis commences with an examination of the controversial events that led to the prosecution, conviction and execution of Derek Bentley for the murder of PC Sidney Miles, and which eventually became the film *Let Him Have It* (1991).[1]

Let Him Have It (1991)

The following section describes the story told within the film, and it is important to note at the outset that there may be disputes concerning their accuracy. The opening shots of *Let Him Have It* (1991) show London during the Second World War, and Derek Bentley being rescued from a bombed building. Having given some context to his early life, the film then goes on to show some other events early in Bentley's short life: petty vandalism, a spell in an approved school and his mixing with 'bad' influences such as Christopher Craig and his older brother, Niven. Derek becomes a member of Niven Craig's entourage and, although initially shown as an outsider and different from the rest of the group, is initiated into the gang. The elder Craig is later sentenced to 12 years'

---

[1] There are several books on the case including: Bentley, WG (1957); Bentley, I and Dening, P (1995); Berry-Dee, C and Odell, R (1990); Parris, EJ (1960); Parris, J (1991); Selwyn, F (1991); Yallop, D (1971). On 30 July 1998 the Court of Appeal set aside Bentley's conviction.

imprisonment for armed robbery. Derek Bentley's family is shown as being concerned about the people he is associating with.

The crux of the film is based on an attempted burglary at a warehouse. Bentley and Craig are spotted on the roof and the police are called. Bentley is arrested, and shouts to his accomplice: 'Let him have it, Chris.' Craig fires the gun, injuring one officer and killing another, before plunging from the roof. The film moves on to the trial, where Craig is sentenced to life imprisonment as he is too young to be hanged, but the older Bentley is sentenced to death. The film then concentrates on the attempts of the Bentley family to overturn this decision, and save Derek Bentley's life. The film culminates in a harrowing portrayal of a confused and scared Bentley being hanged at Wandsworth prison. A priest is shown with Derek when the door opens. Pierrepoint, the executioner, enters, approaches Bentley, loosens his tie, looks him in the eye and says: 'You follow me lad. It'll be all right.' Bentley is then led through to the execution room and a hood is produced from the hangman's pocket which is placed over Bentley's head, the noose is put around his neck and in a matter of moments the trapdoors are opened and Bentley is hanged. This final scene is extremely powerful and, aside from being the vital conclusion to Bentley's life, raises issues about the application and justice of capital punishment. It also clearly affected audiences, as well as Iris Bentley.[2]

There have been a number of books and television programmes made about the Bentley affair, so it was perhaps not surprising that it should eventually be transformed into a film. There were plenty of sources, and the long-running campaign to obtain a pardon had kept the events in the public eye. One of the fundamental problems with the making of the film is that the books themselves take different perspectives. Yallop (1971), for example, makes the case for Sidney Miles being accidentally shot by police fire. After some initial reticence Iris Bentley, Derek Bentley's sister and lifelong campaigner for his pardon, agreed to act as a consultant to the film when she realised that the film would go ahead whether she agreed to it or not. Whilst she technically had some input, her views were not always heeded:

> Whenever I got sent a copy of the script, I sent it back covered in red pencil. So much of it was wrong. They had Derek mixing with Niven Craig. Derek never met Niven Craig. But they took no notice of what I said. That's what upset Chris Ecclestone. He felt they were making Derek out to be more normal than he was ... The film wasn't done in the right order and it wasn't done in Croydon. They didn't get it right ... The house they chose was far too small and poky. I told them. But they took no notice. So much for my being a consultant.[3]

This failure to take account of the views of the participants need not always be the case. For example, Sidney Lumet's *Serpico* (1973) was based on Peter Maas's biography, which detailed the attempt by Frank Serpico to confront police

---

[2] In an interview with Greenfield and Osborn, Iris Bentley indicated that she had never seen the ending. See Greenfield, S and Osborn, G (1996).

[3] Bentley, I (1995: 294).

corruption. According to Cunningham, Frank Serpico himself participated in script conferences and made contributions to the development of the film.[4] Perhaps the greatest bone of contention with respect to *Let Him Have It* (1991) was the title of the film itself, and the way the words 'Let him have it' were used in the courtroom scenes. Both Bentley and Craig always maintained that these words had never been used, and in fact the ambiguity of the alleged words (let him have the gun rather than let him have a bullet) was never explored in court as the film suggests:

> But perhaps the worst was that they were so determined to keep the business of Derek saying 'Let him have it', which by now there was evidence he never said, that they not only kept it in but invented a whole scene in the court where they talk about what it meant. Did it mean 'Shoot him', or did it mean 'Give him the gun'? It was never talked about in court. It couldn't have been because Derek always said he didn't say it. So if he said he didn't say it, there was no point the defence counsel talking about what he meant by it. It was only ever the press who cottoned on to this. What was worse was that calling the film this, having Derek say the line in the film, inventing this scene in court, was sure to leave people thinking that he did say it. And that's the only reason he was hanged, because of those words. And he didn't say them.[5]

Iris Bentley attempted to get some sort of caveat put on the film to this effect, but without success. These were events in which she was intimately involved, but were in the public domain and had been subject to journalistic analysis. Clearly the 'Let him have it' phrase was an effective pitch for the film. After the film had been made, Christopher Craig gave his first interview and took a lie detector test. He was asked a number of questions including whether Derek had uttered the fateful words. Craig indicated that he had not said the words and the polygraph indicated that he was telling the truth. However, the question of whether this was an example of a miscarriage of justice was somewhat overshadowed by the question of the legitimacy of the final sentence.

In the Name of the Father (1993)

Wrongful convictions are a potent source of material for film makers, and the additional mix of the Anglo-Irish conflict can provide a dramatic backdrop. *In the Name of the Father* (1993) begins in Belfast with a youthful Gerry Conlon being mistaken for a terrorist gunman. His life in Belfast is shown as one of minor deviancy and he is only preserved from terrorist punishment through the intervention of his father, Giuseppe. He is portrayed as feckless and non-dependable, certainly not the sort of person who would ordinarily be considered suitable IRA material. Fearing for his son's future safety, Giuseppe encourages his son to

---

[4] Cunningham, F (1991).
[5] Bentley, I (1995: 308–309).

make the journey to England. After meeting up with an old friend, Paul Hill, he is shown becoming involved in the early 1970s hippy scene and living in a squat. He walks out of the squat after an argument and is seen 'sleeping rough' on a park bench, and stealing £700 from the flat of a prostitute. This apparently takes place on the very night when the Guildford bombings occur. Conlon returns to Belfast and is promptly arrested after a tip-off from one of the members of the squat, taken to London and detained under the Prevention of Terrorism Act. He is interrogated and confesses to the bombings, while also implicating his aunt, Anne Maguire, and members of her family. The interrogation process is shown as involving police brutality, which leads to his confession. His father Giuseppe, who has come over to help his son, is arrested at Anne Maguire's house and implicated in the bombing conspiracy. Following their convictions, Giuseppe and Gerry share a cell in prison, and after initial scepticism, Gerry gradually begins to take part in the campaign to prove their innocence. His resolve is further hardened when his father dies. Gareth Peirce, their solicitor, is shown as very proactive and obtains an important file by an act of subterfuge that proves that Gerry Conlon had an alibi and therefore could not have committed the bombings. The evidence is dramatically produced at an appeal hearing and the Guildford Four are freed.

In the Name of the Father (1993) was heavily criticised following its release because of the liberties it took with the facts of the case. Some of these concerned the portrayal of Gareth Peirce, the solicitor for Gerry Conlon, specifically when she appeared at the Court of Appeal. In one of the opening shots of the film, we see the camera pan from a barrister's wig on her car passenger seat to her face as she listens to a tape that Gerry Conlon has sent her. This was perceived as a device very much for American audiences—as a solicitor Peirce would not have had a wig, but to a US audience this image has very real symbolism. Legal commentators particularly picked up on this point, and the fact that she was shown later in the film as appearing as an advocate in front of the Court of Appeal, as gross misrepresentations, particularly as at this time solicitors did not have rights of audience in the higher courts. In addition, other lawyers involved in the case criticised the composite nature of her role, which somewhat decried the efforts of others. Peirce apparently came to the case fairly late in the process and was largely concerned with the appeal.

Other inaccuracies have similarly rankled in some quarters, including the portrayal in the film of Gerry Conlon and Giuseppe Conlon as sharing a cell, and some of the background history that occurred before the bombings took place. Alistair Logan, one of the lawyers involved in the case from the beginning, illustrates this with four problematic portrayals in the film.[6] Logan goes on to

---

[6] These were (1) that Gerry Conlon and Paul Hill were sleeping rough on a park bench on the night of the bombing; (2) that confession evidence was manufactured by forcing Conlon to sign a blank piece of paper, to which the 'confession' was later added; (3) that his father, Giuseppe, was imprisoned along with the Maguire family for assistance in the bomb-making process at a trial involving all 11 people. Finally, (4) that the greatest problem faced by Conlon and Hill was their inability to find the 'tramp' Charlie Burke, who could provide an alibi for their whereabouts on the night in question (Logan 1994).

argue that none of these four assertions is actually true. First, on the night of the bombings, Hill was in Southampton and Conlon at a hostel in London. Charlie Burke, the film's tramp, was a greengrocer who also lived at the hostel. Some six weeks after the arrest of Conlon and the rest of the 'Guildford Four', Burke gave a statement that would have provided Conlon with an alibi. This was the crucial evidence which was not passed on to the defence during the trial, but which was provided by the DPP as part of the appeal process in 1989. The statement was actually found by Avon and Somerset police in 1988 when they were carrying out an inquiry into the case. In fact this evidence was not even presented at the successful appeal hearing where the convictions were quashed.

Additionally, other assertions regarding the confession evidence and the role of the Maguire Seven also do not bear scrutiny. Gerry Conlon did not sign any 'blank confession', but in fact made two detailed written statements, and the Maguire Seven were charged on separate counts from the Guildford Four and tried independently. Logan felt the film was a 'missed opportunity to explain and dignify the struggle of 11 ordinary people who found themselves in a Kafkaesque nightmare where truth was turned on its head and all semblance of reality was replaced by ghastly lies and distortions'.[7]

The Hurricane (1999)

Miscarriages of justice and the consequent wrongful imprisonment of an innocent individual are a fertile source for film-making and the two films above provide compelling accounts about the two cases. These films have a number of different dimensions and a clear element with the latter is the effect of the incarceration on the individual and how the spirit and character of the central figure is affected. A further example is provided by *The Hurricane* (1999). The film tells the story of Rubin Carter who was wrongfully imprisoned for three murders, that took place in the Lafayette Grill in Paterson, New Jersey, on 17 June 1966. Carter was a successful professional boxer who apparently sparred with Sonny Liston, despite a serious weight and height disadvantage.[8] Carter and another young black man, John Artis, were both convicted of the three murders on 26 May 1967. There are a number of sources that tell the story of Rubin Carter. First, there is the autobiography that he wrote whilst in prison, *The 16th Round*. There were further accounts; Sam Chaiton and Terry Swinton's *Lazarus and the Hurricane* and James Hirsch's *Hurricane, The Life of Rubin Carter, Fighter*.[9] The film acknowledges the first two books

---

[7] Logan, A (1994: 295).
[8] Hirsch, JS (2000).
[9] Hirsch's book is the latest of the three and is an authorised biography in that he received full co-operation from Rubin Carter.

as the sources for the film, whilst Hirsch's book was published after the release of the film. Carter seemed somewhat surprised that his story should be of interest:

> I never thought and I still do not think today that my life was one, of which I could have such luminary people, Denzel Washington as the actor, Norman Jewison as the Director, Armyan Bernstein as the president of Beacon Pictures, think that my life was of such a nature that it could be made into a film. I mean that's mind boggling to me. (Interview with Carter included in additional scenes from the DVD, *The Hurricane*.)

The background to the film is racism in American society and the operation of the criminal justice system. It has a number of key issues that are worthy of discussion, including racism, the role of the police, law and justice, punishment, and the strength of the human spirit. The issue here is the nature and reality of the representation, and the relationship between the autobiography, biographies and the cinematic version. The film opens with an acknowledgement of the background: 'While this picture is based upon a true story, some characters have been composited or invented and a number of events fictionalized.' The story of Rubin Carter was much sought after by film companies, and the Director Norman Jewison explained its attraction:

> As a director I've always been, I've always been looking for stories which have a reflection, some reflection, of social conditions and us as a people. After all film really, truly, is the literature of this generation. Therefore at times we should approach film from the standpoint of what the film really has to say of us as a people. (DVD Additional scenes, *The Hurricane*.)

The producer, Armyan Bernstein, was very enthusiastic about filming the story of Carter's life, and spelt out to Rubin Carter that he should make the film with his company because he wanted to tell the story and would write it himself. He made it clear he would accommodate Carter's wishes: 'If you don't like the screenplay I'll throw it away ... we'll keep on doing that until you're happy' (from DVD, *The Making of the Hurricane*). The film is a telling social commentary on a number of areas of the criminal justice system, inherent racism and corruption. It tells with its dramatic story of a miscarriage of justice that is finally righted through the dedication of a small group of supporters, and the self-reliance of Carter. The role and function of Judge Sarokan (Rod Steiger) are vitally important at this point, in marked contrast to the general judicial depiction we outline in Chapter 9. Rubin Carter was also particularly impressed with the performance and dedication of Denzel Washington and the film is a testament to an extraordinary individual who survives an incredible feat of endurance of body and soul, yet Carter explains that is this adversity that has made him who he is:

> I only did what I had to do what I could do and if I had to do it all over again I would do the same thing all over again I wouldn't change a second of it for one moment because I like myself and what I see in this movie, which is a portrayal of myself, I like it very much'. (DVD Additional scenes, *The Hurricane*.)

This is a film that seems to have satisfied all the various, potentially conflicting, interests. The director and writer/producer are clearly happy with the end product and, perhaps most importantly, so is the central figure, Rubin Carter.

Amistad (1997)

Stephen Spielberg's *Amistad* (1997) is a film based upon the mutiny on the ship *La Amistad*, which took place off the US coast in 1839. The film itself deals with an incident which, perhaps surprisingly, had not received much coverage within American history books before this point, something that Waring attributes to American self-denial as regards slavery.[10] The film begins with a depiction of conditions on the ship, centring upon a slave named Cinque who frees himself and leads the subsequent insurrection. Their Spanish captors are killed, but two of the crew are allowed to live so that they could sail *La Amistad* back to Africa. However, the sailors trick the slaves as they sail east (towards Africa) during the day and northwest at night (back towards America), and the ship eventually ends up off the north east coast of America, where it is boarded by Americans and taken to Connecticut.

The slaves are imprisoned and a group of abolitionists mobilise to help them. These number Lewis Tappan (Stellan Skarsgård), Theodore Joadson (Morgan Freeman) and eventually Roger Baldwin (Matthew McConaughey) once their approach to John Quincy Adams (Anthony Hopkins) has proved unsuccessful. The first courtroom scene shows five separate claims being made upon the slaves before a Connecticut Court, a number of international treaties and agreements being cited in support:

> The two surviving crew members and the Spanish government, under whose authority *La Amistad* sailed, each demand the return of the vessel and its human cargo. The United States supports the Spanish, but argues the slaves should be executed as murderous mutineers, giving a criminal flavor to the admiralty proceedings. The crew of the United States warship that recaptured *La Amistad* claims a one-third salvage interest in the vessel, under a maritime law incentive scheme that rewards enterprising seamen, even those in government employ, for retrieving lost property. (Mercifully, Spielberg chose to leave out the similar claims of some opportunistic Long Island residents.) British Naval officers appear as self-righteous witnesses who also ply international waters intercepting slave ships and freeing their prisoners. The movie begins to look like *Roots* meets *Citizen Ruth*, as these competing parties dogmatically pursue their causes, mostly oblivious to the welfare of the Africans whose lives and liberty are at stake.[11]

In the event, the crucial issue centres upon where the slaves were born and their consequent status; it is imperative that testimony from the slaves is heard so that evidence can be adduced. The ship is searched and documents discovered provide

---

[10] Waring, R (1998).
[11] *Ibid*, 3.

some evidence that the ship originated in Africa, and not Cuba (a Spanish colony), and therefore were part of the illegal slave trade.[12] The case has by this time become something of a *cause célèbre*, and the campaigning US President, Martin Van Buren, arranged the release of the trial judge so that his own hand-picked successor can be used in the second trial. Feeling that this further prejudices the slaves' case, John Quincy Adams is approached again for assistance, again they are unsuccessful. As the linguist they have employed proves useless for communicating with the slaves, Baldwin and Joadson conduct a search of the ports looking for someone who can speak their language (Mende). Finding a sailor who can translate, Baldwin takes Cinque through his harrowing voyage and against all odds the judge rules that the slaves should be given their freedom and returned to Africa. Fearing political embarrassment, the Government appeals to the Supreme Court. Again John Quincy Adams is approached to help them, and this time with the stakes increased he agrees. Adams forms a bond with Cinque after he is shown to raise some very pertinent legal questions, and Adams presents his case in the Supreme Court. In an evocative and emotional five-minute oratory, Adams presents the heroic tale of Cinque's life against a moving soundtrack: 'If he were white, he wouldn't be standing [here] fighting for his life. If he were white ... songs would be written about him ... his story would be told and retold in our classrooms.'[13] The slaves receive their freedom and the film closes with the *Amistad* victims sailing back to Africa and some information of what became of the key parties in the film.

Again, *Amistad* (1997) is a film where the 'true' facts of the case and the filmic portrayal differ markedly. First, some of the individuals are represented inaccurately. For example, Baldwin is presented as having a conversion from ambulance chaser (memorably, when he first meets the *Amistad* victims he is described in subtitle as being a 'dung-scraper') to abolitionist, when in fact he was staunchly anti-slavery. Similarly, the linguist who is portrayed as incompetent was in fact highly competent and the person who actually found the sailor who spoke Mende (not Baldwin and Joadson as portrayed in the film).

In addition, there are a number of factual inconsistencies and incongruities within the film. For example, slavery did exist in the north of the US at this point, but the film would have lost some of its impetus had this been acknowledged. Also, certain treaties that were crucial to the trial were not mentioned or considered, the first hearings (aboard the *Amistad* itself) ignored, and the judge 'chose to move the trial from Hartford to New Haven in 1840, a place where people were more likely to be sympathetic to the AMISTAD Africans; the change of venue was simply dropped from the film, as were any subtitles to indicate where events in America occurred'.[14]

---

[12] The slave trade was illegal in Africa, but not in Spain.

[13] Reproduced in Hadden, S (1998). This review and comment is a very useful one and some of Hadden's observations inform this section.

[14] *Ibid*, 3. Other inaccuracies include the replacement by Van Buren's of a 'lackey' judge—this was not the case and Hadden feels that perhaps the most troubling aspect of the film is the agreement made early in 1840 that the slaves would be returned to Cuba whatever the result of the case, 'a strategy that would subvert the entire course of justice, and violate the separation of powers, simply to be rid of a political bombshell before the 1840 election'. Hadden, S (1998: 4).

A curious creation in the film is the character of Joadson. Joadson never existed, and his addition may be seen in the most positive light as emblematic of the role of African-Americans within the abolitionist movement, and at the most negative, as a tokenistic gesture. Certainly it is arguable that such a ploy diminishes the role played by other 'real' figures in the story. There were other less problematic issues, such as the fact that the Amistad was brought into port in August, when it was highly unlikely that it would be snowing. A further area of criticism that has been levelled at the film concerns Adams's speech to the Supreme Court, which provides the finale: 'To add insult to historical injury, Adams's speech actually took eight hours, spread over two days (during which time one of the most odious judges died in his sleep), rather than the five minutes of damp-eyed oration he's allotted in the film.'[15] This returns to the point made earlier concerning the difficulty in cramming an historical event into a short space, geared towards audience toleration.

The examples above deal with particular issues. For example *Let Him Have It* (1991) is concerned with the question of capital punishment both specifically and more generally. *In the Name of the Father* (1993) has as its background the position of the Irish in Britain and the war with the IRA. In both of these films the role and functioning of the criminal justice system is part of the critique. *Amistad* (1997) adopts the issue of slavery as its central theme and is in line with those law films such as *To Kill a Mockingbird* (1962) that have dealt with serious moral questions. There are, though, other examples of films based on factual events that revolve around events that have involved civil justice. Two such films have been based on litigation revolving around environmental damage and personal injury.[16] Here the emphasis is on how the application of the law and the skill, tenacity and determination of the lawyers may enable an otherwise impotent community to obtain redress.[17]

A Civil Action (1998)

A Civil Action (1998), based on the book by Jonathan Harr, charts a dispute over a poisoned water supply in East Woburn between local residents and three companies in the 1980s.[18] It was discovered that wells that served the town had been polluted

---

[15] Jeffries, S and Hattenstone, S (1998).

[16] There is also the earlier film, *Silkwood* (1983). Director Mike Nichols summed up in Halliwell (2008: 1080) thus: 'Despite the historical instance of the case, it is too simple to merit a film of this length, which is filled with pregnant pauses and romantic asides. Nor are the actors quite so charismatic as they think they are.'

[17] In this broad definition we are including the central character in Erin Brokovich played by Julia Roberts as a lawyer even though she was unqualified; it would be churlish to do otherwise.

[18] The book, first published in hard cover by Random House in 1995 and in paperback by Vintage in 1996, won the 1996 national Book Critics Circle award for non-fiction and was a finalist for the non-fiction Book of the Year. The case itself has been used in several law schools as a teaching tool. Dan Kennedy (1999) describes the two vehicles thus: 'the semipopular second-rate movie based on the highly popular, first-rate book'.

with industrial solvents, and the community thought that this was responsible for the higher than average rate of leukaemia. The legal story involved the damages action raised by the local residents, and this forms the core of the film. Although there has been no storm about the accuracy of this film its genesis is itself of interest as it highlights the mediated nature of events. The screenplay was written by Steven Zaillian, and based on the book which indicates that it is 'a work of nonfiction':

> All the characters and events depicted in this book are real. Much of the material comes from my observations over the period of eight years beginning in the winter of 1986, and from repeated interviews with those persons directly involved. The voluminous official record, particularly some fifty thousand pages of deposition and trial transcripts, provided another vital source.[19]

Aware, no doubt, of the whole question of authenticity, Harr provides a significant section on his methodology. He started work on the project in February 1986 before the start of the trial. He met with the main protagonist, Jan Schlichtmann, and his partners when the outlook was rosy: 'When I first started the project all the auguries were great. Jan had gotten a jury. He had the proof that he thought he needed to win the case and he thought the book was going to be a wonderful depiction of an incredible victory.'[20] Schlichtmann agreed to let him follow the events of the lawsuit as 'an observer from within with complete access to his preparation of witnesses'.[21] He also had co-operation from the plaintiffs:

> The Woburn families also graciously gave their consent to my presence and allowed me to sit in on their meetings with Schlichtmann. During the five months of trial, I was excluded only from one early meeting, in April 1986, concerning the firm's dire financial straits. Thereafter, during the summer of the harrowing settlement negotiation and the ensuing four years of the Beatrice appeal, I was permitted unrestricted access to the firm's operation.[22]

This is itself an interesting insight, in that the book and the film show both the upside and downside of expensive and risky speculative litigation. A settlement was reached with one company and the other two were sued. There were attempts to settle the case with the remaining two companies. According to Dan Kennedy (1999), Beatrice offered some $8 million: 'But Schlichtmann, visions of unimaginable riches dancing in his head, walked away from Beatrice's proposed $8 million settlement—$1 million per family. And he reportedly never told his clients about it, apparently because he cut off negotiations before a firm offer could be placed on the table'.[23] The mercurial Schlichtmann risks all the firm's assets and much more that they do not have to bring this case to a successful end. In the short term the

---

[19] Harr, J (1996).
[20] Taken from the website www.movieweb.com/movie/acivilaction (accessed 18 June 2009).
[21] Harr, J (1996: 493).
[22] *Ibid.*
[23] Kennedy, D (1999).

gamble to reject the offer of the polluters backfires and contrary to expectations, the major protagonist does not win out. The residents of Woburn and the firm with expenses of more than $2 million, receive, instead of the $410 million demanded, only $8 million. Schlichtmann ends up bankrupt, quitting the practice of law and narrowly deciding against suicide.[24] In the film the ending is updated to take in the fact that after settling his debts after a number of years Schlichtmann returned to law practice as an environmental specialist in New Jersey.

In addition to the shift of fact into film, *A Civil Action* (1998) contains a number of interesting elements concerning the portrayal of law and lawyers that share much with fictional films. Asimow makes the point that the film deals with a difficult area of law: 'The film dramatizes the human side of litigation, while presenting the realities of complex tort litigation more successfully than any other film.'[25] The film outlines the involvement of a personal injury lawyer, Jan Schlichtmann, who abandons his normal lucrative area of work and eventually throws himself headlong into the case. The Schlichtmann character undergoes a reverse transformation to that normally shown in cinematic lawyers as he is initially unwilling to become involved, though by the end Schlichtmann pays a heavy personal price.[26] As Halliwell notes, the story is 'as much concerned with the cost of the awakening of an individual's social conscience as the case itself'.[27] Aside from the personal transformation, the central feature of the film is the attempt to make the companies legally responsible to the community and the problems of using litigation to obtain redress. The difficulties of framing and winning a legal case are related to issues of causation, and evidence of poisoning, and the vast cost of bringing such an action is stressed throughout.

At the outset the case is seen as uneconomic and the firm is shown as very reluctant to take it on. Schlichtmann goes out to meet the families at Woburn in order to 'get rid of the case'. He meets with them and explains that there needs to be a defendant with deep pockets to provide the apology the families want and pay his firm. He leaves the meeting with his mission accomplished, and is driving back, when he is stopped by the police for speeding. He is in fact shown receiving a ticket both on the way to the meeting and on the way back. He has been stopped on a bridge that goes over the river and he stops and looks into the water. There is some clear symbolism that makes this a cathartic moment. He looks at the water running under the bridge beneath his feet and decides to investigate further. From this point on his life is flowing in a different direction away from the personal injury litigation he regularly settles. He walks, in expensive suit and shoes, along the riverbank to the industrial area that the families had told him about. He notices the names of two companies and returns to the office having found

---

[24] *Ibid.*

[25] Asimow, M (2000a: 533).

[26] One reviewer, Paul Tatara, describes the original portrayal of the John Travolta character at the outset of the film as 'well-dressed scum'. See www.cnn.com/SHOWBIZ/Movies/9901/08/review.civil.action. This has more in keeping with the central role played by Harrison Ford in *Regarding Henry* (1991).

[27] Halliwell, L (2008: 234).

his defendants. He now commits the firm to taking the case and commences the litigation process.

The tensions between law and justice are evident throughout, as is Schlichtmann's changing perception of what matters in the case. This is clearly evidenced at the meeting between the three groups of lawyers (plaintiffs and the two defendants) where a settlement is explored. Schlichtmann is told that Cheeseman (for WR Grace) wants to explore a settlement figure. When he receives the telephone call he is sitting on his car on a freeway bridge in the rain; this takes us back to his first moment of change on the bridge in Woburn. Schlichtmann is shown in a thoughtful manner, reliving one of the family tragedies, the death of one of the children. From this point on his perspective is changing and it is no longer a battle for compensatory damages. As the struggle for his legal conscience is being fought, this widens into a dispute over the practice of law. At the meeting, after pleasantries have been exchanged Schlichtmann indicates the profits made by the two companies in the previous year. He then opens the negotiations about how much should be paid to compensate the families, with a starting position of $25 million in cash, plus $25 million for a research foundation and a further $1.5 million per family per year for 30 years.

This utterly shocks the other parties. Cheeseman adds the total up to $320 million, the meeting quickly breaks up and one of the firm turns to Schlichtmann and says: 'You said this would never go to trial, you've just made certain it will.'[28] Schlichtmann is, however, unrepentant and his ire is reserved for the lawyers: 'They patronise us, they think we're blackmailers, they think they can buy us.' This rejection is fundamental as more than anything else this is a rejection of his own previous existence as a settler of personal injury claims.

This personal abhorrence of a settlement continues through to the final attempts to finish the case after Beatrice has been removed from the action. Schlichtmann goes to a meeting with Al Eustace of Grace's with it having been made clear by his partners that the figure they need to recoup is $8 million. Schlichtmann is offered the $8 million and warned by Eustace not to take this case to the wire, Schlichtmann rejects the offer without consulting his partners, who when they find out, become extremely angry. The filming cuts between the meeting with Eustace and his explanation to the partners. There is unanimity between Eustace and the three others with Schlichtmann the one holding out for more: 'I can't go to the families empty handed,' he explains. 'What families?' is the exasperated reply. By now it is their own domestic circumstances that take centre stage, not the plight of the plaintiffs. Finally a confrontation tales place back at the firm's by now almost completely empty law offices between James Gordon and Schlichtmann, whom he angrily approaches and establishes that

---

[28] According to Dan Kennedy, the William Cheeseman character in the film is a combination of two lawyers. For some unknown reason his name becomes a source of comment by both Facher and Judge Skinner: Kennedy, D (1999).

he is pinned in to a position where he will only accept what he is not going to be offered.

Schlichtmann is in a legal corner as he has been since he deliberately upped the stakes at the settlement meeting; he is not happy to settle because the case is not about money, as Mrs Anderson reminded him at the outset.[29] She repeats this at the last meeting with the families when Gordon explains the settlement. Schlichtmann has been sceptical at first about the solution that was needed and unable to see solutions in anything but financial recompense. After the bridge scene, when he gets news of the desire of the defendants to settle, he realises that this is not about money but the need for the community to know the truth about the death of their children.

The argument with Gordon takes place against the backdrop of a fierce storm, with rain teeming down. Once again Schlichtmann's path of action is symbolised by the storm outside and the storm inside, the connection to water and the course of his life is again established. The settlement is finally accepted by a resigned Schlichtmann, who re-establishes his faith with the practice of law through a symbolic picking up of his certificate, which had previously been thrown on the floor and the glass of the frame broken.

There are two different questions concerning the accuracy of the portrayal. First, the coverage of the physical events that took place in Woburn and second, the characters within the film and most noticeably the central figure, lawyer Jan Schlichtmann. It is, though, a mistake, at the outset, to think that there is a fundamental existing truth that can be found. There are though details that can be verified. For example, Kennedy points out that for some curious reason one of the company's names was changed from JJ Riley to J Riley. In many of the films we have analysed there are some examples of this type of minor change, and it is of course questionable why this should matter at all. The end of the film shows the lawyer handing over his files to the Environmental Protection Agency (EPA), who can then pursue the polluters. Dan Kennedy offers a critical perspective on this ending:

> It makes for an uplifting conclusion to a decidedly downbeat story. It is also completely and utterly false. But, unlike most of the fictionalisations, exaggerations, and dramatizations in the transition from Jonathan Harr's best-seller to the Hollywood screen, the tale of Schlichtmann and the EPA is likely to have a lasting—and distorting—effect on the moviegoers who saw the film over the past few months. The notion that it took one lone ranger to force an uncaring, unresponsive government bureaucracy to act may resonate. But it's not true—or, at least, it wasn't in Woburn.[30]

[29] The Anne Anderson character is an important figure both in real life and the film. Again, according to Dan Kennedy the film version is a mix of the real Anne Anderson and Donna Robins (personal communication with the authors).

[30] Kennedy, D (1999): Kennedy's in-depth knowledge of the case arose from his coverage of the case for the Woburn *Daily Times Chronicle* see http://home.comcast.net/~dkennedy56/woburn.html (last accessed March 9 2010).

The principal resident concurs with this view. Anne Anderson explained:

> I think the picture portrays us as a rather sorry lot … And it makes Jan into a sort of Mighty Mouse who comes in to save the day. It wasn't really like that. I'd done a lot of work before Jan ever arrived on the scene.[31]

The material that makes up the story of *A Civil Action* (1998) is from a variety of sources. First there is the official record. This consists of the pleadings, the witness statements, the court transcript and the published law report. Second there is the amalgamation of these, plus additional material, that was not otherwise recorded in the work of Jonathan Barr. As he had access to the developing case he may have picked out information that has not made its way into the 'official' record, though some must be based on his interpretation of events or discussions that unfolded in front of him. Third, there is the film version based on the book that has a different set of restrictions imposed upon it. Lastly there is the unwritten record that is understood by the participants, on both sides of the case. According to Kennedy, John Harr recalls that Jerry Facher once called the movie 'the fourth degree of separation'. First there were the actual events; then the trial; then the book, and eventually the film.

The film is of course constrained by considerations of time, and it is very difficult to show the complexities of such legal action in much depth. Kennedy argues that the concentration on the law suit and the central figure of Jan Schlichtmann obscures the real lesson of Woburn: 'It raises serious questions about the government's ability to protect the health and safety of its citizens even today, when knowledge of toxic waste's dangers is widespread—questions very different from those the moviegoers were asking one another as they drove home from their local multiplexes in the past few months.'[32]

Given that the film concentrates on the human side of the story, rather than the wider political dimensions, the question is how well is this done. Asimow has praised the film: '*A Civil Action* dramatizes the gritty details of civil litigation better than any other film. Discovery, for example, is shown as it really is—costly, tedious, and exhausting.'[33] This offers a contrast to *In the Name of the Father* (1993), which shows the lawyer finding the 'secret evidence' that dramatically clears the client. Asimow also raises a further interesting point that relates to the aftermath of the litigation and settlement. In the film Schlichtmann is shown thinking about how the pollution could have been caused and he discovers that barrels of toxic waste were taken away from the site prior to a visit by inspectors. According to Asimow, this is a point when the film departs from the truth:

> Here the film pulls its punch by not implicating Beatrice's attorney. According to the book, what actually happened was that Beatrice failed to turn over a consultant's report

---

[31] Randall, K (1999).
[32] Kennedy, D (1999).
[33] Asimow, M (1999).

that would have allowed Schlichtmann to fill the holes in his case against Beatrice. The First Circuit's decision states that Schlichtmann requested all such reports and that Facher's firm replied that none existed. *Anderson v. Cryovac, Inc.*, 862 F.2d 910, 927–28 (1988). If true, this seems like serious discovery misconduct. I don't know why the film-makers fudged this part of the tale, but the full story would have deepened the film's critique of the adversary system.[34]

This point is well made but, by the end of the film, the emphasis has switched away from the litigation towards Schlichtmann's personal life. He is shown passing the case on, a point Kennedy criticises above, and to review this part of the film would mean rewinding the plot somewhat.

Erin Brockovich (2000)

As with *A Civil Action* (1998), the backdrop here is environmental pollution and the consequential physical harm suffered by the surrounding community. The film centres on the central figure Erin Brockovich (Julia Roberts) and her attempts to get to the bottom of water poisoning in the small town of Hinkley, California. The film shows Erin trying to assemble sufficient medical and physical evidence, and the crucial relationship with her boss Ed Masry (Albert Finney). This film is interesting for a number of reasons, not least the emergence of a non-legally qualified woman in the leading role. Erin Brockovich, the central character in the film, is also a somewhat unsettling character because of her dress and behaviour. Furthermore, the emergence of the poisoning of the environment is a new area of cinematic legal dispute where law and lawyers can claim the high moral ground. *Erin Brockovich* (2000) neatly encapsulates some of the problems we discussed previously concerning classifying law films, and the limits of the courtroom drama. As David Gritten observes: 'Other directors might have turned this story into a conventional courtroom drama along the lines of *A Civil Action* or various John Grisham adaptations. But Steven Soderbergh is not other directors, and here he cuts concisely to the story's emotional heart.'[35]

The element of the film that we analyse here is the translation of the real-life events into cinematic action. There are two interesting dimensions to the film from this perspective, first the position of the leading character Erin Brockovich and how the portrayal relates to the 'real' individual and, secondly, how the events are translated into the courtroom action. Erin Brockovich herself has a small cameo role as a waitress in a coffee shop. One of the questions, given the way in which Roberts plays the character, is how far this was embellished,

---

[34] Asimow, M (1999).
[35] Gritten, D (2000).

particularly with respect to her dress and language. However, according to Quentin Curtis this was not manufactured:

> You suspect Robert's get-up to be Hollywood's sexist idea of a woman like Erin—until you see a picture of the real Erin in *Newsweek* magazine showing even more cleavage than Julia. Erin said she had initial fears that Roberts might tone down her frank language. She needn't have worried: Roberts mouths off at blistering pace and with brilliant panache. Like all good swearing, it has pith and point.[36]

Soderbergh actually cut one film that had been filmed with even riper language than Erin Brockovich uses throughout.[37] There is one scene that was cut from the final version that attracts an interesting comment from the director. The scene shows Erin and her children travelling by car to the plant, she stops at the roadside to take some pictures, and her children get out of the car. Two of them play in the dirt with their hands. Erin is looking around and notices that there is some green substance just under the top surface of the ground. Concerned, she gets the children into the car and drives to a store to obtain some water to wash their hands. The point that is being made concerns the spread of pollution and the danger to children. This scene was excluded and in his commentary, Steven Soderbergh explains the rationale for its removal:

> I ultimately felt uncomfortable with it ... Erin sort of rubs her feet over the ground and sees some green dirt underneath, now that did happen, I've seen the photos that Erin took outside the plant where you could see some green underneath the ground but in point of fact it was a lot closer ... and I don't think she had the kids with her and for me I felt uncomfortable with it, it stretched the truth, not completely, but enough that it made me a little uncomfortable, I was trying to not be too creative with the facts and so I lobbied hard to cut it out. (From additional scenes on DVD.)

As with *A Civil Action* (1998), there are debates about how far the film reflects what actually happened to the people of Hinkley, and how they feel about the film. One of the problems that has been raised relates to the distribution of the awards that were determined by arbitration. The case never reached trial:

> Many plaintiffs in the Hinkley case say the movie misrepresents what happened. Far from being the populist victory the movie depicts, the Hinkley lawsuit was a case study in how the rise of private arbitration, as an alternative to costly public trials, is creating a two-tiered legal system that not only favours litigants who can afford it over those who cannot, but is open to potential conflicts of interest and cronyism. The case never went to trial, because Pacific Gas and Electric, the utility accused of polluting Hinkley, and the plaintiff's lawyers agreed to private arbitration before a panel of for-hire judges, some of whom had socialized with the plaintiff's attorneys.[38]

---

[36] Curtis, Q (2000).
[37] The scene that Soderbergh cut shows Erin leaving the law firm and swearing at the other staff using an expletive. Soderbergh commented: 'I felt it was just a little too much.' *Erin Brockovich* DVD additional material.
[38] Sharp, K (2000).

So 'movie-like' is the ending, with Erin Brockovich receiving a bonus of $2 million and a passage into law school, that the main player in a more recent real-life tale of injustice has been billed as 'the real Erin Brockovich'. Here Betty Anne Waters, a divorced mother of two who had not completed high school, went to college, and ultimately to law school, after her brother, Kenny, was jailed for life for murder in 1983. Her research and persistence ended up with him being freed after DNA analysis undermined the case against him, which had been based on motive and blood groups.[39] The notion of this being 'the real Erin Brockovich' reveals the general public's reading of the Julia Roberts film as the character's rags to riches story was fiction rather than actual. The real 'real' story has also inspired the film *Betty Ann Waters* (2010).

Evelyn (2002)

The desire of Pierce Brosnan to 'give something back' to the land of his birth[40] was one of the inspirations in this story based on true events.[41] As Desmond Doyle, he is the father of three young children whose mother leaves for another man in 1950s Dublin. Doyle is unemployed and unable to support his children. They are taken into care by the Church, and put in separate Church-run orphanages. Desmond turns his life around and begins to make a living. He is now in a position to give his children a secure life in the family home. However he comes up against the brick wall of the law. The law requires that the mother must consent before they can be released from the care of the Church. Desmond encounters a barmaid, Bernadette Beattie (Julianna Margulies), who turns out to have a brother, Michael (Stephen Rea), who is a solicitor. With the help of a young American law student with connections, Nick Barron (Aidan Quinn), a challenge is mounted. The case finds a champion in Tom Connolly (Alan Bates), a pugnacious ex-Ireland Rugby Union International and general iconoclast. He is now a senior respected barrister, keen to take on the Establishment out of general devilment.

There is a courtroom scene in which the daughter, Evelyn, satisfies the court as to Desmond's fitness to be a father by explaining that the rays of the sun are her guardian angels, and she can find happiness back with her father. All seems set for an early success but the seeming clear, just result is opposed by the legal requirement for maternal consent. This is absent. The challenge, accordingly, fails at this first hurdle. An appeal is mounted on the basis of the Irish Constitution which, in Article 3, protects family life. The lawyers make their arguments and then, in a dramatic conclusion, the judgment of the Irish Supreme Court is read

---

[39] Tragically he died within six months of being freed in an accident falling off a wall: *Boston Globe*, 19 September 2001.

[40] Two of Brosnan's production company Irish DreamTime's first three productions were set in Ireland—*The Nephew* (1998) and *Evelyn* (2002)—and Ireland also featured in the Brosnan film *Laws of Attraction* (2004).

[41] DVD commentary.

out and relayed to an excited public via a radio link. To the joy of everyone, plucky Desmond has won through against the forces of legal formalism and a blinkered approach to how rules should be interpreted.

This has been described by one blogger as embarrassingly predictable, and certainly we would concur with this view. The idea of the father taking on these two megalithic entities, winning, securing his daughter and a new wife/woman seems most unlikely. The idea that this is based on four life events, makes the viewer consider how for the simplification of the story event. There is perhaps evidence of 'sugarcoating' events to make them conform to the Hollywood narrative style.[42]

The elements of commercialisation do affect the cultural integrity of any indigenous product. They are, however, so ubiquitous that audiences have no difficulties in spotting characters imported for foreign markets. The tidying up of loose ends, so that life is like a fairy tale with happy resolutions all round, is also what we have come to expect. It is one of the things that pre-screenings are designed for. Can the audience face the definite death of characters or would they prefer, like young children whose pets have died, to believe that they have run away to the woods? Sometimes they are unable, it seems, to accept the bitter pill of reality.[43] However at other times, a more upbeat alternative ending is not used.[44]

There is also the question of the misrepresentation of the legal proceedings. The broadcasting of the trial verdict, a little like the ending of *In the Name of the Father* (1993), is a theatrical concoction. This kind of alteration of events can be justified in terms of dramatic focus as no-one is grossly misled by the presentation of the dénouement of the judges reading out their reasons in open court. The writer of the screenplay, Paisley man, Paul Pender, explained his decision to bend reality thus: 'It seemed to me that this way of presenting the decision was justified in terms of the cinema audience.'[45] Evelyn then presents a story that is simplified and altered in such a way that we are both misled and reassured. It is the perfect illustration of how the modern mainstream cinema makes compromises in the interests of drama and, by their estimation, box office.

The Exorcism of Emily Rose (2005)

Although the location was shifted, the story of the death of a young girl living in Bavaria, Anneliese Michel, is very much the basis for this film. Although the trailer suggested this to be a horror film about exorcism, it is also a standard

---

[42] Bordwell, D (1999).

[43] *The Long Kiss Goodnight* (1996)—the original ending kills off private eye Mitch Henessey (Samuel L Jackson).

[44] *Thelma and Louise* (1991)—the alternative ending on the DVD has the protagonists driving off into the distance to the music of BB King.

[45] *The Making of Evelyn*, Scottish Television, 2002.

courtroom drama, as it has all the usual signifying marks. It is, to our minds, strangely still described as a horror/thriller although this was the aim of the writers Derrickson and Boardman. They introduced the courtroom aspect to escape from the long shadow of *The Exorcist* (1973).[46] For our purposes, what is of particular interest is the way in which this sad tale from Germany has been transformed into the transatlantic film, *The Exorcism of Emily Rose* (2005).

In 1968, Anneliese Michel was diagnosed as suffering from epilepsy, and, over the next few years, began to imagine herself to be possessed by demons. She was prescribed medication, her parents rejected the medical treatment, and turned to an exorcism to cure her. Two priests carried out 67 exorcisms, over a 10-month period, which took a physical toll on her body. At Easter 1973, three months before her death, Anneliese began to refuse food and drink. Her convulsions returned with a greater ferocity. No doctors were called. She died in July 1976 of malnutrition and dehydration, and her parents and the priests were charged with negligent homicide. They were found guilty of manslaughter and given a six-month suspended sentence and three years' probation. The prosecution had, in fact, asked only that the priests be fined and the parents found guilty, but not punished. Since the release of *The Exorcism of Emily Rose* (2005) interest in Anneliese's ordeal has grown, including speculation of the possible impact of *The Exorcist* (1973) on her actions.[47] It is possible to hear, online, Anneliese Michel's voice during one of the exorcisms. A German website obtained the audio from one of the 43 taped recordings made during the 67 rites of exorcism that Anneliese underwent.[48]

In *The Exorcism of Emily Rose* (2005) a girl from rural Montana leaves home for college. While the girl, Emily Rose (Jennifer Carpenter) is at university, she suffers from hallucinations and is prescribed various drugs which seem to make her condition worse. She believes that demons are in possession of her soul. She returns home and with the agreement of her parents, the local priest, Father Richard Moore (Tom Wilkinson), carries out an exorcism. Her condition worsens and she has another 'vision'. She refuses to take her medication and a few weeks later dies.

Father Moore is charged with negligence resulting in her death. The trial involves a battle between the religious prosecutor Ethan Thomas (Campbell Scott) and the sceptical but ambitious Erin Bruner (Laura Linney). He is keen to ensure that a clear line is drawn between rational faith and mumbo-jumbo. She wants to become a partner in her law firm, and accepts the challenge of defending Father Moore. She counters the medical experts of the prosecution, who seek to show that Emily was suffering from psychosis, with her own anthropological expert who explains the nature of the beliefs of different cultures about spiritual possession. The film is an exploration of what the stance of rational individuals

---

[46] http://www.hollywoodgothique.com/2005/09/writing-emily-rose-scott-derrickson-paul-harris-boardman/—interview by Steve Biedrowski with Scott Derrickson and Paul Harris Boardman. (last accessed March 9 2010)

[47] Given the timing of the release in Germany of *The Exorcist* (1973) in 1974 and Anneliese's existing symptoms over a number of years previously, this seems unlikely.

[48] The full length tape is available on a variety of websites including YouTube.

should be to those who claim a connection with supernatural forces, where these impact on the lives of the believers. The jury opt for the sympathetic rational response. They find the priest guilty but make a recommendation for mercy. He is sentenced to time served.

Clearly what we have here is the bare bones of the narrative being adapted by the writers to construct a wholly new, and rather simpler, drama. One of the more interesting central characters, Erin Bruner, with her shift from ambitious young lawyer to disillusioned drop-out, is from the wave of new women lawyers. She bears no relation to anyone in the original tale of Anneliese Michel. The priest and parents were in fact defended by one of the most high-profile German defence lawyers. The conflict between what actions should be taken by bystanders, when people put themselves into perceived danger, is a perennial one. We see this explored here in the unlikely context of exorcism. The theme transcends national boundaries, and changes in the representations of the characters and their individual motivations are, we think, marginal. There is a version of the story produced in Germany entitled *Requiem* (2006). This stays much closer to the events in Anneliese Michel's life.

The writers of the film, for their part, saw their film as combining the two genres of horror and courtroom drama, and of creating a fresh product from the basic story with the aim of making the central question 'Why did she die?':

> After we got into it, we ended up fictionalizing it and turning the story into something else. We took certain dramatic licence with it, but we took the basic events and the basic structure of that case as our inspiration.[49]

They were also inspired by having a New York police officer play them a tape of an exorcism which they made a major plank in the film's narrative. This was presented in the context of a debate about how we know what we know:

> We both thought right away that the courtroom was a great arena for debate. We like the film RASHOMON. People talk about 'RASHOMON this and that,' for all these movies, whenever there's multiple points of view. In this case it's actually much closer to that structure, where you present evidence. By doing that, you get to look at something in several different ways.[50]

With one writer a sceptic about supernatural phenomena, and the other a committed Christian, it was perhaps inevitable that the film would end up leaving the audience, like the jury, with no clear view and the writers acknowledge that this is what their film, unlike the death of Anneliese Michel itself, remains a mystery. Both this and the preceding Chapter have shown some of the difficulties in using true stories as the basis for film adaptation. That said, such adaptations, as in the case of Derek Bentley, can be shown to have had a useful impact, notwithstanding problems with the depictions themselves.

---

[49] Biodrowski, S—internet interview cited above (2005).
[50] *Ibid.*

13

Love Vigilantes:[1] Private Eyes and Beyond

In addition to those directly involved in the prosecution, interpretation and enforcement of laws there are two other groups who have emerged, both in film and literature, with distinct relationships to the notion of justice: vigilantes and private detectives. There is a long tradition of literature on detectives in fiction and whilst some are referenced within the text, we do not engage directly with them, both for reasons of space and because the overarching aim of the project is lawyers in *film*. The vigilante has a simple relationship to formal legal system and justice, whilst the private detective has a rather more nuanced stance. We focus here more extensively on the latter but are conscious of their overlapping characteristics. Detectives, of course, have appeared in a variety of different forms and styles and this Chapter is not concerned with the official face of crime detection, the police. The relationship between the legal system and the fictional upholders of law and order should be straightforward; insofar as it is problematic in terms of the issue of vigilantism, this is discussed below. As representatives of the state, police detectives have a defined function in the process. The focus here is not the public professional but rather the private professional. Inside the category of detectives there are a number of 'official' investigators who do not strictly fall into the category of police detectives. For example, pathologists have some history in providing the answers to criminal investigations particularly on television; this has now developed as forensic science has progressed, and the scientist has started to feature both with respect to forensic analysis of evidence, *The Bone Collector* (1999), and psychological profiling, *The Silence of the Lambs* (1991). There are a number of television examples; aside from *Quincy M.E.* (NBC, 1976–1983), who routinely solved cases, there is *Silent Witness* (BBC 1996–2008). On a slightly different level, there is also the issue of criminal psychologists as notably portrayed by Robbie Coltrane's Eddie Fitzgerald in *Cracker* (ITV (UK), 1993–1996), aka *Fitz* (US), and Robson Green's Tony Hill in *Wire in the Blood* (2002). In *The Bone Collector* (1999) the forensic scientist is well respected by the majority of the police officers he has worked alongside to the point where he is treated as a deity. The 'ordinary' cops all attend his bedside (he has been paralysed

---

[1] The title refers to New Order, and the track 'Love Vigilantes', from the LP *Low Life* (Factory Records, 1985).

in an accident) whilst he dispenses his critical analysis of the evidence. By the end of the film Rhyme has rediscovered his will to live and is out of his bed in a wheelchair. Although Agent Starling (Jodie Foster) has interests in psychological profiling, the main source of information in the attempt to catch the killer is the psychotic killer Hannibal Lecter.

This Chapter looks particularly at the changing image of the private eye and the context in which these films were produced. It notes the way in which the role of the private eye, like that of the lawyer, has undergone changes as well as a varied frequency on the screen. In simple terms the private eye has prospered when for a range of reasons lawyers have come under suspicion and have waned in numbers when the lawyer has received positive treatment. It commences, however, with an analysis of the narrower field of the vigilante.

Vigilantes

A familiar type of figure on the crime and justice scene is the vigilante, whose aim is not to solve any great mystery but rather to provide retributive justice. One writer suggests that the central focus of the vigilante film:

> concerns the efforts of a private citizen, man or woman, to operate outside the law in ridding the streets of evil and crime and to seek retribution against specific villains who did harm in the past to him or her.[2]

What we find in the relationship between the vigilante and the law is a breakdown of the system as far as the protagonist is concerned. The vigilante's concern is to right the situation and seek justice for the single event where the law has failed to provide a proper remedy. Thus in *Revenge* (1971) the police arrest a man on suspicion of having raped and murdered a little girl. Released for lack of evidence, the suspect is kidnapped and imprisoned by the girl's parents. Along with the family of one of the man's other 'victims', they seek to extract a confession by torture. The quintessential modern vigilante has been the character of Paul Kersey, and, in particular, the actor Charles Bronson, whose name now effectively signifies a vigilante.[3] In the original *Deathwish* (1974), Kersey is an architect with a belief in the social and political system. It is only when his world falls apart and the system fails to provide him with a satisfactory redress that he takes matters into his own hands. The rape of his daughter and murder of his wife and the laissez-faire attitude of the police lead the previous conscientious objector to decide to use a gun. He starts by responding to muggings by shooting the perpetrators. He is physically overcome by what he has done. Nonetheless he carries on responding

---

[2] Novak, G (1987: 4).
[3] Charles Bronson is the adopted name of Michael Gordon Peterson, a violent British criminal with a long history of incarceration. Bronson, C (2008).

to robbers by shooting them. In the end the police allow him to go free provided he leaves New York. In the four sequels, *Death Wish 2* (1982), *Death Wish 3* (1985), *Death Wish 4 The Crackdown* (1987) and *Death Wish 5: The Face of Death* (1993), Kersey shifts from being a vigilante responding to a specific individual injustice to taking a proactive role in rooting out the evil and depraved—and gunning them down.

Novak suggests we are talking about the normal citizen, who if left alone by criminal elements would have no reason to strike back. The simple revenge theme has cropped up in a whole series of films where the perpetrators are shown as evil, without any redeeming qualities. Their crimes are committed almost as 'sport', as in *Sudden Impact* (1983), *Eye for an Eye* (1995), *Kiss of Death* (1995) and *The Limey* (1999), in which the vigilante seeks to deal directly with a perpetrator whom the legal system has failed to bring to justice. This idea can also operate within a more general law film such as *A Time to Kill* (1996). The 21st century also has its variants on this theme, most recently *The Brave One* (2007). This appears to be more ambivalent than the simple fantasy of revenge of the 'civilised' over the 'savage', in the style of the *Death Wish* series. Here, though, the uniting factor is the complicity of the forces of law and order with the vigilante action of victim Erica Bain (Jodie Foster). It is worth making a distinction between the vigilantism of personal justice, and those individuals under stress, who tip over into mental unbalance like Joe Curran (*Joe*, 1970), or Travis Bickle (*Taxi Driver* 1976),[4] D-Fens (*Falling Down* 1992) or Nick Hume (*Death Sentence* 2007). The targets of their ill-will and action are groups whom they choose to victimise as a result of their bigotry, rather than any reaction to injustice. Also, one should not describe as vigilantes those who are operating loosely as agents of the government, like John Rambo (*First Blood* 1985; *Rambo: First Blood Part II* (1985); *Rambo III* (1988), any more than James Bond, Axel Foley in *Beverly Hills Cop* (1984) or John McClane in *Die Hard* (1988).

There is blurring at the edges where there is a connection between the legal system and the disaffected law officer. The move is from the police who take a cavalier attitude to the rights of suspects like Harry Callahan (*Dirty Harry*, 1971), but still operate within the framework of police powers, to instances where they operate as an extra-legal force like the renegade cops in *Magnum Force* (1973) or indirectly like the disillusioned judges in *The Star Chamber* (1983). Whilst often perceived as a vigilante, Callahan, in *The Enforcer* (1976), *Sudden Impact* (1983), and *The Dead Pool* (1988), metes out justice in a way which is violent but within the framework of his police role. He meets deadly force with deadly force rather than engage in personal revenge. For instance, in *Sudden Impact* (1983), whilst he taunts a robber 'Go ahead, make my day', he does not do what Kersey would have done, and simply shoot him, but arrests him. The actual vigilante is Jennifer Spencer (Sondra Locke), who has been a rape victim and engages in pursuing and killing the perpetrators. Callahan's contribution is to condone this by allowing her to go free.

---

[4] Although Rafter simply describes him as turning 'vigilante', see Rafter, N (2006).

Finally, in *The Dead Pool* (1988), his victims are seeking to kill him and those he is protecting, and it is significant that the series ends when Callahan steps over this line, harpooning to death a man whose gun has run out of bullets. At last he has killed for revenge rather than in the course of his robust version of lawful duty. There can be no more Harry Callahan, tough cop. The link between the wronged private individual and the disillusioned police officer can be strong. In the remake of *Shaft* in 2000, the nephew of the original John Shaft is a police officer who early in the film indicates that he is going to quit the police and become a vigilante. He does this in the light of a court freeing on bail a rich kid who is charged with murder. Shaft gives a stirring speech summing up the essence of the ex-police vigilante position:

> Fuck the job! I'll get him my own way ... I quit ... I took that job thinking that I could fight the good fight from the inside—and you're telling me about all the problems. That colour thing. Too black for the uniform, too blue for the brothers. About how justice gets tangled up in red tape or just bought off by the green. You were right. Fuck that job. Fuck the badge. I'll get this silver spoon motherfucker and I'm going to get him my own way. No lawyers, no politicians, no rules, no regulations ... his ass is mine. (John Shaft (Samuel L Jackson) in Shaft (2000).)

In fact, he stays in the police the whole film to get the bad rich killer by lawful means and then, and only then, quits—to join his uncle, John Shaft (Richard Roundtree) in PI work—as the credits roll. Versions of group action also crop up in a number of different genres. For example, *The Revengers* (1972) is an example within the Western genre that also includes *The Magnificent Seven* (1960). This latter film is based on the classic, *The Seven Samurai* (1954), which provides a fine early example of the provision of self-help and protection. These last two films have defence as their starting point. The shift is from the replacement of random lawlessness, and the individual response, to the emergence of official local law enforcement officers representing the community rather than their own perspective. The introduction of the formality of the law places the vigilante outside the procedures and processes of law enforcement. Hence we see *Shane* (1953) not as a vigilante, but as a proto law officer. In the modern world, the reverse could be said to be appearing. Just as in the Western, the justice of Tom Doniphon was replaced by that of Ranse Stoddart, so in the modern world the challenge to lawful policing comes from alternative individual answers in the form of the vigilante, like Paul Kersey and Erica Bain. It should also be noted that the vigilante theme also finds itself running through other films such as *Daredevil* (2003). More recently, in *Law Abiding Citizen* (2009), there is a vigilante who is not only railing against the murderer of his wife but also the Assistant District Attorney who organised a plea bargain and ultimately the entire criminal justice system. The bulk of this Chapter now turns to a rather different and, arguably, a more nuanced alternative set of values. These are found in the arena of the private eye.

Private Eyes

The private eye seems to offer an alternative to the official version of justice. Cinematic private eyes conjure up a world where men live by their own private code of justice while they ply their trade on the borders of the law.[5] The reason why the moral dilemma has emerged has been the nature of the work of the private investigator (PI). Rather than solving mysteries in the public interest as occurred in the sleuth and police detective model, the PI works as the conduit of the powerful. This has featured consistently throughout the PI film producing a conflict in relation to the path of justice and the interests of the rich client. This has been the bedrock of conflict in the PI film, from *The Big Sleep* (1946) through *Harper* (1966) to *8MM* (1999). The stereotype of the cynical, world-weary private eye with his own standards of ethics standing apart from the sordid fray of daily life may, however, be misleading. How the PI presents to the world has altered and the frequency of their appearance has varied. Our examination of the range of private eye cinema suggests that the 'Chandleresque' perspective on justice and legality within private eye films over the years has not, in fact, been entirely consistent. This is intimately tied up with the nature and type of films about law that co-exist with PI cinema.

Initially the private eye is a figure imbued with a level of scepticism about the efficacy and ethics of forces of law and order, and who provides a moral counterbalance to the corruption of the police, courts and lawyers. In fact, it is the private eye who appears as a form of justice figure. Thus we can contrast the early PI with the lawyer where the latter may be seen as of doubtful moral stature. In the filmic golden age of the hero lawyer, the PI is discarded as the focus for morality. He becomes marginal to the justice enterprise and appears as a minor character rather than a central protagonist. He undergoes a renaissance as films start to once more portray the official legal enterprise as flawed. Along with the rogue cop, the PI is perhaps our only hope of some kind of protection from the forces of evil. Whether it is through the medium of Westerns, Science Fiction, Courtroom Dramas or Private Eye films, there has been a consistent stream of films dealing with the conflict between legality and justice.

In addition to the issue of how representations of institutions within popular culture are of significance in the socialisation process, these PI films provide a perspective on the justice system from a source which is neither part of the institution, nor simply a member of civil society. The private eye is cynical about law, and much like Henry Fonda's Abraham Lincoln before him,

---

[5] A new type of 'private law figure' that has emerged more recently has been the bounty hunter. See *Dog the Bounty Hunter* 2004–2009, which is a reality television show following the exploits of one such bounty hunter.

is cognisant of the fact that the formal goals of law are at odds with the social reality:

> [Lawyers] write the law for other lawyers to dissect in front of other lawyers called judges so that other judges can say the first judges were wrong and the Supreme Court can say the second lot were wrong. Sure there's such a thing as law. We're up to our necks in it. About all it does is make business for lawyers. How long do you think the big-shot mobsters would last if the lawyers didn't show them how to operate?[6]

This Chapter looks at this early critical perspective, expressed by the creator of the most filmed private eye, Philip Marlowe. Chandler explained in connection with the filming of *The Big Sleep* (1946) that he was concerned with the whole question of how to live a moral life in his creation of this central image of the private eye. He complained to John Houseman about the question of the role of moral content in film and the suggestion that Marlowe was 'amoral': 'I feel a little annoyed with you for not realizing that the book had a high moral content ... It is the struggle of all fundamentally honest men to make a decent living in a corrupt society. It is an impossible struggle: he can't win.'[7]

However, this does not represent the full range of private eye views on justice and there have been historical inconsistencies in their portrayal in film. In fact, even Chandler's Marlowe was radically altered in his transition not just from page to screen (see *Murder my Sweet* 1944), but in the final process of cutting. So, for example, a film like *The Big Sleep* 1946 becomes a vehicle for Warner Brothers' new romantic pairing of Bogart and Bacall.[8] It is important to specify that this Chapter is not concerned with the whole range of films stemming from the field of crime/mystery literature. The literary genre classified in Britain under *Crime*, and in the United States under *Mystery*, ranges through police procedurals, courtroom thrillers through to crime novels where amateur sleuths are involved. One of the standard reference works suggests that the field of crime literature can be divided into three basic categories—'the thriller or suspense adventure; espionage; and the crime/detective/mystery novel. This last category breaks into three more divisions: the classic tradition, the private eye and the police procedural.'[9] The literature on crime and detection stories is extensive but does not concern us in this context.[10]

Defining the Private Eye

Our interest in the private eye stems from the role that he plays in the legal process and his relationship to the other participants, notably lawyers and clients. Sometimes the private eye and the lawyer may operate in tandem whilst at other

---

[6] Chandler, R (1953: 267).
[7] Thompson, J (1997: 64).
[8] *Ibid*, 44.
[9] Melvin, D and Melvin, A (1980: xiii).
[10] Woeller , W and Cassiday, B (1988).

times the roles of the two may become blurred as the one adopts the other's traditional role. There are, however, a wide range of individuals who perform an investigatory function with respect to criminal acts or even civil disputes. The most obvious starting point is the public investigator, the police detective.

There are a number of films where the investigatory function is not carried out by the formal state police force. In these it is often carried out by a more shadowy individual, or group. These characters are generally acting to solve some serious matter that threatens the security of the state. They operate outside of normal legal boundaries and rules, and are able to take independent action to secure the outcome. Most obvious of these are the secret agents that deal in the international world of espionage and counter-espionage. There is a group of infamous 'special agents' such as James Bond 007, the *Mission Impossible* crew and most recently Jaron Bourne from the popular *Bourne* trilogy. A particular stream of the semi-official agent has emerged, namely the incarcerated individual who is offered the chance for redemption. This opportunity requires the person to carry out some act of 'justice' to buy his redemption and consequential liberty. An early example of this is the *Dirty Dozen* (1967), with a group of convicted convicts carrying out a tough wartime mission. Individuals who have been assigned this role can be found in, amongst others, *The Assassin* (1993), *Demolition Man* (1993) and *Twelve Monkeys* (1995). This theme, of earning freedom for carrying out a difficult act on behalf of the state, is a variation on a theme of the wrongly convicted individual who seeks to investigate his own miscarriage of justice. *Demolition Man* (1993) combines the notion of the wrongful conviction with a chance to earn freedom. Officials from statutory agencies may have investigative powers and this can be reflected in film, as seen for example in *A Civil Action* (1998). Films may also demonstrate rivalries between different agencies and pit investigators against each other.

Aside from state or quasi-state investigators, there are also the pure independent amateurs. One prominent example of this type of sleuth is the figure at the centre of the mystery melodrama, the quirky eccentric solver of the 'perfect murder'; these are often the product of whodunnit novels by crime writers such as Agatha Christie or Dorothy L Sayers. For example, the Christie novel *Ten Little Niggers* was transformed into three different film versions, *And Then There Were None* in 1945 and in 1974 and *Ten Little Indians* in 1966. Krutnik outlines the constituents of the genre: 'The classical mystery story is often set in a stable, generally conservative social environment—the country mansions and small villages of Christie, for example—and it generally manifests a confidence in the power of the mind to order and thus dispel chaos.'[11]

Intellect is a key component: the mystery can be solved, but only if the detective has sufficient ability. As Poirot observes, it is the application of the 'little grey cells' that matters. The relationship with the formal authorities is ambiguous. Often the detective will, by good fortune, be present in the house when the heinous act

---

[11] Krutnick, F (1991: 39).

takes place or will be invited in by the concerned occupants; a classic example is the *Hound of the Baskervilles* (1939). The great detective is, frequently, a friend. The role is to make up for the deficiencies of the police; however, they are often welcomed by the police themselves, and encouraged to participate and solve the crime.[12] The police are shown as incapable of exercising such intellectual prowess, and are bumbling in comparison. Our amateur investigators often have no particular allegiance but purely have the function of solving the puzzle. They may well help establish guilt or innocence of individuals but the aim is to find the answer to the mystery. It is not so much a question of justice, but the criminal justice equivalent of the cryptic crossword.

The world of the amateur sleuth from the 'Golden Age' of detective fiction like Philo Vance, Poirot, Miss Marple, Father Brown or Lord Peter Wimsey involves nothing of significant interest in its presentation of law and justice. These are worlds where evil or driven people act in their own self-interest, and murder or murders are committed to achieve these ends. There is no moral ambiguity and ethical dilemma between legal acting and personal justice. The amateur sleuths are on the side of law and order. This is not a world where there are political influences in law and this world of crime novels is largely abstracted from any political and social context. This applies from the earliest of the superhuman sleuths, Sherlock Holmes, through to the range of guises in which mysteries were presented from the 1930s to the 1970s including Charlie Chan, Mr Moto, Mr Wong, The Falcon and The Saint. Writings where the commission of crime is socially situated are few and far between.[13] The private eye film, as we know it, developed from the puzzle film. These puzzle films were the cinematic equivalent of the Golden Age detective mystery of Agatha Christie, Van Dine or Dorothy L Sayers. In the 1930s such was their popularity that their key devices became somewhat clichéd. The vehicle through which this kind of puzzle was increasingly presented was the detective series. In most instances these were 'B' features shown prior to the main film, lasting for about an hour instead of the normal 100–120 minutes. One link to the upper-class intellectual sleuth of previous eras is provided by The Saint, who features in numerous films.[14]

The Private Eye: Justice and Politics

The fundamental feature of the private eye is the concept that he is outside of the state system of criminal justice, and is employed privately to perform an investigative role. This need not be confined to criminal matters nor individuals. There are,

---

[12] An interesting twist on this is the use of a hypnotist to solve seemingly impossible criminal puzzles in the TV series *Jonathan Creek* (BBC 1997–2004).

[13] Rendell, R (1995), which deals with the degradation of unemployment and the nature of racism in contemporary Britain.

[14] The Saint was a character developed, in a series of books, by Leslie Charteris. This was turned into a long-running TV series in the 1960s. The character was translated into feature films including *The Saint in New York* (1938), *The Saint in London* (1939), and the contemporary *The Saint* (1997).

however, a number of varieties of private investigator, ranging from the traditional gumshoe through to an insurance company representative. Private eyes may, at times, move in and out of some of the other identified categories but there is a fundamental difference from the start. The private eye is a professional employed by one of the parties and his duty is to that person; however, the private eye may often exceed his mandate and take a wider role. The role of private eyes is rather different from the amateur sleuth. Their role is also quite distinct from that of the police and the lawyers who are involved in the justice process. Here is a man (for the most part in film at least) frequently starting out from a position of ambivalence to authority. They have worked with the authorities, either with the District Attorney or the police. For example, Spade has worked with the Police Department; Marlowe is an ex-investigator for the DA; Hammer has served in the forces; Shaft was with the police; VI Warshawski and Keri Finnegan are from police families. The whole question of masculinity is an important one, as Krutnik observes:

> These stories are most often concerned with the aims, ambitions and activity of a male protagonist who proves and defines himself by his ability to overcome the challenges to his life and to his integrity which the narrative places in front of him. In terms of his active trajectory, the private eye, for example, can be seen as a cross between the traditional hero detective and the type of adventurer-hero found in genres like the Western. The 'hard-boiled' hero seeks to prove his masculine professionalism by outwitting his criminal adversaries, and often triumphing over the dangers presented by the feminine—not just in women themselves but also any non 'tough' potentiality of his own identity as a man.[15]

The ambivalence towards law and legality stems from an alternative moral code that the private eye exhibits. He is placed between officialdom on the one hand and his client on the other. He mediates the meaning of official actions and their impact in the real world. This is a role we are familiar with assessing and analysing in the context of lawyers. It is the contention here that, in film, the private eye has played a similar kind of role. He prevents the full crude armoury of the state being deployed directly on the individual. Like the lawyer, he is a guarantor of due process. There is, however, more to it than this. He is a metaphor for something slightly different—an alternative outlook on the justice that stems from the political and economic interests that dominate the state's laws. The private eye provides a reaction to the excesses of power rather than a full programme of reform or revolution. The creators of the private eye recognise the world for the venal place it is under capitalism:

> Hammett knew what happened to the money politicians did collect, that instead of serving only a few years with full-time careers elsewhere, as Jefferson and others had intended, politics was a lifetime vocation and as ready a way to wealth as the clergy had been in the Middle Ages. His [early unnamed detective protagonist] Continental Op was the common man everyone had on his lips, as befitted the political slogan of the day. He's stood between organised politics and organised crime.[16]

---

[15] Krutnick, F (1991: 42).
[16] Tuska, J (1978: 187).

Insofar as there is a possibility of taking action on behalf of a client, the PI has a resemblance to counterparts both within and outside the law. There is a strong parallel between the approach to justice of Charles Bronson's Paul Kersey (in the *Deathwish* series) and Mickey Spillane's Mike Hammer (*I, The Jury* (1953); *Kiss Me Deadly* (1955); *My Gun is Quick* (1957) *The Girl Hunters* (1963)) as both act as judge, jury and executioner. These of course pre-date what might be termed the post-modern equivalents in figures such as *Judge Dredd* with their blurring of judicial and investigative roles. Even Philip Marlowe does not wait until the police arrive before getting his retaliation in.[17] The ambivalent PI is clearly seen in his movie representations.

The Private Eye in Film

Private eye fiction has been subject to extensive discussion in both book[18] and essay[19] form. When it comes to the detective in film there has been rather less interest since early work in the 1970s.[20] The titles give a clue to the breadth of the coverage. William K Everson surveys the whole field of sleuths, private eyes, gentleman adventurers and police. He recognises the problems in seeking to survey any filmic genre. There are, he notes, some genres such as horror films that have reasonably clearly defined subject boundaries. Others, such as Westerns, are rooted in a geographical locale and a specific period of history. The detective story encompasses 'official' detectives like Holmes and Charlie Chan. Where Dick Tracy and James Bond fit in is less clear. Everson opts to cover a vast filmic area in which the movie detective operates and takes a very wide view of the detective and covers police, amateur sleuths and for the most part 'B' movie series detectives. Work since has not identified the private eye film as a subject for separate analysis.[21] The one work subtitled *A Casebook on the American Detective Film* is, in fact, for the most part an analysis of detective fiction.[22] In the 1990s writing has focused on either broader issues like film noir.[23]

The emergence of the professional private eye as a distinct category started in the 1940s in both main and 'B' features (*Michael Shayne—Private Detective* (1940)).

---

[17] *The Big Sleep* (1946, 1978) ends with Marlowe shooting Joe Brody and sending his boss, Eddie Mars to his death in an ambush. In *Farewell my Lovely* (1944, 1975) he takes out the scheming Velda before Nulty arrives on the scene.

[18] Symons, J (1992); Pyrhönen, H (1994).

[19] Benstock, B (1983); Bell, I and Daldry, G (1990).

[20] Everson, W (1972); Tuska, J (1978).

[21] Cook, P (ed) (1985).

[22] Tuska, J (1988). Although a second edition of the 1978 work, the films covered by Tuska do not extend beyond the date of his earlier work. The private eye coverage goes as far as *Chinatown* (1974) and *The Drowning Pool* (1975).

[23] Cameron, I (1992); Crowther, B (1990); Kaplan, EA (1980); or crime movies Brode, D (1995); or on specific writers Luhr, W (1990).

Although we can find the private eye Sam Spade appearing in the 1930s,[24] it was the cinematic success of the third adaptation of Dashiell Hammett's Maltese Falcon in 1941 which heralded the private eye film as we now think of it. Houston's version of *The Maltese Falcon* was followed by downbeat private eye films which fitted into the vogue for film noir. Film noir has been characterised as a stream of 'haunted visions of doomed men and women for whom love is replaced by blind passion and sexual obsession, which often erupts into violence and cold-blooded murder'.[25] The 1940s private eye representations in 'A' films were within this genre. It has been suggested that there was a certain ambivalence within film noir and that it teased audiences with unhappy endings, but 'even if the hero didn't get the girl, justice was still done and the American way of life remained essentially undisturbed'.[26] Whether one accepts this view of film noir, it is certainly true that PI films in the 1940s seldom exhibited the full features of film noir other than in their overall visual style. Contrast, for instance, the upbeat 'boy gets girl' endings of the 1940s film versions of *Farewell My Lovely* and *The Big Sleep* with their renderings in the 1970s with their greater fidelity to Chandler's original texts and the stress on the angst of existence on the margins of society.

In the post-war era each decade has witnessed a number of private eye films in which the strong central character of the private eye has been the focus rather than the solution of mystery. These are digressions on the nature of existence and living at ease with one's conscience in a hostile world dominated by powerful financial forces.[27] They differ sharply from the plot-centred murder mysteries of a range of film characters who are all technically private investigators. In this sleuthing category, referred to above, are found the modernised Sherlock Holmes and Dr Watson,[28] Charlie Chan,[29] The Saint,[30] The Thin Man,[31] duo Nick and Nora Charles,[32] and Dick Tracy.[33] In addition

---

[24] *The Maltese Falcon* (1941), remade as *Satan Met a Lady* (1936); *Private Detective 62* (1933) with the ubiquitous William Powell.

[25] Crowther, B (1988: 7).

[26] Tuska, J (1978: 361).

[27] Contrast the style and approach of Ricardo Cortez in *The Maltese Falcon* (1931/41) with that of Humphrey Bogart in the 1941 version. The dialogue is the same but in the early version Sam Spade is a light-hearted womaniser with no evidence of the internal torment which Bogart brought to the role.

[28] Twelve 'B' films between 1942 and 1946 with Basil Rathbone and Nigel Bruce.

[29] Forty-four 'B' features between 1931 and 1949 with three different leads.

[30] Eight 'B' features between 1938 and 1943.

[31] A reference to the missing man, Clyde Wynant, sought by Nick and Nora in the first novel rather than to Nick Charles himself. The translation back from the French version avoids this confusion—albeit in favour of another—*A Man Named Thin*—.

[32] Six 'Thin Man' main features were made between 1934 and 1947, with Myrna Loy and William Powell as the upper-class amateur detective team.

[33] Four series of 15 episodes each were produced between 1937 and 1941 as well as a 1945 'B' feature.

some of these early sleuths like The Falcon,[34] Mr Moto,[35] Mr Wong,[36] Michael Shayne,[37] or Philo Vance[38] have faded from view so completely as to be unlikely to be encountered except in specialist outlets. This Chapter does not cover detective spoofs and comic films using the genre as the vehicle for humour, such as in the *Ace Ventura* series. These do not have anything meaningful to say on the theme of the private eye's notion of law, morality and justice. The same applies to the light-hearted genre tributes that have appeared in the past 20 years.[39]

For reasons of finance and social culture the private investigator in Britain is a rare film character, although the private investigator is now a firm fixture in the canon of British fiction.[40] They appear in only a handful of films between 1948 and 1991.[41] These range from a British version of the gentleman sleuth (*Calling Paul Temple*, 1948), a genre tribute (*Gumshoe*, 1971), a traditional crime puzzle (*Unsuitable Job for a Woman*, 1982)[42] and a courtroom drama (*Under Suspicion*, 1991). The paucity of film output means that they do not form a significant part of the evidence in this Chapter. Private eye films are no mere specialist niche interest. Major directors have been involved in working in private eye films: John Huston (*The Maltese Falcon*, 1941), Howard Hawks (*The Big Sleep*, 1946), Edward Dmytryk (*Farewell My Lovely*, 1944), Henry Hathaway (*The Dark Corner*, 1946), Jean-Luc Godard (*Alphaville*, 1965), Robert Altman (*The Long Goodbye*, 1973), Roman Polanski (*Chinatown*, 1974), Arthur Penn (*Night Moves*, 1975), Wim Wenders (*Hammett*, 1982), Alan Parker (*Angel*

---

[34] Sixteen 'B' films between 1941 and 1948—although it should be noted that as part of the Hollywood process *The Falcon Takes Over* (1942) with George Sanders was based on Raymond Chandler's *Farewell, My Lovely*.

[35] Eight 'B' films between 1937 and 1939 with Peter Lorre—one was shown in 1995 on British TV.

[36] Six 'B' films between 1935 and 1940 with Bela Lugosi.

[37] Four 'B' features between 1940 and 1942—one of which, *a Time to Kill* (1942), was based on Raymond Chandler's The High Window. This also appeared as a full feature in 1947 directed by Robert Montgomery, under the title *The Brasher Doubloon* (1947), albeit with a running time of only 75 minutes. For insomniacs the first Michael Shayne film was shown in February 1996 on Channel 4 at 2.40 a.m.

[38] '[N]o other author of detective fiction, save Sir Arthur Conan Doyle, had so meteoric rise in sudden popularity as SS Van Dine; and absolutely no other author of detective fiction eclipsed so swiftly and so completely': Tuska (1988: 50). Jon Tuska also points out that Van Dine's creation, Philo Vance, vanished from the scene of American popular culture from about 1950 to 1980. His whereabouts remain a mystery to us although 15 films were made between 1929 and 1947 starring initially William Powell.

[39] *Shamus* (1973) with Burt Reynolds; *The Cheap Detective* (1978) with Peter Falk as Lou Peckinpaugh; *Dead Men Don't Wear Plaid* (1982) with Steve Martin as Rigby Reardon; *Hammett* (1982) with Frederic Forrest as Dashiell Hammett; *The Gumshoe Kid* (1990) with Jay Underwood.

[40] Sarah Dunant's *Hannah Wolfe*; Alan McDonald's *Rosie Monaghan*; Val McDermid's *Lindsay Gordon*; Liza Cody's *Anna Lee* etc. These recent additions have also featured on the radio and in TV series.

[41] Everson devotes a chapter to the British in his 1972 survey although this consists mainly of police detectives as well as supersleuths like Dick Barton.

[42] *Unsuitable Job for a Woman* (1982) with Pippa Guard as Cordelia Gray—the first woman PI (depending on how Pam Grier's *Sheba, Baby* (1975) is classified).

Heart, 1987) and Karel Reisz (*Everybody Wins*, 1990). Whenever lists of all-time great films are being compiled one or more of the foregoing films always feature. Barry Norman, for example, invariably includes three of the above in his 100 best films.[43] There appears to have been no major director, however, who worked in this field extensively and only two have directed two such films. This fact alone makes it more fruitful to look at these films as a genre rather than in terms of a sustained *auteur* theory.[44] The genres with which they appear to be most closely associated are the Western and film noir. As we shall see, there is no consistent set of themes or style that would allow us to talk of the detective film as a separate genre. Rather we have a subject focus for film-makers over the years.[45]

In the 60 years of the private eye film a variety of different styles have evolved and a division into categories exposes broad trends. The decades since the Second World War appear to have produced a range of private eye films. The styles fit into the prevailing filmic styles, whether it be in thrillers or romances. These changes were driven, then, by box office considerations as were the rise and fall of the private eye as a thriller film sub-genre. There is some reference to other depictions, and these developments will be looked at in terms of their approaches to the question of law and justice.

The Existential Hero

During the 1940s the character-based material in the private eye genre was dominated by the work of Raymond Chandler and his private eye Philip Marlowe.[46] Although the genre started with Sam Spade, he is in fact seen as a more equivocal character, as Tuska notes:

> Spade is no hero; he's just smarter and his greed satisfies itself with being petty rather than monumental. Above all, he won't be played for a fall guy ... Huston ... had to humanise the Spade role somewhat for Humphrey Bogart—Hollywood wasn't quite ready for the notion of dubious heroes.[47]

That said, the Spade of 1941 is rather more ambivalent in his reaction to realising that Miss Wonderley is a character without a moral compass. The contrast between the first and third versions of *The Maltese Falcon* demonstrate

---

[43] See, eg, Norman, B (1992).

[44] Ryall, T (1987).

[45] Cawelti, J (1992).

[46] Humphrey Bogart (*The Big Sleep 1946*), Dick Powell (*Farewell My Lovely 1944*), Robert Montgomery (*The Lady in the Lake 1947*) and George Montgomery (*The Brasher Doubledoon*, (1947)) essaying the role.

[47] Tuska, J (1978: 182).

this with the shift from the triumph of Ricardo Cortez in sending Miss Wonderley to her fate to the regretful resignation of Humphrey Bogart.

Philip Marlowe knows that justice is a commodity that does not flow in the direction of him or his clients. The police are at best his grudging admirers, and his confidence in the operation of the law is at best muted. Marlowe works on the intersection between business and racketeers, and his ethical code is something that he seeks to maintain in the face of temptation. Philip Marlowe struggles to distinguish between what is convenient and what is right. His conscience, nonetheless, sustains him in his encounters with the forces of law and order. The 1940s screen Marlowe is faithful to the spirit of the character expressed by their creator:

> Down these mean streets a man must go who is not himself mean, who is neither tarnished nor afraid … He must be … a man of honour, by instinct, by inevitability, without thought of it, and certainly without saying it … He will take no man's money dishonestly and no man's insolence without a due and dispassionate revenge … If there were enough like him, I think the world would be a very safe place to live in, and yet not too dull to be worth living in.[48]

This upgrading of the happy ending is seen in later films involving the relationship between Marlowe and the females he encounters in his screen life. Light comedy singer/dancer Dick Powell starred very effectively in *Murder My Sweet* in 1944. At the end of this version of *Farewell, My Lovely* (1944) Marlowe is leaving in a taxi with Ann Grayle (Anne Shirely) and it is clear that the romance is leading somewhere other than down the dark, dangerous streets upon which Powell has been beaten up and drugged over the previous 90 minutes. The *Big Sleep* (1946) seems to involve every woman who appears eyeing Marlowe lasciviously. Molly Haskell perceives this upgrading of the sexual allure of Marlowe in a positive light suggesting a 'real … sense of a woman's point of view'. In fact she suggests that since 'the plot … is next to incomprehensible … the women are what it is all about'.[49] Of the seven women who have scenes 'sniffing the honey that is Marlowe', four do not appear in Chandler's book.[50]

The studio's conception of what would sell resulted in changes being made. Certain scenes were re-shot and others inserted in order to cash in on the box office potential of Bogart and Bacall, reprising their roles from *To Have and Have Not* (1944). The re-shooting of scenes included inserting scenes involving Bogart/Marlowe and Bacall/Vivian Reagan in place of plot explanations, after the initial version met with a muted response from troops in the Pacific theatre of war. In fact, the noirish, rain-soaked Los Angeles streets, and elements of the original plot are heavily overlaid by light-hearted scenes and the building

[48] Chandler, R (1950: 198).
[49] Haskell, M (1987: 208).
[50] Thomson, D (1981).

of sexual chemistry between the principal protagonists which Howard Hawks became increasingly convinced would be the unique selling point for the film. Similarly the ending of Robert Montgomery's *Lady in the Lake* (1947) is remarkably cheerful with a remarkably upbeat Marlowe finally revealing his identity in the arms of Adrienne Fromsett (Audrey Totter). This film is remembered principally for the way in which the camera constructs the detective, shooting him from the camera's viewpoint so we only glimpse him during the film. The need for a cheerful conclusion to noirish films is found in another private eye film, *The Dark Corner* (1946). Again, the private eye walks off with his trusty secretary, whose invaluable assets he has come to appreciate during his battle against the forces of greed.

Not all films of this time frame turn out to be playful romps. A rather greater fidelity to the tone of Chandler is reported in the adaptation of *The High Window* in *The Brasher Doubloon* (1947). Robert Mitchum in *Out of the Past* (1947) maintains the sense of doom and threat of the forces affecting the lives of little people. In fact in this instance it is the PI himself who is under threat, having had a fling with the gangster's girlfriend. On balance, however, the principal trope in the private eye film of the 1940s is of an existential hero who discovers that life may be better with a 'sparky sassy partner' and that the danger to society posed by the less than altruistic moral perspectives of the rich and powerful is something that can be forgotten—for the moment, at least.

Fighting Evil

The private eye of 1950s films was a very different kind of animal. With Philip Marlowe, the authorities and establishment are regarded with scepticism. In place of the controlled, self-contained Chandler creation we have a private eye with a strong streak of sadistic violence and a vigilante approach. Mike Hammer's distrust of the authorities is pragmatic rather than principled, and is, in the view of Jon Tuska, the precursor of the vigilantism of the 1970s: 'Once the vengeance films of Clint Eastwood, Charles Bronson and Chuck Norris came upon the scene, Mike Hammer's world-view blazed with an incandescence far surpassing Mickey Spillane's impact.'[51]

Three films were made in the 1950s and one in the early 1960s with Mike Hammer as the protagonist.[52] These involve a variety of simple set-ups: revenging a murdered friend (*I, The Jury*, 1953); seeking the murderer of a woman Hammer gave a lift to, and in the process discovering a nuclear conspiracy (*Kiss Me Deadly*,

---

[51] Tuska, J (1988: 395).
[52] See also *Ring of Fear* (1954), in which Mickey Spillane plays himself to help solve mysterious deaths in a circus.

1955); a secretary going missing and Hammer getting caught up with Communist spies (*Girl Hunters*, 1963). It should be noted that Mickey Spillane was an enthusiastic supporter of Senator Joe McCarthy's anti-communist witch hunt in Hollywood. There is a certain irony in the fact that the writer of the screenplay for *Kiss Me Deadly* (1955), AI Bezzerides, was blacklisted by the House Un-American Activities Committee. Ironically, he takes the opportunity to insert discreet references to the otherness of woman from Simone de Beauvoir's *The Second Sex* into the film's opening sequence.[53]

Mike Hammer knows that justice is a commodity which has to be secured by the individual. The world is a jungle where good and bad contend for primacy. The lone man represents the struggle for right, and evil can be recognised with ease and must be confronted with force. The forces of law and order are a mere sideshow to Hammer's work in righting wrong. The Hammer ethical code is instinctive. There is not much light and shade in the Spillane/Hammer canon, and in the original films these views are expressed by Hammer through reactions to wiser counsel and silence rather than overtly. Even in his 1980s remake of his first film, the same simplicity is found.[54]

One commentator takes a less charitable view of Hammer, regarding him as a fantasy self-image for Spillane. This involves 'marketing garish right-wing fantasies of the threat to the national fibre of communists and homosexuals', stressing the violence whose justification is the need to maintain law and order against 'contaminating foreign elements'.[55] The sales of Hammer's fiction, if not the success of the films, suggest that this may well have reflected the perceptions of the United States in the 1950s. The contrast, nonetheless, with the witty and well-read lawyers, Paul Biegler and Atticus Finch, is remarkable. Nonetheless it is the PI who figures in films during the 1960s and 1970s when the lawyer as a figure of cinematic focus suffers a significant respite of almost 20 years.

The Stylites

The style in the mid 1960s changed again. The lawyer protagonist disappears from the scene with only occasional opportunities to don the wig or white suit. From the mid 1960s the private eye and the spy are who we look to for security. The updated PIs are more at ease with the world than Marlowe, although less

---

[53] The mystery female passenger notes that men are centred on their own interests and that woman is defined in reference to this dominant interest as 'the other'—which is the theme of de Beauvoir.

[54] The 1982 remake of *I, The Jury* has been assessed thus: 'The consummate cynicism of Mike Hammer is drowned in a sea of car chases, automatic weapons, and naked women that have very little to do with either Spillane's original or film noir' (Silver, A and Ward, E (1992: 414)).

[55] Hirsch, F (1981: 37).

certain than Hammer. In the personification of Tony Rome[56] and Lew Harper[57] the approach to life is altogether cooler and more laid back.[58] Even the weather is much better, with the rain and gloom of the early private eye films replaced by the beaches and swimming pools of Florida, Louisiana and Los Angeles. The mean streets are sun-dappled. The characters peopling the streets are mean, in contrast to our wisecracking PI. This not quite the world of the contemporary spy characters such as Derek Flint, with James Coburn starring as a secret agent in *Our Man Flint* (1965) and *In Like Flint* (1967), or Matt Helm,[59] but these are men with personal lives. In *The Moving Target* (1966) Lew Harper is in the middle of a divorce from his wife which he is most reluctant to agree to. His client in *The Drowning Pool* (1975) is an ex-lover. The eponymous *Tony Rome* (1967) lives on a houseboat harboured in Miami and has a passion for betting on horses. Travis McGhee similarly lives on a boat and has a passion for fishing (*Darker than Amber*, 1970). The new Philip Marlowe spends the first 10 minutes of *The Long Goodbye* (1973) trying to feed his hungry cat in the middle of the night. Even the sleazy *Shamus* (1973) (Burt Reynolds) manages to persuade a succession of women to drunken sex on his pool table/bed. These are low-energy all-action heroes.

This emphasis on personal stylishness and detachment from the broad politics of the world is a feature of the two Chandler updates from this period. James Garner plays the eponymous hero in *Marlowe* (1969). He adopts the laid back way in this film version of *The Little Sister* which he utilised in the small-screen portrayal of private eye Jim Rockford.[60] Sharp and worldly on the surface, but at heart soft and playful. This involves crucial character shifts adapting the earlier Marlowe to the changed mores of the 1960s:

> Marlowe was the prudish detective who, in *The Big Sleep*, had torn up the sheets on his bed rather than fornicate with a female suspect and contaminate his apartment with sexuality; and now Garner had to be given a girl friend and idled away his spare time watching the girls in a modeling school across the areaway go through their exercises. The toughness, the loneliness, the sense of claustrophobic isolation gave quarter to only a superficial wittiness.[61]

---

[56] *Tony Rome* (1967); *Lady in Cement* (1968), both with Frank Sinatra playing Marvin H Albert's creation.

[57] *Harper* (1966) with Paul Newman. Lew Archer became Lew Harper as a result of Newman's identification with the letter H after success in *Hud* and *The Hustler*. Tuska, J (1988). The box office hit *Butch Cassidy and The Sundance Kid* (1969) must have been a pleasant surprise.

[58] Lew Harper reappears after a gap in time but the style remains the same in *The Drowning Pool* (1975).

[59] Dean Martin played in a number of spy spoofs: *The Silencers* (1966); *Murderers Row* (1966); *The Ambushers* (1967); and *The Wrecking Crew* (1968). They provided the opportunity for Martin to be surrounded by a series of 1960s 'bombshells': Stella Stevens, Ann-Margret, Senta Berger and Elke Sommer.

[60] *The Rockford Files* (1974–1980), NBC, and five TV movies of the same name between 1994 and 1997.

[61] Tuska, J (1978: 238): the 'suspect' in question was Carmen Sternwood, about whom Marlowe was entitled to entertain major doubts as to her maturity and probably sanity. This incident of bed rage occurs in the 1978 remake with Robert Mitchum.

This inner core of soft lovability is something that Robert Altman sought to subvert in *The Long Goodbye* (1973). Elliott Gould brings his own mumbling, shambling, quirky version of Marlowe to a world with full colour. It has been suggested that by replacing the dark shadows of noir with Hollywood this has the effect of making 'Marlowe a viable character in a contemporary world'.[62] Crowther is less kind and describes it as being; 'out on its own peculiar and sometimes distasteful limb'.[63] Tuska contrasts Chandler's view of *The Long Goodbye*: 'I cared about the people, about this strange corrupt world we live in, and how any man who tried to be honest looks in the end either sentimental or plain foolish'.[64] In the Altman film, Marlowe is neither: he has surrendered to unmotivated and consequently meaningless rage against the world and all that is in it. Altman explained that he saw; 'Marlowe the way Chandler saw him, a loser. But a *real* loser, not the fake winner that Chandler made out of him. A loser all the way'.[65] This leads to a quite distinct perspective:

> There's no reality in the Marlowe character. Marlowe can only exist in the minds of the readers or in the audience. He's an anticharacter. I tried to play him as if he'd been asleep for thirty years. There was a line they cut out which summed him up. Marlowe's friend, Terry Lennox, sees some girls in the next apartment bathing without their tops on. He says to Marlowe. 'I'll bet you have a lot of fun here.' Marlowe replies 'It's no fun anymore, unless I can take off their brassieres.'[66]

David Thomson, commenting on the 1946 (Bogart) Marlowe, takes a more charitable view of the transplant of Marlowe to the late 1960s and suggests that 'Altman's Marlowe is a plausible outcast, a joke and a throwback to the real LA … Elliot Gould … is fine … at conveying the sad, good-natured helplessness of Marlowe, and mounting disquiet that needs to kill Terry Lennox.'[67] For his part Lew Harper knows that justice is a commodity which is elusive. Harper is someone who has things done to him as he struggles to piece together the complex web of intrigue which has resulted in his client's dilemma. Harper, according to Tuska, is scarred by life, but he retains his integrity, not by talking tough, not by being tough, but instead by understanding what it's all about.[68]

His view on law is sanguine. The police are not his close friends. The Harper ethical code is more fragile than that of Marlowe. He is assailed by doubts less because of moral incongruity than through the sheer magnitude of intersecting forces at work in society. At the end of his first film paralleling Spade and Marlowe, and their conflict between the rules and their loyalty to their friends, we find Harper in ambivalent freeze frame. Will he betray his friend of not? The

---

[62] Craddock, J (2009: 574).
[63] Crowther, B (1990: 34).
[64] Tuska, J (1978: 334).
[65] *Ibid*, 328.
[66] *Ibid*, 331.
[67] Thomson, D (1997: 65–66).
[68] Tuska, J (1978).

ambivalence of the undetermined freeze frame is a luxury not permitted to the author of the printed word—in *The Moving Target* (1966) the police have already been sent for by someone else to arrest Lew's lawyer friend, Albert Graves. The only possible ambivalence about which Lew muses is what kind of solace he and Miranda might offer each other for their mutual loss.

In the mid 1970s follow up, *The Drowning Pool* (1975), we are much clearer as to the evils faced—all the protagonists lack a sense of community and it is only Harper who stands against temptation. A fresh twist to the PI outsider is found in the 1970s with a private eye who is a 'black superstar'. Three films were made starring Richard Roundtree as John Shaft in *Shaft* (1971), *Shaft's Big Score* (1972) and *Shaft in Africa* (1973). This reintroduced the more traditional notion of the 'mean streets' being set in the gangster-ridden ghetto. The overwhelming impact of the films is the celebration of black pride and a powerful rejection of the Stepin' Fetchit[69] role for African-Americans in film.[70] John Shaft knows that justice for a black man is something that is a rare commodity which has to be fought for. In addition, he is a less misogynistic version of Hammer. The forces of law and order are largely an irrelevance in the world of Shaft. Our perception of him is one of awe before his ability to both have his roots in the ghetto, and enjoy the respect of gangsters, ordinary people and black revolutionaries. His relationship with Lieutenant Vic Androzzi is markedly different from anything Marlowe ever had; his actions are propelled by his autopoietic ethical code. These philosophical musings are not frequent, however, and he is happier in action rather than entertaining doubts with calm reflection. He alludes obliquely to his concept of justice when weighing up the gangster Bumpy when discussing the possible abductors of the latter's daughter.

The Return to the Politics of Everyday Life and Existential Angst

With the filming of *Chinatown* (1974) and the two updated remakes of Philip Marlowe classics (*Farewell, My Lovely* (1975); *The Big Sleep* (1978)), we have a return of the thoughtful, wry cynic. The world, however, is not the same: 'Chandler's world view no longer held the same currency, because, like the California climate, which had altered from clear skies to smog filled clouds, the world had changed and the social milieu with it.'[71] Marlowe is a man out of his time. The films operate on the assumption that the world continues to be run by rich manipulative people. Only the cars and fashions have changed.

---

[69] The work of Lincoln Perry (Stepin Fetchit) in *Judge Priest* (1934) and *The Sun Shines Bright* (1953).

[70] Tuska, J (1978 & 1988).

[71] Tuska, J (1978: 326).

The private eye works better as a historical relic. Working in 1936 Los Angeles, Jake Gittes knows that justice in a corrupt society is probably no more than a chimera. He has been described as; 'a mass of moral ambiguities, as cynical as Philip Marlowe but far more vulnerable'. His view on law is one of distrust, seeing it as a seat of corruption. The message is gloomy since, according to Tuska, '[c]riminal corruption can at long last be ignored successfully because it has finally thoroughly integrated itself into the American political, judicial, and law enforcement systems: criminal corruption is now synonymous with the American way of life'.[72]

The Gittes ethical code is shaped by operating in a world where; '[t]here are no absolutes, no good guys and bad guys, just guys (male and female) in all of whom innocence and guilt, good and evil are present in lesser or greater degrees'.[73] This notion of an island of honesty in a sordid world is echoed by the director of the 1975 remake of *Farewell My Lovely*, Dick Richards:

> Marlowe is tough, smart but fallible ... Marlowe is a hero ... We debated for months how to handle the last scene, where Marlowe gives the money to the widow. I wasn't so concerned with corruption. There's plenty of that in the picture. I wanted to stress Marlowe's honesty.[74]

Although set in different time periods, the same kind of mood prevails in Gene Hackman's portrayal of deeply troubled private eye Harry Moseby in *Night Moves* (1975). With the emergence of a new kind of redemptive lawyer film in the 1980s the private eye all but disappears from our screens. The PI only appears in strange guises such as Mickey Rourke's Harry Angel in *Angel Heart* (1987) with its Faustian theme and use of noir style. The shift back to the courtroom is presaged by Paul Newman's seedy but ultimately moral Frank Galvin in *The Verdict* (1982). The shifts between these two kinds of justice figures is, of course, not seamless and other figures like all-action heroes,[75] rogue cops[76] and Westerns[77] provide a location for the working through of these moral conflicts—albeit in cartoon, dumbed-down form.

The Postmodern Investigator

There was something of a revival of interest in the detective in film in the 1990s. These include the emergence of women[78] as private eyes[79] as well as unsuccessful operatives (*Kill Me Again* (1989); *From Hollywood to Deadwood* (1991)). These

---

[72] *Ibid*, 409.

[73] Norman, B (1992: 104).

[74] Tuska, J (1978: 335).

[75] See, eg, Sylvester Stallone's *Rambo* films in 1985 and 1988, Arnold Schwarzenegger's *Terminator* (1984), *Predator* (1987), Jean Claude Van Damme's *No Retreat* (1986), *No Surrender* (1986), *Bloodsport* (1988) and *Kickboxer* (1989).

[76] Mel Gibson's *Lethal Weapon* (1987), (1989) and (1992).

[77] Clint Eastwood in *Pale Rider* (1985) and *Unforgiven* (1992).

[78] Tamara Dobson's pathbreaking *Cleopatra Jones* in the 1970s was a Government agent.

[79] *VI Warshawski* (1991) (Kathleen Turner); *Backstreet Justice* (1993) (Linda Kozlowski); *Dancing with Danger* (1993) (Cheryl Ladd).

new detectives typically resist classification and there is no consistent model in the 1990s. We have a misfit detective hired by a woman to find her missing husband. The detective fulfils none of the standard features of the 1940s PI; he is not tough like his 1950s counterpart; he is not stylish like the 1960s version (*Deadly Identity*, 1990). We have a befuddled private eye caught up in a mystery which defies his understanding (*Everybody Wins*, 1990) as well as a traditional down-on-his luck black PI with a wisecracking secretary (*A Low Down Dirty Shame*, 1994). There has also been a remake version, with Jake Gittes encountered in the 1940s 10 years down the road after the events in *The Two Jakes* (1990).

This makes an interesting contrast with a wholly contemporary detective with Bruce Willis' portrayal of Joe Hallenbeck in *The Last Boy Scout* (1991). The traditional trappings of sleuthing and wisecracks soon give way to more familiar scenarios; where *Die Hard* (1988) meets *Lethal Weapon* (1987) in a film with frequent shootouts. The private investigator can function in a world of the blackjack and the occasional handgun, but is not at home when the heavies use Uzis and car bombs. Significantly, then, Walter Mosely's *Devil in a Blue Dress* (1995) is set in 1948 rather than modern-day LA, where Easy Rawlins would be an anachronism.

Similarly in the film version of *Poodle Springs* (1998), the now-married Philip Marlowe operates in 1963 in the shadow of new heroes like the spy James Bond. The advert on the side of the incongruous London bus in Poodle Springs announces 'James Bond is Coming', signalling perhaps the end for the kind of hero such as Marlowe. His demise as the bringer of justice is also presaged by the announcement that the following day Kennedy is visiting Dallas. Not only is Camelot's end being signalled, but the demise of the lower-register justice figure, the PI. Justice for the 1990s PI is a variable commodity just like the PIs themselves, ranging through the Hammeresque Hallenbeck to the characters in *From Hollywood to Deadwood* (1991) and *Deadly Identity* (1990) with their own identity crises. Their views on law are variegated and the 1990s ethical code can be summed up in the sentiment of Easy Rawlins' friend Odell—'in the end all you've got are your friends.'[80]

Often the contemporary private eye in film plays an adjunct role to a central investigative figure, able to offer support in a bit part. What has also developed is the tag that the investigators use, almost as if the film image of the gumshoes has become detrimental to the status of the profession. For example, in *The Client* (1994) the private eye is approached by a member of the mob who needs to find the whereabouts of Mark Sway:

Gronke: You Nance the private investigator?

Nance: Security specialist. Who's asking?

Gronke: Name's Gronke. I need some fast work.

Nance: Who referred you?

Gronke: Sulari. New Orleans.

---

[80] Mosely, W (1990: 189).

Nance is shown as a shady individual, complete with tattooed hands, who is prepared to carry out work for those outside the law. Once it is known through the referral exactly who the type of client is, he is prepared to co-operate and takes on the task of finding the boy. His self-classification takes him outside the traditional definition of the private eye, his title shows he doesn't have any of the ethical limitations of the PI. However, in *8MM* (1999) Tom Welles (Nicholas Cage) is described as a surveillance specialist, perhaps in an attempt to provide a more fashionable and up-to-date technological image.

The Firm (1993) provides a further useful example of the contemporary PI. The central character is the lawyer Mitch McDeere, played by Tom Cruise. Aside from being a lawyer he also carries out a pivotal role in the investigation of the misdemeanours of the firm of solicitors he is an associate with. McDeere's primary concern is to extract himself and his wife from the tentacles of Bendini, Lambert and Locke in such a way that he is free from the mob's later attention. He is the prime mover in the scrutiny of the firm's behaviour. However, he does have assistance. First he explains his fears to his brother, Ray (David Strathairn), when visiting him in prison and Ray advises him to go and see Eddie Lomax (Gary Busy), who is a PI and an ex-cop. That Lomax works on edges of the criminal justice system is explained by the nature of his relationship with Ray, which Lomax tells Mitch when he visits him: 'I was his cell mate, he must have told you? Did he tell you, by the way, it was statutory rape? She was 17, looked 25 and I got a one four.' Lomax is out of his depth, as he admits he is more used to dealing with angry husbands than international money laundering. His inexpertness costs him dearly as the mob find out he has been asking questions about the firm and he receives a visit from two hitmen.

Lomax refuses to reveal the identity of his client and there is an interesting contrast here with McDeere, who is on the verge of doing the exact opposite and breaching the client confidentiality that he is shown swearing to uphold. McDeere then hatches a plot with Tammy Hemphill (Holly Hunter), Lomax's secretary, to find a solution to his and now her entanglement. He sets her up in a nearby office to copy incriminating files that he takes from work. He stumbles across the fact that the firm is over-billing clients and sees this as a fortuitous way out. He rushes in to tell Tammy: 'I think there may be a way of doing this without getting disbarred and without breaking the law.' Tammy's questioning answer, 'Is that our chief concern here?', shows the difference between them. She is ambivalent to the sanctity of law and the ethics of McDeere breaking client confidentiality. She starts to emerge as an important figure, she comes back at the outset to warn McDeere. Tammy fits more satisfactorily into the Erin Brockovich mould than anything we have seen in PI films, VI Warshawski included.

Ridley Scott's *Bladerunner* (1982) is a prominent example of a sign of postmodern culture, in terms of a film that emphasises style and visual image over the actual narrative content. The film is one which mixes architectural and other styles and allows us to slip between different times and genres. Images within the film blend skyscrapers with ancient temples, while clothes, hairstyles and language echo other eras and styles. As Strinati has noted, 'the genre of the film is not clear. It has been defined as a science fiction film, but it is equally defined for us as a detective film: the hero has many of the character traits we associate with the "tough guy" policeman or private eye, and his voice-over which relates the plot draws upon the idioms and tone of film noir'.[81] The film is based on Philip Dick's cult science fiction novel *Do Androids Dream of Electric Sheep*? and set in the year 2019 when 'replicants', effectively human-created robotic slave labour, have been banned from earth, but have infiltrated the city (LA). The phrase Blade Runner is said to be taken from William Burroughs' novel, and Burroughs himself is thought to have appropriated this from an obscure Victorian phrase for a private detective.[82] The film follows Deckard (Harrison Ford), a retired Blade Runner who is called out of his retirement to track down and 'retire' these replicants. The original version of the film released in 1982 had an obvious echo of film noir in its use of a narrative voice-over provided by the chief protagonist—something used in many of the private eye films (see, for example, Mitchum's voice-over in *The Big Sleep* (1978). However, neither Scott nor Ford were keen on the use of the voice-over (rumours persisted after the film was first released that Ford deliberately read the prose in deadpan form in the hope that it would not be used). However, the narration worked on one level in that we identify more with Deckard as he explains his actions and his moral code within which he is operating. This narration was removed by the time the 'director's cut' was released in 1991:

> Both the director and actor, Harrison Ford, disliked Deckard's narration, and lacking this voice-over, the 'director's cut' presents the hero much more objectively and enigmatically, and it is even possible to be nostalgic for Ford's comforting tones when we are left much more to our own devices on the mean streets of the first version, vulnerable to the overpowering, cold visuality of decaying LA.[83]

Tying in with the film's reverence for film noir, Scott said that Blade Runner was a film set 40 years in the future but made in the style of 40 years ago. Indeed:

> The story borrows liberally from the private-eye genre, via the films noir of the 40s and 50s. The voice over narration (which was in fact always part of the conception but was less pervasive), the alienated hero with a questionable moral compass, the femme fatale, the Los Angeles setting, the movement from high-class penthouses to lower-class dives: all of these are familiar—indeed, over familiar—trappings of noir. Dick was openly upset with Fancher's drafts, and had good reason to complain of 'the old cliché-ridden Chandleresque figure' at the center of the narrative (he called early versions 'Philip Marlowe meets the Stepford Wives').[84]

---

[81] Strinati, D (1994: 433).
[82] Wheale, N (1995b); Bukatman, S (1997: 17) adds: 'Scott, revealing an awareness of the textures of science fiction, had been toying with the role of language in his strange new world. He wanted to find new names for the protagonist's profession as well as his targets—detective, bounty hunter and androids were overly familiar terms, no longer evocative enough.'
[83] Wheale, N (1995b: 112).
[84] Bukatman, S (1997: 20).

The setting is noir within a contemporary urban cyberpunk setting, and that just like the earlier antecedents, the concern is for man's quest for humanity—here elevated by the android status of the 'villain', a story of an existential hero fighting urban alienation:

> Jameson wrote that Chandler's narratives reflected an American desire for people to overcome their separation from one another: the detective served as an agent of connection. 'And this separation is projected out onto space itself: no matter how crowded the street in question, the various solitudes never really merge into a collective experience, there is always distance between them.' In *Blade Runner*, this separation extends into the distance between the human and then non-human, the organic and the technological, the natural and the cultural.[85]

Even the ending of *Blade Runner* in the directors cut restored a noirish touch—the happy ending of the original replaced by an ambiguous one where we do not know whether Rachel, a replicant, will live or die. Similarly, extra scenes added to the 1991 version hint at Deckard's own replicant status, further embedding the issue of 'humanity'. In *8MM* (1999), Nicholas Cage plays Tom Welles who is asked, on behalf of a wealthy widow, to investigate the background to a reel of tape found amongst her late husband's possessions. This is an attempt to combine a Chanderlesque setting and task of protecting the rich from the world with an exploration of the way working amongst the dregs of the snuff porn industry can almost destroy an essentially moral human being—the quintessential PI.

Conclusion

There are then two distinct approaches to extra-legal activity. As we have seen, one provides a crude fantasy of problem solution through revenge in a world of unmitigated evil. The other provides a comment on how it might be possible to operate an existential moral code in the midst of a complex world where there is a mixture of weakness, corruption and moral compromise. Since the media portray our world increasingly like the former model, it may be no surprise that the vigilante and the 'officially' sanctioned extra-legal operatives of police or state feature more at the end of the 20th century and in the new millennium. The private eye, although providing a more subtle response to the problems people encounter, is now to be found increasingly in the pages of books rather than films. The back catalogue, though, of such figures continues to cast a giant shadow.

The distinction between film, made-for-TV film, cable, TV mini-series and TV multi-episode series is increasingly blurred with the emergence of satellite television and home DVD use. This allows the development of drama that focuses of 'building characters through small details, its ability to capture the unglamorous

---

[85] *Ibid*, 51.

reality of work and its willingness to confront the big issues of the day, from abortion to affirmative action'.[86] There have been women and ethnic minority detectives in the new cheaper formats with Liza Cody's Anna Lee for example. Notwithstanding that the dominance of TV-orientated portrayals has also given us Stacey Keach as Mike Hammer, this development into greater depth is one which might seem preferable to the trend to remakes of classics in Hollywood.[87] Insofar as they sometimes provide for a slightly detached perspective on the constantly fascinating area of law and justice the private eye component of lawyer fiction and lawyer TV presentations continue to speak to these concerns in the 21st century, albeit in a period setting. This is evidenced in a number of the films above, particularly those such as *Blade Runner* (1982) which blur genres and slip easily between time frames. What we do see in all these films is a displacement of the lawyer, and that the justice figure need not always be the heroic lawyer. As setting and scenes for law films may be varied so indeed can the nature and characteristics of the personnel.

---

[86] Freedland, J (1996).
[87] Although, as mentioned, this was how we got *The Maltese Falcon*.

14

Playing with a Different Sex[1]

The representation of issues of gender and sexuality in film are areas of great interest to film scholars.[2] There is, in the first place, the issue of the distinctive ways that film portrays these identities. This involves looking beyond the range of films that concern law, with which we are principally concerned elsewhere in the text. With these films identified, the role of sex and sexuality in relation to legal issues, and how they appear in relation to the justice system, needs to be considered. Finally, the question of how sex and sexuality are portrayed *specifically* in law films has been the subject of analysis by film and the law scholars. In the context of a book on film and the law there is a greater amount of our space devoted to those areas where law plays a direct part, whilst recognising the importance of the wider context. There has been significantly more scholarship in law and film studies on the quite specific question of how women lawyers appear on screen than there has on how gay lawyers are portrayed. There appear to be only two specific representations of gay lawyers in law films and the covert nature of their sexual identity has been the narrative driver in both these films.[3] There have been no specific lesbian portrayals. Nor, perhaps unsurprisingly, have we seen acknowledged bisexual, transgender or transsexual lawyers. The portrayals of women have been sufficiently varied over the years that it is possible to identify both stages of development as well as recurrent themes. For this reason our coverage of gender and sexuality are separated although both are markers of distinctness from the heterosexual male norm.

This focus is not difficult to understand. Just as women have struggled to obtain proper recognition in the worlds of law, politics and business, so too this long struggle has been reflected in the extent and nature of how they have been portrayed in these areas. Leaving aside the related issues of politics and business in our chosen area of interest the transformation in the visibility of women in the legal profession over the past 50 years has been quite remarkable. These changes are now analysed in more detail. We look first at gender as the area enjoying much more significant coverage, before examining issues of sexuality. These will be

---

[1] The title is an allusion to the title of an LP by post-punk British band Au Pairs (*Playing with a Different Sex*, 1981, Human Recordings), an album that deals in depth with issues of sexual politics through tracks such as 'It's Obvious'.

[2] See, eg, Dyer, R (2002) and the earlier Dyer, R (ed) (1977); Kaplan, E (1983) and Mulvey, L (1989).

[3] *Victim* (1961) and *Philadelphia* (1993).

considered within the context of film generally, before analysing the particular nuances within law and film.

Gender in Film

On one level, the broad portrayal of women in film tells us something about how power is exercised between men and women. This is part of the context determining the specific portrayals of gender in film. In film scholarship, the shift of emphasis from invisibility,[4] through women's objectification,[5] to being the focus of the male gaze[6] is well documented, and it is not intended to rehearse the extent of its debates fully here. This is where the borders of law and film studies blend into film studies more explicitly. If the link to law is absent, and the discussion is of social relations in the broadest terms, the scope of the enterprise expands beyond any manageable boundaries. Women as they appear in romantic comedies, science fiction, fantasy, horror and so on provide an affirmation of the noted trends in relation to justice and law films. This aspect, though, cannot be accorded equal space and should not be the primary focus for law and film scholars. It is, nonetheless, important to see to what extent scholarship on the way film looks at women can assist in getting a better purchase on the role film plays in gender relations. This comes from both the legal sphere, and from film studies. The links between the two, as Lucia and Kamir have noted, have been limited historically.[7]

Most of the collections of essays in law and film contain only limited direct material on gender issues and feminist scholarship has been the principal contributor in this area. Here the focus is on the two distinguishing elements in feminist legal scholarship, noted by Kamir, in her analysis of women's portrayal in law and film.[8] These two strands are radical legal feminism and cultural feminism. Radical legal feminism focuses on the systematic patriarchal domination of women. It calls attention to the prevalent sexual violence against women, and looks for structural changes to address the endemic social oppression of women. In its analysis women are a subordinate class. Cultural feminism has stressed the different ways in which women and men operate.[9] The unique mothering, caring and nurturing tendencies of women express a unique sense of justice. Care-centred feminist jurisprudence advocates greater attention to feminine social functions. Male-dominated law requires reform to equally reflect women's sense of

---

[4] Kuhn, A (1982).
[5] Haskell, M (1987).
[6] Mulvey, L (1975).
[7] Lucia, C (2005); Kamir, O (2006).
[8] Kamir, O (2006).
[9] Johnston, R and Buchanan, R (2007).

justice. Feminist legal scholarship has also, in turn, been critiqued for failing to give a voice to ethnic minority women and lesbian women.[10]

Feminist legal scholars' work in relation to film has tended to focus on the nature of the representation of women lawyers as a visible exemplar of the limitations of the gains of women as professionals. Additional concerns focus on the nature of the rules of a patriarchal legal system. Thus how film portrays rape, child care and sexual harassment, for example, has been the subject of feminist legal scholarship. Feminist film scholars have, Kamir notes, occasionally referred to legal issues enacted on film, but have generally refrained from more comprehensive attempts at a dialogue with feminist legal discourse. The latter has been perceived as overly legally analytic and unreflective.[11] Kamir's work seeks to establish a dialogue between feminist film studies and feminist jurisprudence though Lucia's work on women lawyer films came too late to be part of Kamir's assessment.[12] Lucia has developed a series of readings of films drawing on Lacan's psychoanalytic theory. This might seem a little puzzling given Lacan's work generally. It does, however, foreground the issue of 'essentialising woman', which Lucia's readings of 'women lawyer' films of the 1980s and 1990s appear to do. Her contextualising of the rise of this trend in law films, does, however, seem to be much more clearly derived from a broadly drawn historical materialist perspective.[13] Similarly her readings of these films combine the psychoanalytic and cultural in a way which appears a little confusing. Given the variety of audiences consuming these films, in different countries and in distinct political contexts, the latter observations are more compelling at the general level. In our conclusion we advocate emphasising closer engagement with both producers and viewers of film. This will shift us away from very general observations about the *zeitgeist* to more precise findings about finance and capital return without compromising the possibility of close readings of individual texts.

Gender and the Law in the Cinema

The notion that the law is constructed around the male 'hetero' norm is the unstated paradigm of legal cinema. Specifically, in relation to male focus, it is, argue Spelman and Minow, what *Thelma and Louise* (1991) is about.[14] The key to the series of events that take Thelma and Louise from being quiet, respectable housewife and waitress respectively, to hunted outlaws, is the experience of Louise (Susan Sarandon) being raped in Texas. Who will believe that Thelma (Geena Davis) has not been complicit in the treatment that leads to Harlan being shot? The male-dominated

---

[10] Robson, R (1998).
[11] Kamir, O (2006).
[12] Lucia, C (2005).
[13] *Ibid.*
[14] Spelman, E and Minow, M (1996).

judicial system conspires against women's experience of the law of rape in action. It silences them and their story. We do not need any lawyers to demonstrate exactly how the law is skewed in its construction and application. Like Louise, the audience knows what *would* have happened, *had* they sought the protection of the law. A more extensive and thorough examination of women's oppression under law, and the way in which this can be seen in cinema, is addressed by Kamir in *Framed: Women in Law and Film*, which considers the ways in which women are judged in films.[15] The films she covers are as diverse and far from the traditional fare of law and film studies, for example *Death and the Maiden* (1994), *Pandora's Box* (1929) and *High Heels* (1991). Her goal is to examine the ways films train audiences in the active execution of judgment. This may be supportive or critical of the community. Films can also provide a commentary on the jurisprudence in which they operate, whether it be to discuss notions of community, or corporate responsibility.[16]

Kamir's methodology differs from much of the writing in law and film studies which has a focus on the meaning of the film as divinable in the process of viewing. This is akin to the process whereby lawyers interpret written texts like statutes, constitutions or judicial judgments and opinions. There is some recognition of the role of the film's creators, although work alluding to *auteur* theory has been limited. Arguably greater incursion into genre theory will provide impetus for issues around the ideology of production. Kamir seeks to look at the film as text and the response of the 'implied viewer', that is the 'ideal' person invited by the text. It is questionable whether or not this really advances us beyond the notion of authorial intention. The agglomeration of the responses of film critics, scholars, friends and students does not, in our view, differ substantially from the much simpler notions of context, allied to contested meanings. Thus we are more comfortable with the idea that films may be conceived with a particular message, which may or not be taken on board by any or all of the audience, and that this 'meaning' developed by those reading the film, over time, may come to supplant any original authorial *imprimatur*. Thus the shifts in the assessment of such figures as Atticus Finch come about because later generations see his complicity in the racist society which he serves, as a more significant silence than his self-indulgent, but ineffectual, oratory on behalf of Tom Robinson.

Methodology apart, Kamir centres her analysis of how women's portrayal can be best understood in terms of her distinction between 'honour'—and 'dignity'—based cultures. In the former, honour in relation to the community is the key factor. They may be individualistic or clan-centred. Gender is skewed in such arrangements so that women's honour involves the suppression, restriction and concealment of femininity, while masculine honour is public and aggressive. In dignity-based cultures dignity is universal. It is the contemporary liberal post-Second World War legalistic concept which we all possess merely by being human. This distinction between rights-based social systems and status-based systems is

---

[15] Kamir, O (2006).
[16] *Ibid.*

a familiar one drawn from the analysis of such legal anthropologists as Henry Maine, who considered the shift from status to contract.[17] The expansion of this narrow concept to include the social contract and human rights is not universal and vestiges of traditional roles exist in societies which proclaim gender equality. Child rearing and family care are the most obvious examples. Acknowledging that not all societies have human rights enshrined in the lives of their citizens is a valuable reminder. It provides very little direct assistance in reading films on the issue of gender in the context of Western democracies. Nonetheless there is force in Kamir's suggestion that recognition of the notion that 'honour' may 'expose persistent patriarchal, androcentric, and sexist notions underlying our social system, cultural images and legal standards'.[18] In this sense the shift towards universal rights is the starting point for women in law films. The fascinating issue for us is to assess where there are structural failings, system limitations and whether some of the changes are mere tokenism. In the context of examining women in film, Kamir notes how feminist legal discourse has limited its interest to the portrayal of the female lawyer, and has rarely engaged in feminist film theory.[19] There has been mutual suspicion and Kamir seeks to reintroduce feminist jurisprudence to feminist film scholars. Kamir's reading divides women into 'familiar categories':

> Deadly, sexually brazen Lilith women; timid, domesticated, nurturing, good, sexually subjugated, self-sacrificing Eves; saintly, completely asexual Madonnas; pathetic, manly, unnatural, and unattractive lesbians/feminists.[20]

Central to this analysis is Kamir's suggestion that women are judged in film using these stereotypes, along with viewers being, in effect, invited to actively partake in the cinematic judging process:

> Unbound by restrictive, statutory definitions of offenses, evidentiary rules, and the presumption of innocence, the films use the women's sexuality, as well as sexist stereotypes and prejudices, against them preserving archaic, moralistic notions and subverting social reform.[21]

In the selected films she suggests that these present themes of women's victimisation, delinquency and marginalisation. It is the focus on the men's deaths, and the diminishing of women's sexual victimisation, that renders these films so problematic for Kamir. The tendency of the onscreen fictional legal system is to construct, treat and judge women as guilty objects. This is encountered in relation to rape in *Rashomon* (1950), *Pandora's Box* (1929), *Blackmail* (1929) and *Anatomy of a Murder* (1959). Whether or not there is an agreement with Kamir's reading of these films, it is not entirely clear why this group of films is significant. Kamir does not seek to be representative. Her goal is to provide a feminist reading 'against the

---

[17] Maine, HS (1861).
[18] Kamir, O (2006: 11).
[19] *Ibid.*
[20] *Ibid*, 34.
[21] *Ibid*, 35.

grain' to bring 'to light existing potentially feminist textual elements, emphasizing and using them to read the text's suppressed feminist subtext'.[22] She selects another group of films to challenge this stereotyping. These films let women judge their oppressors on their own terms, inviting viewers to share the women's point of view, and these include *Adam's Rib* (1949), *Nuts* (1987) and *Death and the Maiden* (1994). Finally she looks at films where there are female protagonists, with supportive feminine communities, to emphasise the collective nature of women's plight and the feminist project using *A Question of Silence* (1982), *Set It Off* (1996) and *High Heels* (1991). Of course, Kamir is not trying to suggest that this selection of films is in any way representative of the issue of gender in law, but rather that they illustrate the themes she is concerned to develop. In that respect, although they are for the most part reasonably specialist art house products, they cannot tell us about the extent to which the issues of sexist stereotypes and prejudices prevail in modern mainstream cinema. Other writers have turned their attention to discussing in detail the issues that bear down on women disproportionately, such as rape, childcare and sexual harassment. In relation to issues like divorce and childcare, scholarship has followed the same kind of trajectory outlined in film studies generally. There have been broad overviews examining the different ways cinema has portrayed such matters,[23] as well as a number of studies examining individual films such as *Kramer vs Kramer* (1979)[24] and *It's a Wonderful Life* (1946).[25] The same thing has occurred in relation to rape in *The Accused* (1988),[26] and sexual harassment with *North Country* (2005).[27] This subject-specific, and film-specific, scholarship is likely to continue to flourish since it fits so neatly into the use for which film is made in teaching in law schools.

The Visibility of Female Lawyers

The most striking feature across a wide range of traditional law films is that lawyers have been traditionally portrayed as male. There has, though, been a major shift in our sight of women as lawyers over the year, from a total absence of women in *I Am The Law* (1938) to their omnipresence in *Legally Blonde* (2001). This shift in the number of screen lawyers has to be seen in the context of their presence in the profession, where the first woman lawyer was admitted to practice in Iowa in 1869 and the first woman to graduate from law school did so in 1870.[28]

---

[22] *Ibid*, 38.
[23] Asimow, M (2002).
[24] Papke, D (1996); Asimow, M (2006).
[25] Denvir, J (1996b).
[26] Burr, S (2006).
[27] Korzek, R (2007).
[28] Arabella Mansfield was the first practising woman lawyer. Ada H Kepley of Illinois was the first woman lawyer to graduate from a law school—Union College of Law in Chicago. See also Friedman, JM (1993).

In other parts of the world the progress has followed a similar pattern. In Great Britain, excluded from entry into either branch of the legal profession by myopic judicial interpretation,[29] their numbers progressed slowly,[30] and their elevation to the Bench only made significant progress after the opening up in Britain of Higher Education in 1961. It comes as no surprise that in the Alabama court of the 1930s in which Atticus Finch practised in *To Kill a Mockingbird* (1962), no women are encountered. More noticeable is the absence of any women law students in the classroom of Professor John Lindsay (Edward G Robinson), packed with students and alumni in *I Am the Law* in 1938.[31] By the 1990s we find Joe Miller (Denzel Washington) confronted by a steely Belinda Conine (Mary Steenbergen) in *Philadelphia* (1993). Finally, in what appears to be an ironical comment on the general absence of women from positions of significance in the law, in the concluding trial scene in *Legally Blonde* (2001) there is a reversal of the male default position. This final trial scene with the judge, prosecuting attorney, defence counsel, witness and accused all women may have been a piece of playful irony, but it serves to remind us how rapid recent changes within the legal profession have been. Apart from such 'insider' jokes there is a need to examine what kind of roles women have been given as they have occupied these hitherto male roles. There is a need to adopt a general overview, rather than focus on too narrow a timeframe, since with the lead times for film development and production ascribing trends to clear causes can be a hazardous enterprise. The emergence, for instance, of a tranche of films in the 1980s where women lawyers appear as major protagonists has been seen as both a recognition of the enhanced status of women, as well as part of a conservative backlash.[32]

Narrative Tropes and Female Lawyers

There are various narrative themes which recur in films in which women lawyers act as significant protagonists which we have previously termed 'persistent themes'. In the intervening years this limited range of story trajectories have continued to be used in relation to female lawyers. We have retained our approach of using relevant plot outlines so those who are unfamiliar with these films will gain some basic knowledge even though it may be slightly unwieldy for those already familiar with the films. Whilst there are a limited number of narratives available

[29] *Hall v Incorporated Society of Scotland* 1909 ([1901] 3F. 1059), *Bebb v Law Society* 1913 ([1914] 1 Ch. 286). The first women to pass the qualifying exams to become solicitors were Maud Crofts, Carrie Morrison, Mary Pickup and Mary Sykes in 1922. Carrie Morrison was first to finish her articles, i.e. time as an apprentice. Maud Crofts had been one of the four women involved in Bebb.

[30] In England and Wales only 2.7 per cent of certificated solicitors were women in 1967: Law Society, Friday 19 December 1997, 75th anniversary of women solicitors press release.

[31] The film was based on the racket-busting career of New York district attorney Thomas E Dewey. Edward G Robinson is the Dewey counterpart, here named John Lindsay, who is approached by a group of concerned citizens to act as special prosecutor to rid their unnamed state of big-time lawbreakers.

[32] Shapiro, C (1995).

to writers, the identified tropes here are gender-specific. For example, male lawyers are routinely operating in different ways in relation to emotional subservience, emotional attachment, awe of a father figure and professional 'burnout'. Thus male lawyers are not shown assuming subservient roles; where they occupy a lower rank they challenge the authority figure and demonstrate moral pluck. Mitch McDeere (Tom Cruise) risks his life doing this in *The Firm* (1993). Kevin Lomax (Keanu Reeves) gives up his life challenging his boss in *The Devil's Advocate* (1997). Even the pusillanimous Gavin Banneck (Ben Affleck) forgoes promotion rather than do the bidding of his seniors in *Changing Lanes* (2002). Their judgment is not negatively clouded by emotional attachments. The final scene in *The Verdict* (1982) shows Frank Galvin (Paul Newman) putting temptation, in the form of fellow lawyer Laura Fischer (Charlotte Rampling) firmly behind him. If there are signs of an emotional attachment it is to abstract concepts, like justice and fairness. Normally this is presented in a positive way such as the attachment of Atticus Finch (Gregory Peck) and Jake Brigance (Matthew McConaughey) to racial equality in *To Kill a Mockingbird* (1962) and *A Time to Kill* (1996), and Tom Connolly (Alan Bates) resisting an overarching state in *Evelyn* (2002). When male lawyers do fall from grace, through pressure of work, they are able to redeem themselves through the process of engaging in more law practice, and emerge as revitalised and renewed. Thus there is recovered alcoholic Frank Galvin (Paul Newman) finding solace in coffee and contemplation, having turned his career around, in *The Verdict* (1982) and even Sonny Coufax (Adam Sandler) returning to legal practice after his blank years as a tollbooth attendant in *Big Daddy* (1999).

Subservience in Action

In *First Monday in October* (1981), Ruth Loomis (Jill Clayburgh) appears as a Supreme Court judge. This appears to be the first film where a woman lawyer appears after the Amanda Bonner portrayal in *Adam's Rib* (1949). Ruth Loomis is a broad-brush, cinematic version of Sandra Day O'Connor. She is conservative, against pornography, and the opposite to liberal justice in the form of Dan Snow (Walter Matthau). The film trades on Matthau's capacity to play grumpy characters, and centres on their mutual antagonism. Like disparate cop partnership films, this is a formulaic film in that the audience knows that the two will learn to develop mutual respect. Even given the unlikely material of Walter Matthau, romance is hinted at with the couple ascending the steps of the Supreme Court hand in hand. Whether this is for physical support after Snow's coronary, or as a sign of growing affection, is not certain. The court setting provides a context in which their antagonism can flourish. The process of judging provides a formal context in which the normal conflicts between individuals can be played out and their views on pornography, business responsibility and the environment are explored. This is, however, like its immediate predecessor, a romantic comedy which provides some food for thought rather than some deep Shavian text. There are two encounters where the casual chauvinism of Snow is exposed. Although supposedly the liberal voice on the bench, he finds difficulty adjusting to the reality of a woman's presence. It is against her sex, however, that we see him giving vent to his views as well as her politics, referring to her sneeringly as 'Madame Justess'. The trick of the film is never to let us feel entirely comfortable that the antipathy is political rather than gender-based. Loomis is shown as both tough-minded and pragmatic and is not prepared to meekly allow Snow to make pronouncements on pornography without drawing attention to the limitations of this 'principled' position. Unlike Snow, she shows a capacity for rational debate rather than a rapid retreat into slogans and *ad hominem* attacks. By portraying a woman in a position of significant power, albeit in a romantic comedy, the film started a belated Second Wave for feminism in legal film.

A version of the trope of the shift from mutual antagonism to respect is also found in the next woman lawyer appearance. In *Legal Eagles* (1986) Debra Winger appears as the engaging, but less than impressive, defence attorney Laura Kelly. She comes up against hotshot prosecutor Tom Logan (Robert Redford), who is being groomed by his boss to take over as the next District Attorney. The twist here is that the antagonism is professional rather than personal. Indeed, to Logan, Kelly is a kid sister figure to be patronised and ignored. To Kelly, however, Logan is a big hero as she struggles with her single practitioner business. She admits to him that she copies the way he does a semi-double-take when he wants to cast doubt on testimony from witnesses which does not suit his case. Having encountered her, Logan is unable to sleep, though it is never entirely clear whether this is an incipient romance. Events take over and Logan offers succour to Kelly's vulnerable client, Chelsea Dearden, (Darryl Hannah). Caught in bed with someone who turns out to be a murder suspect, he ends up losing his position. With nothing left, he teams up with Kelly to defend Dearden. In the process of rooting out the truth he begins to appreciate Kelly's gutsy qualities. It is almost the girl with glasses who suddenly grows up without our hero noticing. At the end of the film it is a partnership in law and of love. The difference between this partnership from that of the previous examples, in *Adam's Rib* (1949) and *First Monday in October* (1981), is the imbalance of power in this new relationship. As Mrs Tom Logan, Laura Kelly will be looking after their young children before long. They will have her eyes but his charming grin: this is law practice as an opportunity for pairing rather than for justice. In terms of sexual politics it did not augur well for the type of role women might play.

Emotional Dependence

The next trope that dominates women lawyer films from the mid 1980s is falling in love in such a way as to adversely affect professional judgment. There are five films in seven years with the same underlying narrative device in which the woman lawyer falls for a dangerous charmer. Another aspect of these portrayals is heavily patriarchal in that the woman is seen as being unable to do her job without the outside help of the male—an echo of the portrayals of white civil rights activists helping the helpless ethnic minorities in *Amistad* (1997), for example. In *Jagged Edge* (1985), Teddy Barnes (Glenn Close), a former criminal defence attorney, accepts the brief to defend publisher Jack Forrester (Jeff Bridges). Her willingness to take his case is linked to the promise of partnership at her big corporate law firm. She is an ex-prosecutor whose childhood dream was to grow up to be a prosecutor to carry on the family business as her father was a police officer. Her decision to finally accept Forrester as her client seems to stem directly from a gut feeling that he is innocent, in the face of the circumstantial evidence pointing to his guilt. For reasons which are never entirely clear, the divorced mother of two, Teddy, becomes romantically entangled with her client while awaiting his trial date. Her antipathy to the prosecutor, her old colleague Thomas Krasny (Peter Coyote), stems from the knowledge that he suppressed evidence that would have freed a convicted felon some years before. Whilst she did nothing to remedy this injustice this could be linked to her position of powerlessness as a woman in the male-dominated world of law. Furthermore, at the outset Teddy learns that this individual has committed suicide, thus we have a woman whose decisions and evaluation of the evidence are influenced by her emotional reactions to individuals.

This might be seen as a contrast to the male lawyerly virtues of clear-minded objective pursuit of justice which Paul Biegler (*Anatomy of a Murder*, 1959), Tony Lawrence (*The Young Philadelphians*, 1959), Atticus Finch (*To Kill a Mockingbird*, 1961) and eventually Frank Galvin (*The Verdict*, 1982) demonstrated. It should not be forgotten, however, that Anthony Keane (Gregory Peck) in *The Paradine Case* (1947) illustrated a similar kind of human frailty in his professional application. It might even be argued that Sir Wilfred Robarts has emotional reasons for taking the case of Christine Vole (Marlene Dietrich). He seems to hint at the end of *Witness for the Prosecution* (1957) that it is the attractiveness of his new client that impels him to offer to act as her defence counsel since she has killed his previous client. Of course, it may be that he has doubts about extracting his fee from the Vole estate and adopts a pragmatic course of action.

In what starts as a police corruption drama, *The Big Easy* (1986), Ellen Barkin, assistant District Attorney Anne Osborne, falls for the bayou accent and impressive physique of police lieutenant Remy McSwain (Dennis Quaid). She is providing specialist input in New Orleans, but is too wedded to her work to have a personal life. They sleep together and she is shocked when she subsequently discovers that although employed in law enforcement, he is part of the widespread police protection service available to businesses. His boss is set up by an undercover team but doing him a favour McSwain is the one who actually accepts the bribe and it is Osborne who prosecutes him. Solidarity is strong in the police force and 'damaged' vital video evidence leads to McSwain's acquittal. The rift between them seems complete. There are, however, more significant criminals at work and the two unite against an evil greater than small-time corruption, a conspiracy of murderous policemen involved in drugs. By the end of the picture they are married; he is a changed man and another romantic comedy concludes, albeit one with some dead bodies. Another young female public prosecutor features in *Physical Evidence* (1989); Jenny Hudson (Theresa Russell) is fed up with being treated as a lesser breed of lawyer and given a diet of mundane traffic violations. She demands a chance to shine in dealing with the prosecution of the killer of a local night club owning mobster. Since the chief suspect, police detective Joe Paris, is played by Burt Reynolds, the storyline arrives already written; Hudson 'naturally' falls for Paris. This is a process made easier by Hudson's self-obsessed yuppie boyfriend. The role of solving the case and clearing his name increasingly falls to Paris, with Hudson merely simpering in the background. At the end it is forgotten that she was once a lawyer who demanded to be treated professionally by her colleagues.

Similarly in *Defenseless* (1990) Barbara Hershey starts out as a 'big league attorney', TK (Thelma Knudson) Katwuller, working in a glossy plate-glass corporate law firm. This appears at the outset to be more promising. There is also a slight change to the normal romantic twist. TK has already succumbed to the sleazy charm of businessman Steven Seldes (JT Walsh) before she has to defend him from charges of allowing his property to be used for the making of pornography involving young girls. Having discovered that her lover is indeed a pornographer, she seeks confirmation of his guilt but is attacked by him. She escapes but is forced to return to recover her car keys, which have been displaced in the struggle with her client. When she returns, he has been killed by someone else. The wife is tried but thanks to TK she is acquitted. The lawyer is then framed for the murder. She has successfully defended the wife only to discover that she did the deed all along. With the double jeopardy rule operating, Ellie cannot be retried. She is taken away to be cared for. Hence poor TK is used by both her lover/client, and his cuckolded wife—the film could have been renamed 'Gormless'. The underlying sexual politics of this film have been seen as part of Susan Faludi's 1980s backlash against feminism.[33] Part of the charge includes not only the films mentioned but also, perhaps surprisingly, a film by the director of *12 Angry Men* (1957), *The Verdict* (1982) and *Dog Day Afternoon* (1975), Sidney Lumet.[34] In *Guilty as Sin* (1993), leading attorney Jennifer Haines (Rebecca de Mornay) is selected to represent an alleged wife murderer, David Greenhill (Don Johnson). She accepts the task, falls under the spell of the charming Greenhill and makes serious professional errors of judgment. Having discovered that her client has indeed murdered his wife but appears to be likely to escape justice, she seeks to ensure his conviction by planting evidence against him. Greenhill, however, manages to persuade a woman friend

---

[33] Graham, L and Maschio, G (1995–96).

[34] *The Verdict* (1982), of course, contains the sexually available Charlotte Rampling as a lawyer whose sole narrative function is to distract Frank Galvin (Paul Newman) from pursuing the case.

to provide him with an alibi and the jury is deadlocked. He is released on bail pending a new trial and his character undergoes a transformation from calculating and rational to vengeful. When the ex-client focuses his homicidal attention on her, she is only able to assist him to his death over the side of the block of flats she lives in. Unfortunately he is still holding on to her at this stage; he dies but she survives. How extensively she has been able to benefit from his final role as a human cushion is not clear as the credits roll, although her boyfriend assures her 'she is going to be alright'. Hers is a fitting end to the roster of the misjudgers. An interesting contrast is with the role of Janet Venable (Laura Linney) in *Primal Fear* (1996). Whilst she allows herself to be used by Martin Vail there is a difference; she is acting in the pursuit of justice, albeit at the expense of her career prospects. Their final scene leaves it unclear as to whether their relationship will resume. If it does, however, it will be as equal partners. She has resisted his blandishments in a way in which Teddy Barnes, Laura Kelly, TK Katwuller and Jennifer Haines did not do.

The Repressed Daughter

Tushnet notes that the 'Dominant versus Other' trope often involves 'law versus justice'.[35] In two woman lawyer films, *Music Box* (1989) and *Class Action* (1991), there is a variant concerning father/daughter relationships. Lucia analyses these films as an ideal demonstration of the applicability of Lacan's law of the father.[36] Her reading of the films is both fascinating and interesting though her interpretation is at odds with what might be viewed as a much simpler tale of egocentricity and class conflict. Both films deal with the struggle of daughters to escape from the dominant influence of their fathers. Interestingly, this theme of parental/sibling relationship is one which has been used in other male-centred films. For example, Kaffee (Tom Cruise) in *A Few Good Men* (1992) is constantly striving to live up to the memory of his father and the way other people judge him in relation to this. Certainly, the somewhat obviously schmaltzy riposte at the end of the film that 'his father would have been proud of him' supports this. Thursby (Ian Carmichael) in *Brothers in Law* (1957) has a famously gifted and successful uncle, whose memory haunts him like a spectre, and within the context of which his success or failure will ultimately be judged. From a different angle *In the Name of the Father* (1993) can also be seen on one level as a film about the relationship between father and son.[37] *The Devil's Advocate* (1997) contains a similar, if somewhat unlikely, revelation at the end.

---

[35] Tushnet, M (1996: 244).
[36] Lucia, C (2005).
[37] Jim Sheridan also tackled the mother/son relationship in *My Left Foot* (1989).

These types of relationship may deeply affect how the individuals concerned operate as lawyers. In *Music Box* (1989) Ann Talbot (Jessica Lange) is a successful criminal lawyer, divorced with a son. Her father insists that she undertake his defence against deportation to face war crimes. It is never made entirely clear why the successful and hard-headed Talbot fails to heed the most elementary canon of law concerning the need to avoid emotional entanglement in a case. Her father, Mike Laszlo (Armin Mueller-Stahl), is alleged to have been the leader of a notorious band of Hungarian collaborators, Arrow Cross, who committed atrocities during the Second World War. Of course, Lange pursues the case to prove her father innocent. This sets itself up as a standard vindication of someone falsely accused by shadowy forces of the old Communist Hungarian state who are acting against Laszlo because of his active anti-Communism when in the United States. This has the hallmarks of a take on Kafka's *The Trial*. The documentary and witness evidence which is produced by the government is, however, effectively countered by the production of a Soviet expert in document forgery. There is also the revelation, on cross-examination by Talbot, that some of the witnesses are members of the Communist Party and have an interest in discrediting the anti-communist Laszlo. The final conclusive witness evidence turns out to be a disaster for the government and Laszlo is vindicated. The director is, however, Costa-Gavras and there is more to this story than a simple 'feel-good-brave-lawyer' rescue plot. The evidence which is finally tracked down leads Lange to the inescapable conclusion that her father was indeed a murderer. The bleak ending has her swearing never to speak with him again, and starting life with her son and her extended family destroyed. Throughout the legal scenes Talbot has shown herself to be misguided and at times less than fully competent. Her salvation, however, involves casting her father from her life and that of her son.

By contrast, and slightly less traumatic, is the father–daughter relationship in *Class Action* (1991). Maggie Ward (Mary Elizabeth Mastrantonio) has always craved the approval of her philandering lawyer father, Jedediah Tucker Ward (Gene Hackman). He has been largely absent from her upbringing, fighting injustice and righting wrongs, and yet failing to recognise her efforts. Nothing she has ever done has been good enough and yet she has succumbed to trying to meet the standards of this tyrant. He is portrayed as a man who loves 'the people' as a broad concept, but finds greater difficulties dealing with actual living individuals. As a lawyer unable to meet his exacting standards and confronted by his indifference, she rebels by seeking to make her way in the (different, other) world of big corporations. The path whereby the two achieve eventual reconciliation has two elements. There is first resolution of the conflict of values, in favour of those of the people, against those of capital. The practice of the lawyers for big corporations abusing their power finally sickens Maggie. She is able to stomach it to an extent and she is almost sucked into the maw of the firm with the promise of a partnership. At this point her conscience is finally pricked. As far as the father/daughter relationship is concerned there appears to be a capitulation of the filial revolt in favour of paternal dominance. What is less clear is whether the insufferably self-satisfied Jed Ward has made any adjustments in his personal relationships or whether he will go on using people for the aggrandisement of his humble work of saving the world. These portrayals take as their particular point of departure this paternal/filial conflict, and it is this which provides a significant part of the dynamics of the narrative, along with the questions of freedom of speech, ethnic identity and class which also run through these two films. They provide a richer, more varied kind of backdrop than in some of the films where the legal issue or plot occupies centre stage such as *Anatomy of a Murder* (1959), *Presumed Innocent* (1990) and *Cape Fear* (1962). The contrast with the range of new issues which Martin Scorsese introduces into *Cape Fear* (1991) is itself a valuable insight into the possibilities within a formulaic medium.[38]

Professional Inadequacy

There are few portrayals where women lawyers are displayed as though they could operate as professionals. In none, however, is this shown as anything other than highly problematic. In *Suspect* (1987), Cher, as Washington DC public defender Kathleen Riley, is in danger of losing objectivity as her workload overwhelms her. Her life has become a parody of the workaholic. As she complains to her fellow long-stay public defender Morty Rosenthal (Fred Melamed), her professional life has overtaken her personal life, and she appears tired with the incessant treadmill of her existence. When she asks Rosenthal why he carries on, he replies that it is for the same reason she does: 'For the sake of the one poor bastard who didn't do it.' During the trial her professionalism is constantly under challenge from the judge, Matthew Helms (John Mahoney). However, by the end of the film she has been vindicated and her client is free. She finds contentment in the unlikely arms of political lobbyist, Eddie Sanger (Dennis Quaid). He has assisted her in discovering the real murderer as well as saving her from death and danger, despite being a member of the jury hearing the evidence. Given his background as a manipulative and mendacious schemer, perhaps the prospects are not excellent and Riley's ability to continue to work with murderers and rapists must be doubtful. It is not clear why the overwhelming professional responsibilities should be affected by an emergent personal life, except in the ironic sense that, in fiction at least, sex is an all-purpose problem solver.

The same kind of battle against an impossible workload, with serious doubts about the possibility of securing justice, occurs in *The Accused* (1988). Kelly McGillis as public prosecutor Katheryn Murphy demonstrates sensitivity and skill in dealing with a rape case where the evidence against the perpetrators is such that a plea bargain down to 'recklessness endangerment' is made. Murphy is persuaded by her bosses' scepticism that something less than a rape charge has to

---

[38] Sherwin, R (1996b).

be accepted to secure any chance of conviction. The reason why this is so has to do with the kind of defence which has traditionally been available in rape cases of the double trial. Not only are the accused's actions under consideration but also the defence introduces the lifestyle of the victim into court. This is no longer formally permitted in British trials although there are certain exceptions. Research suggests that there is a high incidence of breach of the 'rape shield laws'—the prohibition against leading character evidence of the claimed victim.[39] The fact that the three accused are all given prison sentences of between two and five years does not mollify victim Sarah Tobias (Jody Foster). Like Meursault in Camus' 1942 novel *L'Étranger*, she is excluded from the process and justice and denied an effective opportunity to tell her story and is incensed that she was not consulted about the plea bargain. When Murphy is made aware of the anger and resentment of the victim at her treatment, she admits this was a mistake, and determines to secure some more equitable outcome. Poring through the texts during an all-night session Murphy discovers the possibility of an obscure crime that she proposes to use against those in the crowd whose cheers 'encouraged' the commission of the crime. However, her boss regards this as a loser and threatens to fire her. Murphy is adamant and says she will leave the department and raise the action as a private prosecution. The feasibility of this course of action is never discovered as next time we see Murphy she is assembling witnesses for the prosecution. The men in the bar who egged on the rapists are charged with 'criminal solicitation'. With the crucial evidence of the college boy who actually called 911, with which the film started, and Murphy's summation, the precedent is set. Unlike most courtroom films, there is almost no coda. All we see is Murphy and Tobias going down the courtroom steps to their separate lives. Tobias is returning to her dog in her trailer home presumably to waitressing. She has achieved some element of redemption and she has escaped from male dominance, at least temporarily, albeit at the cost of dependence on the male institution of the law. This institution has, however, been disrupted by the injection of a new voice into the discourse. Murphy is going back, presumably to carry on her frustrating round of plea-bargaining. Although there are glimpses of Murphy's existence outwith her work, attending a hockey game and hosting a dinner party, the overwhelming sense is of someone, like Riley, whose resolve is being tested. The audience can only speculate as to the change which the precedent-setting episode may have made beyond the specific issue. The absence of a clear view forward is compounded after the fadeout by the screen information preceding the credits. Whether Murphy will be energised by her victory to carry on the struggle or whether her and Sarah Tobias' victory is of any moment in the context of these depressing statistics is, of course, left for the viewer.

As far as burnt-out lawyers are concerned, there is more than a hint in the single-person practice in *The Client* (1994). Reggie Love (Susan Sarandon)

[39] Burman, M, Jamieson, L, Nicholson, J and Brooks, O (2007).

operates as a low-rent people's lawyer more by way of therapy for her own past as a discarded middle-aged, school run Mom. When her husband goes off with another woman, Love has a breakdown and is banned from seeing her children. She seeks to conquer her demons first at law school and then in legal practice. Love lives with her mother and seems to rely on her heavily for support. Her fierce concern for her vulnerable young client, 11-year-old Mark Sway, is apparent. Mark has witnessed the death of a mob lawyer and told a secret which puts his life in danger. The unlikely solution he chooses instead of seeking the protection of the state authorities is to obtain the services of a lawyer. Reggie saves Mark from the clutches of the state. In the original book it is clear that the case will be prosecuted only insofar as it serves the interests of would-be Governor Roy Foltrigg (Tommy Lee Jones). In the film, however, this ambition is moderated and the threat to the child seems less obvious. It does, however, give the lawyer an opportunity to show her forensic as well as her nurturing skills. The changes in the process of adaptation involving as they do a softening of the character of the District Attorney means that we have a hint of a romantic future for Love and Foltrigg.[40] Where will she go from the airport when her client and his family flee to a witness protection scheme? A happier future with another lawyer is one of the possibilities on offer.

That said, it should be pointed out that the male lawyers of the 1980s and 1990s have been provided as more rounded characters with problems and difficulties rather than merely men in white suits slaying the dragons of evil in the manner of Atticus Finch or Sam Bowden. From the alcoholic Frank Galvin haunting funeral receptions and Tom Logan failing to resist vulnerable blondes, to mendacious, cheating Sam Bowden, male lawyers are far from unsullied. Even when they are shown as being less than self-interested, like Rudy Baylor in *The Rainmaker* (1997), they have dark propensities, in this case the willingness to batter to death an unconscious wife abuser. They are not given, however, to much self-doubt and introspection. There is, though, the thoughtful introspective figure of Galvin at the end of *The Verdict* (1982), which is in stark contrast to the thoughtless unethical lawyer at the outset. This provides a positive outcome and allows Galvin to escape from his murky past. Reconsideration of a personal moral position also transforms Joe Miller (*Philadelphia*, 1993) from cold homophobe lawyer to caring supportive friend.

The Changing Role of Female Lawyers

There are far more examples of women lawyers than out gay or lesbian lawyers. Given the quantity of films with women lawyers' material, most of the developments and narrative tropes that follow relate solely to gender and within the

---

[40] Robson, P (2001b).

gay or lesbian lawyer portrayal no such 'progression' can be divined. The first significant film in which a woman appears as a lawyer is *Adam's Rib* (1949).[41] Here, Amanda Bonner (Kathryn Hepburn) is a sole partner with her own law offices. Whether or not this comedic rendition of a woman enjoying a position of equality in professional terms with her husband in a courtroom battle can be seen as liberating or a mere confirmation of an emotional, irrational female stereotype has been subject to debate. An equal partner in law in the 1940s might seem, on the face of it, a sign of a thrust towards equality for women. Sheffield looks at the broader picture and suggests that the film involves Bonner challenging 'custom and convention as to the "proper place" for women'.[42] Molly Haskell described it as 'a commercial "feminist" film that was many years ahead of its time when it appeared ... and remains so even today'.[43] Shapiro speaks of Amanda Bonner as 'an outspoken feminist'.[44] Graham and Maschio are less charitable and suggest that, like so many other women film lawyers, Amanda Bonner's actions are ruled by emotional attachments and that she is 'unwise, stubborn and obstinate'.[45] They are of the view, however, that there is nothing amiss with her attachment to the legal principle of 'equality of rights before the law', which they see as 'utterly correct'.[46] Bergman and Asimow viewed Amanda Bonner as giving women lawyers a 'wonderful start', doing a 'great job' and being a 'dedicated and skilful lawyer'.[47] However, Orit Kamir rejects the reading of *Adam's Rib* (1949) as an optimistic feminist progressive film. She suggests that the character traits embodied in Amanda Bonner and her use of emotion rather than legal rationality outweighs the symbolism of her position in court fighting on behalf of a wronged woman.[48] Kamir makes a distinction both here and elsewhere in her writing between honour-based and dignity-based cultures. In the former, Kamir suggests what is entailed is a structured hierarchy and strict gender roles and the constraint of women. The latter are premised on respect for people as having authentic, diverse, individual needs and aspirations. She suggests that the equality, which Bonner purports to demand on behalf of her client, is in fact the right to replicate the 'honour' basis of the male claim to have an unwritten right to take the life of a woman who betrays him. She also suggests that the film 'does not constitute a community of women'. The film's female characters do not share a unique, distinctive 'feminine culture' and Bonner fails to act in a 'caring, compassionate and empathetic way'. By failing to do this Bonner acts in a 'traditional patriarchal way: cold and dry' thus the message is not a feminist one.

---

[41] Sheffield, R (1993) provides a detailed guide to the women lawyer role encountered between 1930 and 1990.

[42] *Ibid*, 90.

[43] Haskell, M (1987: 228).

[44] Shapiro, C (1995: 963).

[45] Graham, L and Maschio, G (1995–96: 1068).

[46] *Ibid*, 1069.

[47] Bergman, P and Asimow, M (1996: 92).

[48] Kamir, O (2000b).

This mélange of reactions to *Adam's Rib* (1949) demonstrates the notion of multiple questions perfectly. What kind of analysis is likely to seem persuasive depends precisely on the question and the context in which it is asked. By focusing on the symbolic appearance of a woman in court battling on behalf of another woman, it is indeed perfectly possible to cast *Adam's Rib* (1949) as a feminist piece of entertainment and assume that is how an audience is likely to react to it. The fact that one might cast doubt on Bonner's tactics is not necessarily reflective of her whole approach to life and the justice system. The final scene is just such an instance of different 'messages'. Lucia reads the conclusion by suggesting that Bonner has been silenced and that she merely jokes about running against her husband in the upcoming election. Equally, however, this could be viewed as a serious intention rather than her having 'relinquished her position as Adam's competitor'.[49] In a contemporary context it would not be surprising to portray powerful women political figures which would be recognisable to a modern audience.

The Woman Lawyer as a Discreet Object of Desire?

The first time that women lawyers appear on the scene after Amanda Bonner is in a trio of British films. In *The Constant Husband* (1955) we find the philandering Charles Hathaway (Rex Harrison) appearing in court on charges of serial bigamy and his solicitor opting for a smooth and successful woman barrister. Since his crime is against women, he argues that 'the fact that she is prepared to act for you speaks volumes'. Despite all the seven women he has married being individually prepared to take him back, he prefers the peace and quiet of jail and changes his plea to guilty, rather undoing the excellent work his counsel has done on his behalf. The protagonist is seen in the final scene running off with his lawyer, Miss Chesterman (Margaret Leighton), when, on being freed from gaol, he is confronted by all his wives each seeking his company exclusively for themselves.

An attempt to reprise the notion of the battle of the sexes in a courtroom setting sees young barristers Tony Stevens (Michael Craig) and Frances Pilbright (Mary Peach) in *A Pair of Briefs* (1961) being instructed by opposing parties in a comical case where a wife is suing for conjugal rights. This title refers to the slang term for a couple of barristers as well as, racily for pre-Profumo Britain, underwear. The mood is set in the opening shot of the female barrister which shows her addressing the court in her wig and gown. The camera pans back and we see she is merely practising before a mirror, clad only in her underwear. She turns out to be just about to start as a barrister. This light comedy seems to have drawn its structural inspiration from *Adam's Rib* (1949). In this instance,

---

[49] Lucia, C (2005: 34).

however, the slant is firmly towards romantic comedy, and the legal joust, about a declaration of marriage, is no more than a plot device for the lovers to engender conflict prior to a happy marital resolution. There is a thriller in the late 1960s, *Hostile Witness* (1968), where we see a young woman barrister defend her Head of Chambers. She casts doubt on the evidence that seems to incriminate her client and appears a model of competence; the Head of Chambers describes her as having a shining talent. However, the accused insists on calling as a witness a loyal friend prepared to lie to save his friend come what may. She will not agree and he withdraws his instructions and decides to defend himself. This action leaves Sheila Larkin (Sylvia Sims) with a somewhat truncated role. The writer of the screenplay, Jack Roffey, did, however, bring us a fully fledged version of the female barrister as the principal protagonist in the 1970s TV series *Justice*. Margaret Lockwood played the crusading QC after success in a one-off TV play, *Justice is a Woman* (1969). Whilst these examples do not provide any kind of consistent role model, perhaps, they did at least highlight the possible existence of women as part of the legal set-up at a time when lawyers were bemoaning the difficulties of women getting any kind of reasonable treatment in the profession.[50]

Competent Counsel in US Films of the 1980s

Starting some 35 years after Amanda Bonner's court appearance, a number of films from 1985 onwards provide us with a roster of demonstrably competent women lawyers in leading roles. They encompassed defence attorneys—*Jagged Edge* (1985) (Glenn Close (Teddy Barnes)) and *Music Box* (1989) (Jessica Lange (Ann Talbot))—as well as prosecutors—*Suspect* (1987) (Cher (Kathleen Riley)) and *The Accused* (1988) (Kelly McGillis (Katheryn Murphy)).[51] They appear to operate effectively in their professional roles within a male-dominated environment.

They have been critiqued for 'looking for love in the wrong places'[52] and having 'no judgment or common sense'.[53] The question, though, is whether or not this is different from male equivalents. The male lawyers often seem to have character traits which are far from endearing. Paul Biegler (James Stewart) has practically given up law in *Anatomy of a Murder* (1959) in favour of fishing after defeat in the contest to carry on as the local DA. Tony Lawrence (Paul Newman) is not above using his looks and charm to get the business of older women in *The Young Philadelphians* (1959). Atticus Finch (Gregory Peck) is prepared to cover

---

[50] Robson, P (2007a).
[51] This is the way her name is spelt on her office door, although not on the film credits.
[52] Bergman, P and Asimow, M (1996: 90).
[53] *Ibid*, 91.

up a murder with the connivance of another person from the justice system in *To Kill a Mockingbird* (1962). Arthur Kirkland (Al Pacino) in ... *And Justice for All* (1979) displays a reckless disregard for his clients' interests and compromises his own professionalism in a series of ill-judged attempts to expose the shortcomings of the legal system. Even tax lawyer Peter Sanderson (Steve Martin) is not above bribery to secure the affections of a rich client through getting to her dog in *Bringing Down the House* (2003).

There is, however, a variation in the kinds of roles which this wave of films brought the audience in the late 1980s and into the 1990s. Here we have female lawyers as either dependent or gullible. In *Legal Eagles* (1986) Laura Kelly (Debra Winger) is a young lawyer who is star-struck by the Assistant DA Tom Logan (Robert Redford). When we see her in court we are less than overwhelmed with her defence of her client. Her attitude to Redford is to fawn at his feet. Little positive can be said about Jenny Hudson (*Physical Evidence*, 1989), TK Katwuller (*Defenseless*, 1990) and Kate McQueen (*Fair Game*, 1995). The plots are thin and the characters limited and even the touch of veteran director Sidney Lumet does little to encourage us that we have a credible legal performer in Jennifer Haines (*Guilty As Sin*, 1993).[54] This general shift has been remarked upon by a number of writers. Bergman and Asimow suggest women lawyers have received a raw deal at the hands of film makers and Rafter took a similar view in her work on crime films.[55] Lucia also examined the films of the 1980s and 1990s and locates the rise of what she describes as 'woman lawyer films'[56] as part of a deeply rooted 'crisis of patriarchy'.[57] Despite the focus on law, Lucia suggests that the ideological critique implicit in such work becomes supportive of the system being critiqued. Essentially, according to Lucia, these are not feminist films and she locates them in the context of the rise of the Reagan New Right, which established 'an agenda of containment around feminist issues', paying lip service to women's rights whilst at the same time shepherding women back into the home under the rubric of 'family values'.[58] From a European perspective, this backlash against feminism, which provided the title of Faludi's 1992 treatise on the attacks on women's rights in the United States, is rather less convincing.[59] Whilst developments in Britain, for instance, have been slower than one would have hoped, the legislation on such matters as equal pay, discrimination in the workplace, protection from sexual harassment and domestic abuse all improved in the 1980s, 1990s and since. Hence irrespective of whether one accepts the evidence over a 1980s 'backlash' there is the intriguing notion of films being interpreted in a rather different context outwith their country of origin. The sheer volume of female lawyers in this period, along

[54] See the coruscating comments of Rafter, N (2006: 152).
[55] *Ibid.*
[56] Lucia, C (2005: 2).
[57] *Ibid*, 3.
[58] *Ibid*, 8.
[59] Faludi, S (1992).

with their portrayal as encompassing both fighting qualities as well as human frailties, then, provides a less discouraging picture for a non-American observer.

The Woman Lawyer in the Supporting Cast

In contrast with the all male legal world of the 1950s and 1960s in *Witness for the Prosecution* (1957), *Brothers in Law* (1957), *Anatomy of a Murder* (1959) and *To Kill a Mockingbird* (1962), women start to appear on the periphery of male-dominated films like *Philadelphia* (1993)[60] and *The Gun in Betty Lou's Handbag* (1992).[61] Women have, of course, also featured in more minor positions and upwards of 90 films contain women lawyers.[62] Sheffield also noted the absence of African-American female attorneys in mainstream film as well as TV in his assessment up until 1990.[63] There were no records of African-American or ethnic women in a primary, secondary or even an incidental role before 1985. The change since then has been minimal. *Losing Isaiah* (1995) has an African-American lawyer Caroline Jones (LaTanya Richardson) hired for her ethnicity. Both she and her counterpart, Kadar Lewis (Samuel L Jackson) play minor but significant roles in this transracial adoption tug-of-war. There is one African-American female judge in *Primal Fear* (1996) and a young attorney in *The Gun in Betty Lou's Handbag* (1992). The vast majority of lawyer portrayals have been white. The number of women lawyers in the United States was 4,000 in 1940 and of these 57 were African-American. However, by 1990 the number of African-American women practising law had risen to 10,000.[64] It is worth considering not simply the number of female lawyer appearances since the Second Wave of feminism propelled women into law schools in significant numbers in the 1970s but to examine not just what kind of roles women play but the extent to which the gendered nature of law is an issue.

The Demise of the Political

Katheryn Murphy in *The Accused* (1988) and Ann Talbot in *Music Box* (1989) can be considered the 'high-water mark' of the independent modern female lawyer. However, there is a longish line of women lawyers, found in the lesser 1980s films, who appear to embody the notion of the impossibility of an independent woman. In the midst of the critical and commercial blockbuster *A Few Good Men* (1992) involving a smart attorney in pursuit of the truth and a male hierarchy

---

[60] Mary Steenburgen for defence as Belinda Conine.
[61] Alfre Woodard (Ann Orpick) as rookie desperate not to lose her client.
[62] Sheffield, R (1993).
[63] *Ibid.*
[64] *Ibid.*

determined to operate its own rules there is the insertion of a strange piece of throwback sexual politics. Lieutenant Daniel Kaffee (Tom Cruise) is seeking to find out the truth in relation to events leading to the death of a recruit in basic training at the hands of his fellow soldiers. Lieutenant Commander JoAnne Galloway (Demi Moore) is a woman lawyer higher up the pecking order. However, she appears to have little has sense of proportion and devotes an excessive amount of time to minor issues, unable to see the bigger picture. The contrast with casual and self-serving Kaffee is marked. Insofar as she has a role in *A Few Good Men* (1992) Galloway serves to provide the catalyst which awakens in Kaffee's commitment to justice rather than simply avoiding the stress and hassle of legal practice. She is on the team, but her role is reduced to the kind of role one expects would be a feature of the legal practice of Mr and Mrs Tom Logan in their post-*Legal Eagles* (1986) partnership.

Two women lawyers of the new millennium appear to have eating disorders—Lucy Kelson (Sandra Bulloch) binge-eating Chinese food at times of stress in *Two Weeks Notice* (2002), and Audrey Woods (Julianne Moore) in *Laws of Attraction* (2004). Another is a fashion-obsessed future wife of the east-coast establishment—Elle Woods (Reese Witherspoon) in *Legally Blonde* (2001). A failing, career-obsessed mother, Rita Williams (Michelle Pfeiffer), who cannot communicate with her own son other than through buying things, in *I Am Sam* (2001), leaves us with little on the face of it to be encouraged about. The picture looks bleak for women being taken seriously on the basis of their film portrayal. This is, though, to read the films in an over-literal way. Elle Woods may appear in a fluffy rom-com chasing a man as her goals in life, however she transforms. She may still favour a pet chihuahua and wearing pink but she shows herself to be better than the man she was initially pursuing. The reliance on the 'old girl' network rather undermines the sequel *Legally Blonde 2: Red White and Blonde* (2003). Similarly, although Lucy Kelson (*Two Weeks Notice* 2002) appears to be flawed in her personal life, she succeeds in getting her radical community agenda adopted by the property developer with whom she is romantically involved.

Janet Venable (Laura Linney) establishes, in *Primal Fear* (1996), a certain independence and with the role in *The Exorcism of Emily Rose* of feisty Erin Bruner (Laura Linney) there is a roster of women lawyers in major roles which would make Amanda Bonner feel she had indeed started something. The contrast with Erin Brockovich's self-perception in the eponymous film (*Erin Brockovich* 2000) is interesting. Here, the crucial point is that Julia Roberts' character is most definitely **not** a lawyer and her problems begin and end with the profession. Whether or not, though, the audience still see her as a lawyer figure is moot. She is certainly a 'justice figure' in the terms defined by Rafter as a heroine 'who tries to move man-made law closer to the ideal until it matches the justice template'.[65]

---

[65] Rafter, N (2001: 10) and Rafter, N (2006: 136).

Erin Brockovich also spawned a television series *Final Justice with Erin Brockovich* (2003) hosted by the star.

Rebecka Martinsson: An Alternative Role for Women Lawyers?

Rebecka Martinsson (Izabella Scorupco) in *Solstorm* (2007) seems to offer an attractive prospect in the search for a powerful woman lawyer although she exhibits some of the traditional flaws—albeit that they are offset with great(er) strengths. She features as the 'star' in the cinematic adaptation of Asa Larsson's book *The Savage Altar.*[66] In a sense Scorupco is the Hollywood star in an otherwise Scandinavian production having acted in *Golden Eye* (1995) amongst others. Martinsson is a tax lawyer, albeit a junior one, which in itself is somewhat unusual given the masculine tendencies of corporate law. There is no question of her competency as a tax lawyer as she is shown with prospects of partnership. However, she is clearly restless and uncertain about her professional position, unable it seems to commit herself to the firm. When she receives a panic phone call from her childhood friend Sanna Strandgard (Maria Sundbom), Martinsson doesn't hesitate to abandon the firm's party and return to her native Kiruna, a hostile and desolate environment. It is her return to Kiruna that opens up her confrontation with her past. At this point there are strong similarities with a number of other portrayals, notably the idea of the repressed daughter. However, in this case the relationship is broader than with her father. There are several important relationships with men from her deceased grandfather through to the murdered Viktor Strandgard (Andre Sjoberg). However, in the middle are the dominant patriarchal figures that run the religious community that she has 'abandoned'. There is Olof Strandgard (Krister Henriksson), father of Sanna and Viktor, and Tomas Soderberg (Mikael Persbrandt), who it transpires had made her pregnant. It was her subsequent abortion that led to her excommunication from the closed religious group that dominates life in the town.

It is her relationship with these men that demonstrates her strength of character. She is determined to solve Viktor's murder and is convinced that Sanna (who has confessed) is innocent. Martinsson refuses to be browbeaten by them and probes further into the dealings of the church threatening to expose them using tax law by enlisting her boss at the law firm. She is physically threatened and has to keep Sanna's children safe from their own grandparents. Not only is she investigating the church and trying to solve Viktor's murder but is also stepping into the breach and acting as the children's mother. She is shown to be capable of acting both as a 'lawyer' and a mother, albeit a surrogate one. Martinsson does, however, build

---

[66] Martinsson also features as the heroine in Larsson's second book *Blood Spilt* (2008).

a strong relationship with the two children. She is a solitary figure with powerful forces arraigned against her, with her only ally the heavily pregnant police inspector Anna Maria Mella (Lena B Eriksson). Again, a powerful maternal figure who manages to help save Martinsson's life whilst simultaneously giving birth.

However, where Martinsson compares most favourably with the iconic male lawyers of Atticus Finch and Lincoln is her physical defence of the children in the pursuit of justice. Attacked by members of the church she protects the children, although unlike either Finch or Lincoln she is stabbed and ends up in a serious condition in hospital. What this portrayal does show is that a woman lawyer can, contemporaneously, be competent, determined, strong and motherly. There is, however, a slight twist when it transpires that she has misunderstood the nature of the events; there is no Eddie Sanger from *Suspect* (1987) to come to her aid. One of the principal issues though is whether Martinsson can be classed as a lawyer rather than an investigator. She does use her legal knowledge and training and is, perhaps, akin to Erin Brockovich as a justice figure.

The Politics of Gender in Legal Films

The notion of the male construction of law, which is an early theme in feminist jurisprudence, has seldom been encountered in the new roster of legal films with women protagonists. This may be one of the reasons why Kamir looks beyond the standard roster of courtroom dramas for her material on women in film.[67] Bizarrely, however, as early as *Adam's Rib* (1949) the issue was central. In this comic portrayal of the relationship between the sexes there is a gender-based defence. The argument is simple: the reaction of a man to his partner's infidelity would find expression in the defence of provocation and consequently the same should apply to the woman. If there is an unwritten law allowing a man to react to such events with a deadly weapon, the same should be allowed to women. Women are, after all, equal to men. A significant part of the courtroom scenes involve the demonstration of women's equality through their achievements. As Bergman and Asimow (1996) have pointed out, this has little to do with whether or not there is such a defence of provocation available to men. In the final event the device adopted by the lawyer defending the slighted Judy Holliday is to get the jury to reconstruct the law as if it were not simply serving male interests. They are asked to imagine how they would react if the defendant were a man who had discovered his wife in the arms of another man; they immediately acquit. Whilst Bergman and Asimow (1996) are strictly correct, that the defence as portrayed is legally irrelevant, it does serve to draw attention to the question of whose interests the law serves. It suggests, in a deceptively discreet way, that the source of both

---

[67] Kamir, O (2006).

social rules, and the economic and political structure, is patriarchy. Bergman and Asimow also noted that the central figure was in fact a fine role model:

> The most important and the best part of *Adam's Rib* is Amanda. In 1949, there were very few female lawyers at the bar. Law school classes contained only a handful of women, if there were any at all, and the general sense was that the profession was not suitable for women. Thus Amanda was a wonderful role model for women who were considering possible careers in the law. Amanda is loving and committed to her marriage, but equally committed to her politics and to her client, even when it jeopardizes her marriage. The sexual politics so humorously dramatized in *Adam's Rib* remain as fresh today as the day the film was written.[68]

Rather than build on this promising model, subsequent films utilising female portrayals have taken a rather different path. There has been, instead, a concentration on the rather more accessible concept of individual responsibility. Thus we encounter the initial brick wall of male solidarity in the denial of a gang rape in *The Accused* (1988). Here the problem raised is the double bind of the victim reliving the events combined with a trial of her lifestyle and mores. The novelty of women lawyers has not altered the storylines and plots which featured in the 1980s and 1990s from those of the male lawyers. Similarly in the films of John Grisham the gendered nature of law's application as well as its construction does not feature.[69] The writing on the portrayal of women in film has contained one unifying theme, namely the limitations in the filmic portrayal of women lawyers in these films.[70] A range of issues has been examined in both individual films and other selected material. In relation to *Class Action* (1991) Tushnet notes that 'the film preserves the gender relations of dominance and subordination'.[71] Whilst this is undoubtedly true, it stems from the way in which the film combines a courtroom drama and a family drama and seems uncertain whether or not it wants to be about the class of the title or inter-family dynamics. The film could also be treated as a celebration of a lawyer's politicisation and realisation that, since the world is split into warring economic groups, a choice must be made. This political consciousness has been overlaid by a dysfunctional family life.

The broader question of a political backlash during the 1980s has also been discussed. Shapiro suggests that whilst the backlash of the Reagan-Bush era ended in 1992 its legacy lingered on into 1993 and that the movie lawyer has 'neither sexual nor any other kind of power'.[72] She suggests that a better model for Hollywood might be the characterisation of solicitor Gareth Peirce by Emma Thompson in the Irish-directed, British-set, US-financed film *In the Name of the Father* (1993). A broader canvas is the basis for work by Graham and Maschio.[73] Looking at five

---

[68] Bergman, P and Asimow, M (1996: 90).
[69] Robson, P (2001).
[70] Graham, L and Maschio, G (1995–96).
[71] Tushnet, M (1996: 259).
[72] Shapiro, C (1995: 1009).
[73] Graham, L and Maschio, G (1995–96).

of the more significant legal films with women protagonists—*Adam's Rib* (1949); *The Accused* (1988); *Music Box* (1989); *Class Action* (1991); *The Client* (1994)—they conclude that these films indicate that it is at best difficult for a woman to be lawyer and, at worst, a choice must be made between personal fulfilment and acceptability and the profession of law:

> The fables told by these movies stand as a double warning. Women who look too much like successful men displace those men, and thereby risk the loss of love and acceptance from them. Women who reject cloning strategy and seek a different way of working, risk self-assignment to legal areas populated by other, needy women and children.[74]

This work was produced in the context of the Sesquicentenniel of the 1848 Seneca Falls Women's Rights Convention, the theme of which was women's unfinished quest for legal, economic, political and social equality. In that way, as the authors stress, it was firmly located within the approach that reflects the dominant culture's ideology offering suggestions about what external reality ought to be. Thus, as sources of potential role models, these films are lacking.

By contrast there have been overviews of the films, featuring women lawyers, which have seized on certain aspects of the presentations and made bold and sweeping conclusions. It has been proposed that women have been ill-served in the portrayals they have been accorded. Bergman and Asimow suggest that women lawyers as they have been featured have exhibited two character flaws; they are weak and male-dependent in their relationships. This charge covers various forms of unethical sexual relations with either clients or supervisors from Carolyn Polhemus (Greta Scacchi) in *Presumed Innocent* (1990) and Maggie Ward (Mary Elizabeth Mastrantonio) in *Class Action* (1991) to Laura Fischer (Charlotte Rampling) in *The Verdict* (1982) and Teddy Barnes (Glenn Close) in *Jagged Edge* (1985). The female screen lawyer also lacks judgment, common sense and does not understand trial tactics. A long roster is put forward to support this contention including Teddy Barnes (Glenn Close) in *Jagged Edge* (1985), Kathryn Reilly (Cher) in *Suspect* (1987) and uptight Joanne Gallacher (Demi Moore) in *A Few Good Men* (1992) through to the unethical Katheryn Murphy (Kelly McGillis) in *The Accused* (1988). Thus there is a parade of women who display negative qualities. As, however, Asimow has documented, it is possible by noting every single lawyer appearance to produce a perspective on lawyers which allows one to chronicle the appearance of lawyers as including a huge number of 'bad lawyers'.[75] This analysis runs the risk of abstracting certain actions of both major and minor characters and producing a potentially misleading account of the impact of filmic images. It seems mischievous to single out, for example, the moral dubiety of Laura Fischer without seeing her as anything other than the hired hand of the Machiavellian Ed Concannon (James Mason). By contrast, Nevins has suggested that the view in *Reel Justice* that 'almost without exception women lawyers are

---

[74] *Ibid*, 1066.
[75] Asimow, M (2000a).

presented in viciously stereotypical terms is driven by political correctness'.[76] Given the examination of the films which we have undertaken this critique does not seem to be justified. There is much to complain about, but there have been changes. Just as the crude sexism of the 007 Bond films has altered down the years so that he is now often made to appear the junior partner, it is possible to see a difference between Teddy Barnes and Janet Venable. The contrast with televisual portrayals is marked.[77]

In addition, there have been general assessments of how effective as role models these portrayals have been.[78] Caplow assesses the trends in what she describes as the 'six better than average films' that she thinks merit 'more serious scrutiny' as containing interesting common features. The selected films are *Class Action* (1991), *Jagged Edge* (1985), *The Client* (1994), *Music Box* (1989), *Suspect* (1987) *and The Accused* (1988). The lawyers are parodies of the ambitious male lawyer ridiculed in *Regarding Henry* (1991) in which Harrison Ford as workaholic Henry Turner discovers his human side following an accident—a brain injury:

> None of the women lawyers is married allowing them to dedicate long hours to work and leaving them open to sexual temptation ... While the two women with children ... superficially appear to be good mothers with supportive ex-husbands, they spend little time with their children and often put their personal and professional interests ahead of the needs of their kids.[79]

Perhaps more worrying is the persistence of the trappings of the dependence and their presence is what is presented as an essentially male world:

> All (except Sarandon) have either male mentors or professional father figures and protectors. Several have a male protégé such as the junior associate in Class Action and the paralegal in The Client. All have male adversaries in court, and appear to be the only women lawyers, and only professional women at their respective jobs.[80]

In addition, as part of the concern with law-related individual films as opposed to assessing broader areas of film a whole range of assessments have been put forward in relation to films where the law and gender interact. *Thelma and Louise* (1991) has been the subject of coverage although it features no lawyers. Its particular interest in this context is that the genesis of the flight of two protagonists is the lack of faith in the judicial system's ability to deal with the kind of 'everyday violence' visited on Thelma by Harlan. It has been suggested that this exhibition of feminist consciousness links with that demonstrated in *Adam's Rib* (1949) and highlights the daily operation of patriarchy.[81] Similarly, another film in which law lurks in the background, *Fatal Attraction* (1987), has been described as a film which reaffirms

---

[76] Nevins, F (1996c).
[77] Corcos, C (1998).
[78] Caplow, S (1999).
[79] *Ibid*, 64.
[80] *Ibid*, 64—this is 'corrected' in the TV series of *The Client*, where Foltrigg becomes Reggie's male mentor.
[81] Spelman, N and Minow, M (1996).

the ideology of patriarchy and part of the backlash against the social changes fostered by the women's movement from the late 1960s. It is structured according to the conventional assumptions of male spectatorship.[82] This notion from Freudian psychoanalytic theory that mainstream cinema is constructed around the domain interests of men and assumes that female characters are the object of that 'male gaze' allows us to see this gross increase of female lawyer protagonists in a slightly different light. The question of the style of portrayal needs to be considered. Rather than simply being celebrated as an emergence from behind the secretarial desk or the domestic arena the modern woman lawyer seems capable of being seen as an obscure object of desire rather than as a powerful professional.

The problem, though, in assessing films relating to female representations parallels the struggle against women's traditional oppression. The paucity of the films and the nature of the representations can be seen as reflecting structural failings. The stories, where they highlight limitations of the socio-political system, can be seen as no more than tokenism. As we have noted in relation to the 'good lawyer/ bad lawyer' debate, we are sceptical about any simple kind of binary categorisation. We would concur with Asimow and Mader's view that films 'contain many examples of tough, competent, hard-working, successful, and committed female lawyers'.[83] Whilst we would also agree that the films 'abound with negative stereotypes about female lawyers', the overall portrayal in the 21st century is similar to that of male lawyers. When looked at in detail over the whole range of films we get a mix of altruism, self-interest, competence and incompetence. Whether or not that is the reading of members of the public or those setting out on a legal career is another matter.

Gay, Lesbian and Bisexual Portrayals

In relation to the portrayal—or rather, for the most part, non-portrayal—of gay, lesbian and bisexual images in mainstream cinema this is primarily a tale of silence, or their presence has been coded.[84] That said, there are notable exceptions, such as *Different from the others* (1919), that provided an affirmative exposition of homosexuality.[85] Sometimes the coding has been limited but their sexuality is irrelevant to the narrative as with Joel Cairo and Wilmer in *The Maltese Falcon*

---

[82] Babener, L (1992).

[83] Asimow, M and Mader, S (2004: 185).

[84] Russo, V (1999). Assessments of coded representations are, of course, highly subjective and may be no more than idiosyncratic readings. In *The Young Philadelphians* (1959) is Robert Vaughn a bad (gay?) apple and what of Martin Landau in *North by NorthWest* (1959)?

[85] Jones C (1996: 258) notes that '*Different from the others* (1919) was a success on its first release. Even though the main character, a homosexual musician, finally poisons himself, the dour storyline is strongly countered by sections of the film in which Dr Magnus Hirschfield puts forward an affirmative view of homosexuality.' He goes on to note that Hirschfield was a well-known researcher whose institute was later destroyed by the Nazis and that only a few fragments of the film still exist.

(1941). Non-heterosexual identities and themes are found in a somewhat oblique form in such films as *Adam's Rib* (1949) and *Tea and Sympathy* (1956) from the 1940s and 1950s. In the former the character of piano-playing Kip is cute and camp. Adam Bonner makes homophobic disparaging remarks about him. The references, though, are sufficiently oblique and the would-be affair with Amanda so integral to the revenge plotline that his sexual identity is subsumed within the hetero norm.

In the latter there is a sensitive young man interested in arts and drama and uninterested in rough male bonding sports like American football being ostracised for his cissy nature and lack of keenness to date young women. His ability to play tennis, though, gives him a certain status and protection from harassment. The plot takes a wild twist, however, when an older woman sets herself the goal of 'saving' him. Being the 1950s this is a success and when we catch up with Tom 10 years down the line he is happily married, having put his youthful sensitive 'whatever it was' behind him.

In the 1960s, Sheila Delaney's portrayal in *A Taste of Honey* (1961) of an unmarried pregnant girl was shocking enough in itself that almost no attention was paid to the 'otherness' of her friend, Geoffrey. It is not until the 1970s that we have any clear mainstream films with characters not hidden, or compromised, in relation to their sexuality. Films, however, such as *The Boys in the Band* (1970) and *Sunday, Bloody Sunday* (1971) remain memorable because they involved frank portrayals of the existence of the concepts of lesbianism, homosexuality and bisexuality, rather than the films that followed. A little bit like *Philadelphia* (1993) in a later era, it was as if Hollywood could point to the existence of the films to show that it canvassed the full range of life's experience, without going overboard and doing any further portrayals. That was left to specialist markets and art house cinema.

The one pre-decriminalisation appearance of a gay lawyer in *Victim* (1961) has homosexuality portrayed as a furtive clandestine world. Dyer makes a valid point on the cultural importance of the film in the chronology of gay cinema:

> It was, in gay terms, a first—the first film to defend homosexuality as a cause in a mainstream context, the first to deal with gayness explicitly (earlier examples demand a good deal of 'reading in'), the first to have a major star playing a gay character.[86]

The film had its difficulties passing the censor, even in what appears to be the bland and oblique presentation of the gay world found in the film.[87] The problem here is seen as the existence of blackmail and its impact on people's lives. As Dyer notes: 'The film is organized around the investigation of crime (theft, then blackmail) and the agents of investigation are the agents of law. This means that the victim image (victims of blackmail, victims of the law) is reinforced by the gay characters' narrative passivity'.[88] It is only the lawyer, Farr (Dirk Bogarde) who is able to exert

---

[86] Dyer, R (1993: 93).
[87] Robertson, G (1989).
[88] Dyer, R (1993: 99).

any autonomy. However, he is caught in the contradiction between his profession and the application of the law is applied against homosexuality. Although the context to the film is the criminalisation of gay existence, this is addressed within the context of the detective thriller genre rather than as a direct social issues film.[89]

As Moran (1998) points out, however, the lawyer protagonist is presented positively as he struggles to live his life morally in a climate of fear and repression. However, issues of equal treatment and gay rights are still some way off in the early 1960s.[90]

It is perhaps unsurprising that sexuality has not been focused upon to any great degree within legal film. The courtroom drama might be expected to feature lawyers dedicated to the law for whom sexuality is not really imaginable. Certainly one reading of *Young Mr Lincoln* (1939) sees Lincoln choosing the law over any romantic attachment he may have had; essentially he is sexless. It is almost as if other emotions may get in the way of a quest for justice and there is not time for a distraction from a lawyer's vocation. That said, we see Cher in *Suspect* (1987) outwardly bemoaning that her commitment to her job has cost her the chance to have a relationship, and perhaps a child, and she is resentful of this. There are, of course, dedicated lawyers for whom the personal life is secondary to doing justice. These include Sir Wilfred Robarts in *Witness for the Prosecution* (1957) and Atticus Finch in *To Kill a Mockingbird* (1962). Many of the subsequent lawyers do, however, have emotional entanglements complicating their professional lives. These range from Paul Newman in *The Young Philadelphians* (1959) and *The Verdict* (1982), Tom Cruise in *The Firm* (1993), Gene Hackman in *The Firm* (1993) and *Class Action* (1991). Insofar as they possess sexuality, these non-*Philadelphia* lawyers are, without exception, clearly straight. Few instances are encountered when we look at gay or lesbian characters in law films. Moran has identified the two major roles of the barrister in *Victim* (1961) and corporate litigator in *Philadelphia* (1993). Even when added to this are the two friends of Sonny Coufax in *Big Daddy* (1999), this is not a significant cohort.

In *Victim* (1961) it is as a threatened figure in a British society where homosexual acts in private are criminalised that we encounter Melville Farr. He is subject to blackmail demands through his involvement with a young man who has disappeared and then commits suicide. Farr is married and has a successful career. We see him hopeful of being recognised as a leader in his profession as a court practitioner being made a QC. He shows courage and regard for others in his actions, being prepared to sacrifice his career and marriage to bring the blackmailers to justice. What is significant about the film, though, is its being made at all.

It is a long time from *Victim* (1961), however, until we have another heroic protagonist in the shape of Andrew Beckett (Tom Hanks) in *Philadelphia* (1993). Thirty years separate Melville Farr and Andrew Beckett. The first stages in the struggle for equal treatment have taken place, without impinging on the legal film.

---

[89] Kuzina, M (2001).
[90] See, eg, Eskridge, WN (1997) and Britton, P (1998).

It is the theme of AIDS and its impact on a high-flying young corporate lawyer that brings us a gay lawyer in *Philadelphia* (1993). Andrew Beckett's sexuality is what drives the narrative since he loses his employment when it is discovered that he is gay. There is, however, an alternative explanation put forward by his employers. He has, according to them, been sacked because he has not able to perform his duties satisfactorily and cannot 'cut the mustard'. This conflict provides the essence of the court action he raises against his erstwhile employers for discrimination. What we know of Andrew might lead us to believe that he is a dedicated hardworking lawyer. To what extent he is the sort of lawyer that Atticus Finch or Jed Ward would approve of is not clear. Miller asks him whether he is a 'good lawyer'. On being told that he is an excellent lawyer he inquires as to what makes Beckett such a lawyer. Apart from knowing the law and excelling at practising it Beckett loves the law; he loves it for its inclusivity and for the way in which it makes him feel part of something bigger, something important.

We see him at the start resisting a nuisance suit against his clients, Kendo Construction. They are building a skyscraper and damaging the health of those in the immediate neighbourhood. The issue which generates the dismissal of the action is a copyright infringement of a spreadsheet system. Whilst this may be a quintessential 20th-century version of basic human rights, this kind of work does not seem likely to produce those thrilling moments of justice of which Andrew waxes so lyrical when on the witness stand later on. Perhaps he is no more than a hotshot corporate figure like Mitch McDeere or Tony Lawrence. He has certainly never sought to challenge the oppressed nature of those who share his sexuality. Indeed, while he patently would not have agreed or concurred with the locker room banter he was subjected to (anti-gay jokes etcetera), he chose to suffer in silence for fear of putting the steep trajectory of his career in jeopardy. This portrayal of the law as a bastion and reflection of male values is reinforced in a number of films. For example in *The Firm* (1993) there is a distinction draw between the male lawyers and their partners. The women are expected not to work but to produce a family in order to encourage stability. In *A Civil Action* (1998) it is the woman (possibly a lawyer though her status is not clear) who wants to hear the details of the case when the male lawyers want to ditch it as uneconomic. If Beckett is, as he suggests, thrilled by exposing injustice, the need to live a double life in the late 1980s does not make him a legal hero for a generation out of the closet.

Unfortunately it is as the bearer of AIDS rather than as a lawyer in his own right that we encounter him. The lawyers active in the courtroom in *Philadelphia* (1993) are Joe Miller and, to a lesser extent, Belinda Conine (Mary Steenburgen). Those who start as lawyers, such as Andrew Beckett, Charles Wheeler (Jason Robards, Jnr) and Walter Kenton (Robert Ridgely), rapidly fade into the background as regards their lawyer input. Interestingly the first major portrayal of a gay lawyer in fact portrays him as a victim, and along with other key legal players at the beginning of the film, he features only as a witness (in his case defendant) to the action. Beyond these two films, however, the appearance of the gay world in legal films is confined to three versions of the Oscar Wilde case which effectively demonstrated the cruelty and hypocrisy of Wilde's treatment by a homophobic legal regime (see *Oscar Wilde* (1959); *The Trials of Oscar Wilde* (1960) and *Wilde* (1997).[91] Moran emphasises that there is more to Andrew Beckett's appearance as a lawyer than the according of this status to a gay character.[92] He notes that he has transcended merely appearing to transforming the institution of law into something homosocial. He is able to do this convincingly through the deployment of the buddy relationship between him and another previously invisible lawyer, the African-American Joe Miller.

When women finally appear frequently as protagonists in law films, the same sexual presumption applies to them. Although, as Moran has pointed out, in other areas of popular culture like TV and novels, gay characters appear either as lawyers or other legal figures there are, as indicated, only two films in which gay lawyers appear as major protagonists.[93] It is not easy to add to this list looking to lesser roles. All we have is occasional gender displacement. Reggie Love employs a male secretary in *The Client* (1994), but this is no more than a device to allow young Mark Sway to draw attention to the fact that, young as he is, he expects lawyers to be men. The fact that lawyer Love has a reasonably standard male name may also have something to with his error. The range of sexuality in law films seems to be restricted to the heterosexual.

---

[91] There are of course comedies like *Jeffrey* (1995) and *In and Out* (1997) which, according to Russell, 'might serve as effective complements to a courtroom drama like Philadelphia' Russell, M (1998: 2).

[92] Moran, L (1998).

[93] *Ibid.*

15

Minority Report? Ethnicity in Film

There is a range of issues involved in the representation of ethnicity in film generally in addition to the more specific interest of the narrower law and the justice system. Bell Hooks makes an important point in accepting the importance of both the extent and the nature of the representation, as well as its ambivalence. She notes that:

> [o]ften multiple standpoints are expressed in an existing film. A film may have incredibly revolutionary standpoints merged with conservative ones.[1]

Interestingly the examination of law films in relation to ethnicity suggests that, historically, there has been a relative lack of subtlety in this area. There are three aspects to consider, starting with the broad issue of ethnic minority representation in film. Secondly there is the depiction of minority ethnic matters within law films and finally the extent and nature of the portrayal of ethnic minority lawyers. Who and what matters has been significantly skewed. Gender, race and class have been major signifiers in the picture of society that emerges from film and contributes to the construction and content of popular culture. It is important to indicate precisely why the nature and extent of that representation in film is deemed to be significant.[2] Hollywood film and British film are covered separately here as this highlights the contingency of these images and their power. What resonates in one culture will be perceived through a different lens elsewhere. The operation of Britain's empire has provided a backdrop for a range of films, though most interestingly this has more recently been subject to domestic interpretation through Bollywood offerings. See, for example, *The Rising: the Ballad of Mangal Pandey* (2005), which deals with the 1857 Seepoy Mutiny with the usual Bollywood touch of flamboyance.

Ethnic Minority Representation in Film

There have been a number of overviews of how films have represented the African-American experience. The second-class citizenship that has been the lot of

---

[1] Hooks, B (1996: 3).
[2] Ferguson, R (1998).

the ex-slave community has had its expression in the kinds of roles that have been available to them and how they have featured in these films. The starting point is, of course, controversial. On the one hand there is a perception that reform of the rules and operation of institutions was appropriate, through legal challenges facing a more radical challenge from critical studies. This involves:

> [a] call for context, critique of liberalism, insistence that racism is ordinary not exceptional, and the notion that traditional civil rights law has been more valuable to whites than blacks.[3]

The reality of representation, as opposed to an appropriate strategy to alter this, must be undertaken. This can be seen in a number of surveys of black Hollywood with slightly different focuses. Surveys of ethnic minority participation in cinema go back as far as 1940, with Peter Noble's *The Negro in Film*.[4] In the 1970s Cripps produced *Slow Fade to Black*[5] looking at the films between 1900 and 1942. He completed his review with *Making Movies Black*—the latter's subtitle indicates its scope—*The Hollywood Message Movies from World War II to the Civil Rights Era*.[6] Cripps related the differences between the representation of ethnicity, to changes in political context in both the United States and Britain. He also showed how these films both reflected and altered ideas about race. This makes the analysis subtle, but also, at the same time, rather elliptical. Hence the court victory of Pinky Johnson in *Pinky* (1949) is described as a vindication of the Southern justice system rather than a victory of Negro 'rights'.[7]

Bogle takes a slightly different approach recording the different ways in which black actors appeared in Hollywood films in the 20th century. As the title *Toms, Coons, Mulattoes, Mammies & Bucks* implies, much of the available work has been restricted to playing stereotypes from Stepin' Fetchit to Will Smith.[8] Fetchit remains a highly controversial figure due to the acting style and the roles he played.[9] On a legal theme his roles in the John Ford films about Judge Priest are prominent examples of his Minstrel style of clowning—*Judge Priest* (1934) and *The Sun Shines Bright* (1953). Bogle sought in his work to recognise and record this but also to explore what actors had managed to do within the context of the stereotype. Starting from the faithful Uncle Tom from Harriet Beecher Stowe's portrait of plantation life there were other ways of representing blackness in Hollywood films from the very start:

> After the Tom's debut, there appeared a variety of black presences bearing the fanciful names of the coon, the tragic mulatto, the mammy, and the brutal black buck.[10]

---

[3] Delgado, R (1995: xviii).
[4] Noble, P (1940); for an early American Marxist analysis see Jerome, VJ (1950).
[5] Cripps, T (1977).
[6] Cripps, T (1993).
[7] *Ibid*, 233.
[8] *The Legend of Bagger Vance* (2000) discussed in Bogle, D (1997).
[9] Clark, C (2005). Clark refers to Jar Jar Binks from the *Phantom Menace* (1999) being described by one acerbic critic as 'a Rastafarian Stepin Fetchit on platform hoofs' which Clark took to be a way of describing the character as an 'Uncle Tom'.
[10] Bogle, D (1997).

The Tom, despite his problems, remains 'hearty, submissive, stoic, generous, selfless and oh-so-very kind'.[11] Although this has been the most dominant type of representation, Bogle notes that 'he had serious competition from a group of coons ... presenting the Negro as amusement object and black buffoon'.[12] Women characters came as either the 'tragic mulatto' who is a victim of her divided racial inheritance or more frequently as the fiercely independent 'Mammy'. Finally there is the 'subhuman and feral ... barbaric black brute' from *The Birth of a Nation* (1915) to *Shaft* (1971) and *Superfly* (1972).[13] What Bogle argues is that these basic types appeared in various guises from servants to angry militants:

> With the Griffith spectacle, audiences saw the first of the guises. The brutes, bucks, and the tragic mulatto all wore the guise of villains. Afterwards during the 1920s, the audiences saw the toms and coons dressed in the guise of plantation jesters. In the 1930s and 1940s, the types were dressed in servants' uniforms. In the early 1940s they sported entertainers' costumes. In the late 1940s and the 1950s, they donned the gear of troubled problem people. In the 1960s, they appeared as angry militants. Because the guises were always changing, audiences were sometimes tricked into believing the depictions of the American Negro were altered, too. But at heart beneath the various guises, there lurked the familiar types.[14]

Spike Lee's satire on these stereotypes, *Bamboozled* (2000), involves a bizarre post-modern take on reviving these stereotypes in a television format. The film concludes with a three-and-a-half-minute montage of a large number of the African-American stereotypes from film and TV from the 1930s through to the 1950s and is perhaps more powerful than the film that precedes it. By applying Bogle's categories to law films and the portrayal of minority ethnic lawyers below the overall issue of note, beyond the issue of stereotyping, is the relatively small number of actors and directors who have actively contributed to American cinema. It is in this context that the specific issue of ethnic minority representation arises in relation to law films and more specifically as lawyers.

A slightly different scenario operates in Britain where the ethnic minority experience has been somewhat different. Its extent has, however, also been modest and has involved some stereotyping. In Britain the non-white population grew from 10,000 to a little over 4 million in 50 years as an imperial power relinquished a major empire during this time. There is a wealth of material here for cinematic treatment. However, the sheer lack of non-white faces in film means that the stereotypes Bogle identified have no equivalent. To counter this we adopt a 'time-frame' approach. British cinema has examined racial and ethnic issues in three quite specific and distinct ways during different eras.[15] These approaches correspond quite closely with particular concerns in cultural and political life and can

---

[11] *Ibid*, 6.
[12] *Ibid*, 7.
[13] *Ibid*, 13.
[14] *Ibid*, 18.
[15] For a different way of assessing the changes in filming of the black experience see Pines, J (2001).

be characterised as the confident imperialist perspective/funny foreigners phase, the integration or blending-in phase and the era of ethnic self-examination and self-confidence.

Race in British Film: The Imperialist Era

The existence of a significant Empire, covering large parts of Africa and the Indian sub-continent, continued after the Second World War. Imperialism was keenly espoused by a number of prominent politicians, such as Enoch Powell, well into the 1950s, and it was only with reluctance, often in the face of armed struggle, that the process of de-colonisation was completed. Movements for self-determination bore fruit principally after the Second World War notably in the Indian sub-continent in 1947 and Africa and the Far East throughout the 1950s and 1960s.[16] Films were made in the inter-war period which embraced the notion of Empire as a civilising force and which were still found in the 1960s. A mirror image of this issue has also been fascinatingly documented in the context of censoring cinema in colonial India.[17] Typical of this approach to other ethnic groups as uncivilised but mouldable is the filming of Edgar Wallace's story of a District Officer restoring peace amongst the child-like natives *Sanders of the River* (1935). Thus we have the film starting with a tribute to the notion of civilising colonialism and the role of men like Sanders:

> Africa ... tens of millions of natives under British rule, each tribe with its own chieftain, governed and protected by a handful of white men whose everyday work is an unsung saga of courage and efficiency. One of them was Commissioner Sanders.

The tone of interchange and relationships between Sanders (Leslie Banks) and the assembled chiefs is typified by Sanders' pep talk prior to taking a 12-month sabbatical: 'In my place the Lord Ferguson shall stay and give the law to all the peoples of the river. I want you to obey him as if you were his own children.' The condescension and obviously assumed inferiority of the 'natives' is the crux of this story about how the tribes are unable to respond to anything other than a mighty charismatic white man. He, Sanders, is the fount of all order and when other unscrupulous foreigners seek to subvert this control for their own profit they do so by putting out a cryptic message which underlines the limited and childlike nature of the native tribes. His successor, Ferguson, is urged to treat the natives as you would unruly schoolchildren when they run amok on discovering that the

---

[16] India and Pakistan, August 1947; Ghana, 1957; Malaya, 1957; Cyprus, 1960; Nigeria, 1960; Sierra Leone, 1962; Tanganyika (Tanzania), 1962; Somaliland, 1962; Uganda, 1962; Nyasaland, 1963; Northern Rhodesia (Zambia), 1963.

[17] Prasad, M (2004: 61).

charismatic white ruler is no more.[18] The main star of the film, Paul Robeson, is reputed to have been outraged at the final portrayal of Africans in the final version of the film.[19] In fairness, without going into the rest of the film, the lines which he himself was provided with make it pretty clear that his character was going to be portrayed as a wheedling self-serving servant of imperialism, albeit with charm. The content, though, has been altered in such a way as to shift it from reflecting producer Zoltan Korda's apparent passionate concern with African culture into a 'glorification of British colonial rule'.[20]

The same contrast between the western and 'native' culture is found in *Song of Freedom* (1936). This seemed to offer a rather more significant role for Paul Robeson by providing him with the chance to do more than sing and smile. The accidental overhearing of London stevedore John Zinga's stunning voice by the Opera impresario, Donozetti, results in Robeson touring the world. By chance he discovers that he is a descendant of Queen Zinga and is the lost King of the West African island of Casanga. This unusual film, nonetheless, despite having a black actor in the leading protagonist role still portrays African tribal life as riven with ignorance and superstition.[21] Contentment is to be found by acceptance of Robeson as the true King of the islanders whence his ancestors came so that he can lead them with his Western ways from being 'backward, uncivilized and impoverished'.

A related later feature of the Empire is the relationship between colonisers and colonised in the dog days of the colonial era. In *Bhowani Junction* (1956), Victoria Jones, a woman of Anglo-Indian parentage discovers that she is tolerated but not fully accepted due to her 'half-caste' status.[22] She rejects the suits of her anglified fellow 'half caste', Patrick Taylor, and of Nationalist activist Ranjit Kasel, and becomes the mistress of a white army officer. Told in flashback the audience sees the way in which Britain's military and gubernatorial withdrawal from the Indian sub-continent is reflected in the problems of identity she experiences due to this racial status. The conclusion of the film suggests an upbeat ending with love winning out against prejudice from both communities. The dominant mood in the film is of an isolated and problematic situation for the young couple in the new India and for Anglo-Indians generally rather more in keeping with John Masters' original text and the analysis of Ranjit Kasel's mother:

> Have you ever met an Englishman that didn't insult you? Haven't your own people worked for them for a hundred years and how are they going to reward you? They are going to leave you here with us. And what do you think we are going to do with Anglo-Indians? We're going to make you realise that you are Indians. Inferior Indians. Possibly

---

[18] The self-serving nature of this portrayal did attract oblique criticism at the time, notably in the Will Hay spoof *Ol' Bones of the River* (1938).

[19] Bourne, S (1998).

[20] Bogle, D (2001).

[21] Bourne, S (1998).

[22] See also *North West Frontier* (1956) with 'wise' imperialists counterposed to simple destructive native hordes.

disloyal because you spent the last hundred years licking England's boots and kicking us with your own boots.

A number of films during this late colonial era looked at these cross-cultural relationships including the British *The Wind Cannot Read* (1958). This rehearses the notion of forbidden love between Suzuki, a Japanese female translator, and Dirk Bogarde's military student during the Second World War. The problem of social disapproval that the couple seeks to overcome is elided by the death, from a mysterious illness, of Suzuki.[23] Thus, the trope is played out in these films superficially as one of a culture clash, with the crucial problem being acceptance by the dominant white society.

Foreignness on the Home Front

There has continued to be a strong adherence in locally situated family comedy and drama to racial and ethnic stereotypes. From the 1940s through to the 1970s Scottish, Irish, Welsh and English stereotypes abound along with 'funny foreigners'. An alternative treatment is to be found in *Pool of London* (1950), where a subplot involves a tentative relationship between a black sailor and a white theatre cashier. Problems of integration into a white society and cultural acceptance are hinted at as the story occupies a very brief amount of screen time compared with the machinations of the smuggler Bonar Colleano. Typically, in an otherwise undistinguished musical vehicle for a trio of British popsters, there is a sequence in the social security benefits office in *What a Crazy World* (1963) which is firmly in the tradition of the American black servant stereotyping.[24] All kinds of foreigners are shown disrupting the normal process of British youth avoiding work by themselves turning up and seeking state financial assistance. The Dole Office song features pig-tailed Chinese, singing Italian waiters, long-robed Africans, Arabs in headdress, Caribbean dancers, an Irish navy and a drunken kilted Scotsman. What makes it particular noteworthy is the way it feeds into a populist right-wing concept of 'dole-scrounging foreigners', who in this instance are principally non-white.[25] A sequence from the world of work, whether factory, restaurant or café, could have achieved the notion of nascent multiculturalism equally well. Crude stereotyping abounds in this period. It may be fondly meant but canny

---

[23] See also *The World of Suzie Wong* (1960) about a Hong Kong prostitute, Nancy Kwan, who attracts the attention of by two western men, William Holden and Michael Wilding.

[24] Joe Brown (hit with film's title song), Marty Wilde (father of Kim) and Susan Maughan (cover of Lesley Gore's Bobby's Girl).

[25] In the 1990s the Conservative Social Security Secretary, Peter Lilley, entertained his party's Annual Conference with his tales of immigrants knowing only a few words of English—'social security' and 'housing benefit' were in this alleged vocabulary. This notion finds a place in the Dole Office sequence in *What a Crazy World* (1963).

Scots,[26] devious Welsh,[27] feckless Irish[28] and hidebound English[29] are the staple of dramas and comedies.[30] Other ethnic groups are similarly treated whether they are amusing servile Indians[31] or onion-toting Frenchmen.[32] It has to be said that an absence of light and shade in characterisation is not unusual at this time with trade unionists as ogres in both comedy and drama.[33] There are some exceptions, like the reflection on the nature of inherent national, as opposed to individual characteristics, in the context of the initial ostracism and subsequent acceptance of a wartime German bride by her RAF hero husband's family and home town.[34]

The Question of Integration

In response to increasing immigration and the re-emergence of neo-fascist politics in Britain in the 1950s, there is an initial tendency to simply ignore racial issues, as in *Saturday Night and Sunday Morning* (1960). The casual, good-natured but offensive, racial stereotyping of the Seaton family in their encounter with a black soldier found in Sillitoe's book does not appear in the film version.[35] Sillitoe himself explained that the book was originally written as short stories and poems featuring the character of Arthur Seaton.[36] The omission of the section involving the visit of Sam, the black soldier visiting Arthur's relatives at Christmas, does not detract from the narrative flow of Arthur Seaton's passage from a carefree young philanderer to a married man with responsibilities.

By the same token, the mother of Doreen, Arthur's fiancée, is presented as a simple petit bourgeois mother-in-law stereotype. Her enigmatic Indian lodger/ lover, Chumley, does not feature although, again, this does not affect the narrative thrust of the story. These absences can be taken to signify the relative invisibility of ethnic minorities in most parts of Britain in the late 1950s, albeit Arthur Seaton's Nottingham was the scene of some of the 1958 race riots.

Race and its impact on the existing society are, however, found in a couple of films made in the wake of the riots. These adopt a liberal equal treatment agenda. In *Flame in the Streets* (1961) there is a clear rejection of discrimination in the

---

[26] *Geordie* (1955); *Sailor Beware* (1956); *The Fast Lady* (1963).
[27] *A Run for Your Money* (1949); *Doctor in the House* (1954); *Lucky Jim* (1957).
[28] *Captain Boycott* (1947); *The March Hare* (1956).
[29] *The Admirable Crichton* (1957); *The Man in the White Suit* (1951); *The League of Gentlemen* (1960).
[30] Contemporary TV satirised the same crude stereotypes with Johnny Speight's bigot Alf Garnett (*Till Death Us Do Part* (1966–68 passim) and Clement and Le Frenais' *The Likely Lads* (1964–66).
[31] *The Millionairess* with Peter Sellers (1960); *North West Frontier* (1959).
[32] *Summer Holiday* (1962).
[33] *I'm All Right Jack* (1959); *The Angry Silence* (1960).
[34] *Frieda* (1947).
[35] Sillitoe, A (1956). Some characters were either simplified or omitted in the film version of the book.
[36] *Ibid*, 1.

workplace related to the promotion of a black foreman. This occurs after the espousal of a clear anti-racist stance by the trusted trade unionist Jacko Palmer (John Mills). This is a man who, despite his years of service, refuses to take promotion within the union and leave the factory floor. His call to his comrades is impassioned and wins the day. Palmer's own reaction to discovering his daughter wants to marry a black teacher from Africa is to warn against the relationship 'for the sake of the children'. Interestingly this was almost exactly the response the author, Edward Braithwaite, records receiving from his girlfriend's father (Braithwaite 2005). Palmer then has to confront the ugly and, to him, unexpected racism of his wife when she discovers that their daughter is planning marriage with a black teacher:

> I'm ashamed of you. When I think of you and that man sharing the same bed ... It's filthy, disgusting, it makes my stomach turn over and I want to be sick.

There is a contrast with workplace racists motivated by the fear of losing work alongside the wife whose loathing of the black teacher is purely irrational. The film was not well received by some critics who saw it is a simplistic 'issues' film and it did not do well at the box office.[37] It has also been criticised for failing to engage properly in the debate between cultural integrationists and separatists.[38]

Race also appears within the generalised social prejudice against the unmarried teenager in *A Taste of Honey* (1961). The film, based on the 1959 stage production, addresses serious and controversial issues that were seldom openly discussed at the time of its production: single parenthood; inter-racial relationships and the treatment of gays. The father of the child of the pregnant Jo (Rita Tushingham) is black: a 'coloured naval rating' from Cardiff. He has proposed marriage and when Jo is left by her feckless mother they have sex. He duly disappears, not knowing of Jo's pregnancy. On discovering that Jo is pregnant her mother's concern is crude, suggesting either that the child be adopted by the black midwife or 'Put it on stage and call it a Blackbird'. This resignation indicates rather less faith in 'integration' than the liberal writer Ted Willis had implied in *Flame in the Streets* (1961), where the young couple were left facing the difficult future together.

It is in the context, then, of these cultural and political developments that the adaptation of *To Sir with Love* (1967) needs to be seen rather than as some feeble British version of *The Blackboard Jungle* (1955), which had led to riots when screened. *To Sir with Love* has a very mild underlying theme that the outlook for humanity is broadly positive. Edward Braithwaite's British Guyanan teacher wins over his unruly class of mildly rebellious young students with his personality.[39]

---

[37] Murphy, R (1992).
[38] Cripps, T (1993).
[39] Slightly more obliquely, racism emerges in a film where the issue is avoiding assumed racism by 'passing white'—*Sapphire* (1959).

Strangely enough for a London-set mid-1960s film, apart from Sidney Poitier there are only three other non-white faces.[40] This reflects the situation when Braithwaite wrote about in the early 1950s, but not 15 years later. One critic of the film was scathing:

> The sententious script sounds as if it has been written by a zealous Sunday school teacher after a particularly exhilarating boycott of South African oranges.[41]

As indicated below, race does not feature through most of the film until the question of flowers for the dead mother of Seales, the mixed race boy in the class, emerges. No one is initially prepared to deliver these because they would not want to be seen visiting such a house. In an unlikely-seeming denouement all the children cast off their bigoted views and turn up at the house for the funeral. This scene is not, as the above film critic implies, a nod towards a strained liberal agenda, but a faithful re-enactment of Braithwaite's original text.[42]

The issue of bigotry was covered in an explicit way in a feature film of the early 1970s, derived from a half-hour situation comedy series running between 1972 and 1976, *Love Thy Neighbour* (1973). The situation derives from the premise that the two bigoted factory workers, Eddie (Jack Smethurst) and Bill (Rudolph Walker) are neighbours. Eddie is a white trade unionist, and Bill is a black, boss-orientated Conservative. They insult each other with gusto but beneath the insults there is both a permanent stand-off as well as a possible resolution. There is the symbiosis of mutual entrapment in their jobs and houses. In addition there is the promise of ultimate respect for each other, since the obviously sensible wives get on just fine. The actors, Jack Smethurst and Rudolph Walker, reviewed this work 25 years later after the rise of racist politics and racial attacks and murders in the interim. They suggested that this series and film did nothing to support racist abuse since each use by Eddie of the word 'coon', 'nignog' or 'sambo' was balanced with Bill getting to say 'honky' and 'spook'.[43] Despite the 1958 riots and Enoch Powell's prophecy of 'rivers of blood' in 1968 the actors suggested that racism and racial issues had not really surfaced when the series started in 1972. There is some oblique support for this kind of insensitivity in the continuation throughout the 1970s of the Black and White Minstrel Show. This had started, ironically perhaps, in 1958 and its black-face white cast did not leave our screens until 1978—10 years after race relations legislation was introduced outlawing discrimination in jobs and housing.

---

[40] A follow-up, *To Sir With Love II*, takes Poitier out of retirement after a further 30 years in education in London—to south side Chicago in 1997—released straight through to budget video. Lulu retains a cameo role singing the title song.

[41] *Halliwell* (2008).

[42] The author had made a similar assessment until checking back with the original text. In his entry in the *Cambridge Guide to English Literature*, Braithwaite's third volume of autobiography is, however, described as 'self-congratulatory'.

[43] *History of British Comedy*, BBC2, March 1999.

The Black and Asian British Experience

In the era when the number of non-white citizens had grown beyond 5 per cent of the overall British population the focus shifts from the reactions of indigenous Britons to non-white faces to life from the point of view of Black and Asian Britons.[44]

The ever-present theme, in the films reflecting the Asian experience, centres on the problems of living across two distinct cultures. This experience is initially found in *My Beautiful Laundrette* (1985) and *Sammy and Rosie Get Laid* (1987), both written by Hanif Kureishi, and directed by Stephen Frears. Both films document the impact on Pakistani family life of movement to Britain, in the first example because of the father's radical politics. The question of identity and the relationship between immigrants, Britain and Pakistan, is the theme shared by both films. In a variety of different ways, the film reflects on the complexity of being Asian in Thatcher's Britain, uncomfortable in both the minority Pakistani immigrant ethnic culture, and within the predominantly white host 'British' culture. By the end of *My Beautiful Laundrette* (1985), despite the attack by Johnny's (Daniel Day Lewis) ex-mates on the laundrette, it seems that Omar's (Gordon Warnecke) love for Johnny has made his decision for him. He is committed to this relationship with the problems it entails for both of them. His Uncle Nasser (Saeed Jaffrey) has problems in deciding where his loyalties as a member of an ethnic minority lie. Nasser is also prepared to employ Johnny, the white former fascist, engaged to help out in the 'laundrette' of the title by Omar, with whom he went to school. The work for Omar's Uncle Nasser involves doing odd jobs which include 'unscrewing': the illegal eviction of tenants or squatters. Johnny draws attention to the paradox of evicting a black tenant on behalf of Nasser, a successful Pakistani businessman:

Johnny: Aren't you giving ammunition to your enemies doing this kind of … unscrewing. To people who say Pakis just come here to hustle other people's lives and jobs and houses …

Nasser: But I'm a professional businessman not a professional Pakistani. There's no race question in the new enterprise culture.

Receiving equal treatment means being treated as badly as anyone else in the interests of profit. There is also fracturing between the non-white communities referred to later in *Bhaji on the Beach* (1993). At the end of *My Beautiful Laundrette* (1985) the oblique ending favoured by Kureishi in his screenplay leaves unclear the future of the other major 'in between', Omar's Uncle Nasser. Is he able any longer to continue living within two distinct and grating cultures, separated as he is from both his family and his white mistress, but reconciled with his brother? Omar's prospective marriage partner, his cousin Tania (Rita Wolf), has made her

---

[44] For fascinating coverage of early black-directed films see Young, L (1996) and Pines, J (2001).

decision for full rejection of the traditional female Pakistani role. It is fair to say, however, that this seems to centre more on claustrophobic restrictions of family as opposed to embracing the host culture.

The tone is darker, and more overtly about class and gender politics as well as race, in *Sammy and Rosie Get Laid* (1987). The return of Sammy's (Ayub Khan-Din) father Rafi (Shashi Kapoor) to his beloved London to find riot-torn streets and the change in the culture is the initial context for the exploration of identity of immigrants. The wider problem of belonging to a place that no longer exists is a persistent notion throughout the film:

Rafi: For me England is hot buttered toast on a fork in front of an open fire.

This is said in the context of criss-crossed motorways, flyovers, huge direction indicators, and swirl of fast-moving traffic, dreamlike, noisy, strange. This is not the England that Rafi remembers and a place of such endemic conflict that he ends up taking his own life. The film portrays an England not sympathetic to individuals, or groups, with values residing outside the mainstream. A more affirmative, but critical view of minority ethnic experience is found in *Bhaji on the Beach* (1993). This traces the problem of the second generation adjusting to a different environment and creating a new self-confident distinctive culture. For once the white world is marginal to the issues explored which are more concerned with generational and gender conflict. The coach trip from the Midlands to Blackpool has as its underlying theme a series of subtle challenges by the Indian daughters and nieces to the disapproving older women of their families. Coupled with this is a portrait of the narrower authority structure within the patriarchal family unit. The attempt by one husband to persuade his wife to return to her servile abused position for the sake of their son, but really to save face for him in the community, is unsuccessful when he reverts to his true violent nature. The threats, though, to these traditional forms of determining how life is to be lived have their source not in the specific prescriptions of white society but in the alternative glimpse of another way afforded by that society. The source of potential ethnic conflict is located not in a story about white racism but rather the novel question for British cinema of a black/Asian romance. Here it echoes, in a rather more optimistic light, the theme of *Mississippi Masala* (1992).

Conflict within cultures is a question that is explored in two films examining how young people react to being part of two distinct worlds. The theme of belief in a secular society emerges in Hanif Kureishi's sombre *My Son the Fanatic* (1997). The film portrays youth seeking certainty in a society without fixed moral certainties. The rejection of pleasure is central to this exploration of the appeal of fundamentalism in which taxi-driving middle-aged Parvez (Om Puri) is at a loss to understand why young people wish to surrender the right to think for themselves. The authoritarian nature of Islamic thought is what the immigrant father cannot bring himself to accept. The fact that this breaks up his family and leaves him at the end of the film adrift from his wife, son and mistress means, as he admits, 'I have managed to destroy everything. I have never felt worse … or better'.

Similar issues are covered in *East is East* (1999), with the various children from a mixed Anglo-Pakistani marriage developing their lives within a predominantly white culture. Set in early 1970s Salford, one son is an entrepreneur cut off by his father, and his younger brothers and sister have to decide the parameters to their lives. The fundamental question is whether this will be within what they see as their repressive communities, or in the hostile, but seemingly freer, white world? This tension is reflected in three of the brothers' dual identities as Tariq/Tony, Nazir/Nigel and Abdul/Arthur. Although this is a comedy, the pull of two very different cultures, and the potential for personal conflict, is the central trope in all aspects of the film. Setting the film in the early 1970s allows the theme to present an era when issues seemed starker. The virulent repatriation racism of 'Powellism' and the restrictive moral certainties and rules of the Muslim world are interspersed with broad comic moments which have been described as unexpectedly crude.[45] Ultimately the different members of the family make different choices.

The choice between different cultural pressures is a feature of the most recent exploration of the British Asian experience, directed and co-written by the director of *Bhaji on the Beach* (1993), Gurinder Chadha. In *Bend it Like Beckham* (2002), a light, almost sitcom touch is brought to the tale of a young girl, Jess Bhamra (Parminder Nagra), who has a talent for playing football. Football does not fit in with the submissive marriage-orientated path prescribed by Sikh culture which is being taken by Jess's older sister. The dominant aspect of both Sikh and lower-middle-class English cultures which the film reveals is the need to keep up appearances and pay attention to what the community may think. There is also a complicating love interest for Jess in the shape of her football manager, Joe (Jonathan Rhys Meyers), across the racial divide. This, however, comes from a man from a minority group himself, as Joe is Irish. Jess's family have come to Britain from East Africa and her father was a keen cricketer; it turns out the discrimination he suffered on arrival in relation to playing cricket has caused his opposition to sport. This then segues into a Hollywoodesque touch with a magical melting away of all other opposition to the proposed California football scholarships of both Jess and her white teammate Jules (Keira Knightley). The tidy happy resolution might seem to smack of target audience expectations but Hanif Kureishi's Parvez would have fully approved. Most recently in this same mould is the adaptation of Monica Ali's *Brick Lane* (2007). The film documents the culture shock not within the numerically dominant white community but within a different kind of urban British minority ethnic community. Here a young woman arrives in 1980s London, leaving behind her family in Bangladesh, for an arranged marriage to a middle-aged man and a new life of restriction in the midst of apparent freedom.

From the black perspective there has been no real equivalent to the blaxploitation films of the 1970s or the canon of work of Spike Lee which have achieved

---

[45] McFarlane, B (2001).

wide distribution or video status. Looking at independently produced black British films, Lola Young notes the way that culture became racialised in the late 1970s in a subtle new way around the nation as an indivisible unit with race lurking beneath the surface rather than made explicit.[46] This racialisation, she argues, can be identified in such films as *Pressure* (1974), *Black Joy* (1977), *Burning an Illusion* (1981) and *Playing Away* (1986). These were not focused on dismantling or deconstructing the discourse of 'race' but centred on attacking racism.[47]

Much of this work has allegedly suffered from the increasing concentration of advertising and promotion on a handful of films.[48] *Young Soul Rebels* (1991) and *Babymother* (1996) were, however, produced with the financial support of Channel Four Films and are available in video format. Like British Asian films, they are concerned with the experiences of individuals from ethnic backgrounds and their inter-relationships. These films are as close as possible to a black British cinema in the terms indicated by Cripps.[49] The status and issue of citizens of mixed race is briefly raised in *Young Soul Rebels* (1991), where one of the two main soul DJ protagonists has a white mother. Racism and homophobia within the black community are touched on as in the discussion of the identity of the murderer of a young man found in a park shortly before the 1977 Silver Jubilee celebrations.

> Carlton: Can't trust dem 'alf caste bwoy ye no. Ye don't know which side them on. I could well believe it was one a dem kill that black bwoy … as far as I and I concern, musa be a white bwoy, an' if it wasn't a white bwoy, I'll lay on money it was a 'alf caste …

Caz (Mo Sesay) is suspect because he associates with Chris (Valentine Nonyela), who is the son of a black father and a white mother, as well as white people. This is deemed problematic whilst the relationship between race and homosexuality is left uncertain.

> Caz: You're fulla shit Davis! The bruvva dat got killed on the park—he was what you call an anti-man, a bwatty bwoy. Dat make it alright no? You concerned 'bout who did it now?

Davis hesitates.

Caz throws down his cloth, leaves the garage, not waiting for one.

The marginalisation of black interests in white dominated culture has a much more extensive focus in the film. The white world is peripheral in the daily lives of the protagonists except as the force that moulds black experience. Similarly in *Babymother* (1995) the struggle of Anita (Anjela Lauren Smith) to escape from the influence of her partner, Byron (Wil Johnson) and to succeed as an artiste in her

---

[46] Young, L (1996).
[47] *Ibid.*
[48] Todd, P (2000).
[49] Cripps, T (1978).

own right in the world of reggae is not mediated by race or the white world. The conflict is between traditional male chauvinism and her perception of a woman's role and potential. She finds strength from the successful struggle of her supposed sister Rose (Suzette Llewellyn), who managed to obtain professional employment through support from her own mother and self-belief after giving birth to Anita.

A steady flow of films which have centred on the experience of ethnic minority youth and their lives beyond the law have continued to be produced and become increasingly commercial. Using a member of rappers So Solid Crew, *Bullet Boy* (2004) is a film concerned with gun crime and the impact on the lives of all members of a family. The theme of gangs and rivalries is also encountered in *Kidulthood* (2006), which shows young people from different backgrounds presented with different life chances and choices. The picture is bleak and yet engaging with its presentation of young people as real human beings with frailties and goals. More traditionally there is a Romeo and Juliet romance between a south London DJ (Ashley Walters from So Solid Crew) and 'a young woman aligned to another crew Carmen (Louise Rose) in *Life and Lyrics* (2006). The life of one of the characters from *Kidulthood* (2006) is taken up again in *Adulthood* (2008). Here some six years later with the character convicted of murder and released from prison and finding stopping the cycle of violence which put him away hard to confront.

This, then, is a cinema of self-confidence which does not rely on the validation of the dominant white culture. Themes centred on how the cultures intersect are dealt with principally from the minority viewpoint. The issues of interest in Asian and Black British cinema are how those communities relate to each other. This is not to say that racism and the impact of white Britain is not important. This is something which may be merely sketched out as in the car park taunting in *Bhaji on the Beach* (1993) or so ingrained in life that it hardly needs emphasising. Explaining his decision to cut the pub fight scene in *East is East* (1999), director Damien O'Donnell explained:

> The whole idea of them being surrounded by racism is made abundantly clear earlier on in the film and done with humour so why should we have it again in a serious sense.[50]

Indeed in the most recent film that contemplates life in Britain for minority ethnic communities, *Adulthood* (2008), there is a representation of white middle class drug users as deliberately crude stereotype. The director and writer, Noel Clarke, however, has explained that his decision to include this sequence was as a reminder of all the crude stereotypes black people had suffered down the years.[51]

Critical race theory alters the focus of previous work to the whole starting point for analysis and rather than concentrate on the nature of representation of minority groups and the extent to which such groups are excluded from the mainstream

---

[50] *East is East* (1999) DVD deleted scenes—director's comments.
[51] *Front Row* interview, Radio 4, 13 June 2008.

it starts with the social construction of race.[52] According to Russell films exemplify the 'dominant gaze'.[53] Drawing on Mulvey's concept of the 'male gaze' she suggests this involves 'the tendency of mainstream culture to replicate, through narrative and imagery, racial inequalities and biases which exist throughout society'.[54] Russell described how this is done not just in clearly racist material like *The Birth of a Nation* (1915) but through to warm and popular material like *Driving Miss Daisy* (1989) and even romantic comedies like *Soul Man* (1986).

Ethnicity and the Law Film

The kind of issues encountered from the commencement of the film industry in the United States described by Bogle and Cripps are less obvious at first sight when we look at law films. Instead, the picture is of almost complete invisibility in mainstream legal cinema until the 1980s except as victims,[55] and a very limited representation since then. Ethnic minority protagonists started out solely as victims, saved from the lynch mob in *The Sun Shines Bright* (1953) and *To Kill a Mockingbird* (1962). If not victims of the mob they are victims of the legal process. In Bogle's terms, Tom Robinson (Brock Peters) is the loyal and noble submissive Uncle Tom—although that is not how Atticus Finch (Gregory Peck) characterises him in his defence. As part of this, a subtext often emerges of the ethnic minority character being helpless without the aid of the white 'crusader'; even recent years have seen films such as *Mississippi Burning* (1988) and *Amistad* (1997), which arguably fall into this stereotypical portrayal. This perspective, of the supremacy of the white lawyer, also appears in *A Time To Kill* (1996), though with a degree of refinement.[56] It can also be seen in *A Dry White Season* (1989) with Ian McKenzie (Marlon Brando) as the radical white lawyer, and the courtroom is shown as racially divided as it was in *To Kill a Mockingbird* (1962).[57] Interestingly in *The Hurricane* (1999) Carter employs a (prominent) black lawyer to *fight* his corner, as does Andrew Beckett (Tom Hanks) in *Philadelphia* (1993). Though this latter case does not start out as a cause célèbre for Joe Miller (Denzel Washington), it is essentially a relationship borne out of desperate circumstances.

In *12 Angry Men* (1957) the accused is unspecified, but in the word of juror number 10 (Ed Begley), 'one of them', and this casual racism becomes an aspect of the jury's deliberation. It is, however, far more muted than that encountered in

---

[52] Delgado, R (1995).
[53] Russell, M (1991).
[54] *Ibid.*
[55] Sheffield, R (1991). Although Sheffield does record films aimed at black audiences featuring a number of black lawyers favourably.
[56] Interestingly in the critically acclaimed TV show *The Wire* the defence lawyer for the arrested black gang members is the white Maurice Levy.
[57] Bogle, D (1988); Young, L (1996); Hill, J (1999).

To Kill a Mockingbird (1962), which deals with the absence of any justice in the south for African-Americans and the very real threat of lynching. The film is discussed by Bogle, however, only in the context of the career of Brock Peters and not mentioned by Cripps.[58] Bogle does, however, subsequently suggest that this film influenced Joel Schumacher's *A Time to Kill* (1996), and notes that the latter:

> was set in the 1990s but had the look and feel of a movie from the late 1940s or 1950s. It's like a Negro Problem Picture that makes a big deal over the fact that (even at this late date) the white attorney has to inform the white jury of its own racism.[59]

The focus of the film is on the white character's nobility in replicating the feat of Atticus Finch and taking the case of a black man: 'Throughout, we're to feel for the poor white attorney's welfare and that of his family because he's so heroic in defending this black man.' Arguably, both in the film and in the John Grisham book on which it was based, Jake Brigance lacks Finch's 'nobility'. Rather he is motivated by the possibility of escaping the grind of daily legal practice—a trope which features in a number of Grisham's books and their film adaptations. Bogle does point out, however, that the subject of Jake Brigance's charity, Samuel L Jackson, has, in a number of films, been able to transcend the material he has to work with:

> What usually distinguished his performances was his ability to give each part an ethnic marker and also to inject humour and irony into characters that might otherwise be forgettable or old-style types.

His role as revenge killer Carl Lee Hailey in *A Time to Kill* (1996) is singled out as such an example with Jackson's strong uncompromising playing and the intensity of his performance energising the film. What Bogle has sought to do is chart the tortuous path of black actors to reach a situation in which mainstream American cinema might be invigorated with 'new rhythms, insights, perspectives and a new aesthetic'. Coming from an African-American point of view and focusing on these aspirations and goals he concludes: 'African-American films can liberate audiences from illusions, black and white, and in so freeing can give all of us vision and truth.'[60] Whether or not any elements of this process can be identified in relation to ethnic minority lawyers in law films is one of the key tasks for further exploration.

As far as British law films are concerned, the position reflects the very different make-up and background of British society and the British film industry. There have been far fewer films over the years centring on legal themes.[61] In only one of these films are there issues of ethnicity and the justice system making an appearance. The personnel of the dramas that have been portrayed have otherwise been white British. *In the Name of the Father* (1993) makes it clear that the personnel

---

[58] Bogle, D (2001).
[59] *Ibid*, 418.
[60] *Ibid*, 433.
[61] Greenfield, S, Osborn, G and Robson, P (2007).

operating the British system of justice have no difficulty in making decisions based on crude stereotypes and xenophobia. As the impassioned lawyer Gareth Peirce (Emma Thompson) expresses it in relation to the fitting up of her client: 'He was in the wrong place at the wrong time. He was guilty of being Irish.' This is in stark contrast to the ways in which ethnicity and the legal system have been covered in fictional lawyer series over the years from Rumpole in the early 1970s, through Black Silk in the 1980s and Kavanagh QC in the 1990s to Outlaws in the 2000s.[62]

Ethnic Minority Lawyers

The first appearance of a black lawyer in a mainstream film is the appearance of Juano Hernandez as the Honourable Judge Theodore Motley in *Trial* (1955). Rather like the appearance of Katharine Hepburn as a woman lawyer in *Adam's Rib* (1949), this breakthrough was followed by nothing for the next 20 years. Sheffield records that:

> Even when fictional African American lawyers did appear, albeit infrequently, in movies in the late 1970s and 1980s, they assumed the role of the loyal assistant. They were almost always an assistant district attorney; rarely a defense attorney ... It was also unheard of for filmmakers to cast a Black actor as a corporate attorney or as a partner in a major law firm.[63]

The films which revived the sub-genre of the courtroom drama reflected a white world. Thus the racial element which was an element in the trial on which *The Accused* (1988) was based does not feature in the film.[64] There is room for ethnic minorities in the role of the accused in ... *And Justice For All* (1979) and the District Attorney in *Suspect* (1987) bears the non-WASP name of Charlie Stella (Joe Mantegna). There have been Jewish lawyers in a number of films such as *Reversal of Fortune* (1990) with Ron Silver as Alan Derschowitz and *Presumed Innocent* (1990) with Raul Julia as Sandy Stern.[65] The Jewish roots of Sandy Stern are not clear from the film, with Raul Julia's full name Alejandro and his strong Latino accent. The book is rather more oblique: Stern's ethnic background is revealed in Turrow's next novel, *The Burden of Proof*, where his name and accent are located as coming from his birthplace in Argentina, although his parents speak Yiddish at home.[66] From near invisibility in these films and others such as *Body Heat* (1981) and *Suspect* (1987), though, the road to a positive model has been slow. Poor Dan Hislan (Michael Dorn) is restricted to a handful of lines in *Jagged*

---

[62] Robson, P (2007c).
[63] Sheffield, R (1991).
[64] Bergman, P and Asimow, M (1996).
[65] Crowdus, G (1994).
[66] Turow, S (1990).

Edge (1985) whilst at the same time being responsible, or at least being on the end of the accusing glares of his white boss, Krasny (Peter Coyote), for failing to secure cast-iron evidence against Jack Forrester. His role as whipping boy and his facial expression brings back Bogle's 'coon' category.[67]

It is in the 1990s that a consistent number of African-American judges and attorneys appear with roles of some symbolic significance. This followed on from the 1980s television breakthrough for ethnic minority lawyers in *LA Law*, with Blair Underwood and Jimmy Smits playing an African American and Hispanic lawyer. A small speaking role is given to Jerome Green (Obba Babatunde), who plays Belinda Conine's (Mary Steenburgen) assistant in *Philadelphia* (1993), though we only discover his identity in the credits. Whilst the significance of the part may be somewhat limited, there is at least a presence which signifies a shift for ethnic minority lawyers from the dock to bar or bench. Not all the portrayals are, of course, entirely positive. Paul Winfield, for instance, is the corrupt, but powerful, Judge Larren Lyttle in *Presumed Innocent* (1990). In the same film, Rusty Sabich (Harrison Ford) chooses Alejandro Stern (Raul Julia), not part of the white establishment, as his defence lawyer although he is only seen briefly in court. The narrative is only tangentially concerned with forensic skill and focuses more on missing evidence and the 'whodunnit' aspect of the death of assistant prosecutor Carolyn Polhemus (Greta Scacchi) as well as the politics of re-election of a District Attorney. Morgan Freeman plays the paradoxically named Judge White in *Bonfire of the Vanities* (1990), presiding over the trial of a wealthy white man. Similarly in *The Client* (1994) the main judicial figure is Harry Roosevelt (Ossie Davis). He is a strong figure who will not tolerate interference by the powerful would-be Governor and current District Attorney Roy Foltrigg (Tommy Lee Jones). It is interesting to note the emergence of black judges though the judicial role generally is seldom a focal point in legal films. Lawrence Fishburne as Nick Holbrook features in a modified 'Tom role' in *Class Action* (1991) although it is his boss, Jed Ward (Gene Hackman) who is shown in action.[68] Nick, though, is loyal, supportive and selfless. There are no records of African-American or ethnic women in a primary, secondary or even incidental role before 1985 and the vast majority of lawyer portrayals are white. Alfre Woodard makes two appearances in the 1990s, first as fresh-out-of-college attorney Ann Orkin in *The Gun in Betty Lou's Handbag* (1992), where her wide-eyed sassyness places her in a slimmed-down Mammy role of the fiercely independent kind.[69] Second, she appears as Judge Miriam Shoat in the murder trial in *Primal Fear* (1996). However, the scantiness of the part leaves little room for analysis. Of rather more substance is the role of attorney Caroline Jones (La Tanya Richardson) in *Losing Isaiah* (1995).[70] This is the novel situation, for a law film, where the lawyers for both sides

---

[67] Bogle, D (1988).
[68] *Ibid*, 4–7.
[69] *Ibid*, 9.
[70] Sheffield, R (1993).

in an adoption challenge are African-American. Kadar Lewis (Samuel L Jackson) is an attorney retained to take cases where significant issues are at stake for the African-American community. In this instance it is a cross-racial adoption which took place without the true consent of the young crack-addicted mother Khaila Richards (Halle Berry). Representing the white adopting parents is Caroline Jones (La Tanya Richardson), who is aware that her clients have chosen her to represent them because of the colour of her skin. Her clients lose, but there is a *Kramer vs Kramer* (1979) type resolution. Joe Miller (Denzel Washington) appears as leading counsel for lawyer Andrew Beckett (Tom Hanks) in *Philadelphia* (1993), and the team facing him includes an African-American attorney. An earlier example of an ethnic minority lawyer, this time from the period of Reconstruction in the 1860s, is James Earl Jones' portrayal of Judge Isaacs in *Sommersby* (1993), exhibiting a firm hand to those in his courtroom.[71] Also of note is *Separate But Equal* (1994), an Emmy-award-winning TV movie, featuring the pioneering African-American actor Sidney Poitier. The film charts the struggle against racial segregation culminating in the Supreme Court case *Brown v Board of Education*. There are also African-American women judges in *Big Daddy* (1999)[72] and *Legally Blonde* (2001).[73]

The shift from victim, through bystander, to major figure has been catalogued in respect of African-American,[74] Asian[75] and Latino[76] actors and themes. Indeed, as regards Latino portrayals, Roman has noted that:

> [d]espite the fact that there are dozens of Latina and Latino law professors, thousands of attorneys with such backgrounds ... a Latina or Latino in a major Hollywood film will almost always be played as a hot-blooded gang member, musician or illegal alien. A Latina or Latino will rarely be portrayed as a working professional such as a physician or attorney ...[77]

The culmination in the role of Joe Miller in *Philadelphia* (1993) shows that there need not be a simplistic use of an Atticus Finch type figure as a model for portrayal. Neither can Miller be categorised within any of Bogle's definitions.[78] Miller is not subservient, submissive or stoic nor by any means a 'comic wheedler' or 'subhuman brute'. With him, at last, there is a character who transcends the stereotypes and appears as full-rounded protagonist. His initial portrayal is a small-time lawyer keen to take anything that comes his way and is not beyond the use of corny television advertisements, though it is not entirely clear whether it is the unusualness of these in Philadelphia or their nature that results in almost everyone

---

[71] Although doubt has been cast on the historic likelihood of this, Bergman, P and Asimow, M (1996).
[72] Judge M Healy (Carmen De Lavallade).
[73] Judge Marina R Bickford (Francesca P Roberts).
[74] Smith-Kahn, C (1998).
[75] Russell, M (1998).
[76] *Ibid.*
[77] Roman, E (2000: 41).
[78] Bogle, D (1988), chapter 1 particularly.

he meets identifying him as the 'TV guy'. He distributes his business cards like confetti and is keen to build up what seems to be a small, hungry business. He is not, however, so cynical about success that he is prepared to do anything to get publicity and his motive is not, however, noble. Rather he initially rejects the Beckett brief on the basis of fear and loathing of homosexuality. He is not the only lawyer to have expressed such sentiments as a previous nine lawyers have already rejected Becket's case. Miller expresses homophobic sentiments privately and it is only when he sees Beckett in the Law Library researching his own case that Miller changes his mind and decides to represent him. What actually changes his mind is never made explicit: it is not simply seeing Beckett hunched and looking ill that arouses his compassion. When he sees Beckett being hassled by the librarian he shows solidarity by talking with him and becomes more excited about the case when he discusses the precedents that Miller has unearthed. With the uncomfortable atmosphere created by the librarian, the description of what discrimination implies in theory and the reality of how people with AIDS are treated as pariahs, Miller's attitude starts to change. Conflating those with AIDS with the gay community, his treatment of the bearer of both of what Miller would term these 'conditions' crucially changes. He takes the case, but whilst this may be the first part of his transformation and the beginning of a shift in his perceptions of gay identity and lifestyle, his full transformation is far from swift. He does, for example, continue to feel uncomfortable in the presence of other gays: this is notably portrayed in a meeting with a young black man in a pharmacy. By the end of the film Miller has undergone a slow transformation from tolerance to acceptance to true appreciation of his client as a human being, not as a category. He is a good courtroom performer with a clear grasp of how to hone in on the issue underlying the case and Taubin argues that the Miller character is the more significant of the two:

> Joe is the central character. The narrative of Philadelphia is less about being gay and living with Aids than about being heterosexual and homophobic. Joe comes to understand how his homophobia, which he regards as integral to his manhood, underlies his fear and loathing for people with Aids. But Philadelphia is a breakthrough film, not only because it deals with Aids and homophobia, but because it is the first major non-action Hollywood movie in which a black man personifies mainstream America. Joe's homophobia is a sign of his normality (he's a regular Joe): Andrew's white skin privilege is cancelled by his homosexuality and his disease.[79]

This is an interesting reading of a film which has generally been discussed as a film concerning HIV and Aids. The point about Miller as a representative of mainstream American opinion raises the question as to why he need be bigoted rather than possess an 'Atticus Finch' type wisdom over controversial issues. The uncomfortable racism in *To Kill a Mockingbird* is substituted with homophobia. The issue is of course not clear-cut, as Finch's purity is by no means assured and there is often the need for our screen lawyer to undergo a personal transformation.

---

[79] Taubin, A (1994, 24).

With his portrayal as a fully rounded person, warts and all, and his transition from success-orientated bigot to humane and caring individual, there emerges a classic version of a heroic but recognisable lawyer. Smith-Khan indicates that the depiction of Miller is subtle as 'an African-American attorney' is depicted as 'a professional wrestling to overcome biases that threaten his ethical and moral being'.[80] Miller is thus in the mould of the more complex, less one-dimensional lawyers encountered in Harris's early golden age. He is in the later tradition of flawed lawyers achieving redemption through law, like Tony Lawrence (*The Young Philadelphians* (1959)), Frank Galvin (*The Verdict* (1982)) and, even at a stretch, Tom Logan (*Legal Eagles* (1986)). Taubin also makes the point that the casting of Washington guaranteed a black audience that 'otherwise might not have had much interest in the problems of a rich white homosexual with Aids'.[81] This question of targeting casting at audiences is also raised by Sheffield. Quoting *The Coloured American Winning His Suit* (1916), *Murder in Harlem* (1935) and *Life Goes On* (1938) he argues that 'films aimed at Black audiences in the early twentieth century presented black lawyers favorably'.[82]

Given that *Philadelphia* (1993) was both an artistic and a commercial success it is surprising that there has been no attempt to centre a subsequent legal film on an ethnic minority protagonist. Washington himself appears in another legal thriller, *The Pelican Brief* (1993), but as a journalist rather than enjoying the status of lawyer. The only major ethnic minority lawyer who figures as the cinematic focus is Robert Dean (Will Smith) in *Enemy of the State* (1998). This is a political thriller, with Smith cast as a Washington labour lawyer who without his knowledge gets involved with the cover-up of a political assassination. He is only shown on the run from those who are seeking to recover the evidence which he does not realise he has and never operating as a lawyer. Dean runs into an old college friend in a big hurry. Unknown to him, that friend secretly drops a disc containing footage of a political assassination overseen by the senior advisor to the National Security Agency. Unfortunately, that politician soon learns what Dean has in his possession and secretly uses the vast resources of the NSA to find, investigate and stop him before he goes public. Soon, Dean finds himself on the run, with his assets frozen, his loved ones watched and actively hunted by NSA agents using all the surveillance technology they have available. This is *Three Days of the Condor* (1975) for a new era.

Conclusion

The limited inclusion of ethnic minority characters within domestic law films reflects both the limited number of English films and the historic development of

---

[80] Smith-Kahn, C (1998: 130).
[81] Taubin, A (1994).
[82] Sheffield, R (1993).

British society.[83] The presence of non-white actors in this limited range of films is restricted to the appearance of eight Indian lawyers walking through a shot in *Eight O'Clock Walk* (1953). They may symbolise the end of Empire and the take-over of imperial institutions by the once-colonised and arguably the embodiment of the universality of the Anglo-American adversarial system. A small but perhaps significant change is encountered in *Life and Lyrics* (2006), where the object of the blandishments of one of the rap crews, a former soul vocalist Carmen (Louise Rose), has given up music to study law. Unfortunately she is a member of the rival gang of DJ Danny 'D-Biz' Lewis (Ashley Walters) and the scene is set for a Romeo and Juliet climax, South London style. An interesting development is the emergence of Bollywood as a source of films with a legal dimension. There are two particular strands that cross over that are noted here. First the narration of historical events charting India's colonial relationship with Great Britain and the portrayal of law, lawyers and legal institutions. *The Rising: the Ballad of Mangal Pandey* (2005) centres on the 1857 Seepoy uprising and the subsequent Courts Martial of Mangal Pandey, the instigator of the rebellion. Second there are similar themes to other films with the white 'crusader' attempting to 'save' the black victim. *Shaurya* (2008) is another contemporary Bollywood offering that also contributes to the category of courts martial films but provides the opportunity for two Asian lawyers to engage in a 'remake' of *A Few Good Men*. The focus on the 'plagiarism' of the plot distracted from the subtle changes to the original and the prominent role for the woman non-lawyer played by Minissha Lamba. The two lawyers enjoy some of the stereotypical traits of screen lawyers notably as Siddhant (Rahul Bose) develops from a playboy uninterested in the law to a fighter for the truth and human rights. What these films indicate is that there is enormous potential for alternative portrayals of both events and people. This is an area which lends itself to more detailed and specialist analysis. A more fruitful exploration closer to home is to be found in television drama where there have been rather more appearances on television in both major and supporting roles for black actors.[84] For example in 1985 Rudolph Walker played black QC Larry Scott in *Black Silk* in an eight-episode run on BBC2. Similarly the series *Kavanagh QC* in 1995, where 10 episodes featured Jenny Jules as pupil (trainee) barrister Alex Wilson. The short run of *Trust* (2003), one season of six episodes, had Chiwetel Ejiofor as Ashley Carter, though there were no ethnic minority lawyers in *New Street Law* (2006).[85]

---

[83] Greenfield, S, Osborn, G and Robson, P (2007).

[84] Robson, P (2007).

[85] In the 1980s Rudolph Walker played black QC Larry Scott in *Black Silk* in an eight-episode run on BBC2 in 1985. The series *Kavanagh QC* in 1995–98 featured Jenny Jules as pupil (trainee) Barrister Alex Wilson in 10 episodes; *Trust* (2003) had Chiwetel Ajiofor as Ashley Carter but there were no ethnic minority lawyers in *New Street Law* (2006).

16

Future Trajectories and Possibilities

In order to make some kind of informed judgment on the future of law and film it is essential to remind ourselves how the area emerged and what scholars have been seeking to do as the area has developed. The sustained scholarship, and development of courses in the area of law and film, originated from an initial acknowledgement of the importance of the area in a variety of significant journal articles in the late 1980s.[1] These sought to identify, and develop, the idea of the significance of popular culture within the context of the law. In simple terms the version of law that was entering popular culture was derived from and reflected back by the media, and there was recognition that this was an area worthy of study. The comments did not provide a systematic overview of the field, but rather provided inspiration for others to interrogate the relationship between law and popular culture, and also urged an alternative to the alleged sterility of critical legal studies.[2] The work produced thereafter mapped out a whole host of areas of interest on both a national and international level. There have also been developments in the area of film and television within European scholarship. Since an earlier survey of work in law and film assembled in 2003,[3] there has been further work analysing individual films such as *Casablanca* (1942)[4] and *Adam's Rib* (1949).[5] There has also been a traditional practice-based collection,[6] as well as two essay collections which explicitly seek to develop different perspectives.[7] Earlier Chapters deal in depth with a number of issues around representations of law and lawyers, and highlight some of the difficulties that have been encountered. In addition to considering the role of European studies in the future of law and film, this Chapter starts by considering some possibilities with *futurescapes* of law, in a section termed celestial justice. This outlines some of the possibilities of film making, and law and film scholarship, freed from the constraints of the traditional courtroom, or the tyranny of the real-life event. We then consider the development of the European scholarship and the possibilities that this has unearthed, before concluding with some likely future directions for the area.

[1] Macaulay, S (1987); Stark, S (1987) and Friedman, L (1989).
[2] Chase, A (1986b).
[3] Robson, P (2005).
[4] Almog, S and Reichman, A (2004).
[5] Sanderson, P and Sommerlad, H (2006).
[6] Epstein, M (2004b). Also Asimow, M and Mader, S (2004).
[7] Moran, L (2004); Sarat, A, Douglas, L and Umphrey, M (2005a).

Sometimes I, Fantasise: Celestial Justice

It is useful to contrast mimetic approaches to justice with symbolic representations of the justice issue. Celestial justice would seem to add an imagined world of how justice might be constructed and viewed by being de-historicised and de-contextualised. A mirror image can be encountered in the methods used in the 1930s to avoid the censors' aversion to social issues being portrayed in film and the British Board of Film Censors sought to exclude social conflict from the cinema screen.[8] A similar situation existed in the USA with the application of the Hays Code in the 1930s.[9] One way of side-stepping conflict with regulators was for film makers to shift the temporal context of their work.[10] This defused, for example, the types of problems encountered by films attempting to deal with contemporary anti-semitism in Germany and Austria.[11] The notion that only naturalistic portrayals can be used as vehicles for effective critique, and comment on the questions of law and justice, is not only theoretically suspect, but also demonstrably false. Various essays in the Denvir collection show how legal issues can be effectively highlighted by looking beyond legal sources.[12] Here are questions that are central to the legal/justice enterprise being addressed in a whole range of different kinds of 'non-law' film. These include gangster and cop films, Westerns, comedy dramas as well as law-centred films. This point, of course, returns to issues around genre and its use. Since our concerns are a good deal broader than looking at the range of possible images of justice on which one might draw for legal training purposes, then this need to limit our analysis to naturalism ceases to have its principal rationale. Hence we examine a number of mainstream films where there are projections into the future, or a discussion about the way in which justice might be dispensed in a more or less recognisable world.

Further examples of the phenomenon can be located firmly within the world of science fiction. In dystopian visions of the future such as *Waterworld* (1995) and *Mad Max* (1979) there are vestiges of justice systems. *Judge Dredd* (1995) provides a good example of the role of law and justice in the futurescape, and the merging

---

[8] The BBFC was known as the British Board of Film Censors until 1984. It changed its name to the British Board of Film Classification in 1985 and its ambit extended to video recordings after the Video Recordings Act 1984. For a history of the BBFC see Trevelyan, J (1973), and for a more recent history, the BBFC website: www.bbfc.org.uk, last accessed 22 May 2010.

[9] The Motion Pictures Producers and Distributors Association, which later became the Motion Picture Association of America, adopted a Production Code in 1930, which it finally abandoned in 1968 in favour of the subsequent MPAA film rating system. The Production Code, named after its first chair, spelled out what was morally acceptable and morally unacceptable content for motion pictures produced for a public audience in the USA. Crucially for law films, amongst the general principles were two issues: (1) No picture shall be produced that will lower the moral standards of those who see it. Hence the sympathy of the audience should never be thrown to the side of crime, wrongdoing, evil or sin. (3) Law, natural or human, shall not be ridiculed, nor shall sympathy be created for its violation.

[10] Robertson, J (1985).

[11] Richards, J (1982).

[12] Denvir, J (1996a).

of traditional categories within the legal system in the anarchic, totalled state that is the year 2136. Here the margins between law and justice have been blurred, with many arms of the state mechanism contained within one body. Whilst law should be totally objective, and adherence to the law should be seen as sacrosanct (the law cannot make mistakes in the world of Judge Dredd), what happens when a mistake is actually made? The notion of an abstract 'pure' justice has been located in a number of films looking to some kind of alternative future. The stance which has generally been adopted favours liberal values of tolerance and freedom of expression. The settings include the relatively prosaic interrogation of how society might best treat those who are perpetrating intolerance, as well as more imaginative works. The different characteristics within a celestial setting permit film makers the opportunity to explore broad ethical issues without the constraints of specific historical, or contemporary contexts. In a sense this provides the freedom that is sometimes lacking in films based on 'real life' events or those constrained by genre. A key point is the different ways in which abstract concepts of fairness and justice are constructed within these alternative *fora*. Some of the more adventurous projects in film have included within their compass a consideration of what law is seeking to achieve. The relationship between overarching moral principles, and legal systems created by society, is an issue that emerges in these celestial or futuristic courtrooms. In most of the academic work encompassing the portrayal of law and legality, analysis has centred on 'naturalistic portrayals' of lawyers. This stems from the specific contexts in which law and film writing emerged, which includes reflections on how law films can illustrate particular points in practice. The emphasis here is on the way things have been done, or how they are done, rather than on the very nature of the concept of law. Similarly, work centred on the nature of the likely impact of film portrayals on the public perception of the law is concerned with the actual, not the possible. A law film constructed on this basis will centre predominantly on the US court system. These films are concerned with crime, principally murder and, less frequently, civil matters. The joy of films set in the future, or in some other-worldly context, is that they offer a possibility for reflection on the fundamental principles of life. There are films where the issue of justice, and how human beings should make judgments about what is permissible behaviour and what is not, is aired in a rather different way.

One naturalistic treatment of a novel form of justice was essayed in *None Shall Escape* (1944). The film was produced, and released, during wartime and presages the legal and moral dilemmas facing victors and vanquished in peacetime where cruel and unusual policies have been practised. Although this is set in the future, this is a clearly recognisable as the near future. It was located after the end of the Second World War, and involved a new method of bringing those responsible for crimes against humanity to justice. The novel factor here is the forum and the issue. In place of national courts there is an International Commission with judges from a whole range of nations. The camera pans around a semi-circular Bench and the panel is seen to comprise some 18 judges. Interestingly the issue of being forced to act against one's own conscience is not the point here. Rather, the accused, the Reich's Commissioner for Western Poland, William Grimm, is portrayed as a fanatical Nazi, whose views about the ethics of his personal involvement in genocide is unmodified. He does not seek to hide behind others and warns that Nazism will not die. The film ends with the stern question to the jury from the Chair of the Bench firmly locating the responsibility for action with those whom he addresses:

> You are the jury. What do you want to happen? It is your choice.

As he utters these words the camera closes in on the judge for the final shot and it becomes clear that the jury is not a small group of men and women in the court-room but those watching the film. The issue is a contemporary debate about what should happen after the war to the perpetrators of death in the camps, although the terms 'extermination camp' or 'concentration camp' are not actually used. Scenes from actual camps are included in the evidence against Grimm. This is a vision of an altered kind of justice, one into which a new set of criteria have been introduced, albeit obliquely—how should one deal with the defence of 'superior orders'? The film was scripted by Lester Cole who was to come to public attention as one of the 'Hollywood Ten' under Senator Joseph McCarthy's House Un-American Activities Committee hearing in the 1940s and 1950s.

In Powell and Pressburger's *A Matter of Life and Death* (1946) a whole range of interesting issues are raised.[13] Some of these are pragmatic, such as the concern of the film makers to address the question of post-war Anglo-American relations, others are more philosophical and reflective, such as the metaphysical issue of the nature of life after death. It is the denouement, which takes place in a futuristic court with an English-style judge in full-bottomed wig, that is of particular interest. The trial stems from a failure of a celestial 'conductor' to locate a person at the time of his appointed death. This individual's task is to accompany the person to the next stage for disposal. A problem emerges when the conductor fails, due to fog, to locate the subject. Can there be an exception to the assigned date of death by virtue of the 'deceased' obtaining new responsibilities in the additional period before the conductor locates him? In this case, the English Second World War pilot Peter Carter (David Niven) has fallen in love with the American radio operator seeking to guide his doomed aeroplane safely back to base. This apparently innocent entanglement provides a platform for Abraham Farlan (Raymond Massey) to argue that the principles of freedom will be harmed by such a debasing of American stock. He points to the repressed and anti-democratic spirit abroad in Britain and mocks cricket. Portrayed as virulently anti-imperialist, this character debates with the doctor who was trying to save the life of the crashed airman. The discussion before a celestial court takes place in the afterlife: Dr Reeves (Roger Livesey), having been killed on his way to operate, is able to operate in the 'afterlife'.

---

[13] We are indebted to the comments of the anonymous reader of an early manuscript before the first edition who pointed out that there is in fact an inversion of celestial justice in this film, with heaven as the site of conflict and the earth in 'Edenic form'.

The trial evolves into an inquiry about national identity and the responsibility of people for the misdemeanours of their forbears. It uses the forensic forum for examining notions of national guilt, and here the jury is representative of Britain's colonial and imperial history. It consists initially of a range of people from places Britain had in the past subjected to her power: French, Dutch Boers, Russians, Chinese, Irish, and the people from the Indian sub-continent. In a neat debate between the prosecutor and the British defence, a new jury is offered consisting of freedom-loving Americans. All the oppressed characters transform into American citizens from America's melting pot: French chef, Dutch farmer, Russian worker, Chinese student, Irish policeman and African-American soldier. The audience is multi-national, stretching over time, and representing different groups who are fighting against the Nazi threat as well as those who have taken collective action in the past: Puritans, American Independence militia, regiments from British India, etc. The plea for keeping the 'dead' airman alive succeeds when the parties both prefer to take the other's place and die rather than lose their partner. The principle which trumps law is love. Prosecutor Abraham Forlan protests: 'This is not the way of the law.' The response from the bewigged judge is, however, clear, if less than clear in its source:

> Here on earth love is supreme and law must give way to love.

The judge proceeds to cite the novelist, and lawyer, Sir Walter Scott to the effect that 'love conquers all'. Why this should be so is not explained but, at least, it has the narrative function of leaving the 'deceased', Peter Carter, to enjoy a long life with his new-found love. This is less surprising given the source of the film with its origins in a semi-autobiographical novel in which the narrator recounts the onset of hallucinations, and the brain operation he had in order to get rid of them. Thus, the trial in heaven is the figment of a highly imaginative mind, and its way of coping with dangerous brain surgery. The film is, however, grounded in a real struggle for the life of the doomed pilot between the forces of life and of fate. It is a trope which is encountered in a number of films at this time as Christie points out.[14] The difference here is that the resolution of this scenario takes place without the intervention of law and legal protagonists.

A further encounter with judicial tribunals, albeit of a rather more earth-orientated type, is portrayed in an Albert Brooks film, *Defending Your Life* (1991). Here is a process whereby individuals are able to advance up the tree of life beyond the earth once they have learned to live better. This is rather vaguely sketched out through the encounter of Daniel Miller (Albert Brooks). His task is to show that he conquered his fear of confrontation and is able to stand up for himself.

---

[14] Christie, I (2004). See *Here Comes Mr Jordan* (1941)—man due to survive has to find a body to inhabit after mistake in taking him to heaven early—remade, confusingly, with the title as *Heaven Can Wait* (1978); *Heaven Can Wait* (1943)—playboy dispatched from Hell to Heaven; *A Guy Named Joe* (1944)—dead pilot returns to supervise girlfriend's romance with a friend—remade as *Always* (1989). See also the BBC series *Life on Mars* and *Ashes to Ashes*. *Life on Mars* was also made for the US television market in 2008.

The procedure is described thus: 'even though this feels like a trial, it's just a process which helps us to decide'. It involves the replaying of incidents from his life by the prosecutor who wishes him returned to earth. On his behalf, his defender, is Bob Diamond (Rip Torn), seeks to show how what appears as fear can be seen in fact as strength. The prosecutor takes a rather different view of Daniel:

> Over the course of the next four days I will attempt to show that Daniel Miller, while he is a quality human being, is still held back by the fears that have plagued him lifetime after lifetime. I believe I will be able to show that he should be returned to earth to work on this problem.

Miller seeks to avoid confrontation and is prepared to take the blame for a friend's actions. This American-style, *in camera* hearing is interspersed with a burgeoning romance between Miller and Julia (Meryl Streep). She wins her case and is allowed to proceed, whilst Miller is to return to earth aboard different driverless trams. Miller's final attempt to board the tram that Julia is on, at great danger to himself, is proof that he is brave enough and does not lack courage. The concept of what people are on a trial for is rather vague. The underlying notion encapsulates elements of 'human potential fulfilment' or even Scientology's 'going clear'.[15]

The first film version of science fiction writer Pierre Boulle's *Planet of the Apes* (1968) includes a trial section. The film focuses upon life on a planet where human astronauts have landed, and the trial scene takes place at the National Academy of Science and involves these 'outsiders'. The hearing involves charges against the young scientists whose theory, that a more advanced non-Ape civilisation predated their own, is regarded as heretical. In a mirror of the Christian biblical tenets, their God made ape-kind in his own image and set him to rule over the animals including the mute human beings whom they have enslaved. The hearing is before the President and Secretary of the National Academy of Science and the Chief Minister of Science; interestingly, the latter is also described as Defender of the Faith. However, the Tim Burton re-imagination, also entitled *Planet of the Apes* (2000), dispenses with the trial. The trial, whilst set in the future, harks back to the purposive justice systems encountered under the Inquisition and with various witchcraft trials. This is territory that has been dealt with in film, for example *The Hour of the Pig* (1993) and *The Crucible* (1996). By its nature, this return to a less advanced civilisation is not able to add anything to a perspective on how justice might be sought in a future world. It does highlight the concept of formal natural justice. The separation of powers between executive and judiciary, and the notion of decision making by bodies which have no direct personal interest in the outcome of deliberations, is cogently illustrated. The impact of cinematic 'celestial justice's' perspective on how human behaviour might be judged is, on the present

---

[15] Leonard Cohen's *Famous Blue Raincoat* (1971) from *Songs of Love and Hate* finishes:
And Jane came by with a lock of your hair
She said that you gave it to her
That night that you planned to go clear
—Sincerely, L Cohen.

evidence, rather underwhelming. It may be that when other films are examined they may shed light on this process. Until then the conclusions are rather limited. Other material covering non-worldly courts, and ripe for future analysis, includes futuristic ones: *Rashomon* (1950), remade as *The Outrage* (1964); *Morgan* (1966); *One Way Pendulum* (1964); *Alice in Wonderland* (1933); *The Balcony* (1963); *The Wonderful World of the Brothers Grimm* (1962); *All that Money Can Buy* (1941) (aka *The Devil and Daniel Webster* (2004)); *The Remarkable Andrew* (1942), based on a novel by Dalton Trumbo; and prophetic ones: *Outward Bound* (1930), remade as *Between Two Worlds* (1944); *The Trial* (1962) (Orson Welles, from Kafka's novel); *The Trial* (1993), remake scripted by Harold Pinter; *The Flight that Disappeared* (1961); *1984* (1956), the British version of Orwell's novel.

Certainly the expectation that certain patterns would emerge by observing almost 20 films where celestial justice exists has been frustrated and leaves one interesting perspective, for the rest is something of a Barmecidal feast. The conclusion to *None Shall Escape* (1944), with its judge-to-camera 'challenge to the viewer', leaves us with a plain and undisguised 'message'. In a new moral future, decisions about morally deviant behaviour need to be judged across national boundaries rather than by pragmatic considerations of national and economic interest. This is a challenge that has been accepted with varying degrees of commitment in the subsequent years. Its cry resonates down from Nuremberg, through the corridors of the International Court of Justice and the International War Crimes Commission of the 1990s dealing with Rwanda and the Balkans, to the International Criminal Court.

By contrast, the arguments about the nature of national identity canvassed in *A Matter of Life and Death* (1946) are of more interest in specific debates about supposed inherent national characteristics. Beyond this the arguments illustrate the rhetorical nature of legal argumentation, at least where juries are involved. The contribution of *Planet of the Apes* (1968) is less of a 'future film' than one, in reality, set in the past. Here the identification of justice with the dominant ethnic group's interests is plain. These interests define the whole goal of law to support 'apekind'. It is a warning about speciesism that is encountered in a variety of modern contexts from those seeking to maintain biological diversity to those committed to co-existence with fellow creatures. The least obvious interest can be derived from *Defending Your Life* (1991), which can, at best, be seen as an oblique critique of psycho-babble and the narcissistic cult of self-absorption that is sustained by psychoanalysis.

Cyber Justice

Progressing into the future in a slightly different way from 'celestial justice' are those films which envisage a different kind of social order, and allow us to reflect on how justice might operate in these typically bleak settings. Whilst it is arguable that *Judge Dredd* (1995) is an alternative perspective on the traditional legal theme, it is important to place the film in terms of where its antecedents lie. Dredd (Sylvester Stallone) is a figure who not only acts in a traditional legal role, but who also performs the function of lawyer and police. Given this amalgamation, the ways in which the police have been portrayed and constructed are a useful starting point:

> Indeed, for some commentators [the present and immediate future] is a period in which the community 'plod', epitomized by Ted Willis's PC George Dixon, first in the 1950 film *The Blue Lamp* and later in the BBC television programme *Dixon of Dock Green*, has been replaced by the 'reactive pig' or 'reluctant bobby', with a visored 'Robocop' or 'Darth Vader' armed and waiting around the millennium corner.[16]

In terms of their portrayal within popular culture, policemen were rarely the heroes within film or other fictional treatments, as Reiner has noted:

> Until the late 1960s, a professional policeman was rarely the hero of a film. In the early days of Hollywood, the Keystone Cops were portrayed as clumsy buffoons, causing much protest from the law-enforcement establishment about this imbecilic image. At the 1913 convention of the International Association of Chiefs of Police, a resolution was passed to stop such movie misrepresentation.[17]

Indeed, within fictional portrayals of private detectives, the policeman was most often utilised as the foil that illustrates the impotence of the police, and the stunning forensic ability of the PI. This is a device notably employed between Inspector Lestrade and Sherlock Holmes, for example. Professional police began to appear in films in a more central role towards the end of the 1940s, although depictions in the 1950s illustrate that often the 'corrupt cop' was the dominant form of portrayal (*The Prowler* (1951) and *Rogue Cop* (1954)). The 1960s saw some heroic portrayals of police, notably Poitier's performance in *In the Heat of the Night* (1967) along with other similar portrayals.[18] A significant development was seen in films such as *Dirty Harry* (1973), with its concentration on internal workings and the failings of the system, and the move in films such as *Magnum Force* (1973) to a higher level of 'vengeance policing'. Perlmutter, in an excellent ethnographic analysis of the links between police portrayals, analyses the way in which the police see and construct themselves. Borrowing Shakespeare's phrase, he argues in addition that the police play out a role not dissimilar to an actor, and that 'all the street's a stage':

> Such a dramaturgical metaphor is not meant to slight police work. Rather, it allows the observer to note how cops, their superiors, and the public at large have expectations about the kind of character types, narratives, denouements, plot twists, lines, tones of voice, and assorted dramatic devices that will appear in the performance. In asserting that, to paraphrase Shakespeare, 'all the street's a stage', we argue that the demands of the publicly viewed acting role and its contradictions to the police officer's private beliefs

[16] Reiner, R (1978: 706).
[17] Reiner, R (1978: 706).
[18] Reiner, R (1978).

produce the essential tension that affects the principles, principals, and processes of modern law enforcement.[19]

The concept of street justice is taken a stage further by the *RoboCop* series (*RoboCop* (1987), *RoboCop 2* (1990) and *RoboCop 3* (1993)) and by *Judge Dredd* (1995). Similarly *Daredevil* (2003) depicts a blind lawyer, who spends his nights as an avenging superhero out to deliver justice to those who have escaped the gaze of the formal law. In terms of the *fora* in which the law is played out, this presents a marked shift in location. Although other shifts are considered, the central purpose here is to illustrate the shifting nature of the arena in which the process is conducted. The *RoboCop* trilogy and *Judge Dredd* (1995) might be termed as part of a move towards techno law films, and these in turn could be seen as part of a wider filmic depiction of 'futurescapes' that would embrace dystopian visions as portrayed by Kubrick and others. There is certainly a lineage from the cop films, via *Dirty Harry* to *RoboCop*, with a blurring of roles in terms of what a 'cop' actually does. Certainly in *Judge Dredd* (1995) there is the apotheosis of a separation of powers: Dredd is police, judge, jury and executioner all in one. Based on the character from the cult comic *2000 AD*, Dredd is a dispenser of justice in the 22nd century. As a curious counterpoint to *Robocop*, a cyborg with human tendencies, Dredd is a human, although cloned, and with an almost computer-like unreflexive and dogmatic approach to law enforcement. He has a rigid adherence to the Mega City law book, the rules and regulations he has as his coda behind the outward exclamation of 'I am the Law' as illustrated by his speech during his training of cadets at the Academy. After showing the cadets some of the tools that will be theirs when, or if, they qualify he continues:

> All of these things are nothing but toys. End of the day, when you're alone in the dark, all that counts ... is this (He takes something down from the lectern shelf, throws it down. It's the all-but-holy book: THE LAW). And you will be alone when you swear to uphold these ideals.[20]

This highly formalistic approach is underpinned by a belief that the law is always right, and must be strictly adhered to. This is very much in evidence when Dredd first meets a supporting character in the film, Fergie (Rob Schneider), after being called to a block riot. Fergie, recently released from jail, was in the vicinity as an innocent bystander and is asked by Dredd why he is there. Whilst Fergie argues that the only thing he could have done to avoid being there was to jump from a window to certain death, Dredd retorts that this action would have at least been legal. This rigid adherence is predicated on a belief that the law cannot be wrong and that the rule of law must be adhered to. Dredd still even appears to subscribe to this once he is sentenced to life for a crime he knows he did not commit, and once again meets Fergie; whilst he still believes he was wrongly convicted he still maintains that the law cannot make mistakes. However, this attitude shifts once

---

[19] Perlmutter, D (2000: 21).
[20] Wisher, W and De Souza, S (1995: 52–53).

Dredd starts to appreciate the wider context of the situation, and the notion of justice begins to outweigh rigid ideas of formal, doctrinal law. Here he becomes more like Lincoln, with his idealised notion of what is right and wrong, and less rigidly bound to the rule-book. In terms of the *fora* itself there is a military, futuristic courtroom portrayed in the film when he is charged with murder, and subsequently sentenced to life imprisonment. However, what is also identified here is that just as there are different types or forms of courtrooms that have been utilised for filmic depictions, the ideas of what a courtroom should be are not static. Here the sidewalk is the courtroom, the sidewalk is legitimised as an arena for dispensing justice, and Dredd is just as much the judge as his robed ancestors. There is still the formalism of law, and an acknowledgement of due process, but the parameters of the courtroom are no longer fixed. This shifting nature of the courtroom is evidenced in other films, and perhaps echoes a shift within contemporary legal practice to different *fora* for dispute resolution.

Safe European Home? Law and Film in Europe

Contemporaneously to the anglophone world examining the products of Hollywood, scholars from Europe have been busy engaging in law and film studies in a rather different way. Central control of the syllabus, and the dominance of the profession on its content have, until very recently, inhibited the kinds of courses available to students of law, particularly in Spain.[21] The work which has been produced in these circumstances is an interesting mix of analysis of indigenous cinema, and the much more familiar American films. The scholarship is evidence of the huge impact of Hollywood on national cinemas, both in general terms as well as specifically in relation to issues around justice. The significance of national cinema in the future is a matter for serious concern. It should be noted that, in Britain, in addition to the engagement with debates about the nature and direction of law and film studies, there has been some focus on material outwith the Hollywood mainstream. For instance Moran has examined the construction of the films centring on the trials of Oscar Wilde of both the 1960s and 1997.[22] Similarly films such as *M* (1931)[23] and *Henry V* (1944, 1989)[24] have been analysed.

This section provides a brief introduction to the most accessible material from Europe, focusing on France, Germany and Spain. This work is of particular significance because it stresses different approaches to the interrelationship between law and film, away from the dominant American practice-orientated approach. It takes the cinematic, as well as the legal, aspects to be much more central to the

---

[21] Rivaya, B (2006).
[22] Moran, L (2004).
[23] MacDonald, A (2004).
[24] McNamee, E (2004).

scholarship and the focus is likely to shift onto a different roster of films. The contribution of British scholarship here is a slight paradox, perhaps paralleling previous political alignments. British work has hitherto been very much focused on the products of Hollywood.[25] The indications are, however, that links with Europe and work on local British and European issues may well dominate in the future and these possible developments are covered below.

France

The range of subjects encountered in French scholarship is wide, and the perspectives have varied considerably. It ranges from documentaries,[26] through various readings of individual films, to an unsurprising interest in the work of *auteurs* like Fritz Lang and Alfred Hitchcock.[27] French scholars have also taken the opportunity to explore the world of courtroom reality in the coverage of the Yugoslavian War Crimes trials.[28] Other work traces the development of issues such as film censorship in America, justice in the Western, and prison films.[29] In addition to these historical approaches, the vast majority of the scholarship takes a reasonably consistent approach. The films are analysed as texts in their political and social context. Although French scholars have examined the products of their own film industry, there is in their work a significant proportion of the material with a focus on American films. The impact of Hollywood, and resistance to its hegemony, are themselves issues that have preoccupied commentators.[30] For instance in the essays collected under the title *Screen Justice*, of the 30 essays only four are solely concerned with non-American films.[31] These examine French justice films, the Eichmann trial, German legal cinema and Italian judges in films. Some of the other essays deal with themes that recur in different national cinemas; there is an overview of films on the trial of Joan of Arc as well as coverage of the Inquisition and First World War courts martial. Other essays examine both individual American films—*12 Angry Men* (1957), *Anatomy of a Murder* (1959), *Sergeant Rutledge* (1960) and *Erin Brockovich* (2000)—as well as themes such as the role of the vigilante in American films, and the struggle between the North and South. There is also coverage of other material that deals with justice-related issues, such as the coverage on the screen of superheroes, described by Marc-George Boulanger as 'silent "agents" of good'.[32] Of interest also is coverage of the nature

---

[25] Greenfield, S, Osborn, G and Robson, P (2001).
[26] Delage, C (2005).
[27] Puaux, F (2002).
[28] See http://justice-images.ihej.org/, last accessed 11 June 2009.
[29] Puaux, F (2002).
[30] CinémAction, 2002, Quelle diversité face à Hollywood.
[31] Puaux, F (2002).
[32] CinémAction (2004: 214).

of the state—the army on the screen[33] and Utopia,[34] which discuss films covered in other national debates like *Blade Runner* (1982). There has also been discussion of the broader related question of what constitutes French legal culture.[35] Law and film has made limited inroads into the hitherto constrained French legal curriculum. Support is found, though, at the level of professional training for judges and magistrates through the Institut de Hautes Études sur la Justice whose research is ongoing. There has also been inclusion of Law and Film in the professional training for the judiciary.

Germany

The nature and scope of the German scholarship is also of interest and is broadly speaking concerned with textual analysis in a cultural context. The material German scholars have examined has been sourced from the United States as well as Germany. Their approach has been to situate the films and issues in their concrete political and historical framework. Böhnke, for example, looks back to three of John Ford's Westerns in a search for the inherent qualities of law he suggests they reveal. His analysis of these films is centred on an examination of the legal and political issues in law achieving legitimacy.[36] This whole question of the legitimacy recurs in the work of Kuzina in relation to the politics of American law films,[37] social issues films,[38] and the portrayal of military justice.[39] A rather different form of legitimacy, sought through the strength of cinema's images, is discussed by Drexler.[40] He provides a close reading of the law-centred films produced during the Nazi period whose goal was to create consensus through the concept of the pre-political *Volksgemeinschaft*—an idealised version of law deriving from the people. Finally, Machura and Ulbrich describe the phenomenon of American legal images extending their reach into German culture and how this process occurs.[41] Their analysis draws on Niklas Luhmann's systems theory with its echoes of Kuhn's paradigms and discourse theory. German scholarship is to an extent inhibited by the tendency of German legal scholars to view sociology of law as outside their concerns, and for sociology to view such work as not 'real' sociology. This is the context in which this work needs to be evaluated.

---

[33] (L'armée à l'écran] CinémAction (2004), vol 113.
[34] Utopie et cinéma CinémAction (2005), vol 115.
[35] Garapon, A (1995).
[36] Böhnke, M (2001).
[37] Kuzina, M (2000).
[38] Kuzina, M (2001).
[39] Kuzina, M (2005).
[40] Drexler, P (2001).
[41] Machura, S and Ulbrich, S (2001).

Spain

In terms of publications Spain has been the most systematic and productive country. It offers a complete self-contained world of scholarship and teaching and there is much to learn from the scholarship here, both in terms of focus, and material covered. Although the first work is recorded as appearing in 1996,[42] most has been published since 2003. This extensive literature of some 25 books does not appear to have received coverage in the English language literature. American films have, not surprisingly perhaps, dominated hitherto, but there is much other material under discussion. It is interesting to note also that, like the English language scholarship, the material analysed goes far beyond the narrow world of the courtroom and the lawyer-centred drama, into science fiction *Bladerunner* (1982)[43] and into historical material: *Macbeth* (1908, 1971); *A Man for All Seasons* (1966); *The Scarlet Letter* (1995) and melodrama *The Hours* (2002).[44]

This work appears in three particular forms. First in a series of over 20 monographs under the title *Cine y Derecho*, from the Valencian publishing house *Tirant Lo Blanch*, there is coverage of individual films. These are extended essays ranging from 25,000 to 40,000 words with varied emphasis. Some focus on the historical context of the films and the socio-political issues they address such as the works on *El Verdugo* (The Hangman) (1963), *Paths of Glory* (1957), *The Leopard* (1963) and *JFK* (1991). The focus ranges from the role of the state in punishment in *The Scarlet Letter* (1995) to the nature of legality under the Nazis in *Schindler's List* (1993). Others are much more concerned with aspects of legal philosophy and legal concepts such as the coverage of *Blade Runner* (1982), *Macbeth* (1971), *Anatomy of a Murder* (1959) and *The Matrix* (1999). The final group including *Judgment at Nuremberg* (1961), *A Man for All Seasons* (1966) and *Three Colours Red* (1999) separate out the coverage of the legal issues within the work and give distinct treatment to cinematic techniques (aspectos cinematográficos; análisis fílmico).

There is a second kind of work in the *Cine y Derecho* series which focuses on specific themes. To date there have been volumes on the death penalty, prostitution and the law, torture and the jury in film. In the collection *Film and the Death Penalty*, there are essays on 10 different films where the death penalty arises as an issue.[45] Some 57 films are listed in the Filmography, of which 40 are American, and the coverage includes both legal and moral matters. The films commented on include Fritz Lang's *M* (1931) as well as classic Hollywood works like *Intolerance* (1916), *Young Mr Lincoln* (1939), *I Want to Live!* (1958), *In Cold Blood* (1967) and *Dead Man Walking* (1995) along with less familiar works like *El Verdugo*

---

[42] Varios, (1996).
[43] De Lucas, J (2003).
[44] Benítez, OS (2006).
[45] Rivaya, B (ed) (2003).

(The Hangman) (1963) and *Sacco e Vanzetti* (1971). *Prostitution and the law in film* brings together seven writers each looking at the work of a British, Spanish, French, Italian, Japanese, German and American director.[46] Only one of the films, *Taxi Driver* (1976), is a product of the United States. The approach centres much more heavily on cinematic techniques. *Torture in Film* looks at 10 films, with three from Britain, two from France, one each from Italy, Spain, United States, and Germany with one Franco-British co-production.[47] The approach here again is much more on the filmic aspects of the works along with an analysis of such issues as social implications of torture and its historical significance. Most recently we have an extended essay on *The Profile of the Jury in Film* (El perfil del jurado en el cine).[48] By contrast, the focus is on a discussion of 14 films, all from the United States, and the hidden way in which juries are selected. This is based on a textual analysis of a range of familiar films from *The Paradine Case* (1947) and *Adam's Rib* (1949) through *12 Angry Men* (1957) to *The Juror* (1996) and *A Time to Kill* (1996). There is also a brief note on the implications of the jury selection process in the context of a modern Spanish practitioner.[49]

The most recent work from the *Cine y Derecho* series is entitled *A Cinematic Introduction to Law*.[50] This provides a brief overview, and indicates that the context in which the Spanish scholarship has been produced is the sceptical world of professional law training.[51] It consists of a dozen essays looking at different areas of law. These range from constitutional law, international law, family law and environmental law through to commercial law, procedure, criminal law and labour law. There is also treatment of broader themes like the nature of law, the goals of punishment, and the relationship between law and violence. The approach is somewhat akin to that adopted by Anthony Chase in *Movies on Trial*, where he explored a range of themes in the American legal curriculum, through film.[52] In the Spanish collection, there is an exploration of how film can assist in the business of law teaching. The Spanish style of law teaching with its almost exclusive reliance on the didactic tradition is identified as a problem and film is seen as a way to provide departure points for reflections on bigger themes such as the death penalty and the family.[53] The tone is, to an extent, defensive in that a spectrum of approaches to law and film is identified which ranges from simply using film as an excuse for enlivening classes to using the material to provide a legal commentary within the film.

A slightly different approach is found in a further Spanish publication, *Images and Justice: law through film* which examines 21 individual films with two separate

---

[46] Berenguer, E Orts (2003).
[47] Amado, JA García and Castañón, JM Paredes (2005).
[48] Colomer, JL Gómez (2005).
[49] *Ibid.*
[50] Linera, M, and Rivaya, B (eds) (2006).
[51] Rivaya, B (2006).
[52] Chase, A (2002).
[53] Rivaya, B (2006).

commentaries for each film.[54] There is a legal commentary from the magistrate author and a cinematic commentary from the journalist author. The films have been selected because the authors consider they provide a good introduction to the legal and juridical themes in them and with one exception are well known to the general public. The films are predominantly mainstream products of Hollywood, extensively discussed in the existing literature, along with a couple of less well-known works.[55] The rest of the volume is made up of a discussion of Vittorio de Sica's classic *Bicycle Thieves* (1948) and two Spanish films, *Muerte de un Ciclista* (1955) and *El Crimen de Cuenca* (1979). The cinematic commentary seeks to offer a critical evaluation of the film and situates it within its historical context as well as relating it to other films and the other work of the director. Thus we discover, *inter alia*, why Billy Wilder did not like *The Fortune Cookie* (1966) and the nature of the film's structural weakness. The notion of 'one man against the herd' as a theme in the films of Sidney Lumet is noted in *12 Angry Men* (1957) with reference to *Serpico* (1973), *Prince of the City* (1981) and *Night Falls on Manhattan* (1996). Interestingly, separating director from screen writer, David Mamet's script is critiqued for relying on stereotypes for judge and defence lawyer in *The Verdict* (1982) though it is noted that the director is ultimately responsible for the final product.[56]

The two Spanish films are particularly fascinating, offering a glimpse of the influence of Italian neo-realism on cinema under Franco. This was more or less limited to historical epics, cheery comedies and some crime thrillers. *Muerte de un Ciclista* (1955) looks at the issue of the failure to help the victim of an accident, and provides a veiled critique of Franco's post-1939 dictatorship. *El Crimen de Cuenca* (1979) comes after the end of the regime and just after the transition to democracy and is based on actual events from the 1920s. It also provides a critique of the oppressive power wielded by the wealthy landed classes, the Church and the forces of the state. It centres on the 18-year imprisonment of two men for a crime that did not actually take place when a young shepherd boy went missing. The young boy turned up 14 years later after the release of the 'criminals'. In these, as in the other films, the legal commentary examines the legal issues and how Spanish law would deal with such a matter. For instance, in *12 Angry Men* (1957), the nature and role of the jury in Spain is explained at some length. In *Witness for the Prosecution* (1957), the nature of the lawyer's duty to the profession is discussed.

This approach of Nieto and Fernandez complements the emergence of law and film studies as a part of professional legal education in Spain, and the need

---

[54] Nieto, FS and Fernández, FJ (2004).

[55] The 'mainstream' films are *A Civil Action* (1998); *Anatomy of a Murder* (1959); *12 Angry Men* (1957); *Cape Fear* (1961); *The Paradine Case* (1947); *The Fortune Cookie* (1966); *The Wrong Man* (1957); *Adam's Rib* (1949); *The Firm* (1993); *To Kill a Mockingbird* (1962); *Dead Man Walking* (1995); *I want to Live!* (1958); *Witness for the Prosecution* (1957); *A Man for All Seasons* (1966); *Judgment at Nuremberg* (1961); *The Verdict* (1982). The two lesser known works are *A Simple Plan* (1998); *The Confession* (1999).

[56] Nieto, FS and Fernández, FJ (2004).

to show that analysis of film has a practical as well as aesthetic purpose which is underscored by Rivaya.[57] This is precisely what we find in volume 20 of the *Cine y Derecho* series.[58] This provides an overview of the whole focus on law and film in a book which offers commentaries on 100 legal films (películas jurídicas). Although structurally it draws its inspiration from Bergman and Asimow (1996) the commentaries are preceded by an extensive 100-page Introduction to Law and Film by Rivaya. The debates and issues discussed include many of those which are noted above. The object of its study is not, for the most part, different. The same Hollywood films and occasional European classics are covered and there are, nonetheless, some fascinating and thoughtful insights.

Rivaya explains that the work is a guide to the most important 'law films' and the focus is on those films which have used legal themes and thinking.[59] In addition to functioning as a specific course guide, the aim of the work is to popularise studies of law and film (Derecho y Cine) in Spain. Rivaya's overview of the field of law and cinema involves a discussion of the nature of genre and whether legal cinema (cine jurídico) is a discrete category. Rivaya is concerned to lay out the value of cinema to those involved in a range of areas of legal teaching such as procedural law, labour law, international law, private law and legal philosophy. There is recognition that within law and film studies, law is not the only factor and that engagement with film theory is required to enrich the scholarship. Finally, Rivaya returns to the whole core question of what is the usefulness or value of law and film studies. He considers the insights from sociology of law on 'law as image' valuable, and that law and film provides a way of enriching law teaching. This is one of the most sustained explanations of what is involved in the struggle for academic recognition, in an environment which is often sceptical.

The 100 films are selected from every decade from *Intolerance* (1916) up to *The Navigators* (2001) and include some 73 films from America, nine from Spain, seven from Italy, four from Great Britain, three from France, two from Japan and one each from Colombia and Germany. The basis for the choice of films is not necessarily the artistic quality of the film, but whether they encompass a significant legal concept.[60] Thus we have some of the standard films with major courtroom action, *Young Mr Lincoln* (1939), *12 Angry Men* (1957), *Anatomy of a Murder* (1959), alongside *The Birdman of Alcatraz* (1961) and *The Truman Show* (1998). There are some initially surprising choices. *Straw Dogs* (1971), for instance, is selected because it deals with the notion of extenuating circumstances in relation to people's actions. The comments on the films contain three elements. There is a list of legal themes by heading; for example in the film about euthanasia *Johnny Got his Gun* (1971) these are noted as Critique of law, Human rights, Explanation/justification, Euthanasia, Command theory, Liberalism/authoritarianism, Social

---

[57] Rivaya, B (2006).
[58] Rivaya, B and Cima, P de (2004).
[59] Rivaya, B (2006).
[60] Rivaya, B and Cima, P de (2004: 448) on *17 and under*.

morals/critical morals, obedience to the law, ideology of positivism, separation of moral and legal, internal point of view/external point of view, legal security and moral utilitarianism. This is followed by a commentary on the narrative and the social issues raised in the film. Finally there are suggestions for further reading of other writings on the film and/or director. All this has taken place in the context of a legal curriculum which has only in the 21st century begun to emerge from rigid central direction and a strong professional focus. Whilst there are extensive references to English language scholarship in the Spanish literature, few references to the non-English language material in the English language scholarship are encountered. This is to be regretted since the insights and perspectives provided, and material covered, are of no little interest. It is hoped that this account of the work here may assist in the dialogue from which both linguistic traditions could benefit.

Current Debates

There are two principal observations, with implications for the future, to be made at this juncture. One is that 'law and film' is a significant subject in its own right, the other that it has internal divisions. First, writers talk of a 'law and film move-ment' that is constituted by the critical mass of work that has been published and courses that exist.[61] To the central body of work can now be added further essays and books centring on various aspects of the portrayal of justice within film.[62] Some writers have gone further, however, to suggest that, in effect, an 'orthodoxy' has emerged.[63] The 'orthodoxy' is based in law schools and its predominant approach is a concern with narrative and textual analysis.[64] 'Narrative' is used here to denote a principal focus on outlining the plots of films and adding little by way of analysis. The role of narrative work is a difficult question at an early stage in a field of study. There is no doubt that texts which do no more than précis the story of the film are somewhat limited. It is, however, frustrating to read an analysis of unfamiliar material without being able to critically evaluate the attached analysis through linking it to allied material. Equally frustrating is to read narratives which are no more than descriptive. For that reason we have attempted, throughout the book, to use description where necessary, but to add a critical or analytical glaze to this where at all possible. When, however, one looks at the scholarship, it is hard to actually identify any work which *purely* recites the plots of the films under discussion. For instance, Levi's account of modern legal cinema does not

---

[61] The phrase 'law and film movement' should be credited to Richard Sherwin. See here Rivaya, B (2004); Almog, S and Aharonson, E (2004); Kamir, O (2006).

[62] Moran, L (2004); Levi, RD (2005); Sarat, A (2005a); Kamir, O (2006).

[63] Moran, L, Sandon, E, Loizidou, E and Christie I (eds) (2004: xii); Seymour, D (2004).

[64] *Ibid.*

purport to be an academic text.[65] It has no bibliography, makes reference to no other work, and provides a résumé of various aspects of the courtroom experience from judge, to juries, to lawyers. It is, nonetheless, informed by a particular perspective. Levi is concerned that the important area of lawyers in film has been ignored by American culture's cinematic consciousness, and seeks to show how important films have featured the legal system. As one commentator indicates, there is limited, explicit theory referred to within much of the early law and film scholarship, possibly due to the lack of theory traditionally encountered in legal education generally.[66] Even where a contextual element has been introduced into law teaching, this does not always go much beyond a historical 'topping and tailing' before teachers get down to the 'serious business'.[67]

One further critique is that American film is assumed to be a national cinema for all and its dominance is often ignored.[68] Continental scholars have, in the past, looked for much of their subject matter from this source. Similarly, British scholars have been slow to examine in depth the contribution of the British film industry to law's portrayal although the issue has been discussed in conferences.[69] A contributing factor, of course, has been the relative paucity of national film material.[70] There are, however, other reasons. Law and film studies emerged within law schools as a part of the challenge to the uncritical didactic 'black letter' approach to legal education.[71] To focus, initially at least, on such central issues as the ethical standards of lawyers, or the racial nature of the justice process, seemed entirely understandable. Where these issues were encountered was less important than to debate the issues, given the dominance of American film in Europe. Further, as has been pointed out in a range of contexts, law and film has no prescribed focus or methodology.[72] Those who teach and write in the area have a range of reasons for linking film and law. As was noted above, interest in the use of film has been taken up by those involved in professional legal studies, social theory and legal philosophy. The need to go back to basics, and explore what one critic described as the core question of 'what is film', would probably have seemed a step back too far.[73]

Nonetheless, the suggestion that what was needed was to put more emphasis upon the cinematic and tone down the legal makes sense if one's principal concern

---

[65] Levi, RD (2005).

[66] Robson, P (2005).

[67] Although the approach of Kingsfield in *The Paper Chase* (1973) is not to be taken literally in the 21st century it is still reflected in many of the examination questions which are encountered in modern-day Britain.

[68] Moran, L, Sandon, E, Loizidou, E and Christie I (eds) (2004).

[69] Robson, P, Osborn, G and Greenfield, S, Paris, November 2003; Robson, P, Bologna, January 2006—meetings organised under the auspices of the Images of Law Group.

[70] Robson, P (2007c).

[71] Osborn, G (2001).

[72] Machura, S and Robson P (eds) (2001); Robson, P (2005). See also Elkins, J (2004) for the US perspective on this.

[73] Biber, K (2006).

is with the area as a branch of film studies.[74] Exactly what is implied, though, in terms of writing by this change of emphasis is less than clear. An examination of the *Law's Moving Image* essays seems to involve a very similar mix to what we find in the *San Francisco* collection, the *Reel Justice* collection, and the *Law and Film* collection.[75] There is a mix of socio-political theory,[76] historical overviews,[77] and close textual analysis of a range of non-mainstream films,[78] as well as one essay which does not *really* appear to be about media but provides a political/social reading of 'deviance'.[79] The essays' texts, although scholarly, are, for the most part, characterised by density.

The complaint that analysis in 'orthodox' law and film studies has been textual is interesting. Assuming this is a reference to a failure to engage with literary and film theory, it has some substance. There has been some work on the process of adaptation of fiction to film that noted the flattening of narrative style, from the personal, to the objective, in the context of adapting James Ellroy.[80] At the same time this work observed a heightening of certain critical elements in Grisham adaptations.[81] This could be said to have produced material, however, which might be of some interest within literary studies, but which added little to the concerns of law and film studies. Whilst clearer theoretical positions need to be articulated, care needs to be taken.

One of the early attractions of law and film studies was the liberating effect on law students of using film as part of study. They were no longer so clearly in the traditional, supine relationship to their 'expert' teachers when it came to interpreting films, as opposed to standard legal texts.[82] If the scholarship is too dense, or covers highly esoteric issues, this opportunity for mass engagement is in danger of being lost, however admirable the scholarship may be.[83] Essentially, it should be possible to produce work that is penetrable, accessible and meaningful. For instance, the parallel between legal performance and cinematic productions is captured most accessibly in the examination of 'law as film' by Almog and Aharonson.[84]

On the other hand, the call for interdisciplinary study is one which appears already to have been heeded. A survey of scholarship shows that the principal academic approach is historical textual analysis. Seymour specifically bemoans the absence of critique in the work produced by the 'orthodoxy', and suggests a way

[74] Moran, L (2004).
[75] Sherwin, R (1996a); Denvir, J (1996a); Machura, S and Robson, P (eds) (2001).
[76] Loizidou, E (2004).
[77] Douglas, L (2004); Grieveson, L (2004); Prasad, M (2004).
[78] Christie, I (2004); MacNeil, W (2004); McNamee, E (2004); Botting, F and Wilson, S (2004).
[79] Young, A (2004).
[80] Meyer, P (2001a).
[81] Robson, P (2001).
[82] Denvir, J (1996a).
[83] Black, D (1999); MacDonald, A (2004).
[84] Almog, S and Aharonson, E (2004), Part I.

forward for a critical method of the study of law and film.[85] What this amounts to is, however, expressed in a manner which is far from lucid, involving a textual analysis of Antigone and the film *The 6th Sense* (1999). What is radical about this is not immediately obvious.

A call to 'broaden the focus' of law and film studies was made in 2005 by Sarat, Douglas and Umphrey.[86] Here they urged scholars to focus on 'undervalued areas', and they were particularly keen that the relationship between law and film, as distinct narrative forms, be explored. What this actually has produced appears to be further work in the mould of earlier influential comments like those of Sherwin[87] and Kamir.[88] Whilst most of the films are not courtroom-centred, there is no move away from the tradition of individual film analysis which has characterised much of the previous work. These are interesting in themselves, but it is not entirely clear in what way this differs from past practice. Whilst the collection is divided into *Studies of Representation* and *Studies of Reception*, these categories are, in fact, remarkably similar. What one might have expected is evidence which would make a link with the very broad statements of the earlier writers like Macaulay, Friedman and Sherwin that had noted that popular culture was a major source for the public's knowledge and understanding about law.[89] This is absent. What we do not have in great supply and what is lacking here is any discussion of the impact of film. The notion of reading for meaning in the literary tradition is what seems to be practised here. It is seductive and well executed but it does not unlock the key to the question of film's actual significance in people's lives. We cannot simply take Macaulay, Friedman and Sherwin as read—although we may well suspect they are probably right.

This is precisely the missing element in Kamir's recent book that covers the portrayal of women in film.[90] She eschews the overview/survey approach in favour of concentrating on an analysis of eight individual films and contrasting two other pairs of films. This involves a mixture of textual analysis, contextualisation and cinematic techniques. She echoes the thinking of the earlier pioneering writers up to two decades before with her suggestion that law films are important and worthy of being read as jurisprudential texts because they are overwhelmingly influential in moulding public actions. Kamir posits competitiveness and egalitarianism as alternative bases for society's value systems under the guises of honour and dignity. Taking her own readings of various films involving women involved in sexual encounters she seeks to unravel the hold on viewers of earlier readings.[91] As with her previous work these readings are both fascinating and

---

[85] Seymour, D (2004).
[86] Sarat, A, Douglas, L and Umphrey, M (2005).
[87] Sherwin, R (1996a, b).
[88] Kamir, O (2000).
[89] Macaulay, S (1987); Friedman, L (1989); Sherwin, R (2000).
[90] Kamir, O (2006).
[91] Kamir, O (2006).

controversial, and mean that debate in this area is enlivened and invigorated.[92] How influential these current debates are likely to be is a theme we pursue below. At this juncture we want to say a little about the context in which this scholarship has been flourishing. Just as films are conceived in specific economic, political and cultural contexts, so scholarship is produced within determined situations. We have noted some of the driving forces which have led to the emergence of law and film as an area of extensive and very diverse scholarship in the past decade. Whilst these factors have shaped the nature and extent of this work it should be noted that changes in both legal professional interests, academic criteria and within the culture industry mean that we can expect shifts in the nature and patterns of scholarship in the future. These may not, however, be the ones called for by other commentators.[93]

Future Directions

We have already indicated that further empirical work is potentially a fruitful direction in which to expand the scholarship and move it into new areas of significance. Currently, though, work is continuing to be developed despite the institutional problems faced by areas outwith the narrow range of professional legal education. One very muted feature in these debates and discussions of the future is the role of television, which has received scant attention in the scholarship. Whilst scholarship on law and film has flourished in the past two decades, there has been relatively little work published on the small-screen lawyer. There has been some work carried out in the United States but only a limited examination of the images of law and justice found on television. The study of law has been slow to look beyond its narrow professional concerns, and consider the social cultural context in which it operates. In the past decade, some work has been conducted in the cultural field, particularly as regards literature and film. Lawyers figure prominently in film, and have been the focus of a significant body of scholarship, but TV lawyers have been largely overlooked. There is a paradox here as television reaches the vast majority of the population. It provides news, dramas, documentaries and comedies seven days a week, 24 hours a day. Cinema, the previous major player, has declined from being the major source of popular entertainment and visiting the cinema is now a feature in the lives of a relatively small proportion of the population in Western societies. In the studies that have been undertaken into the role and impact of popular culture on people's legal consciousness, the overwhelming majority of this work has taken place on film. The rise of television and what the future is likely to hold as interest in law and popular culture continues to expand requires consideration.

[92] Kamir, O (2000a, b, c).
[93] Moran, L (2004); Sarat, A (2005a).

Academics, both within law schools and in cognate areas of scholarship, have engaged with various areas of popular culture. Courses have been developed which encompass law and literature as well as law and film. There is also evidence of some interest in other areas such as music, cartoons, and legal humour. Insofar as there has been engagement and activity in relation to law and television it has occurred within the broader area of law and popular culture. This, as indicated in Freeman's *Law and Popular Culture* edited collection, has involved writers engaged in debates about pressing moral and legal issues in their work and such themes continue to be found in modern literature.[94] As Freeman noted, however, a considerable body of the scholars attracted to contribute to the 2003 Colloquium focused their study on the more intellectually prestigious genre of film. Of the essays published from this meeting, some seven were on literature,[95] fourteen on film and only three mentioned television.[96] There has been little attention paid to the phenomenon of television in relation to lawyers in general. The portrayal of other aspects of the justice process on television have figured, such as the police and the prison system.[97] Whilst the operation of the law includes the apprehension, deliberation and disposition phases of the legal process, the separation of these phases within popular culture means that it is not unrealistic to consider each of these phases separately. In simple terms, the deliberation phase featuring lawyers does not feature in the vast majority of police or prison dramas. Inaccurate though this is, there is no sense from popular culture that the various phases inter-relate. This is worthy of a separate study which is being undertaken.[98] This seeks to explore the connections between the various phases of what comes under the umbrella of the 'justice system', and the portrayal of institutional isolation encountered in television programmes.[99] The separateness, then, of the trial process, is a consistent feature of a considerable body of programmes in Britain as well as the United States, and the lawyer sub-genre ranks along with

---

[94] *Ibid.*

[95] To indicate the lack of link with TV the titles are noted here: Where the Wild Things *Really* are: Children's Literature and the Law (Desmond Manderson); The Absence of Contradiction and the Contradiction of Absence: Law, Ethics and the Holocaust (David Seymour); Popular Fiction and Domestic Law (East Lynne), Justice and the Ordeal of the Unpredictable' (Marlene Tromp); Law's Agent: Cultivated citizen or Popular Savage? The Crash of the Moral Mirror (Melanie Williams); Law's diabolical Romance: Reflections on a New Jurisprudence of the Sublime (Leslie Moran); Re-Imagining the Practice of Law; Popular Twentieth-Century Fiction by American Lawyers (David Ray Papke); The Materiality of Symbols (JG Ballard) and Jurisprudence; Law Image, Reproduction (Adam Gearey); L'Oeil qui pense: The Emotive as Grounds for the Pensive in Phenomenological Reflection (Claire Vallier); Public and Private Eyes (Lawrence Friedman).

[96] Kuzina, M (2005).

[97] Rafter, N (ed) (2000).

[98] *TV Lawyers Today* Robson, P (forthcoming 2012).

[99] The linked approach of GF Newman's *Law and Order* series is the exception and is only occasionally mirrored in miscarriages of justice themes which have featured in such series as *Rumpole* and *Kavanagh QC*. Most recently *Outlaws* featured some interplay between the lawyer protagonists, the Crown Prosecution Service and individual police officers in the context of plea-bargaining and securing clear-up rates. The underlying narrative drive of *Judge John Deed* is the active role of the 'Establishment' in seeking to determine judicial decision making to favour their interests.

other dramas such as the cop show, the prison drama, hospital programme and the neighbourhood soap.[100] There has been a slow, and only partial recognition, of the significance of television in this area.[101] The expansion of DVD and other 'home cinema' devices pose interesting challenges. Quite what the significance, for example of the alternative delivery technology for film both in cinemas and the home is not yet clear.

There are dangers, however, if home viewing does burgeon. Television does not measure up to film in terms of academic kudos, however, and the academic output is, to date, relatively meagre. Apart from the general overview, *TV Lawyers Today*, there has been a brief focus on *LA Law* and another popular series has been commissioned.[102] Some crime and law studies do cover the two mediums in single studies but the different nature of the viewing experience and the distinct nature of the product would seem to militate against this and it would be surprising were this to become the norm.[103]

There is, though, an interesting paradox about legal scholarship and television as much of the early work focused on television rather than film.[104] Other commentators made no distinction between images in the different formats.[105] In the 1990s, however, the vast majority of the scholarship was on film and TV largely neglected. There is also a question of volume. The sheer quantity of material, even in the most modest series, is a banal but serious barrier to research. Typically even a modest run of a series involves a dozen one-hour episodes. The attractions of looking at a single 90–120 minute film are obvious in terms of containability. In both British and American series, there has been, historically, limited easy access to material. Only three of the pre-2000 British fictional shows appeared in video/DVD format although such release now appears to be standard even when the series is not re-commissioned.[106] The vast majority of programmes from 1958 to the present have not been preserved, or are available only at considerable cost. The same appears to be the case in the United States. At the time of writing there appears to be no availability of such programmes as *The Defenders*, *LA Law* or *Petrocelli*.[107] Although these are not insuperable obstacles, they reinforce the unarticulated hierarchy in cultural products in which television comes way below literature and film.[108]

---

[100] Even the apparent exception to this convention of phase separation, *Law and Order*, comprises effectively free-standing components of apprehension and trial.

[101] Rapping, E (2003); Villez, B (2005); Robson, P (2007a and b).

[102] Asimow, M (ed) (2009).

[103] Brown, S (2003); Lenz, T (2003).

[104] Stark, S (1987); Rosen, R (1989).

[105] Macaulay, S (1987); Friedman, L (1989).

[106] *Rumpole, Kavanagh QC and Sutherland's Law*. By contrast four of the post-2000 shows have gone to DVD: *Judge John Deed; Outlaws; New Street Law* and *Kingdom*. The pioneering series *Law and Order* (1978) is also now available.

[107] Although *Perry Mason* is available in no less than 48 discs! Matlock's first series is also released in the UK with Seasons 2 and 3 available on import.

[108] Robson, P (2007a).

There is of course no logical reason for this state of affairs. Insofar as part of law and film has concerned itself with the nature and impact of the image of justice, there would seem to be more reason for scholars with these interests to examine the ubiquitous television lawyer, rather than the much less popular forms of films or books. There are signs that the initial interest which was shown in the past is reviving.[109] In the empirical work carried out on what law students think about law and lawyers, television was the sole focus of one of the studies and featured alongside film in the other.[110]

Law and Film Studies does face problems: it is popular with students, and thriving in terms of courses and publications.[111] There is, however, the danger of it being sidelined as no more than an irrelevant sideline within law schools. The past 20 years have seen the emergence of a recognised area of scholarship around law and popular culture generally, and law and film in particular. We have reflected on the nature and health of this academic development, and have attempted to assess its prospects and vitality. Perhaps the key thing we have found is that, whilst America is where the first significant work was carried out, is where much of the production has taken place, and has perhaps been dominant in writing in the area, it is not, any more, the only game in town.

---

[109] Robson, P (2007a and b).
[110] Salzmann, V and Dunwoody, P (2005); Asimow, M (2005).
[111] Denvir, J (2005).

BIBLIOGRAPHY

Abrahamson, J (2000) 'The jury and popular culture' 50 DePaul Law Review 497

Abramson, J (2007) 'Anger at angry jurors' 82(2) Chicago-Kent Law Review 591

Adams, J and Brownsword, R (1987) 'The ideologies of contract' 7(2) Legal Studies 205

Adorno, TW, Adorno, G and Tiedemann, R (eds) (2004) Aesthetic theory (London: Continuum)

Alloway, L (1963) 'On the iconography of the Movies', Movie 7 in Neale (2000)

Almog, S (2006) 'Creating Representations of justice in the third millennium: legal poetics in digital times' 32 Rutgers Computer and Technology Journal 184

Almog, S and Aharonson, E (2004) 'Law as film: representing justice in the age of moving images' 3 Canadian Journal of Law and Technology 1

Almog, S and Reichman, A (2004) 'Casablanca: judgment and dynamic enclaves in law and cinema' 42 Osgoode Hall Law Journal 202

Althusser, L (1971) Lenin and philosophy (London: New Left Books)

Altman, R (1999) Film/Genre (London: BFI)

Amado, JA García (2003) La Lista de Schindler: abismos que el derecho dificilmente alcanza (Schindler's List; the abyss which law scarcely reaches) (Valencia: Tirant Lo Blanch)

Amado, JA García and Castañón, JM Paredes (2005) Torturas en el cine (Torture in film) (Valencia: Tirant Lo Blanch)

Anolik, R Beinstock (2000) 'Horrors of possession: the gothic struggle with the law' 24 Legal Studies Forum 667

Aoki, K (2006) 'Is Chan still missing? An essay about the film Snow Falling on Cedars (1999) and representations of Asian Americans in US films' in Strickland R, Foster, T and Banks, T (eds) (2006)

Appelo, T (1992) 'Atticus doesn't live here anymore' 8 California Lawyer 174

Ashford, C (2005) 'Law, film and the student experience' 4 Web JCLI
http://webjcli.ncl.ac.uk/2005/issue4/ashford4.html

Asimow, M (1996) 'When lawyers were heroes' 30 University of San Francisco Law Review 1131

—— (2000a) 'Bad lawyers in the movies' 24 Nova Law Review 533

—— (2000b) 'Film commentary' 24 Legal Studies Forum 335

—— (2001) 'Embodiment of evil: law firms in the movies' 48 UCLA Law Review 1339

—— (2002) 'Divorce in the movies: from the hays code to Kramer vs Kramer' 24 Legal Studies Forum 221

—— (2005) 'Popular culture and the American adversarial ideology' in Freeman, M (ed) (2005)

—— (2006) 'Kramer v Kramer (1979): Family Law in the movies' in Strickland R, Foster, T and Banks, T (eds) (2006)

—— (2007) '12 Angry Men: A revisionist view' 82(2) Chicago-Kent Law Review 711

—— (ed) (2008) TV lawyers (Washington: American Bar Association)

Bibliography

Asimow M, Greenfield, S, Guillermo, J, Machura, S, Osborn, G, Robson, P, Sharp, C and Sockloskie, R (2005) 'Perceptions of lawyers: A transanational study of student views on the image of law and lawyers' 12 *International Journal of the Legal Profession* 407

Asimow, M and Mader, S (2004) *Law and Popular Culture: A Course Book* (New York: Lang)

Asner, E (ed) (1994) *The Political Companion to American Film* (Chicago, London: Fitzroy Dearborn)

Babcock, B and Sassoubre, T (2007) 'Deliberation in 12 Angry Men' 82(2) *Chicago-Kent Law Review* 633

Babener, L (1992) Patriarchal Politics in Fatal Attraction, 26 *Journal of Popular Culture* 25 (Winter)

Bander, E (1993) 'The lawyer as devil's advocate', in Gunn, D (ed) (1993)

Bankowski, Z and Mungham, G (1976) *Images of law* (London: RKP)

Banks, T (2006) '*To Kill a Mockingbird* (1962): lawyering in an unjust society' in Strickland, R, Foster, T and Banks, T (eds) (2006)

Barker, M and Brooks, K (1998) 'Dredd' 8 *Sight and Sound* 16

—— (1998) *Knowing audiences: Judge Dredd – its friends, fans and foes* (Luton: University of Luton Press)

Barnouw, E (1974) *Documentary: a history of non-fiction film* (Oxford: OUP)

Barton, B (2006) 'Harry Potter and the half-crazed bureaucracy' 104 *Michigan Law Review* 1523

Batt, J (1990) 'Law, science and narrative: reflections on brain science, electronic media, story and law learning' 40 *Journal of Legal Education* 19

Bell, D (1999) 'The power of narrative' 23 *Legal Studies Forum* 315

Bell, I and Daldry, G (eds) (1990) *Watching the detectives: essays on crime fiction* (London: Macmillan)

Bender, S (2006) 'Savage fronteras and the tribal boundaries: chasing success in Hollywood's *Bordertown*' in Strickland, R, Foster, T and Banks, T (eds) (2006)

Benítez OS (2006) *Las Horas: El Tiempo de las Mujeres* (The Hours: the time of women) (Valencia: Tirant Lo Blanch)

Bennett, R (2006) 'Compulsion (1959): death as different' in Strickland R, Foster, T and Banks, T (eds) (2006)

Benstock, B (ed) (1983) Essays on detective fiction (London: Macmillan)

Bentley, WG (1957) *My son's execution* (London: WH Allen)

Bentley, I and Dening, P (1995) *Let him have justice* (London: Sidgwick and Jackson)

Berenguer, E Orts (2003) *Prostitución y Derecho el el cine* (*Prostitution and the law in Film*) (Valencia: Tirant Lo Blanch)

Berch, M (2006) 'Worst of the worst: which, if any, circle of hell: Dostoevsky's *Crime and Punishment* (1983)' in Strickland R, Foster, T and Banks, T (eds) (2006)

Berets, R (1996a) 'American films depicting domestic violence' 20 *Legal Studies Forum* 175

—— (1996b) 'Changing images of justice in American films' 20 *Legal Studies Forum* 473

—— (1997) 'Legal Reelism: movies as legal texts (Book Review)' 21 *Legal Studies Forum* 399

—— (1998) 'Lawyers in film' 22 *Legal Studies Forum* (Nos 1/2/3), 99

Berger, A (1995) *Cultural Criticism* (London: Sage)

Berger, J and Pratt, C (1998) Teaching Business-Communication Ethics with Controversial Films, 17 *Journal of Business Ethics* 16 1817–23

Bergman, P (1996a) 'Pranks for the memory' 30 *University of San Francisco Law Review* 1235

—— (1996b) 'A bunch of circumstantial evidence' 30 *University of San Francisco Law Review* 985

—— (2001) 'The movie lawyers' guide to redemptive legal practice' 48 *University Of San Francisco Law Review* 1393

Bergman, P (2005) 'Emergency! Send a TV show to rescue paramedic services!' in Freeman M (ed) (2005), *Law and popular culture*

Bergman P and Asimow, M (1996) *Reel justice—the courtroom goes to the movies* (Kansas: Andrews and McMeel)

Berring, R (2006) '*Defending Your Life* (1991): due process in the afterlife' in Strickland, R, Foster, T and Banks, T (eds) (2006)

Berry-Dee, C and Odell, R (1990) *Dad, help me please* (London: WH Allen)

Biber, K (2006) 'Review: Law's Moving Image' 15 *Social and Legal Studies* 607

Birks, P (1995) 'Compulsory subjects: will the seven foundations ever crumble?' 1 *Web Journal of Current Legal Issues*

—— (ed) (1996) *Pressing problems in the law Vol II: what are law schools for?* (Oxford: Oxford University Press)

Black, D (1999) *Law in film: resonance and representation* (Urbana and Chicago: University of Illinois Press)

—— (2005) 'Narrative determination and the figure of the judge' in Freeman M (ed) (2005)

Blinder, M (1984) 'Picking juries: social psychological and behavioral factors to consider' in Warshaw, B (ed) 1984.

Bloom, M (1995) Using Early Silent Film to Teach French: The Language of Cinéma Muet, 1 *ADFL Bulletin 27* (Fall 1995) 25–31

Blum, CP (1996) 'Images of lawyering and political activism in *In the Name of the Father*' 30 *University of San Francisco Law Review* 1065

—— (2005) 'Film, culture and accountability for human rights abuses' in Freeman, M (ed) (2005)

Bohler-Muller, N (2010) 'The Justice of the Heart in Little Brother' *Entertainment and Sports Law Journal* Vol 7 No 2

Bogle, D (1988) *Blacks in American films and television: an Encyclopedia* (New York, London: Garland)

—— (1997) 'Black beginnings: from Uncle Tom's Cabin to The Birth of a Nation' in Smith, V (ed) (1997)

—— (2001) *Toms, coons, mulattoes, mammies, and bucks: an interpretive history of Blacks in American films* (New York: Continuum)

Böhnke, M (2001) 'Myth and law in the films of John Ford' in Machura, S and Robson, P (eds) (2001)

Bolla, A (2000) 'The portrayal of "Admiralty Law" in films' 31 *Journal of Maritime Law and Commerce* 539

Bordwell, D (2006) The Way Hollywood Tells It: Story and Style in Modern Movies (Berkeley Los Angeles: University of California Press)

Borrie, G (1969) Courts-martial, Civilians and Civil Liberties, 32(1) *Modern Law Review* 35–52

Booth, M (1991) 'Fact and fiction in film' 15 *Legal Studies Forum* 233

Bordwell, D (1999) *The way Hollywood tells it: story and style in modern movies* (Berkeley; Los Angeles, California: University of California Press)

Botting, F and Wilson, S (2004) 'Toy law toy joy, Toy Story 2' in Moran, L, Sandon, E, Loizidou, E and Christie I (eds) (2004)

Bounds, D (1995) *Perry Mason, the authorship and reproduction of a popular hero* (Westport, CT; London: Greenwood Press)

Bourne, S (1998) *Black in the British frame* (London: Cassell)

Bradney, A (2003) *Conversations, choices and chances. The liberal law school in the twenty-first century* (Oxford: Hart)

—— (2006) 'The Case of Buffy the Vampire slayer and the politics of legal education' in Greenfield, S and Osborn, G (eds) (2006)

Bray, S (2005) 'Not Proven: Introducing a third verdict' 72 *University of Chicago Law Review* 1299

Britton, P (1998) 'The rainbow flag, European and English law: new developments on sexuality and equality' 8 *Indiana International and Comparative Law Review* 261

Brode, Douglas (1995) *The films of Steven Spielberg* (Kenington: Citadel Press)

Bronson, C (2008) Bronson (London: John Blake Publishing)

Brooks, J (1997) 'Will boys just be boyz n the hood? African-American directors portray a crumbling justice system in urban America' 22 *Oklahoma City University Law Review* 1

Brown, S (2003) *Crime and law in media culture* (Buckingham and Philadelphia: Open University Press)

Browne, R (1993) 'Why lawyers should study popular culture' in Gunn, D (ed) (1993)

Browne, N (ed) (1998) *Refiguring American film genres: history and theory* (Berkeley, Calif and London: University of California Press)

Bukatman, S (1997) *The Blade Runner* (London: British Film Institute)

Burket, R (1999) 'The state law enforcement apparatus as America: authority, arbitrariness and the "Force of Law" in Vineland' 24 *Oklahoma City University Law Review* 727

Burkoff, J (1997) 'If god wanted lawyers to fly, she would have given them wings: life, lust & legal ethics in *Body Heat*' 22 *Oklahoma City University Law Review* 187

Burman, M, Jamieson, L, Nicholson, J and Brooks, O (2007) *Impact of Aspects of the Law of Evidence in Sexual Offence Trials—An Evaluation Study* (Edinburgh: Scottish Executive)

Burns, T (2006) 'The role of securitisation in financing film production in the United Kingdom' 1 *Juridical Review* 69

Burns, R (2007) 'A jury between fact and norm' 82(2) *Chicago-Kent Law Review* 643

Burr, S (2006) 'Screening justice in *The Accused* (1988)' in Strickland, R, Foster, T and Banks, T (eds) (2006)

Cameron, I (1992) *The movie book of film noir* (London: Studio Vista)

Caplow, S (1999) 'Still in the dark: disappointing images of women lawyers in the movies' 20 *Women's Rights Law Reporter* 55

—— (2006) '*Reversal of fortune* (1990) affirmation of ambiguity' in Strickland, R, Foster, T and Banks, T (eds) (2006)

Carlen, P (1976) *Magistrates' justice* (London: Martin Robertson)

Carriere, J (2006) 'Cold comfort: law and community in Ethan and Joel Coen's *Fargo* (1996)' in Strickland, R, Foster, T and Banks, T (eds) (2006)

Cartmell, D, Hunter IQ, Kaye, H And Whelehan, I (eds) (1996) *Pulping Fictions* (London: Pluto Press)

Carter, R (1974) *The 16th Round: from No 1 contender to No 45472* (New York: Viking)

Castillo, M del Mar Ruiz and Gutiérrez, J Escribano (2007) *La Huelga y el Cine: Escenas del Conflicto Social* (*The cinema and strikes: scenes of social conflict*) (Valencia: Tirant lo Blanch)

Caughie, J (ed) (1981) *Theories of authorship* (London: Routledge and Kegan)

Cawelti, J (1992) 'Chinatown and the generic transformation in American films, in Mast G *et al* (1992)

Chaiton, S and Swinton, T (1999) *Lazarus and the Hurricane: the freeing of Rubin 'Herricane' Carter* (New York: St Martin's Griffin)

Champoux, J (1999) Film as a Teaching Resource, 8(2) *Journal of Management Inquiry* 240–51

Chandler, R (1950) *The simple art of murder* (reprinted in *P Pearls are a Nuisance (Stories from 'The Simple Art of Murder')* (London: Hamish Hamilton)

—— (1953) *The long goodbye* (Harmondsworth: Penguin)

Chase, A (1986a) 'Lawyers and popular culture: a review of mass media portrayals of American attorneys' 11 *American Bar Foundation Research Journal* 281

—— (1986b) 'Towards a legal theory of popular culture' *Wisconsin Law Review* 527

—— (1997) 'Subterranean government, underground film' 22 *Oklahoma City University Law Review* 167

Chase, A (1997) 'Review essay on Bergman and Asimow's Reel Justice and Past Imperfect: history according to the movies' 9 *Cardozo Studies in Law and Literature* 107

—— (1999) 'Civil action cinema' *Law Review of Michigan State University—Detroit College of Law* 945

—— (2000) 'International law on film' 24 *Legal Studies Forum* 559

—— (2002) *Movies on trial: the legal system on the silver screen* (New York: The New Press)

Cheung, A (2005) 'What law cannot give: from the Queen to the Chief Executive' in Freeman M (ed) (2005)

Christie, A (1954) *Witness for the Prosecution* (London: Samuel French)

Christie, I (2004) 'Heavenly justice' in Moran, L, Sandon, E, Loizidou, E and Christie I (eds) (2004)

Clark, C (2005) *Shuffling to Ignominy.* New York: iUniverse

Clark, G (1994) 'The lawyer as hero?' in Gunn, D (ed) (1993)

Clover, C (1998a) 'Movie juries' 48 *DePaul Law Review* 388

—— (1998b) 'Law and the order of popular culture' in Sarat, A and Kearns, T (eds) (1998)

Clover, C (1998c) 'God bless juries!' in Browne, N (ed) (1998)

—— (2000) 'Judging audiences: the case of the trial movie' in Gledhill, C and Williams, L (eds) (2000)

Coffman, CS (1998) 'Gingerbread women: stereotypical female attorneys in the novels of John Grisham' 8 *Southern California Review of Law and Women's Studies* 73

Colomer, JL Gómez (2005) *El perfil del jurado en el cine (The profile of the jury in film)* (Valencia: Tirant Lo Blanch)

Comer, DR (2001) 'Not just a Mickey Mouse exercise: using Disney's *the Lion King* to teach leadership' 25(4) *Journal of Management Education* 430

Cook, P (ed) (1985) *The cinema book* (London: BFI)

—— (1993) '"Cape Fear" and feminity as destructive power' in Cook, P and Dodd, P (eds) (1993)

—— (2005) *Screening the past: memory and nostalgia in cinema* (London: Routledge)

Cook, P and Dodd, P (eds) (1993) *Women and film: A Sight and Sound reader* (Philadelphia: Temple UP)

Cooke, L (1996) 'British cinema: representing the nation' in Nelmes, J (ed) (1996a)

Cooke, P and Oughton, D (1998) *The Common Law of Obligations* (London: Butterworths)

Corcos, C (1997) 'Presuming innocence: Alan Pakula and Scott Turow take on the great American legal fiction' 22 *Oklahoma City University Law Review* 129

—— (1998) 'Women Lawyers' in Jarvis, R and Joseph, P (eds) (1998)

—— (2000) 'Sea-TV: admiralty law on television' 31 *Journal of Maritime Law and Commerce* 545

—— (2001) '"I am not a number! I am a free man!": Physical and Psychological Imprisonment in Science Fiction' 25 *Legal Studies Forum* 471

—— (2003a) 'Legal fictions: irony, storytelling, truth and justice in the modern courtroom drama' 25 *University of Arkansas at Little Rock Law Review* 503

—— (2003b) 'Prosecutors, prejudices, and justice: observations on presuming innocence in popular culture and law' 34 *University of Toledo Law Review* 793

Corner, J (ed) (1986) *Documentary and the mass media* (London: Edward Arnold)

Corrington, J (2002) 'Logos, lex and law' 26 *Legal Studies Forum* 709

Cotterrell, R (1992) *Sociology of law* 2nd edn (London: Butterworths)

Coughlin, C (1998) 'Law at the OK Corral: reading Wyatt Earp films' 22 *Legal Studies Forum* 133

Coyne, R (1997) 'Images of lawyers and the three stooges' 22 *Oklahoma City University Law Review* 247

—— (2006) 'Disorder in the court' in Strickland R, Foster, T and Banks, T (eds) (2006)

Craddock, J (2009) *VideoHound's Golden Movie Retriever* (Gale Cengage Learning: Detroit)

Crespino, J (2000) 'The Strange Career of Atticus Finch', 6(2) *Southern Cultures* 9

Cripps, T (1977) *Slow fade to black* (Oxford: OUP)

—— (1978) *Black film as genre* (Bloomington and London: Indiana University Press)

—— (1987) *Making movies black* (Oxford: OUP)

Crowdus, G (1994) Foreword by Asner, E, *The political companion to American film* (Chicago; London: Fitzroy Dearborn)

Crowther, B (1984) *Hollywood faction: reality and myth in the movies* (London: Columbus)

—— (1988) *Film noir* (London: Columbus)

—— (1989) *Captured on film: the prison movie* (London: Batsford)

—— (1990) *Film noir* (London: Virgin)

Cunningham, F (1991) *Sidney Lumet: film and literary vision* (Kentucky: University Press of Kentucky)

Curtis, L (1984) *Ireland: the Propaganda War* (London: Pluto Press)

Darbyshire, P (1991) 'The lamp that shows that freedom lives—is it worth the candle?' Oct *Criminal Law Review* 740

De Lucas, J (2003) *Blade Runner: El Derecho, guardián de la diferencia (The law, protector of difference)* (Valencia: Tirant Lo Blanch)

Delage, C (2005) 'Image as evidence and mediation: The Experience of the Nuremberg Trials' in Freeman M (ed) (2005)

Delgado, R (1995) *Critical race theory: the cutting edge* (Temple University Press)

Denton, K (1981) *The Breaker: The Novel Behind Breaker Morant* (New York: St Martin's Press)

Denvir, J (1991) 'Frank Capra's First Amendment' 15 *Legal Studies Forum* 255

—— (ed) (1996a) *Legal reelism: movies as legal texts* (Urbana: University of Illinois Press)

—— (1996b) 'Capra's Constitution' in Denvir, J (ed) (1996a)

—— (1996c) 'Introduction: one movie no lawyer should miss' 30 *University of San Francisco Law Review* 1051

—— (2000) 'Law, lawyers, film and television' 24 *Legal Studies Forum* 343

—— (2004) 'The slotting function: how movies influence political decisions' 28 *Vermont Law Review* 799

—— (2005) 'What Movies Can Teach Law Students' in Freeman M (ed) (2005)

Devlin, PA (1956) *Trial by Jury* (London: Stevens & Sons Ltd)

Dimmock WC (2005) 'Science Fiction as a World Tribunal' in Freeman M (ed) (2005)

Disalvo, C (1997) 'Ghandi: The Spirituality and Politics of Suffering' 22 *Oklahoma City University Law Review* 51

—— (2006) '*Gandhi* (1982): The Spirituality of Politics and Suffering' in Strickland, R, Foster, T and Banks, T (eds) (2006))

Douglas, L (2004) 'Trial as documentary: images of Eichmann' in Moran, L, Sandon, E, Loizidou, E and Christie I (eds) (2004)

Douzinas, C and Nead, L (eds) (1999) *Law and the image: the authority of art and the aesthetics of law* (Chicago: Chicago University Press)

Dow, D (2000) 'Fictional documentaries and truthful fictions: the death penalty in recent American film' 17 *Constitutional Commentary* 511

Drexler, P (2001) 'The German Courtroom Film During the Nazi Period: Ideology, Aesthetics, Historical Context' in Machura S and Robson P (eds) (2001)

Dunlop, C (1991) 'Literature Studies in Law Schools' 3 *Cardozo Studies in Law and Literature* 63

Dyer, R (1993) *The Matter of Images* (London: Routledge)

—— (2002) *The culture of queers* (London: Routledge)

—— (ed) (1977) *Gays and film* (London: British Film Institute)

Edwards, M and Handley, J (2006) *Captured!: Inside the World of Celebrity Trials* (Santa Monica: Santa Monica Press)

Elkins, J (2002) 'A great gift: on reading John William Corrington' 26 *Legal Studies Forum* 425

—— (2004) 'Reading/teaching lawyer *films*' 28 *Vermont Law Review* 813

Epstein, M (1994) 'The evolving lawyer image on television' 27 *Television Quarterly* 18

—— (2001) 'Judging Judy, Mablean and Mills: how courtroom programs use law to parade private lives to mass audiences' 8 *UCLA Entertainment Law Review* 129

—— (2003a) 'For and against the people: television's prosecutor image and the cultural power of the legal profession' 34 *Toledo Law Review* 817

—— (2003b) 'From Willy to Perry Mason: the hegemony of the lawyer statesman in 1950's television' 53 *Syracuse Law Review* 1201

—— (2004a) 'Law and the supernatural: how one film's truth compulsion conceit critiques and redeems the post-OJ lawyer' 28 *Vermont Law Review* 881

—— (2004b) 'Symposium: law in film/film in law: introduction' 28 *Vermont Law Review* 797

Eskridge, WN Jr (1997) 'Privacy jurisprudence and the apartheid of the closet 1946–1961' 24 *Florida State University Law Review* 703

Esquibel, A (2000) 'Be led not into temptation: ethics lessons from *The Rainmaker*' 26 *University of Memphis Law Review* 1325

Everson, WK (1972) *The detective in film* (Citadel Press)

Faletti, H (1982) 'The workings of law in Kafka's *Der Prozess* and Böll's *Die Verlorene der Katharina Blum*' 6 *ALSA Forum* 149

Faludi, S (1992) *Backlash: the undeclared war against women* (London: Vintage)

Fedirka, S (1999) 'Crossing boundaries: social borders and alternative realities in *The Crying of Lot 49*' 24 *Oklahoma City University Law Review* 609

Bibliography

Felix, R (2000) 'The ox-bow incident' 24 *Legal Studies Forum* 645

—— (2006) 'The ox-bow incident (1943) justice denied' in Strickland, R, Foster, T and Banks, T (eds) (2006)

Ferguson, R (1998) *Representing 'race': ideology, identity, and the media* (London: Arnold)

Fineman, M and McCluskey, M (eds) (1997) *Feminism, Media and the Law* (New York; Oxford: Oxford University Press)

Fiske, J (1996) 'Admissible postmodernity: some remarks on Rodney King, O Simpson, and contemporary culture' 30 *University of San Francisco Law Review* 917

Fiske, J and Glynn, K (1995) 'Trials of the postmodern' 9 *Cultural Studies* 505

Fitzpatrick, P (ed) (1991) *Dangerous supplements: resistance and renewal in jurisprudence* (London: Pluto)

Fludemik, M and Olson, G (eds) (2004) *In the grip of the law: trials, prisons, and the space between* (Frankfurt am Main; New York: P Lang)

Foster, T (1997) '*I want to live!* Federal judicial values in death penalty cases: preservation of rights or punctuality of execution?' 22 *Oklahoma City University Law Review* 63

Foucault, M (1975) *Discipline and punish* (London: Penguin)

Fredman, S (1997) *Women and the law* (Oxford: OUP)

Freedman, M (1992) 'Atticus Finch, *Esq, RIP*' 40 *Legal Times* 20

—— (1994) 'Atticus Finch—right and wrong' 45 *Alabama Law Review* 473

—— (2005) *Introduction* in Freeman M (ed) (2005)

—— (ed) (2005) *Law and popular culture* (Oxford: Oxford University Press)

Friedman, JM (1993) *America's first woman lawyer. The biography of Myra Bradwell* (New York: Prometheus Books)

Friedman, L (1985) *Total Justice* (New York: Russell Sage Foundation)

—— (1989) 'Law, lawyers and popular culture' 98 *Yale Law Journal* 1579

Friedman, LM and Rosen-Zvi, I (2001) 'Illegal Fictions: mystery novels and the popular image of crime' 48 *University of California at Los Angeles Law Review* 1411

Frolik, L (2006) '*The Grapes of Wrath* (1946): can justice be found on route 66' in Strickland, R, Foster, T and Banks, T (eds) (2006)

Fukurai, H (1999) 'Social deconstruction of race and affirmative action in jury selection' 11 *La Raza Law Journal* 17

Galanter, M (1998) 'The faces of mistrust: the image of lawyers in public opinion, jokes, and political discourse' 66 *University of Cincinnati Law Review* 805

Gallagher, T (1986) *John Ford: the man and his films* (Berkeley and London: University of California Press)

Garapon, A (1995) 'French legal culture' 4 *Social and Legal Studies* 492

Garfinkel, H (1956) 'Conditions of successful degradation ceremonies' *American Journal of Sociology* 61, 420

Gertner, N (2007) 'Angry men (and women) in federal court' 82(2) *Chicago-Kent Law Review* 613

Gest, JM (1913) *The Lawyer in Literature* (London: Sweet and Maxwell)

Getches, D (2006) 'A wealth of water law, not a drop of justice: *The Milagro Beanfield War* (1988) and *Chinatown* (1974)' in Strickland, R, Foster, T and Banks, T (eds) (2006)

Ghosh, S (2003) 'Gandhi and the life of the law' 53 *Syracuse Law Review* 1273

Gilbert, WS (1991) *Spiked* (Gay Men's Press)

Gillers, S (1989) 'Taking LA law more seriously' 98 *Yale Law Journal* 1607

Glass, DM (1990) 'Portia in primetime: women lawyers, television and LA law' 2 *Yale Journal of Law and Feminism* 271

Gledhill, C and Williams, L (eds) (2000) *Reinventing film studies* (London: Arnold)

Goldman, W (1983) *Adventures in the screen trade: a personal view of Hollywood and screen-writing* (Boston: Warner Books)

Goodrich, P (1990) *Languages of law: from logics of memory to nomadic masks* (London: Weidenfeld and Nicolson)

—— (1996) 'Of Blackstone's Tower: Metaphors of distance and Histories of the English Law School' in Birks (1996)

—— (1999) 'Law in the courts of love of the law: intimate observations on an insular jurisdiction' 10(3) *Law and Critique* 343

—— (1996) *Law in the courts of love: literature and other minor jurisprudences* (London: Routledge)

Graham, L and Maschio, G (1995–6) 'A false public sentiment: narrative and visual images of women lawyers in film' 84 *Kentucky Law Journal* 1027

Grant, J (1996a) 'Morality and liberal legal culture: Woody Allen's *Crimes and misdemeanours*' in Denvir, J (ed) (1996a)

—— (1996b) 'Lawyers as superheroes: The Firm, The Client and The Pelican Brief', 30 *University of San Francisco Law Review* 1111

Grantham, B (2004) 'Cultural 'patronage' versus cultural 'defence': alternatives to national film policies' in Moran, L, Sandon, E, Loizidou, E and Christie I (eds) (2004)

Greenfield, S (2001) 'Hero or villain: cinematic lawyers and the delivery of justice' in Machura, S and Robson, P (eds) (2001)

Greenfield, S and Osborn, G (1993) 'Lawyers in film: where myth meets reality' 143 *New Law Journal* 1791

—— (1995a) 'The living law: popular film as legal text' 29 *The Law Teacher* 33

—— (1995b) 'Where cultures collide: the characterisation of law and lawyers in film' 23 *International Journal of the Sociology of Law* 107

—— (1995c) 'The empowerment of students: the case for popular film in legal studies' 10(2) *American Bar Association Focus on Law Studies* Special Issue

—— (1996) 'Pulped Fiction? Cinematic parables of (in)justice' 30 *University of San Francisco Law Review* 1181

—— (1999) 'Film, law and the delivery of justice: the case of Judge Dredd and the disappearing courtroom' 6 *Journal of Criminal Justice & Popular Culture* 35

—— (2005) 'The double meaning of law: does it matter if film lawyers are unethical' in Freeman M (ed) (2005)

—— (eds) (2006) *Readings in law and popular culture* (London: Routledge)

Greenfield, S, Osborn, G and Robson, P (2001) *Film and the Law* (London: Cavendish)

—— (2007) 'Genre, iconography and British legal film' 36 *Baltimore Law Review* 371

Grieveson, L (2004) 'Not harmless entertainment: state censorship and cinema in the transitional era' in Moran, L, Sandon, E, Loizidou, E and Christie, I (eds) (2004)

Guery, C (2007) *Justices à l'écran (Justice on the screen* (Paris: Institut des Hautes Etudes sur la Justice)

Gunn, D (ed) (1993) *The lawyer and popular culture: proceedings of a conference* (Littleton, CO: Fred B Rothman)

Gutoff, J (2000) 'The law of piracy in popular culture' 31 *Journal of Maritime Law and Commerce* 643

Haddad, T (2000) 'Silver tongues on the silver screen: legal ethics in the movies' 24 *Nova Law Review* 673

Hadden, S (2002) 'New directions in the study of legal cultures' 33 *Cambrian Law Review* 1

Haldar, P (1994) 'In and out of court: On topographies of law and the architecture of court buildings' 7(2) *International Journal for the Semiotics of Law* 185

—— (1999) 'The function of the ornament in Quintillian, Alberti and court architecture' in Douzinas, C and Nead, L (eds) (1999)

Halliwell, L (2008) *Halliwell's Film Video and DVD Guide* 2008 (London: Harper Collins)

Haltom, W (1998) 'Laws of god, laws of man: power, authority, and influence in *Cool Hand Luke*' 22 *Legal Studies Forum* 233

Hambley, G (1992) 'The image of the jury in popular culture' 12 *Legal Reference Services Quarterly* 171

Hamer, D and Budge, B (eds) (1994) *The Good, the Bad and the Gorgeous: Popular Culture's Romance with the Lesbian* (London: Pandora)

Hans, V (2007) 'Deliberation and dissent: 12 Angry Men versus the empirical reality of juries' 82(2) *Chicago-Kent Law Review* 579

Harding, R (1996) 'Celluloid death: cinematic deceptions of capital punishment' 30 *University of San Francisco Law Review* 1167

—— (2005) 'Reel violence: popular culture and concerns about capital punishment in contemporary American society' in Freeman M (ed) (2005)

Harr, J (1999) *A Civil Action* (New York: Arron)

Harris, T (1987) *Courtroom's finest hour in American cinema* (New York and London: The Scarecrow Press, Inc Metuchen)

Harrison, J (2006) 'Law and rage in *Do the Right Thing* (1989)' in Strickland, R, Foster, T and Banks, T (eds) (2006)

Harrison, J and Wilson, S (2000) 'Advocacy in literature: storytelling, judicial opinions, and *The Rainmaker*' 26 *University of Memphis Law Review* 1285

—— (2006) 'Harry Potter and the law' 12 *Texas Wesleyan Law Review* 427

Haskell, M (1987) *From reverence to rape* (Chicago: University of Chicago Press)

Hauserman N, (1995) 'Learning can be fun: high tech meets undergrad law' ABA, Focus on Law Studies

Hay, B (2007) 'Charades: religious allegory in 12 Angry Men' 82(2) *Chicago-Kent Law Review* 911

Hegland, K (2003) 'If Stephen King discovers Cujo, can judges discover law?' 27 *Legal Studies Forum* 97

Herman, D (2005) 'Juliet and Juliet would be more my cup of tea' in Freeman M (ed) (2005) *Law and popular culture*

Herman, S (2006) '*Philadelphia* (1993): law in the city of brotherly love' in Strickland, R, Foster, T and Banks, T (eds) (2006)

Herz, R (2007) 'Portrayal of justice on German television' in Masson, A and O'Connor, K (eds) (2007)

Hickman, G (2001) 'The writing and filming of *The Penalty Phase*' 48 *University of California at Los Angeles Law Review* 1583

Hill, J (1999) *British cinema in the 1980s: issues and themes* (Oxford: Oxford University Press)

Hirsch, F (1981) *The Dark Side of the Screen* (New York: Da Capo)

Hirsch, JS (2000) *Hurricane: the life of Rubin Carter, fighter* (London: Fourth Estate)

Hodge, H and Hodge, J (1984) *Famous Trials* (London: BCA/Penguin)

Hoff, T (2000) 'Anatomy of a murder' 24 *Legal Studies Forum* 661

Hoffman, M (2007) 'The myth of factual innocence' 82(2) *Chicago-Kent Law Review* 663

Hoggart, R (1958) The uses of literacy: aspects of working-class life with special reference to publications and entertainments (Harmondsworth, Middlesex: Penguin Books, in association with Chatto and Windus)

Horkheimer, M (1972) *Critical theory: selected essays* (New York: Herder & Herder)

—— (1974) *Critique of instrumental reason; lectures and essays since the end of World War II* (New York: Seabury Press)

Horkheimer, M (1993) *Between philosophy and social science: selected early writings* (Cambridge, MA; London: MIT Press)

Holt, W (2006) 'Can labor law produce justice?: *Matewan* (1987), *Norma Rae* (1979), and *Shout Youngstown* (1984)' in Strickland, R, Foster, T and Banks, T (eds) (2006)

Hudock, A and Gallagher Warden, S (2001) 'Using Movies to Teach Family Systems Concepts' 9(2) *The Family Journal* 116–121

Hunt, A (1987) 'Jurisprudence, philosophy and legal education—against foundationalism' *Legal Studies* 92

Hunter, IQ (1996) 'Capitalism most triumphant Bill and Ted's Excellent History Lesson' in Cartmell, D, Hunter, IQ, Kaye, H and Whelehan, I (eds) (1996)

Hyde, HM (1954) *The Trial of Craig and Bentley (Notable British Trials series)* (Glasgow: William Hodge and Co)

Insdorf, A (1983) *Indelible shadows: film and the holocaust* (New York: Vintage Books)

Isralowitz, J (2000) 'Lonely hearts and murderers: the fourth amendment through Hitchcock's lens' 24 *Legal Studies Forum* 99

Jackson, C (2000) 'Film & TV drama commentary' 24 *Legal Studies Forum* 321

Jarvis, R (1998) 'Legal tales from Gilligan's Island', 39 *Santa Clara Law Review* 185

—— (1998) 'Situation comedies' in Jarvis, R and Joseph, P (1998)

Jarvis, R and Joseph, P (eds) (1998) *Prime time law: fictional television as legal narrative* (Durham, NC: Carolina Academic Press)

Jay, M (1993) *Downcast eyes. The denigration of vision in twentieth century thought* (Berkeley, CA: University of California Press)

—— (1999) 'Must Justice be blind? The challenge of images to the law' in Douzinas, C and Nead, L (eds) (1999)

Jenkins, S (1994) 'Stories that get in the way of the facts' *The Times* and *The Sunday Times* compact disc edition

Jerome, VJ (1950) *The negro in Hollywood films* (New York: Masses & Mainstream)

Jerry II, R (2000) 'Health insurance coverage for high-cost health care: reflections on *The Rainmaker*' 26 *University of Memphis Law Review* 1347

Jimeno-Bulnes, M (2007) 'A different story line for 12 Angry Men: verdicts reached by majority rule—the Spanish perspective' 82(2) *Chicago-Kent Law Review* 759

Johnson, R and Buchanan, R (2001) 'The insider's story out: what popular film can tell us about legal method's dirty secrets' 20 *Windsor Yearbook of Access to Justice* 87

Johnson, R and Buchanan, R (2007) 'Strange Encounters: Exploring Law and Film in the Affective Register' in Sarat, A (ed) (2007)

Johnson, SL (1985) 'Black Innocence and the White Jury' 83 *Michigan Law Review* 1611

Johnson, V (1987) 'Audiovisual enhancement of classroom teaching: a primer for law professors' 37 *Journal of Legal Education* 97

Johnson-McGrath, J (1998) 'Witness for the prosecution: science versus crime in twentieth century America' 22 *Legal Studies Forum* 183

Jones, JP (2000) 'Into the wind: Rhett Butler and the law of war at sea' 31 *Journal of Maritime Law and Commerce* 633

Bibliography

Joseph, P (1998) *'Science Fiction' in Prime Time Law: Fictional Television as Legal Narrative* (Durham, NC: Carolina Academic Press)

—— (2000a) 'Introduction: law and popular culture' 24 *Nova Law Review* 527

—— (2000b) *'Pleasantville*: an essay on law, power, and transcendence in our cultural mythological past' 24 *Nova Law Review* 619

—— (2003) 'Saying goodbye to Ally McBeal' 25 *University of Arkansas at Little Rock Law Review* 459

Joseph, P and Carton, S (1992) 'The law of the federation: images of law, lawyers and the legal system in Star Trek: the next generation' 24 *University of Toledo Law Review* 43

Kahn, P (1999) *The cultural study of law: reconstructing legal scholarship* (Chicago: University of Chicago)

Kairys, D (1990) *The Politics of law: a progressive critique* (New York: Pantheon Books)

Kamir, O (2000a) 'Feminist law and film: searching for imagery of justice in popular culture' 75 *Chicago-Kent Law Review* 899

—— (2000b) 'X-raying Adam's rib: multiple readings of a (feminist?) law-film' 22 *Studies in Law, Politics and Society* 103

—— (2000c) 'Judgment by film, socio-legal functions of Rashomon' 12 *Yale Journal of Law and the Humanities* 39

—— (2005a) 'Anatomy of Hollywood's hero-lawyer: a law-and-film study of the western motifs, honor-based values and gender politics underlying *Anatomy of a Murder*'s construction of the lawyer image' 35 *Studies in Law, Politics, and Society* 67

Kamir, O (2005b) 'Why law-and-film and what does it actually mean? A perspective' 19 *Continuum: Journal of Media and Cultural Studies* 255

—— (2005c) 'Cinematic judgment and jurisprudence: a woman's memory, recovery, and justice in a post-traumatic society (a study of Polanski's *Death and the Maiden*)' in Sarat, A, Douglas, L and Umphrey, M (eds) (2005)

—— (2006) *Framed: women in law and film* (Durham, NC: Duke University Press)

Kaplan, EA (1983) *Women and film: both sides of the camera* (London: Methuen)

—— (1980) *Women in film noir* (London: BFI)

Kaplan, L (2006) 'Welles and Jones: Kafka's *The Trial* (1962 and 1993) and its legal significance' in Strickland, R, Foster, T and Banks T (eds) (2006)

Kavanagh, D (1980) *Duffy* (London: Cape)

Kaye, J (2007) 'Why every chief judge should see 12 Angry Men' 82(2) *Chicago-Kent Law Review* 627

Kempf, DGJ (2001) 'Reel courtroom dramas' 27 *Litigation* 25

Kennedy, E (1994) 'The gorgeous lesbian in LA law: the present absence?' in Hamer, D and Budge, B (eds) (1994)

Kennedy, H (1992) *Eve was framed: women and British justice* (London: Random House)

Kesrshen, D (1997) 'Breaker Morant' 22 *Oklahoma City University Law Review* 107

Kidwell, J (2001) *'The dock brief'* 25 *Legal Studies Forum* 287

King, D (ed) (1999) *Legal education for the 21st century* (Littleton: Fred B Rothman)

Kluge, AA, Retrospective (The Goethe Institutes of North America, 1988), quoted in Minh-ha (1995), 268

Korzek, R (2007) 'Viewing *North Country*: sexual harassment goes to the movies' 36 *University of Baltimore Law Review* 303

Krutnick, F (1991) *In a Lonely Street: film noir, genre, masculinity* (London; New York: Routledge)

Bibliography

Kuhn, A (1982) *Women's pictures: feminism and cinema* (London: Routledge Kegan Paul)

Kuzina, M (2000) *Der amerikanische Gerichtsfilm: Justiz, Ideologie, Dramatik* (*The American law film: justice, ideology, drama*) (Göttingen: Vandenhoeck und Ruprecht)

—— (2001) 'The social issue courtroom drama as an expression of American popular culture' in Machura, S and Robson, P (eds) (2001)

—— (2005) 'Military justice in American film and television drama: starting points for ideological criticism' in Freeman, M (ed) (2005)

Larner, D (1998) 'Justice and drama: historical ties and "thick" relationships' 22 *Legal Studies Forum* 3

—— (1999a) 'Justice and drama: conflict & imagery' 23 *Legal Studies Forum* 417

—— (1999b) 'Teaching justice: the idea of justice in the structure of drama' 23 *Legal Studies Forum* 201

Landsman, S (2007) 'Mad about 12 Angry Men' 82(2) *Chicago-Kent Law Review* 749

Langford, D and Robson, P (2003) 'The representation of the professions in the cinema: the case of construction engineers and lawyers' 21 *Construction Management & Economics* 799

Laster, K with Breckweg, K and King, J (2000) *The drama of the courtroom* (Leichhardt, NSW: Federation Press)

Laurence, R (1989) 'Last night while you prepared for class I went to see light of day: a film review and a message to my first year property students' 39 *Journal of Legal Education* 87

Lebel, P (2006) 'Giving voice to anger: the role of the lawyer in *The Sweet Hereafter* (1997)' in Strickland, R, Foster, T and Banks, T (eds) (2006)

Ledwon, L (2006) '*Zoot Suit* (1981): realism, romance and the anti-musical—film as social' in Strickland, R, Foster, T and Banks, T (eds) (2006)

Lenz, T (2003) *Changing images of law in film & television crime stories* (New York: Peter Lang)

Leonard, D (1988) 'From Perry Mason to Kurt Waldheim: the pursuit of justice in contemporary film and television' 12 *Legal Studies Forum* 377

Lesnick, H (1990) 'Infinity in a grain of sand: the world of law and lawyering as portrayed in the clinical teaching implicit in the law school curriculum' 38 *University of California at Los Angeles Law Review* 1157

Levi, RD (2005) *The celluloid courtroom: a history of legal cinema* (Westport, CT; London: Praeger)

Linder, D (2000) 'Salvaging Amistad' 31 *Journal of Maritime Law and Commerce* 559

Linera, MA Presno and Rivaya, B (eds) (2006) *Una introducción cinematográfica al derecho* (*A Cinematic introduction to law*) (Valencia: Tirant Lo Blanch)

Logan, A (1994) 'In the Name of the Father' 144(6637) *New Law Journal* 294

Loizidou, E (2004) 'Rebel without a cause' in Moran, L, Sandon, E, Loizidou, E and Christie I (eds) (2004)

Lott, T (1997) 'A no-theory theory of contemporary black cinema' in Smith, V (ed) (1997)

Lubet, S (1999) 'Reconstructing Atticus Finch' 97 *Michigan Law Review* 1339

—— (2000) 'The man who shot Liberty Valance: truth or justice in the old west' 48 *University of Southern California Law Review* 353

Lubet, S (2001a) 'The forgotten trial of Wyatt Earp' 72 *University of Colorado Law Review* 1

—— (2001b) 'Slap leather! Legal culture, Wild Bill Hickock, and the Gunslinger myth' 48 *University of California at Los Angeles Law Review* 1545

—— (2004) 'Murder in tombstone: the forgotten trial of Wyatt Earp' (New Haven: Yale University Press)

Lucia, C (1992) 'Women on trial: the female lawyer in the Hollywood courtroom' 19 *Cineaste* 32

—— (1997) 'Women on trial: the female lawyer in the Hollywood courtroom' in Fineman, M and McCluskey, M (eds) (1997)

—— (2005) *Framing female lawyers: women on trial in film* (Austin: University of Texas Press)

Luhr, W (1990) *Raymond Chandler and film* (Tallahassee: Florida State University Press)

Lull, J and Hinerman, S (eds) (1997) *Media scandals: morality and desire in the popular culture marketplace* (Oxford: Polity)

Lurvey, I and Eiseman, S (1996) 'Divorce goes to the movies' 30 *University of San Francisco Law Review* 1209

Macaulay, S (1987) 'Images of law in everyday life: the lessons of school, entertainment and spectator sports' 21 *Law and Society Review* 185

McAdams, T (2000) 'Blame and *The Sweet Hereafter*' 24 *Legal Studies Forum* 599

McCann, M and Haltom, W (2008) 'Nothing to Believe In—Lawyers in Contemporary Films About Public Interest Litigation' 230 in Sarat, A and Scheingold, S (2008)

McCarron, B (1999) '*Catch 22, Gravity's Rainbow* and lawlessness' 24 *Oklahoma City University Law Review* 665

McColgan, A (1999) *Women under the law: the false promise of human rights* (Harlow: Longman)

MacDonald, A (2004) 'Endless streets, pursued by ghosts' in Moran, L, Sandon, E, Loizidou, E and Christie I (eds) (2004)

McDowell, James (2000) 'From "Perry Mason" to *Primary Colors*: using fiction to understand legal and political systems' 24 *Legal Studies Forum* 73

McFarlane, B (2001) 'The more things change ... British cinema in the 90s' in Murphy, R (ed) (2nd edn)

McKenna, A (1991) 'The law's delay: cinema and sacrifice' 15 *Legal Studies Forum* 199

McKenna, J (1981) 'The judge as dramatist' 5 *ALSA Forum* 40

McNamee, E (2004) 'Once more unto the breach: Branagh's Henry V, Blair's war and the UK Constitution' in Moran, L, Sandon, E, Loizidou, E and Christie I (eds) (2004)

MacNeil, W (2004) '"It's the vibe!": the common law imaginary Down Under' in Moran, L, Sandon, E, Loizidou, E and Christie I (eds) (2004)

Machura, S (2005) 'Procedural unfairness in real and film trials: why do audiences understand stories placed in foreign legal systems?' Freeman M (ed) (2005)

Machura, S (2007a) 'A scheme for analysis of legal film' 36 *University of Baltimore Law Review*

—— (2007b) 'The German response to 12 Angry Men' 82(2) *Chicago-Kent Law Review* 777

Machura, S and Robson P (eds) (2001) *Law and Film* (Oxford: Blackwell)

Machura, S and Ulbrich, S (1998) *Recht im Film (Law in Film)* (Baden-Baden: Nomos Verlagsgesellschaft)

—— (2001) 'Law in film: globalising the Hollywood courtroom' in Machura, S and Robson, P (eds) (2001)

Maine, HS (1861) *Ancient law: its connection with the early history of society, and its relation to modern ideas* (London: John Murray)

Malloy, R (2003) 'Symposium on the image of lawyers in popular culture: an introduction' 53 *Syracuse Law Review* 1161

Mansfield, M (1994) 'Jurassic justice' *7 Sight and Sound* 3

Marder, N (1997) 'Deliberations and Disclosures: a study of post-verdict interviews of jurors' 82 *Iowa Law Review* 465

—— (2006) 'Why *12 Angry Men*? (1957): the transformative power of jury deliberations' in Strickland, R, Foster, T and Banks, T (eds) (2006)

—— (2007a) 'Introduction to the 50th anniversary of 12 Angry Men' 82(2) *Chicago-Kent Law Review* 557

—— (2007b) 'The banality of evil: a portrayal in 12 Angry Men' 82(2) *Chicago-Kent Law Review* 887

Marek, J (1999) '"The Practice" and "Ally McBeal": a new image for women lawyers on television' 22 *Journal of American Culture Spring* 77

Martinez, R de Vicente (2003) *El Color de la Justicia (Tres Colores: rojo) (The colour of justice (Three Colours: red))* (Valencia: Tirant Lo Blanch)

Masson, A and O'Connor, K (eds) (2007) *Representations of Justice* (New York and London: PIE Peter Leng)

Mast, G *et al* (1992) Film theory and Criticism (Oxford: Oxford University Press)

Mastrangelo, P (1983) 'Lawyers and the law: a filmography' 3 *Legal Reference Services Quarterly* 31

—— (1983) 'Lawyers and the law: a filmography' 3(4) *Legal Reference Services Quarterly* 31

—— (1985–86) 'Lawyers and the law: a filmography II' 3 *Legal Reference Services Quarterly* 5

Melvin, D and Melvin, A (1980) Crime, detective, espionage, mystery, and thriller fiction and film (Westport: Greenwood Press)

Menkel-Meadow, C (1999) 'The sense and sensibilities of lawyers: lawyering in literature, narratives, film and television, and ethical choices regarding career and craft' 31 *McGeorge Law Review* 1

—— (2000) 'Telling stories in school: using case studies and stories to teach legal ethics' 69 *Fordham Law Review* 787

—— (2001) 'Can they do that? Legal ethics in popular culture: of characters and acts' 48 *University of California at Los Angeles Law Review* 1305

—— (2005) 'Legal negotiation in popular culture: what are we barganing for?' in Freeman M (ed) (2005)

Mersky, R (1993) 'Introduction to the lawyer and popular culture' in Gunn, D (ed) (1993)

—— (1998) 'Law and popular culture in the film collection at the Tarlton Law Library' 22 *Legal Studies Forum* 109

Meyer, P (1992) 'Law students go to the movies' 24 *Connecticut Law Review* 893

—— (1993) 'Visual literacy and the legal culture: reading film as text in the law school setting' 17 *Legal Studies Forum* 73

—— (1996) 'Desperate for love ii: further reflections on the interpretation of legal and popular storytelling in closing arguments to a jury in a complex criminal case' 30 *University of San Francisco Law Review* 931

—— (2001a) 'Why a jury trial is more like a movie than a novel' in Machura S and Robson P (eds) (2001)

—— (2001b) 'Criminality, obsessive compulsion, and aesthetic rage in "Straight Time"' 25 *Legal Studies Forum* 441

Meyer, P (2003) 'Darkness visible: litigation stories and Lawrence Joseph's *Lawyerland*' 53 *Syracuse Law Review* 1311

—— (2004) 'Using non-fiction films as visual texts in the first-year criminal law course' 28 *Vermont Law Review* 895

—— (2005) 'Adaptation: What post-conviction relief practitioners in death penalty cases might learn from popular storytellers about narrative persuasion' in Freeman M (ed) (2005)

Mezey, N (2005) 'Screening the law: ideology and law in American popular culture' 28 *Columbia Journal of Law & the Arts* 91

Miguel, I (2005) *The Matrix: La humanidad el la encrucijada* (*The Matrix:* humanity at the crossroads) (Valencia: Tirant Lo Blanch)

Millbank, J (2005) It's about *this*: lesbians, prison, desire in Freeman, M (ed) (2005) *Law and popular culture*

Miller C (1994) 'What a waste. Beautiful, sexy gal. Hell of a lawyer. Film and the female attorney' 4 *Columbia Journal of Gender and Law* 203

Miller, W (1998) 'Clint Eastwood and equity: popular culture's theory of revenge' in Sarat, A, and Kearns, T (eds) (1998)

Milles, J (1992) 'Rules, facts and hidden narratives' 16 *Legal Studies Forum* 63

Minh-Ha, T (1995) 'The totalizing quest of meaning' in Wheale, N (ed) (1995a)

Minow, N (1996) '"An idea is a greater monument than a cathedral": deciding how we know what we know in *Inherit The Wind*' 30 *University of San Francisco Law Review* 1225

Miskin, C (1999) 'Death by Entertainment' 7 *Entertainment Law Review* 259

Mnookin, J (2005) 'Reproducing a trial: evidence and its assessment in *Paradise Lost*' in Sarat, A, Douglas, L and Umphrey, M (eds) (2005)

Mogg, K (1999) 'The Paradine Case' in Mogg, K (1999) *The Alfred Hitchcock Story* (London: Titan Books)

Moiseiwitsch, M (1962) *Five famous trials. With Commentaries by Lord Birkett* (London: Heinemann)

Moran, L (1998) 'Heroes and Brothers in Law: the male homosexual as lawyer in popular culture' 18 *Studies in Law, Politics and Society* 3

—— (2004) 'On realism and the law film: the case of Oscar Wilde' in Moran, L, Sandon, E, Loizidou, E and Christie I (eds) (2004)

—— (2004) Review of Law and Film *Entertainment and Sports Law Journal* Vol 2 No 3

Moran, L, Sandon, E, Loizidou, E and Christie, I (eds) (2004) *Law's Moving Image* (London: Glasshouse Press)

Mosely, W (1990) *Devil in a Blue Dress* (London: Pan)

Mulvey, L (1975) 'Visual pleasure and narrative cinema' 16(3) *Screen*

—— (1989) *Visual and other pleasures* (London: Macmillan)

Munt, S (1988) 'The investigators: lesbian crime fiction' in Radstone, S (ed) (1988) *Sweet dreams: sexuality, gender and popular fiction* (London: Lawrence & Wishart)

Murchison, K (2006) 'Heroism in the Midst of Tragedy: *Judge Horton and the Scottsboro Boys* (1976) TV' in Strickland, R, Foster, T and Banks, T (eds) (2006)

Murphy, R (1992) *Sixties British Cinema* (London: British Film Institute)

—— (ed) (1997) *The British cinema book* (London: British Film Institute)

—— (ed) (2000) *British cinema of the 90s* (London: BFI Publishing)

—— (ed) (2001, 2nd edn) *The British cinema book* (London: British Film Institute)

—— (ed) (2008, 3rd edn) *The British cinema book* (London: British Film Institute)

Murphy, S (2002) 'Scott Turow' in Their World is Law: bestselling lawyer/novelists talk about their craft (New York: Berkeley Books)

Murphy, T (1999) 'Britcrits:subversion and submission, past present and future' 10(3) *Law and Critique* 237

Musser, C (1996) 'Film truth, documentary, and the law: justice at the margins' 30 *University of San Francisco Law Review* 963

Napper, L (1997) 'A despicable tradition? Quota quickies in the 1930s' in Murphy, R (ed) (1997)

Natale, R (1987) 'Going Hollywood: writing screenplays, producing tv shows, dominating the boardrooms—lawyers are suddenly center stage' 7 *California Lawyer* 38

Neale, S (2000) *Genre and Hollywood* (London: Routledge)

—— (ed) (2002) *Genre and Contemporary Hollywood* (London: British Film Institute)

Nelmes, J (ed) (1996a) *An introduction to film studies* (London: Routledge)

Nelmes, J (1996b) 'Women and film' in Nelmes, J (ed) (1996a)

Nelmes, J (ed) (2007) (4th edn) *An introduction to film studies* (London: Routledge)

Nevins, F (1993) *The lawyer in popular culture: proceedings of a conference* (Littleton, CO: Fred B Rothman & Co)

—— (1994) 'From Darwinian to biblical lawyers: the stories of Melville Davisson Post' *Legal Studies Forum* Vol XVIII, No 2, 177

—— (1995) 'Mr Tutt's jurisprudential journey: the stories of Arthur Train' 19 *Legal Studies Forum* 57

—— (1996a) 'Through the Great Depression on horseback: legal themes in western films of the 1930s' in Denvir, J (ed) (1996a)

—— (1996b) '*Man In The Middle*: unsung classic of the Warren court' 30 *University of San Francisco Law Review* 1097

—— (1996?) 'Book Review of Reel Justice' 20 *Legal Studies Forum* 145

—— (1998) '"Westerns" in prime time law: fictional television as legal narrative' (Durham, NC: Carolina Academic Press)

—— (1999) 'Using fiction and film as law school tools' in King, D (ed) (1999)

—— (2000a) 'Cape Fear dead ahead: a thrice-told tale of lawyers and law' 24 *Legal Studies Forum* 611

— (2000b) 'Samurai at law: the world of Erle Stanley Gardner' 24 *Legal Studies Forum* 43

—— (2001) 'Tony Richardson's *The Penalty Phase*: Judging the judge' 48 *University of California at Los Angeles Law Review* 1557

—— (2004) 'Reconnoitring juriscinema's first golden age: law and lawyers in film 1928–34' 28 *Vermont Law Review* 915

—— (2005) 'When celluloid lawyers started to speak: exploring juriscinema's first golden age' in Freeman M (ed) (2005)

Newcomb, H (1993) 'The lawyer in the history of American television—an overview' *in* Gunn, D (ed) (1993)

Newman, D and O'Brien, J (2006) 'Sociology: exploring the architecture of everyday life' (Thousand Oaks, CA: Pine Forge Press)

Nichols, B (1996) 'Unseen jury' 30 *University of San Francisco Law Review* 1055

Nichols, M (1998) 'Law and the American western: *High Noon*' 22 *Legal Studies Forum*, 591

Nieto, FS and Fernández, FJ (2004) *Imágenes y Justicia: el derecho a través del cine* (*Images and Justice; law through cinema*) (Madrid: La Ley)

Noble, P (1940) *The negro in films* (London: Skelton Robinson)

Norman, B (1992) *100 best films of the century* (London: Chapmans)

Novak, G (1987) 'Social ills and one-man solution: depictions of evil in the Vigilante film' *International Conference on the Expressions of Evil in Literature and the Visual Arts* (Atlanta, GA)

Nowell-Smith, G and Ricci, S (eds) (1998) *Hollywood and Europe: economics, culture national identity 1945–1995* (London: British Film Institute)

Olivas, M (2006) '*El Norte* (1983): immigration mythology as crossover dream' in Strickland, R, Foster, T and Banks, T (eds) (2006)

Omrod, J (1971) Report of the Committee on Legal Education, Cmnd 4595, HMSO

Orth, J (1992) 'The law in Spoon River' 16 *Legal Studies Forum* 301

Osborn, G (2001) '*Borders and Boundaries: Locating the Law in Film*' in Machura, S and Robson, P (2001)164.

Osborn, G and Sutton, T (1996) 'Of new orders and new dawns: freewheeling returns to negligence' 12(1) *Professional Negligence* 2

Osborn, J (1996) 'Atticus Finch—the end of honor: a discussion of *To Kill a Mockingbird*' 30 *University of San Francisco Law Review* 1139

Owens, J (2001) 'Grisham's legal tales: a moral compass for the young lawyer' 48 *University of California at Los Angeles Law Review* 1431

Packard, A and Davenport, C (1995) 'Mercy and justice in a capital murder trial' 19 *Legal Studies Forum* 411

Painter, R (2000) 'Irrationality and cognitive bias at a closing in Arthur Solmssen's *The Comfort Letter*' 69 *Fordham Law Review* 111

Pannick, D (1987) *Judges* (Oxford: Oxford University Press)

Papas, E (2000) 'Legal ethics: lawyers' duties to clients and clients' rights and the media—teaching legal ethics using a media studies lesson plan' 24 *Nova Law Review* 701

Papke, D (1980) 'Advertisements for the legal self: a review of contemporary lawyers' auto-biographies' 4 *ALSA Forum* 57

Papke, D (1996) 'Peace between the sexes: law and gender in *Kramer vs Kramer*' 30 *University of San Francisco Law Review* 1199

—— (1999a) 'Conventional Wisdom: the courtroom trial in American popular culture' 82 *Marquette Law Review* 471

—— (1999b) 'The American courtroom trial: pop culture, courtroom realities and the dream world of justice' 40 *South Texas Law Review* 920

—— (2001) 'Law, cinema, and ideology: Hollywood legal films of the 1950s' 48 *University of California at Los Angeles Law Review* 1473

—— (2003a) 'Cautionary ales: the woman as lawyer in contemporary Hollywood cinema' 25 *University of Arkansas at Little Rock Law Review* 485

—— (2003b) 'How does law look in the movies (reviewing Anthony Chase, Movies on Trial)' 27 *Legal Studies Forum* 439

—— (2003c) '*Mr District Attorney*: the prosecutor during the golden age of radio' 34 *University of Toledo Law Review* 781

—— (2004) 'Crusading hero, devoted teacher, and sympathetic failure; the self-image of the law professor in Hollywood cinema and in real life, too' 28 *Vermont Law Review* 957

—— (2006) 'Genre, gender and jurisprudence in *Adam's Rib* (1949)' in Strickland, R, Foster, T and Banks, T (eds) (2006)

—— (2007) '12 Angry Men is not an archetype: reflections on the jury in contemporary popular culture' 82(2) *Chicago-Kent Law Review* 735

Parker, R (2006) 'The good lawyer: *The Verdict* (1982)' in Strickland, R, Foster, T and Banks T (eds) (2006)

Parris, EJ (1960) *Most of my murders* (London: Frederick Miller)

Parris, J (1991) *Scapegoat: the inside story of the trial of Derek Bentley* (London: Duckworth)

Payne, M (1997) '*The Ten Commandments*—the movie: freedom extolled' 22 *Oklahoma City University Law Review* 193

Peltz, R (2003) 'On a wagon train to Afghanistan: limitations on *Star Trek*'s prime directive' 25 *University of Arkansas at Little Rock Law Review* 635

Penney, S (2004) 'Mass torts, mass culture: Canadian mass tort law and Hollywood narrative film' 30 *Queen's Law Journal* 205

Perlmutter, D (2000) Policing the Media: Street Cops and Public Perceptions of Law Enforcement (London: Sage)

Pew, C (2000) 'Mutiny on the bounty (ex-Bethia)' 31 *Journal of Maritime Law and Commerce* 609

Phillips, J (2005) 'Law's Moving Image' 16(6) *Entertainment Law Review* 162

Phillips, P (1996) 'Genre, star and auteur: an approach to Hollywood cinema' in Nelmes, J (ed) (1996a)

Pines, J (2001) 'British Cinema and Black Representation' in Murphy, R (ed) (2001) (2nd edn)

Podlas, K (2009) Impact Of Television On Cross-Examination And Juror 'Truth', 14 *Widener Law Review* 483

Porter, V (2001) 'Methodism versus the market-place: the Rank Organisation and British cinema' in Murphy, R (ed) (2001) (2nd edn)

Post, R (1987) 'On the popular image of the lawyer: reflections in a dark glass' 75 *California Law Review* 379

Prasad M (2004) 'The natives are looking: cinema and censorship in colonial India' in Moran, L, Sandon, E, Loizidou, E and Christie I (eds) (2004)

Projansky, S (2001a) *Watching rape: film and television in postfeminist culture* (New York: New York University Press)

—— (2001b) 'The elusive/ubiquitous representation of rape: a historical survey of rape in US film 1903–1972' 41 *Cinema Journal* 63

Puaux, F (2002) 'La justice à l'écran' ('Justice on screen') 105 *Cinéma Action* (Corlet-Telerama, Conde-sur-Noireau)

Pyle, R (1984) 'Orwell's Nineteen Eighty-Four and law' 8 *ALSA Forum* 167

Pyrhönen, H (1994) *Murder from an academic angle: an introduction to the study of the detective narrative* (Columbia: Camden House)

Rafter, N (2001) 'American criminal trials films: an overview of their development 1930–2000' in Machura, S and Robson, P (eds) (2001)

—— (2005) 'Badfellas: movie psychos, popular culture, and law' in Freeman, M (ed) (2005)

—— (2006) (2nd edn) *Shots in the mirror* (Oxford: Oxford University Press)

—— (ed) (2000) *Shots in the mirror* (Oxford: Oxford University Press)

Rahmatian, A (2006) 'Law's Moving Image' 3(2) *Entertainment and Sports Law Journal*

Rapoport, N (2000) 'Dressed for excess: how Hollywood affects the professional behaviour or lawyers' 14 *Notre Dame Journal of Law Ethics and Public Policy* 49

—— (2006) '*Lord of the Flies* (1963): the development of rules within an adolescent culture' in Strickland, R, Foster, T and Banks, T (eds) (2006)

Rapping, E (2003) *Law and justice as seen on TV* (New York: NYU Press)

Bibliography

Redhead, S (1995) *Unpopular cultures: the birth of law and popular culture* (Manchester and New York: Manchester University Press)

Reiner, R (1978) 'The new blue films' 43 *New Society* 706

Rendell, R (1995) *Simisola* (London: Arrow)

Reynolds, O (1997) 'Review of *Cool Hand Luke*' 22 *Oklahoma City University Law Review* 97

—— (2006) '*Cool Hand Luke* (1967) rebellion and illusion' in Strickland, R, Foster, T and Banks, T (eds) (2006)

Richards, J (1982) 'The British Board of Film Censors and content control in the 1930s' 1 *Historical Journal of Film, Radio and Television* 39

Richmond, M (1988) 'The cultural milieu of law' 13 *Nova Law Review* 89

—— (2006) 'Kenneth Branagh's *Henry V* (1989)' in Strickland, R, Foster, T and Banks, T (eds) (2006)

Menchú, R, Burgos-Debra, E (ed) (1984) *I, Rigoberta Menchú: an Indian woman in Guatemala* (London: Verso)

Rivaya, B (ed) (2003) *Cine y pena de muerte (Film and the death penalty)* (Valencia: Tirant Lo Blanch)

—— (2004) *Derecho y Cine (Primer Plano) (Law and film: introductory guide)* in Rivaya, B and Cima, P de (2004)

—— (2006) *Derecho y cine: sobre las posibilidades del cine como instrumento para la didáctica jurídica (Law and film: on the possibilities of film as a tool in law teaching)* in Linera, MA Presno, and Rivaya, B (eds) (2006)

Rivaya, B and Cima, P de (2004) *Derecho y Cine en 100 peliculas (Law and cinema in 1000 films)* (Valencia: Tirant Lo Blanch)

Robertson, J (1985) The British Board of Film Censors. Film Censorship in Britain 1896–1950 (*London: Croom Helm*)

—— (1989) *The hidden cinema: British film censorship in action* (London: Routledge)

Robertson M (2005) 'Seeing blind spots: corporate misconduct in film and law' in Freeman M (ed) (2005)

Robinson, M (1982) 'The law of the state in Kafka's *The Trial*' 6 *ALSA Forum* 127

Robson, P (1979) *Housing and the judiciary* (Glasgow: University of Strathclyde)

—— (1996a) 'Images of law in fiction of John Grisham' in Morison, J and Bell, C (eds) (1996) *Tall stories?: reading law and literature* (Aldershot: Dartmouth Publishing)

—— (2001b) 'Adapting the modern law novel: filming John Grisham' in Machura, S and Robson P (eds) (2001)

—— (2002) 'Fade to Grey: portraying the ethnic minority experience in British film' 3 *International Journal of the Sociology of Law* 235

—— (2005) 'Law and film studies: autonomy and theory' in Freeman M (ed) (2005)

—— (2006) 'The justice films of Sidney Lumet' in Greenfield, S and Osborn, G (eds) (2006)

—— (2007a) 'Lawyers and the legal system on TV: the British experience' 2(4) *International Journal of Law in Context* 333

—— (2007b) 'Developments in law and popular culture: the case of the TV lawyer' in Masson, A and O'Connor, K (2007)

—— (2009) 'Law, Hollywood and the European experience' 46 *Studies in Law, Politics, and Society* 117

——, *Lawyers Today* (forthcoming 2012)

Robson, P and Watchman, P (eds) (1981) *Justice, Lord Denning and the Constitution* (Farnborough, Hants: Gower)

Robson, R (1998) *Sappho goes to law school* (New York: Columbia University Press)

Rosen, R (1989) 'Ethical soap: *LA Law* and the privileging of character' 43 *University of Miami Law Review* 1229

—— (2006) '*A Few Good* (and angry) *Men* (and women) (1992)' in Strickland, R, Foster, T and Banks, T (eds) (2006)

Rosenberg, C (1989) 'An LA lawyer replies' 98 *Yale Law Journal* 1625

—— (2000) 'The myth of perfection' 24 *Nova Law Review* 641

Rosenberg, N (1991) '*Young Mr Lincoln*: the lawyer as super-hero' 15 *Legal Studies Forum*, 215

—— (1994) 'Hollywood on trials: courts and films 1930–1960' 12 *Law and History Review* 341

—— (1996a) 'Professor Lightcap goes to Washington: rereading *Talk Of The Town*' 30 *University of San Francisco Law Review* 1083

—— (1996b) 'Law Noir' in Denvir, J (ed) (1996a)

—— (2000) 'The Caine Mutiny: not just one but many legal dramas' 31 *Journal of Maritime Law and Commerce* 623

—— (2001) 'Looking for law in all the old traces: the movies of classical Hollywood, the law, and the case(s) of film noir' 48 *University of California at Los Angeles Law Review* 1443

—— (2002) 'Constitutional history and the "cultural turn": cross-examining the legal-reelist narratives of Henry Fonda' in Van Burkleo, SF (ed) (2002)

Russell, M (1991) 'Race and the dominant gaze: narratives of law and inequality in popular film' 15 *Legal Studies Forum* 43

Russo, V (1987) *The celluloid closet: homosexuality in the* movies (New York: Harper & Row)

Ruud, M (1958) The Townes Hall Film Forum, 11 *Journal of Legal Education* 551

Ryall, T (1987) *The Gangster Film* (London: British Film Institute)

Ryan, C (1996a) 'Print the legend: violence and recognition in *The Man Who Shot Liberty Valance*' in Denvir, J (ed) (1996a)

—— (1996b) 'Lawyers as lovers: *Gold Diggers Of 1993* Or "I'd rather you sue me than marry me"' 30 *University of San Francisco Law Review* 1123

—— (2006) '"Across the border—again?" The labyrinth of law in Orson Welles's *Touch of Evil* (1958)' in Strickland, R, Foster, T and Banks, T (eds) (2006)

Salzmann, V and Dunwoody, P (2005) 'Do portrayals of lawyers influence how people think about the legal profession?' 58 *Southern Methodist University Law Review* 411

Sanderson, P and Somerlad, H (2006) 'Gender, power and law in screwball comedy: re-viewing *Talk of the Town* and *Adam's Rib*' in Greenfield, S and Osborn, G (eds) (2006)

Sarat, A (1999) 'Rhetoric and remembrance: trials, transcription, and the politics of critical reading' 23 *Legal Studies Forum* 355

—— (2000) 'Imagining the law of the father: loss, dread and mourning in the Sweet Hereafter' 34 *Law and Society Review* 5

—— (2007) 'Fathers in law: violence and reason in 12 Angry Men' 82(2) *Chicago-Kent Law Review* 863

—— (2009) *Studies in Law, Politics and Society*, (Amherst: Emerald) Vol 44

Sarat, A, Douglas, L and Umphrey, M (eds) (2005a) *Law on the Screen* (Stanford: Stanford University Press)

Sarat, A, Douglas, L and Umphrey, M (2005b) 'On film and law: broadening the focus' in —— (eds) (2005)

Sarat A, and Kearns, T (eds) (1998) *Law and the Domains of Culture* (Ann Arbor: University of Michigan Press)

Sarat, A and Scheingold, S (2008) *The Cultural Lives of Cause Lawyers* (Cambridge: Cambridge University Press)

Saunders, K (1997) '*Billy Budd* and the Federal Sentencing Mandates' 22 *Oklahoma City University Law Review* 211

—— (2006) '*Budd* (1962) and Mandatory Sentences' in Strickland, R, Foster, T and Banks, T (eds) (2006)

Savage, N and Watt, G (1996) 'A "House of Intellect" for the profession' in Birks, P (ed) (1996)

Schatz, T (1981) *Hollywood genres: formulas, filmmaking, and the studio system* (Boston: McGraw-Hill)

Schmill, U (2005) *Macbeth: La Tragedia del Poder* (*Macbeth: the tragedy of power*) (Valencia: Tirant Lo Blanch)

Schraf, MP and Robert, LD (1994) 'The interstellar relations of the federation: international law and "*Star Trek: the Next Generation*"' 25(3) *University of Toledo Law Review* 577

Schwabach, A (2006) 'Harry Potter and the unforgivable curses: norm-formation, inconsistency and the rule of the law in the Wizarding World' 11 *Roger Williams University Law Review* 309

Scottoline, L (2000) 'Get off the screen' 24 *Nova Law Review* 655

Seaton, J (1996) 'Review of Bergman and Asimow's Reel Justice' 20 *Legal Studies Forum* 145

Selinger, C (1997) 'Dramatizing on film the uneasy role of the American criminal defense lawyer: True Believer' 22 *Oklahoma City University Law Review* 223

Selwyn, F (1998) *Gangland: the case of Bentley and Craig* (London: Routledge) (reprinted as —— (1991, 1998) *Nothing but revenge: the case of Bentley and Craig* (London: Penguin)

Seymour, D (2004) 'Film and law: in search of a critical method' in Moran, L, Sandon, E, Loizidou, E and Christie, I (eds) (2004)

Shale, S (1996) 'The conflicts of law and the character of men: writing *Reversal of Fortune* and *Judgment at Nuremberg*' 30 *University of San Francisco Law Review* 991

Shaman, J (2006) '*On the Waterfront* (1954): cheese-eating, HUAC and the First Amendment' in Strickland, R, Foster, T and Banks, T (eds) (2006)

Shapiro, C (1995) 'Women lawyers in celluloid: why Hollywood skirts the truth' 25 *Toledo Law Review* 955

—— (1996) 'Do or die: does *Dead Man Walking* run?' 30 *University of San Francisco Law Review* 1143

Shapiro, C (1998) 'Women lawyers in celluloid: rewrapped' 23 *Vermont Law Review* 303

—— (2006) 'Whose *True Crime* (1999) is it anyway? (A meditation on the death penalty' in Strickland, R, Foster, T and Banks, T (eds) (2006)

Shapiro, M (2005) 'The racial-spatial order and the law: *Devil in a Blue Dress*' in Sarat, A, Douglas, L and Umphrey, M (eds) (2005)

Sharp, Cassandra (2005) 'The "Extreme Makeover" effect of law school: students being transformed by stories' 12 *Texas Wesleyan Law Review* 233

Sheffield, R (1991) 'A social history of black lawyers in popular culture' 7 *Focus on Law Studies* 4

—— (1993) '*On* film: a social history of women lawyers in popular culture 1930 to 1990' 14 *Loyola of Los Angeles Entertainment Law Journal* 73

Sherman, D (1999) 'A case study in legal deconstruction: history, community and authority in *The Crying of Lot 49*' 24 *Oklahoma City University Law Review* 641

Sherman, R (1991) 'Small screen takes shine to lawyers' 13 *The National Law Journal* 9

Sherwin, R (1994) 'Law frames: historical truth and narrative necessity in a criminal case' 47 *Stanford Law Review* 39

—— (1996a) 'Introduction: symposium: picturing justice: images of law and lawyers in the visual media' 30 *University of San Francisco Law Review* 891

—— (1996b) '*Cape Fear*: law's inversion and cathartic justice' 30 *University of San Francisco Law Review* 1023

—— (1996c) 'Framed' in Denvir, J (ed) (1996a)

—— (2000) *When law goes pop: the vanishing line between law and popular culture* (Chicago: University of Chicago Press)

—— (2001) 'Nomos and cinema' 48 *UCLA Law Review* 1519

—— (2005a) 'Law's enchantment: the cinematic jurisprudence of Krzysztof Kieslowski' in Freeman, M (ed) (2005)

—— (2005b) 'Anti-Oedipus, Lynch: initiatory rites and the ordeal of justice' in Sarat, A, Douglas, L and Umphrey, M (eds) (2005)

Sherwin, R, Feigenson, N and Spiesel, C (2006) 'Law in the digital age: how visual communication technologies are transforming the practice, theory and teaching of law' 12 *Boston University Journal of Science & Technology Law* 227

Silbey, J (2001) 'Patterns of courtroom justice' in Machura, S and Robson, P (eds) (2001)

—— (2002) 'What we do when we do law and popular culture' 27 *Law and Social Inquiry* 139

—— (2004) 'Judges as film critics: new approaches to filmic evidence' 37 *The University of Michigan Journal of Law Reform* 493

—— (2005) 'Filmmaking in the precinct house and the genre of documentary film' 29 *Columbia Journal of Law and the Arts* 107

—— (2006) 'Videotaped confessions and the genre of documentary' 16 *The Fordham Intellectual Property, Media and Entertainment Law Journal* 789

—— (2007a) 'Criminal performances: film, autobiography and confession' 37 *New Mexico Law Review* 189

—— (2007b) 'Truth tales and trial films' 40 *Loyola of Los Angeles Law Review* 551

—— (2007c) 'A history of representations of justice: coincident preoccupations of law and film' in Masson, A and O'Connor, K

Silver, A and Ward, E (1992) (2nd edn) *The film director's team* (Los Angeles: Silman-James Press)

Simon, WH (2001) 'Moral pluck: legal ethics in popular culture' 101(2) *Columbia Law Review* 101

Smith, R (1997) 'What price propaganda? When *The Paths of Glory* led but to the pulpit' 22 *Oklahoma City University Law Review* 89

Smith, S (2006) '*The Fortune Cookie* (1966) and "Whiplash Willie"—the image of lawyers' in Strickland, R, Foster, T and Banks, T (eds) (2006)

Smith, V (ed) (1997) *Representing blackness: issues in film and video* (London: Athlone Press)

Smith-Khan, C (1998) 'African-American attorneys in television and film: compounding stereotypes' 22 *Legal Studies Forum* 119

Smoodin, E (2005) '"Everyone went wild over it": film audiences, political cinema and *Mr Smith Goes to Washington*' in Sarat, A, Douglas, L and Umphrey, M (eds) (2005)

Sokolow, D (1991) 'From Kurosawa to (Duncan) Kennedy: the lessons of Rashomon for current legal education' *Wisconsin Law Review* 97

Sokolsky, A (1990) 'The case of the juridical junkie: Perry Mason and the dilemma of confession' 2 *Yale Journal of Law & the Humanities* 189

Spelman, N and Minow, M (1996) 'Outlaw women: Thelma and Louise' in Denvir, J (ed) (1996a)

Spitz, D (2000) 'Heroes or villains? Moral struggles vs. ethical dilemmas: an examination of dramatic portrayals of lawyers and the legal profession in popular culture' 24 *Nova Law Review* 725

Stachenfeld, A and Nicholson, C (1996) 'Blurred boundaries: an analysis of the close relationship between popular culture and the practice of law' 30 *University of San Francisco Law Review* 903

Stark, S (1987) 'Perry Mason meets Sonny Crockett: the history of lawyers and the police as television heroes' 42 *University of Miami Law Review* 229

Stoll, D (1999) *Rigoberta Menchú and the story of all poor Guatemalans* (Boulder, CO; Oxford: Westview Press)

Stone, A (2000) 'Teaching film at Harvard Law School' 24 *Legal Studies Forum* 574

Storey, J (ed) (1994) Cultural theory and popular culture: a reader (New York; London: Harvester Wheatsheaf)

Storkey, E (1985) *What's right with feminism* (London: SPCK)

Street, S (1997) British national cinema (London: Routledge)

Strickland, R (1993) 'The Hollywood mouthpiece: an illustrated journey through the courtrooms and back-alleys of screen justice' in Gunn, D (ed) (1993)

—— (1997) 'The Cinematic Lawyer: the Magic Mirror and the Silver Screen' 22 *Oklahoma City University Law Review* 13

—— (2006a) 'The Cinema of Law: The Magic Mirror and the Silver Screen' in Strickland, R, Foster, T and Banks, T (eds) (2006)

—— (2006b) 'Bringing bogie out of the courtroom closet: law and lawyers in film' in Strickland, R, Foster, T and Banks, T (eds) (2006)

—— (2006c) 'Tonto's revenge revisited: Jim Thorpe—all American (1951) as Seen from the Cutting Room Floor' in Strickland, R, Foster, T and Banks, T (eds) (2006)

Strickland, R, Foster, T and Banks, T (2006) *Screening justice—the cinema of law: significant films of law, order and social justice* (Buffalo, NY: Hein)

Strinati, D (1994) 'Postmodernism and popular culture' in Storey, J (ed) (1994)

Sugarman, D (1991) 'A hatred of disorder: legal science, liberalism and imperialism' in Fitzpatrick, P (ed) (1991)

Suggs, J (1990) 'Epistemology and the law in four African American fictions' 14 *Legal Studies Forum* 141

Sullivan, T (2003) 'Imagining the criminal law: when client and lawyer meet in the movies' 25 *University of Arkansas at Little Rock Law Review* 665

Sussex, E (1976) The rise and fall of the British documentary (California: University of California Press)

Symons, J (1992) *Bloody Murder* (London: PAN)

Taylor, J (1978) *Hitch* (London: Faber and Faber)

Taylor, K (1999) 'The festival of justice: Paris, 1849' in Douzinas, C and Nead, L (eds) (1999)

Teubner, G (ed) (1988) *Autopoietic law: a new approach to law and society* (Berlin: de Gruyter)

Thain, G (2001) 'Cape Fear' in Machura, S and Robson, P (eds) (2001)

Thaman, S (2007) 'The good, the bad, or the indifferent: 12 Angry Men in Russia' 82(2) *Chicago-Kent Law Review* 791

Thomas, J (2001) 'Legal culture and the practice: a postmodern depiction of the rule of law' 48 *University of California at Los Angeles Law Review* 1495

Thompson, EP (1980) *Writing by candlelight* (London: Merlin Press)

Thompson, J (1997) 'Scandal and social theory' in Lull, J and Hinerman, S (eds) (1997).

Thomson, D (1981) 'At the Acme Book Shop' (Spring) *Sight and Sound* 122

Thornton, M (2002a) 'Law and popular culture: engendering legal vertigo' in Thornton, M (ed) (2002b)

—— (ed) (2002b) *Romancing the tomes* (London: Cavendish)

Todd, P (2000) 'The British film industry in the 1990s' in Murphy, R (ed) (2000)

Torres, ÁP González (2005) *Salò o las 120 jornadas de sodoma* (*120 Days of Sodom*) (Valencia: Tirant Lo Blanch)

Trevelyan, J (1973) *What the censor saw* (London: Michael Joseph)

Tudor, A (1974) *Theories of film* (London: Secker and Warburg/BFI)

Turner, G (1996) British cultural studies: an introduction (London: Routledge)

Tushnet, M (1996) 'Class action: one view of gender and law in popular culture' in Denvir, J (ed) (1996a)

—— (2006) 'M (1931) and the serial killer's humanity' in Strickland, R, Foster, T and Banks, T (eds) (2006)

Tuska, J (1978) *The detective in Hollywood* (Garden City, NY: Doubleday)

—— (1988) In manors and alleys: a casebook on the American detective film (New York: Greenwood Press)

Tyler, J and Reynolds, T (1998) 'Using feature films to teach group counselling', 23(1) *The Journal for Specialists in Group Work* 7–21

Uelmen, G (1996) 'Trial as a circus: *Inherit the Wind*' 30 *University of San Francisco Law Review* 1221

VanBurkleo, SF (ed) (2002) *Constitutionalism and American Culture: Writing the New American History* (Lawrence Kan: University Press of Kansas; London: Europan)

Varios (1996) *Abogados del cine: leyes y juicios en la pantalla* (*Lawyers in films: legal acts and judgements on screen* (Madrid: Illustre Colegio de Abogados de Madrid y Castalia)

Vetri, D (2006) '*Victim* (1961)—no more!' in Strickland, R, Foster, T and Banks, T (eds) (2006)

Vidmar, N, Beale, S, Chemerinsky, E and Coleman, J (2007) 'Was he guilty as charged? An alternative narrative based on the circumstantial evidence from 12 Angry Men' 82(2) *Chicago-Kent Law Review* 663

Villez, B (2005) *Séries télé: visions de la justice* (*TV series: visions of justice*) (Paris: Presses Universitaires de France)

—— (2007) 'Representation of the legal profession on television. Professional ethics and client expectations' in Masson, A and O'Connor, K (2007).

Vogel, J (1997) '*Bonfire of the Vanities*: the thinking man's redneck: an upper class white man's fall from grace' 22 *Oklahoma City University Law Review* 203

Von Zharen, W (2000) 'Human contraband: stowaways in popular culture' 31 *Journal of Maritime Law and Commerce* 601

Waldman, D (2005) 'A case for corrective criticism: *A Civil Action*' in Sarat, A, Douglas, L and Umphrey, M (eds) (2005)

Walker, J (ed), Halliwell, L (1993) *Halliwell's film guide* (London: HarperCollins)

Waring, R (1996) '*Z*' 30 *University of San Francisco Law Review*, 1077

——— (2000) 'Film Commentary' 24 *Legal Studies Forum* 301

Warshaw, B 1984 (ed) *The Trial Masters* (New Jersey: Prentice Hall)

Watt, G (2006) 'The soul of legal education' 3 *Web Journal of Current Legal Issues*

Weber, M, Roth, G and Wittich, C (eds) (1979) *Economy and society: an outline of interpretive sociology* (Berkeley; London: University of California Press)

Weiner, S (1993) 'True crime: fact, fiction and law' 17 *Legal Studies Forum* 275

Weisselberg, C (2007) 'Good film, bad jury' 82(2) *Chicago-Kent Law Review* 717

Wells, P (1996) 'The documentary form: personal and social realities' in Nelmes, J (ed) (1996a)

Westling, W (2006) 'Trial as theater: *Witness for the Prosecution* (1957)' in Strickland, R, Foster, T and Banks, T (eds) (2006)

Wexman, V (2005) 'Right and wrong; that's (not) all there is to it!: Young Mr Lincoln and American law' 44 *Cinema Journal* 20

Wheale, N (ed) (1995a) *The postmodern arts: an introductory reader* (London: Routledge)

——— (1995b) 'Recognising a "human-thing": cyborgs, robots and replicants in Philip, K Dick's *Do Androids Dream of Electric Sheep?* and Ridley Scott's *Bladerunner*' in Wheale, N (ed) (1995a)

Wheeler, D (1995) *It looks at you: the returned gaze of cinema* (Albany: State University of New York Press)Widiss, A (2000) '"Bad Faith" in fact and fiction: ruminations on John Grisham's tale about insurance coverage, punitive damages, and the great benefit life insurance company' 26 *University of Memphis Law Review* 1377

Wiegand, S (1997) 'Deception and artifice: Thelma, Louise, and the legal hermeneutic' 22 *Oklahoma City University Law Review* 25

Wilkinson, A (2006) 'The Protest Singer: ten purposes of music' 44 *New Yorker* (17 April 2006) www.peteseeger.net/new_yorker041706.htm

Williams, P (1991) *The alchemy of race and rights* (Cambridge: Harvard University Press)

Williams, R (1958) Culture and society (London: Chatto and Windus)

Wilsher, W and De Souza, S (1995) *The Art of Judge Dredd* (London: Boxtree)

Wilton, T (1995) *Immortal, invisible: lesbians and the moving image* (London: Routledge)

Winer, L (2006) 'Don't bogart that witness: *The Caine Mutiny* (1954) and trial by jury' in Strickland, R, Foster, T and Banks, T (eds) (2006)

Woeller, W and Cassiday, B (1988) *The literature of crime and detection: an illustrated history from antiquity to the present* (New York: Ungar)

Wright, G (2001) 'The pale cast of thought: on the legal status of sophisticated androids' 25 *Legal Studies Forum* 297

Yallop, D (1971) *To encourage the others* (London: WH Allen)

Yoder, E (2000) 'Fated boy: Billy Budd and the laws of war' 31 *Journal of Maritime Law and Commerce* 615

Young, A (1996) *Imagining crime* (London: Sage)

——— (1997) 'Murder in the eyes of the law' 17 *Studies in Law, Politics and Society* 31

——— (2004) '"Into the blue": the cinematic possibility of judgment with passion' in Moran, L, Sandon, E, Loizidou, E and Christie, I (eds) (2004)

Young, L (1996) *Fear of the dark: 'race', gender and sexuality in the cinema* (London: Routledge)

Web material

Asimow, M (1998) 'A free soul: drunk lawyers in the movies' *UCLA Law School*. Available at: www.usfca.edu/pj/archive.htm [Accessed 31 March 2010]

—— (1999) 'In toxic tort litigation, truth lies at the bottom of a bottomless pit' *(Feb) Picturing Justice* [online] Available at: http://www.usfca.edu/pj/articles/Civil_Action-Asimow.htm [Accessed 15 June 2009]

—— (2000) 'Return of the heroic lawyers … and the heroic client: *The Winslow Boy* and *The Castle*' *(Jan) Picturing Justice* [online] Available at: http://www.usfca.edu/pj/winslow_boy.htm [Accessed 15 June 2009]

Biodrowski, S (2005) 'Writing Emily Rose: Scott Derrickson and Paul Harris Boardman', *Hollywood Gothique*, 9 September 2005 [available at: http://www.hollywoodgothique.com/screening/writing-emily-rose-scott-derrickson-paul-harris-boardman [accessed 9 September 2005]

Child, B (2009) Spielberg's Abraham Lincoln project to go ahead despite competition http://www.guardian.co.uk/film/2009/sep/15/abraham-lincoln-spielberg-redford

Curtis, Q (2000) 'True story turned into movie magic' Electronic Telegraph 13 March

Denvir, J (1998a) 'Chinatown' *(Mar) Picturing Justice* [online] Available at: http://www.usfca.edu/pj/articles/chinatown.htm [Accessed 15 June 2009]

—— (1998b) 'The Last Wave' *(May) Picturing Justice* [online] Available at: http://www.usfca.edu/pj/articles/LastWave.htm [Accessed 15 June 2009]

—— (1999) 'The law of rules' *9 (Nov) Picturing Justice* [online] Available at: http://www.usfca.edu/pj/ruleoflaws.htm [Accessed 15 June 2009]

Edelstein, D (2003) 'His Father's Son: The haunted men of 'Capturing the Friedmans' *Slate Magazine* 5 June 2003 www.slate.com/id/2094025 (last visited 06/08/08)

Freeman, P (2005) 'The Exorcism of Emily Rose: destroying demons the old fashioned way … In a courtroom' (independentfilm.com interviews with writer/director Scott Derrickson and writer Paul Harris Boardman) 31 August

Grant, J (1997) 'The Rainmaker' *(Dec) Picturing Justice* [online] Available at: http://www.usfca.edu/pj/articles/Rainmaker2.htm [Accessed 15 June 2009]

Gritten, D (2000) 'Women on the verge of greatness' Electronic Telegraph 7 April

Hadden, S (1998) 'Amistad', Film Review' *Jan H-Net Film Review*

Haviland, D (2004) Capturing the Friedmans Culture Wars www.culturewars.org.uk/2004-01/friedman.htm visited 06/08/08

Horowitz, D (1999) 'I, Rigoberta Menchu, Liar' *26 (Feb) FrontPageMagazine* [online]. Available at: http://www.frontpagemag.com/readArticle.aspx?ARTID=24278 [Accessed 18 June 2009]

Jackson, C (1999) 'Judging *Judging Amy*' *(Dec) Picturing Justice* [online] Available at: http://www.usfca.edu/pj/amy.htm [Accessed 15 June 2009]

Jackson, C (2000) 'Mamet's *The Winslow Boy*: traps and loopholes' *(March) Picturing Justice* [online] Available at: http://www.usfca.edu/pj/winslow-jackson.htm [Accessed 15 June 2009]

Johnston, P (2000) 'Republican writes BBC's Irish drama' *01 Dec Electronic Telegraph* [online]. Available at: http://www.telegraph.co.uk/news/uknews/1376477/Republican-writes-BBCs-Irish-drama.html [Accessed 18 June 2009]

Kennedy, D (1999) 'Civil inaction' The New Republic, 2 http://home.comcast.net/~dkennedy56/woburn_tnr.html

Bibliography

Randall, K (1999) 'Civil Action: a compelling tale loses much of its impact' 21 Jan 1999 World Socialist Web Site http://www.wsws.org/articles/1999/jan1999/civ-j21.shtml [Accessed 13 06 2009]

Robson, P (1996b) 'Globalising Atticus Finch' (Law and Society Association, Glasgow, July 1996 (available at www.imagesofjustice.eu)

Sharp, K (2000) 'Erin Brockovich: the real story' *14 (Apr) Salon Arts and Entertainment* http://www.salon.com/ent/feature/2000/04/14/sharp/index.html (accessed 08-01-2010)

Suggs, J (1998) 'Adams Ribs: get 'em while they're hot' *(Mar)* http://www.usfca.edu/pj/articles/TimetoKillAdamsRib.htm [Accessed 15 June 2009]

Sundermann, H (2002) 'Judges in Film' *(Mar) Picturing Justice* [online] Available at: http://www.usfca.edu/pj/judges_sundermann.htm [Accessed 15 June 2009]

Waring, R (1997a) 'Amistad (Van Buren's Folly)' *(Dec) Picturing Justice* [online] Available at: http://www.usfca.edu/pj/articles/Amistad.htm [Accessed 15 June 2009]

—— (1997b) 'The Devil's Advocate' *(Nov) Picturing Justice* [online] Available at: http://www.usfca.edu/pj/articles/devilsad.htm [Accessed 15 June 2009]

—— (1997c) 'The Winemaker' *(Nov) Picturing Justice* [online] Available at: http://www.usfca.edu/pj/articles/Rainmaker.htm [Accessed 15 June 2009]

—— (1998) 'The Sweet Hereafter' *(May) Picturing Justice* [online] Available at: http://www.usfca.edu/pj/articles/sweethearafter.htm [Accessed 15 June 2009]

—— (1999a) 'A Civil Action—another government bailout?' *(Feb) Picturing Justice* [online] Available at: http://www.usfca.edu/pj/articles/Civil_Action-Waring.htm [Accessed 15 June 2009]

—— (1999b) '*Not for Ourselves Alone* and *Salt of the Earth*: the interplay of gender and race' *(Dec) Picturing Justice* [online] Available at: http://www.usfca.edu/pj/gender.htm [Accessed 15 June 2009]

—— (1997) 'Amistad (Van Buren's Folly)' http://www.usfca.edu/pj/articles/Amistad.htm

Webster, R (2004) '"Capturing the Friedmans": art, truth and marketing' 20 April [at www.richardwebster.net/print/xfriedmans last visited 06/08/08]

Websites

http://www.amctv.com/ontheair/realtoreel/archives/trial.html
http://tarlton.law.utexas.edu/lpop/legstud.htm
http://www.okcu.ed/law/lrev.htm#articles
http://www.wvu.edu/~lawfac/jelkins/lawyersfilm.htm

Newspaper and other material

Bawdon, F (1994) 'The truth is far worse than fiction' *The Times* and *The Sunday Times* compact disc edition, 37

Burkeman, O (2008) 'High noon in the middle east' *The Guardian* Film and Music Supplement 5

Derschowitz, A (1986) 'Legal eagles; ten tapes that have their day in court' 12 *American Film* 59

Dooling, R (1997) 'Sue Hollywood for false representation!' 19 *The National Law Journal* A18

Freedland, J (1996) 'The Recurring Dream Factory' *The Guardian* 25 January

Jeffries, S and Hattenstone, S (1998) 'In the light of history' *The Guardian* 6 February

Joseph, P and Carton, S (1995) 'Perry Mason in space: a call for more inventive lawyers in television science fiction series' in *Imaginative Futures: Proceedings of the 1993 Science Fiction Research Association Conference* (San Bernardino, Califormia: SFRA Press)

Katsh, E (1976) 'Filmsy evidence' *1 (Jan) ALSA Newsletter*, 17

Margolick, D (1993) 'The cinematic law firm of greedy, vain & immoral' 142 *The New York Times* 9

Marks, PD (2001) 'Magic in the movies: do courtroom scenes have real-life parallels?' 73 *Journal of the New York State Bar Association* 40

Newman, K (1993) 'See you in Court!' *Empire*, 118

ORC International (2003) *Court Working Dress in England & Wales. Public Consultation by the Department for Constitutional Affairs* [electronic source] Ministry of justice/Information/Documents. Available at: http://www.justice.gov.uk/information/docs/Court-working-dress-in-England-and-Wales.pdf [Accessed May 16, 2009]

Porter, R (2002) 'Lawyers on the big screen: consider whether moviegoing jurors buy a ticket for an imitation of life or a large cup of hot buttered entertainment' 38 *Trial* 54

Robson, P (2001a) 'Adapting and re-adapting—the case of 12 Angry Men' (Critical Legal Studies Conference, Kent)

—— (1995) 'Watching the detectives' Glasgow: University of Strathclyde (mimeo)

Stracher, C (2001) Reality TV 23 *American Lawyer* 138

Taubin, A (1994) 4 'The Odd Couple' 24

INDEX

Index

Index